Essays in the History of Youth and Community Work

Discovering the Past

Edited by

**Ruth Gilchrist, Tony Jeffs,
Jean Spence and Joyce Walker**

RHP

Russell House Publishing

First published in 2009 by:
Russell House Publishing Ltd.
4 St. George's House
Uplyme Road
Lyme Regis
Dorset DT7 3LS

Tel: 01297-443948
Fax: 01297-442722
e-mail: help@russellhouse.co.uk
www.russellhouse.co.uk

British Library Cataloguing-in-publication Data:
A catalogue record for this book is available from the British Library.

ISBN: 978-1-905541-45-4

Typeset by TW Typesetting, Plymouth, Devon

Printed by the MPG Books Group in the UK

Contents

In memory of Bert Jones,
1935–2006

About the Authors

Linnea A. Anderson, *University of Minnesota, Minneapolis, Assistant Archivist, Social Welfare History Archives.*

Simon Bradford, *Brunel University, School of Sport and Education.*

Barry Burke, *YMCA George Williams College London.*

Michael Butterfield, *National Association of Youth Clubs Chief Executive 1975–1986.*

Dan Conrad, *retired high school and college teacher, the latter with the Center for Youth Development and Research, University of Minneapolis. Two of his aunts, Ruth and Ruby Johnson, were captains of Cokako High School girls' basketball team in the early 1920s.*

Filip Coussée, *Ghent University, Department of Social Welfare Studies.*

Tania de St Croix, *detached youth worker in London; has spent the last 15 years attempting to combine youth and play work with Anarchist and environmental activism.*

Ruth Gilchrist, *UK Youth, Education, Training and Development Officer.*

John Holmes, *Newman University College, Birmingham, Community and Youth Work Department.*

Tony Jeffs, *Durham University, School of Applied Social Sciences and visiting Tutor Ruskin College, Oxford.*

Richard G. Kyle, *Lancaster University, Institute of Health Research.*

George Lovell, *contributing author to 'The Church and Community Development Work Trust, Avec'.*

Eliz McArdle, *team leader of the Gender Equality Unit within Youth Action, Northern Ireland.*

Susan Morgan, *University of Ulster, School of Sociology and Applied Social Studies. Young Women's Development Worker in Youth Action, Northern Ireland, 1997–2003.*

Keith Popple, *London South Bank University, Department of Social Work; and a founder member of the 'Youth and Policy' editorial board.*

Sue Robertson, *Chichester University College, Community and Youth Work Studies.*

Mark K. Smith, *YMCA George Williams College London, Rank Research Fellow and Tutor.*

Jean Spence, *Durham University, School of Applied Social Sciences.*

Tony Taylor, *writes and researches on youth policy and youth work. Co-ordinator of the 'Critically Chatting' website.*

Joyce Walker, *University of Minnesota, Extension Center for Youth Development.*

Tom Wylie, *National Youth Agency Director, 1996–2000.*

Withywood Centre

Preface

We can draw from a deep well. Community and youth workers are fortunate in being able to learn from and relate to a long history that stretches back unbroken to the very beginnings of industrialisation and the birth of the modern state. Both youth workers and community workers, operating in ways we would recognise and understand, have been around for over two hundred years. They were not only functioning before the emergence of mass schooling and the birth of universal welfare but importantly many leading youth and community work practitioners helped create contemporary welfare structures in Europe and the United States. In particular they did much to shape the social movements which played an essential part in driving forward ideas that eventually influenced and moulded the social policies which gave us our contemporary welfare structures. Yet the contributions of many of those individuals and agencies has been forgotten or overlooked.

Although a rich vein of history lies beneath our feet youth and community workers have tended to be rather negligent when it comes to mining it. As a consequence, contemporary practitioners, and most of the preceding generations have been unable to learn from both the successes and failures of the past. Each generation has tended to believe that they are creating new approaches and methods when in fact these have a long history. The arrogance of the assumption of present superiority has hindered the development of theory and made youth and community work prey to fashion and short-termism in relation to policy. Moreover, it has meant that we have failed to claim the rightful stature which our calling deserves: by overlooking the enormous achievements of those who went before, community and youth work has lost an opportunity to claim its place alongside related welfare professions – notably social work and teaching. Historical self-awareness is a pre-requisite for the long term survival of a profession and a discipline. For that reason it is important to invest time and resources upon the study of our history.

The prime purpose of this collection of essays is to help recover the history of youth and community work and lay it before a new generation of practitioners. We hope to encourage colleagues to cast a backward glance towards those who went before as they set about the task of creating practice appropriate to the contemporary environment. This is the fourth volume of such essays and like the earlier collections, it is an eclectic mix, drawing on research into youth and community work as well as aspects of adult education, play work and social history that relate closely to our central area of interest. Previous editions have overwhelmingly focused on the historical development of youth and community work in England and Wales. We are therefore delighted to include in this edition material on Belgian youth work, girls' work in Northern Ireland and two chapters specifically drawing on the American experience. A topic overlooked in the past has been the professional training of practitioners, but this volume begins to address that gap with two contributions which deal with aspects of this particular history.

In order to encourage and foster the study of the history of youth and community work, during the last decade the British journal *Youth and Policy* has sponsored five bi-annual conferences on the topic, each held at Ushaw College Durham. Since 2006 the Extension Center for Youth Development at the University of Minneapolis has hosted a similar initiative in the United States. Most of the essays in this volume first emerged as papers given at the two most recent conferences organised by the Extension Center for Youth Development and *Youth and Policy*. The growth in the number of delegates attending these conferences and the sales of earlier collections of essays, point to a growing interest in this area of study.

Given the close relationship between this publishing venture and the conferences that preceded its appearance, the editors would like to acknowledge the contributions made by Tracey Hodgson and Colleen Byrne. Colleen, in Minneapolis, and Tracey, in Durham, were responsible for the administration of the last two conferences held in those cities. We suspect that without their efficient administration neither conference would not have produced the range of papers that provide the bedrock upon which this book rests. Two new members of the *Youth and Policy* editorial group, Aylssa Cowell and Naomi Stanton have made significant contributions to the ongoing work of the journal which has allowed us more space to complete the book.

Observant readers will note that for the first time we do not include an essay by Bert Jones on the history of Welsh youth work. Sadly Bert died suddenly just before the last Durham conference. We missed his enthusiasm and intellect at that gathering and will continue to do so in the future.

Ruth Gilchrist, Tony Jeffs, Jean Spence and Joyce Walker

1897 Basketball Team *Basil Yeaxley* *Mary Burnie 1933,*
Warden of Westhill College

Withywood

CHAPTER 1

Why History?

Mark K. Smith

The popularity of this series of books, and the conferences connected with them, poses some obvious questions. Has there been increased interest in historical exploration – and if there has why has it occurred? What is it that people are gaining from researching and reading about the history of youth work? I want to suggest some tentative answers to these questions and set the experiences and anxieties of workers and academics within the youth work field within a broader context. In particular, I want to argue that there has been a general turn to history; and that it reflects fundamental concerns around identity, shifts in the nature of the work, and about what is to be done. Further, I suggest that history, carefully approached, offers illumination and hope. But first we need to ask 'what is history?'[1]

What is history?

For many the answer to this question is obvious. History is the past; it is that which has gone before. In our web browsers it is a record of the pages we have visited and when we downloaded them; in our families the stories of previous and present generations. We often make sense of such things by setting them in time – ordered from the earliest to the most recent. In this way we can make some sense of the impact of the past on subsequent events. But this begs all sorts of questions. How are we to know whether something did actually happen in the way it is described to us? Who is to say how things were?

When E.H. Carr approached these questions in the early 1960s his initial answer was that history is 'a continuous process of interaction between the historian and his facts, an unending dialogue between the present and the past' (Carr, 1964, 30). It rests on the belief, as Evans (1997, 157) put it, that the present differs from the past and derives from it. Evans continues:

> It also points to the future, which will be different again. In the end, everyone knows that the present is affected by the past, that what happens today can affect or cause what happens tomorrow or the day

after, and that the texts and other material objects which we produce today provide the basis on which the future can attempt to know us.

Inevitably though, as we dig deeper, issues arise. There have been arguments, for example, about what sort of events and stories count as history, the nature of historical evidence and facts, and indeed, whether it is possible to do history in any meaningful way at all. The last problem, of course, was raised by the turn to postmodernism and deconstruction in social theory in the last quarter of the twentieth century. It involved, in Ralph Samuel's (1992) words, an invitation to see history 'not as a record of the past, more or less faithful to the facts' but 'as an invention, or fiction of the historians themselves'.

A useful starting point when approaching these questions is the work of Leopold von Ranke – partly because he helped to establish history as a separate discipline in the mid-nineteenth century; partly as his studies have provided a key reference point for later generations of historians. Three particular ideas have been significant. That history:

1. is fundamentally concerned with establishing what actually happened (*wie es eigentlich gewesen ist*) – how it essentially was;
2. involves adopting an objective and non-moralising stance. The past cannot be judged by the standards of the present. The task is to 'try to understand the past as the people who lived in it understood it, even while deciphering hieroglyphs of interconnectedness of which they had been largely unaware' (Evans 1997, 17);
3. is based in the use of an appropriate range of primary sources – documents and materials of the time that can be shown to be consistent with other documents etc. from the same period. Secondary sources such as histories and memories that are produced later are not to be relied on.

A century and a half later this empirical approach still provides a basis for much historical research. However, it has been the focus of debate. Secondary sources, for example, can offer particular illumination when reading primary materials; there are questions around the nature of 'objectivity' and who is to define it – and so on. Here I want to look at three areas of exploration that have helped to shape conversations around the nature of history in more recent times – and that have special relevance to us when thinking about youth work history.

On time and historical interpretation

First, it is important to reflect on the extent to which understandings can be deepened by drawing upon insights, models and theories generated by other disciplines – most especially economics, anthropology, geography and, later, sociology. Here the work of Fernand Braudel, writing in the mid-twentieth century, has been of particular note. Amongst other things, he was able to show the ways in which historical time might move at different speeds. In *The Mediterranean* (which first appeared in 1949) Braudel makes a case for attending to three levels or dures (durations of time). At each level different things become revealed:

- The *Événementielle*. These are the events that are reasonably easily seen and often reported in news broadcasts and feeds, and newspapers. They can be seen as part of the political sphere – and can change fairly quickly. Another way of viewing them is as 'surface disturbances'. This is sometimes known as 'individual time' – the things that happen, often very quickly, in the lives of individual actors.
- The *Conjonctures*. These are 'durations' of intermediate length (by which Braudel meant less than 50 years). They involve reasonably slow moving economic and social trends, changing technologies and shifting social structures and institutions. These durations are sometimes called 'social time'.
- *The Longue*. This durée – which is a particular focus of Braudel's interest – is deep and slow-moving and can be counted in centuries. The movements and changes are often imperceptible to those living within it. It involves repetition and constant cycles. Some have described this as 'geographical time' as this durée is wrapped up with environmental change.

Braudel's work has been subject to criticism – especially around the extent to which his treatment of the third dure over-estimates the constancy of forces that make for stability and little change; and difficulty in disentangling and agreeing on the levels. However, the idea that history moves at different speeds retains considerable power as Corfield (2007) has recently shown. Furthermore, this sort of categorisation has the merit of problematising the way we view historical time and of exposing some of the gaps in the sorts of history linked to areas such as youth work.

The utility of the social sciences to historians was also championed by E.H. Carr (1964) and others. In addition, Carr turned the spotlight on those writing history. He understood that historians reflected something of their times, and their ideological orientation, in their writing. 'The historian', Carr argued, 'is engaged in a continuous process of moulding his facts to his interpretation and his interpretation to his facts' (1964, 29). Neither, he concluded, has primacy over the other.

The historian starts with a provisional selection of facts, and a provisional interpretation in the light of which that selection has been made – by others as well as himself. As he works, both the interpretation and the selection and ordering of facts undergo subtle and perhaps partly unconscious changes, through the reciprocal action of one or the other. And this reciprocal action also involves reciprocity between present and past, since the historian is part of the present and the facts belong to the past. The historian and the facts of history are necessary to one another. The historian without his facts is rootless and futile; the facts without their historian are dead and meaningless.

(Carr, 1964, 29)

In this we find an echo of the philosophical hermeneutics of Gadamer and of Geertz's approach to anthropology. What it leaves to one side is what actually counts as history i.e. what historians choose to study, and to what extent that is a product of dominant ideologies and power relations. As Winston Churchill is reported to have said (although it is not documented), 'history is written by the victors'. Historians were becoming much more attuned to the ways in which people in groups and institutions build versions of the past to serve their own ends (see, for example, Hobsbawm, 1983).

History from below

During the 1960s – and especially following the publication of E.P. Thompson's *The Making of the English Working Class* in 1963 there was a growth in what Georges Lefebvre (1939, 2005) described as 'history from below'. The focus shifted from a concern with the machinations of the powerful, to an interest in the experiences of 'ordinary' people, and to groups, institutions and regions that had not previously been considered important within the dominant historical discourses.

There had, of course, been a tradition of researching and writing about social history. Rather than focusing on political events, military campaigns and the lives of 'great men and women' it looked to the everyday experiences of people and to changing social behaviours and mores – and found a large popular audience. For example, G.M. Trevelyan's *English Social History* (first published in 1942) was the best selling English history book for a significant period of time (Cannadine, 1992). However, it looked at the past through a lens that was literary – making writers such as Chaucer and Shakespeare the touchstone. As a result, it – and other books like it – failed to engage with social theory, and did not look to underlying causes and dynamics. Furthermore, as

Evans (1997, 163) has noted, Trevelyan and other similar writers tended to adopt a 'paternalistic and condescending stance towards the lower orders in history'.

Thompson's *The Making of the English Working Class* had grown out of a strand of social history that made the emergence and development of the working class and the labour movement its focus. The contrast with Trevelyan couldn't have been stronger. Thompson drew upon social theory, his text was rooted in a Marxist analysis, and viewed 'ordinary' people as actors, organisers and creators. The book quickly became the focus of debate and activity. It has subsequently been recognised as one of the most influential books published in the second half of the twentieth century (*Times Literary Supplement*, 1995). Over the following twenty years or so there was an explosion in social history scholarship – and the development of some important and distinctive strands of exploration. Interest in these was fed and accelerated by the growth of key social and political movements in the late 1960s and through the 1970s. The wish to explore and make known that which had been 'hidden from history' (Rowbotham, 1973) was powerful. Thus, for example, we see the development of women's history, gay and lesbian history, and Black history. Alongside this continuing research into the experience of working class people, the growth of oral history produced a rich vein of scholarship. Of particular note here, was the range of work appearing around the history of childhood and youth, and local communal institutions (e.g. Taylor, 1972; Roberts, 1973; Gillis, 1974; Laqueur, 1974; Clarke *et al.*, 1979; White, 1980; Dyhouse, 1981; Humphries, 1981; Roberts, 1984; Davin, 1996). Significantly, many of these writers were involved with the *History Workshop Journal* founded by Ralph Samuel and others in 1976.

The postmodern challenge

The splintering of the study of history into a wider range of more clearly demarcated strands – and the critiques that grew within them – challenged a number of cherished ideas within the discipline. However, perhaps the most fundamental questioning of the traditions of historical research that had emerged, came from 'postmodern' commentators. Keith Jenkins (2006) looking back on the changes within the discipline over 40 years comments, 'No one in 1966 foresaw the impact of the various linguistic and literary theories known as "post-structuralism" and "postmodernism". With linguistic theorists such as Roland Barthes (1968) talking of the 'death of the author' and disputing historians' claims to be able to reconstruct past reality (see

Thompson, 2000, 96–127), and Jacques Derrida discussing the infinite play of significations and hence the meaning of texts changing each time they are read, it seemed to some that there was little possibility of achieving any certain knowledge of the past (Jenkins, 2006). This was reflected in a series of academic texts that drew on literary theory to study historical themes (most significantly the work of Hayden White, 1973, 1978, 1987); to a questioning of the notions of truth and objectivity (Hutcheon, 1988 being one of the most influential); and of the need to reconceptualise or reform time in line with the discourse of the postmodern (Ermarth, 1992) (for a collection of some of the key thinkers see Jenkins, 1997).

The critique of postmodern thinking is well known. Most crucially, key proponents tend to contradict themselves through self-reference, and presuppose concepts they seek to undermine (Habermas, 1987). However, as an intellectual fashion it gained considerable ground – in part because it seemed to chime with the times, and because it appeared to offer some interesting areas for exploration. An 'incredulity to metanarratives', as Lyotard (1984: xxiv) characterised the postmodern, and the associated focus on self-reflexivity and literary construction, did offer insight. One important element of this has been around the way that historical texts are made. Another concerns the insights that can be gained into the role that the focus of history has in terms of constructing the identity of those that read and study it (see Purkiss, 1996). At the same time though, the 'postmodern turn' also involved a retreat away from 'primary sources' into textual analysis and into specialist language and narcissism. Richard Evans, one of the central critics of 'postmodernist history', has argued that postmodernism's legitimation of subjectivity in the historian's work, 'encourages historians to intrude into the text to such a degree that in some cases their presence all but obliterates the historical subject' (1997, 200). His attack on postmodern history excited considerable debate (see Institute of Historical Research, undated) but also met with considerable acclaim from those wanting to defend the worth of historical exploration.

The turn to history and the rise of popular history

Interestingly at the same time that postmodernists were questioning the truth and worth of doing history there was an explosion in the numbers of people wanting to read and learn about it and engage in it. At present, in any one year some 10,000 people publish books or articles on British and Irish history (Thomas, 2006, 4). Amazon.co.uk has approaching 470,000 books categorised under 'history' on its database. While a number of these are the products of what might be called 'academic' historians and are aimed at, or at least have, a limited readership, alongside this there has been a marked growth in publishing and programme-making that looks to the mass market. Indeed, such is the demand that we now have a number of digital channels solely devoted to historical programming and history has also found its way into peak-time viewing slots on the main general channels.

The growing appetite for 'popular history' appears to have accelerated in the 1990s. According to Stella Tillyard (2006) the market 'grew hugely'. Following the success in 1987 of Paul Kennedy's *The Rise and Fall of the Great Powers* and Simon Schama's *The Embarrassment of Riches*, publishers and programme makers were on the look out for writers who could package and present material to a growing audience of people who on the one hand had received 'higher' levels of education, but on the other had suffered from patchy history teaching (Tillyard, 2006: 9). Writers like Simon Schama (2000, 2001, 2002, 2005), David Starkey (2000, 2003, 2004, 2006) and Niall Ferguson (2004, 2005, 2006) had huge sales via television tie-ins. Generalist writers like Norman Davies (1996, 1999), Eric Hobsbawm (1994) and Roy Porter (1999, 2000) also gained a large readership. With this came a whole raft of books aimed at the mass market often with one word titles and a particular focus e.g. *Longitude* (Sobel, 1998), *Stalingrad* (Beevor, 1999), *Rubicon* (2004) and *Birth* (Cassidy, 2007).

When thinking about popular history it is important to look beyond the blockbusters. The interest in history has also involved a growth in 'doing' it. Three particular forms dominate – local, enthusiast, and family. There has been a long-standing tradition of 'amateur' history research and writing in these areas – but the range of titles that are now published, and the opportunities and tools open to 'memory workers' does appear to have expanded and reflects a passion for the past. Crucially it also offers a deep well of 'unofficial knowledge' (see Samuel, 1996).

Most local libraries will have a number of books that explore the history of the surrounding area. These include collections of historical pictures (usually with commentaries), explorations of particular institutions and industries, accounts of local life and more academic histories. Along with this there are various local projects and initiatives examining different aspects of the pasts. Some engage young people and flow out from school work, others might be linked to work with older people (e.g. reminiscence workshops) or to recovering or celebrating things past. Recent examples local to me have included making a collective history of a local large biscuit factory; exploring the experience of docklands both through the building of an exhibition and the gathering of oral history; the celebration of 100 years of the state old age pension (Herbert Stead, a local settlement worker was a key instigator of the campaign for their establishment); and a library-based book group examining more recent political events (in this case, the contest between Peter Tatchell and Simon Hughes in the Bermondsey by-election of 1983). The local paper has a history page each week; and the council a participatory blue plaque scheme where local people vote for whom or what they want to see celebrated. This study of local history has also created demand for methodological texts aimed at general readers and enthusiasts (e.g. Riden, 1998; Blatchford and Blatchford, 2008; Brooks, 2008).

Enthusiast history is equally as vibrant. Many thousands of books and DVDs are published each year ranging from explorations of the history of different sports and teams, through accounts of the development of railways, roads and canals (and the vehicles and ephemera that are associated with them), to histories of different crafts and hobbies. A search on Amazon brings up over 5,000 titles on railway history alone. However, the scale and scope of publishing around history of enthusiasms is not its most notable feature – it is the extent to which it flows from, and remains located in, civil society. Enthusiast groups, which are a shining example of mutual aid in leisure (see Bishop and Hoggett 1986), are also one of the key forms that civic society takes and are fundamental to its health. They are also, somewhat strangely, under-represented in the research that has taken place around civil society.

While local history and the history of enthusiasms have been important areas of endeavour, genealogy and family history have become a major social phenomenon. The histories of different families regularly become best sellers – a recent example being Jane Mulvagh's *Madresfield* (a study of the Lygons who provided the basis for *Brideshead Revisited*) – but it is the numbers of people who are engaged in researching their own families' histories that is of particular note. With the development of specialist computer software, the ability to access public records on-line, and the creation of user-friendly internet gateways such as genealogy.com/ancestry.co.uk and FamilyRecords.gov.uk there has been an explosion in active exploration. The Ancestry website operates across nine countries and in any one week around eight million people add something to their family tree (ancestry.co.uk 2008). Family history has also become a focus for programme makers – perhaps the best known recent example being the BBC's *Who do you think you are?* and its family history web portal.

The scope and scale of this turn to popular history is of considerable interest – and later I want to speculate on what some of the underlying reasons for this movement may be. However, for the moment we need to look to what has been happening around the history of youth work.

Developments in the history of youth work

Again, attention to the history of youth work is not new. There have been a number of landmark texts that have looked to the development of the work. Mostly produced to celebrate a particular point in the history of a youth organisation, they provide a fascinating insight into the organisations, the work associated with them, and concerns and interests at the point of publication. Examples include C.J. Montague's (1904) account of the ragged school movement, Mary Heath Stubbs' (1926) study of the Girls' Friendly Society, Gwennat Davies' (1973) history of the Urdd (The Welsh League of Youth), and the history of the Boys' Brigade written by John Springall *et al.* (1983). There have been a smaller number of more general texts that chart key aspects of the development of work with young people. Five stand out: Alicia Percival's (1951) account of voluntary youth organisations, W. McG. Eagar's *Making Men* (a study of the development of boys' club work) published in 1953, John Springhall's discussion of youth, empire and society, Tony Jeffs' (1979) exploration of young people and the youth service, and Michael Rosenthal's (1986) exploration of Baden-Powell and scouting. Of all of these books Eagar's remains the most comprehensive study – but it is obviously limited by its focus. There have also been a number of useful biographies published, notably Barclay Baron (1952) on John Stansfeld, Clyde Binfield (1973) on George Williams, Tim Jeal (1989) on Baden-Powell, and Sybil Oldfield (2008) on Jane Senior. Memoirs are also a rich source of material – for example Basil Henriques (1937), Leslie Paul (1952) and, more recently, Sidney Bunt (1990) and Dennis Burgess (1996). (See Smith, 1996, 2008 for a more substantial listing of texts.)

While there has been a tradition of studying youth work history, a number of indicators point to an increased interest. One of the most obvious expressions of this has been the establishment of the history of youth work conferences at Durham beginning in 1998 (Gilchrist, Jeffs and Spence, 2001a, 2003, 2006). These conferences have produced a number of fascinating local studies – often linking discussion with broader movements and shifts in thinking, (e.g. Buckland, 2006; Spence, 2001, 2003), some longer-run analysis of agencies and phenomenon (e.g. Bolton, 2006; Cranwell, 2001; Fabes and Skinner, 2001), interesting explorations of key moments for policy (e.g. Bradford, 2006; Holmes, 2001), one or two significant re-appraisals of key figures (e.g. Jeffs, 2003) plus some helpful reflections on youth work history itself (Davies, 2001, 2006; Gilchrist *et al.*, 2001).

Another indicator of the health of youth work history is the number of dedicated publications that have appeared over the last decade or so that focus on youth work history. Notable contributions over the last decade include Celia Rose's account of the the Clapton Jewish Youth Centre (1998); Bernard Davies' three volume history of the youth service (1999a, 1999b and 2008); Sharman Kadish's (1995) examination of the Jewish Lads and Girls' Brigades; and Pete Ward's (1996) exploration of evangelical youth work. Alongside this there have been numerous examples of explorations of local institutions such as Newcastle YMCA (Jeffs with Gilchrist, 2005), the Oxford and Bermondsey Club (Say, 1997), Dockland youth ministry (Griffiths, 2008) and Devon Association of Youth Clubs (Booth and Corben, 2008). *Youth and Policy* also ran a popular series for a number of years that explored the contribution of classic youth work texts. In addition, proper archives have been established for the YMCA movement in England, and the National Organisation of Girls' Clubs and its successor bodies (both at the University of Birmingham). In addition, a new on-line archive and resource has been established for girls' clubs and youth work (ukyoutharchive.org). The centenary of the Scouts also prompted some significant publication, notably a new edition of *Scouting for Boys* (Baden-Powell, 2004).

When surveying this literature a number of things stand out. First, we lack a comprehensive study of the history of youth work and work with young people. The two major studies that are contenders look to specific arenas. Bernard Davies explores the changing state of the youth service between 1939 and 2007; and Waldo McG. Eagar boys club and associated work up to 1953. We have nothing on any scale that looks at *youth work* and work with young people per se.

Second, the vast bulk of the work has been undertaken by enthusiasts or by academics who are not primarily historians. There are one or two obvious exceptions here, notably Binfield (1973) and Springhall (1977, 1983), but the pattern is clear. Youth work history has largely been an exercise in popular history.

Thirdly, and flowing in part from the above, much of what has been written has operated at the level of what Braudel (1949) described as the Événementielle. The focus is on events and things that happen, often quickly, in the lives of individual actors. A small number of studies have attended to 'durations' of intermediate length involving deeper economic and social trends, changing technologies and shifting social structures and institutions. None, as far as I can see, have got to grips with the *Longue*.

Fourth, as an expression of popular history much of the work in this area has escaped the linguistic turn. As such it has retained many of the characteristics that Ranke would have recognised as history: a concern to establish what happened; holding on, more or less, to an 'objective' stance; and paying attention to primary sources. There are some deviations in this, for example, in the tendency to gloss over embarrassing aspects of an institution's history or individual's biography. Compare, for example, the accounts of the development of Scouting and of the life of Baden-Powell that were produced by insiders or that were official accounts with the studies of Rosenthal (1986) and Jeal (1989). There have also been examples of cherry-picking in order to bolster the case being made. Further, while the study of youth work history may have avoided much of the narcissism and abstraction of postmodern discourses, it has lost something – most particularly attention to the exploration of truth claims, the process of writing 'history', and the impact of the person of the history writer.

Why the turn to history?

Here I want to make some tentative suggestions as to why people appear to have been drawn to the study of history – and especially the study of youth work and associated movements. Before looking at some deeper running themes it is worth noting that a small number of people who have had a long-standing concern with historical analysis and with the exploration of contemporary youth work practice have put a considerable amount of effort into inviting people to explore history. Tony Jeffs and *Youth and Policy* have been key in terms of stimulating the work, organising conferences, and in publication; Bernard Davies has opened up a number of strands of exploration in his writing; and the archive groups associated with the YMCA and UK Youth have been able to make material available in accessible forms. This invitation was not primarily driven by changing circumstances but arose out of a conviction on the part of those involved that history matters. While there may be deep running changes in social life and some profound movements in policy, as Davies (2008, 6) put it, 'the unfolding of historical events cannot be treated as "natural" or "inevitable" '. Things have been 'shaped by the actions and intentions of people' (op. cit.) although not necessarily in the way they hoped.

To understand what has been going on it is necessary to recognise that youth work is essentially both the product of, and only makes sense when it is connected with, or embedded in, civil society (see Jeffs and

Smith, forthcoming). It has arisen out of what David Marquand has discussed as the public domain: 'the domain of citizenship, equity and service whose integrity is essential to democratic governance and social well-being' (2004, 1). This is reflected in the literature. The written history of youth work and of work with young people is overwhelmingly focused on the activities of individuals, groups and organisations who operated within civil society and who were concerned with the public domain. There has been some tension within this. As the public domain grew – and professionalism and professional society developed (Perkin, 1989) – the discourse and organisation of youth work gradually distanced itself from the language and forms that were prevalent within faith and community-based groups. In more recent years, far from diminishing faith-based work, there has been a major renaissance in the work which has been expressed in a large rise in the numbers employed by local religious organisations (Brierley, 2000), and in the literature of the area (see Ward, 1997; Brierley 2003; and Passmore, 2003). Unfortunately the same cannot be said of community-based work which has suffered both from a withdrawal of state-support (as things have become centralised), and from declining levels of traditional forms of civic engagement. However, as Liz Richardson (2008) has shown, within local communities a significant disposition remains to organise things for and with young people where funding is provided without any of the traditional state-strings.

The public domain and professionalism has, in turn, come under profound attack from the state. In Britain, Marquand (2004, 2) has argued, the last twenty years or so has seen 'an aggressively interventionist state systematically enfeebling the institutions and practices' that nurtured the public domain and that it is now in crisis. The degree of discretion afforded front-line workers within state-sponsored institutions has been dramatically curtailed through mechanisms such as targets, inspection and data-collection. Within this process of centralisation there was a growing view of education and welfare as problems of management, rather than processes of 'working with'. State agencies became the commissioners or buyers of services rather than seeking to act in partnership with civil society. It made the practice of youth work as it came to be defined by the post-war settlement very difficult to sustain within many areas of the state.

Linked to these movements was organisational change – especially in England, but also in different forms in other parts of the UK. With the organisational focus on children's services and the location of state-sponsored work with young people within the social work-dominated *Every Child Matters* strategy (see Jeffs and Smith, forthcoming) many practitioners, managers and trainers experienced significant disruption. They were required to present and define themselves differently.

As we have seen, these changes were linked into longer term movements and shifts. It was clear twenty years ago that state youth services would wither away (Jeffs and Smith, 1988, 252–6; Smith, 1988, 65–87). It was also clear that youth work could continue to flourish within civil society (*op. cit.*) – although civil society itself would continue to come under attack from the market mechanism. As Karl Polayni (1957, 73) put it over fifty years ago, 'To allow the market mechanism to be the sole director of the fate of human beings and their natural environment, indeed, even of the amount and use of purchasing power, would result in the demolition of society'. There is a significant sense in which this has happened. Growing commodification and corporate takeover in welfare and education; de-localisation and the adoption of problematic new technologies; and a growing focus on branding and on the way in which we now define ourselves by what we consume, have left their mark (Smith, 2002). The issues facing managers, workers and young people, and the environment in which they have to make sense of these is very different to the post-Albemarle period. In this context, four dynamics are worth looking at as drivers of a turn by individuals to a concern with history.

The search for identity

As Gilchrist *et al.* (2001b: 1) have commented, 'lack of attention to the contribution of predecessors in the work 'has fuelled an insecurity and an unwarranted tendency towards self-deprecation'. With shifts and changes in the direction of work with young people there has been an increased desire on the part of many workers to name and own what they are. For faith-based workers operating within Christian churches and settings, for example, there has been an expressed need to locate their activities and to build a distinctive identity as practitioners. For some it has been necessary to explore the history of the work in order to counter the demands of their churches or agencies to focus on church building, and to ignore social engagement. For more, I suspect, an interest in history has arisen out of a sense of alienation from secular youth work discourses. Much of the literature neither speaks their language nor looks to spirituality. Being able to connect back with earlier generations has allowed Christian workers to name youth work as their own and to counter the claims of secular and more bureaucratic forms. Attention has tended to focus, though, on earlier and more evangelical forms and institutions (e.g. Ward, 1996; Griffiths, 2008). This is hardly surprising given the current overall orientation of much Christian youth work – but in so doing some key traditions have been overlooked. Perhaps the most significant of these is Methodist youth work and the contribution of people like Butterworth (1932), Barnett (1951, 1953, 1962) and Milson (1963, 1980). The latter two are particularly interesting – Barnett because of his explicit commitment to informal education, Milson because of his exploration and embracing of groupwork and of political education.

The need to assert a youth work identity has also been a concern of some those working within, or influenced by, state-sponsored work. While many practitioners have simply got on with their new roles or have taken on state definitions of their activities, a number have felt profoundly uncomfortable with what they were being told to do, and uneasy with the professional identity they were being encouraged to adopt. Returning to the thinking, commitments and practice of earlier generations can be both refreshing and liberating. However, it can also be frustrating and dispiriting if people understand and see themselves as youth workers and there is little room to express this within their state-sponsored roles. Not a few have left state youth services to see what is possible in other environments.

Charting and honouring that which has past

One of the strongest impetuses to writing history appears to be the wish to honour the achievements of earlier generations and to record the work so that others may appreciate what was done. This certainly appears to be the dominant concern in many of histories and explorations of local institutions. For example, if we look at the various books and articles written about, or touching on, the work of the Oxford and Bermondsey Club (Paterson, 1910; Secretan, 1931; Baron, 1952; Eagar, 1953; Day, 1997; Davies, 2006), they largely provide descriptive material about the personalities involved, the work undertaken, and the underpinning concerns and beliefs. The great strength of this is the rich and illuminating stories and examples that appear. For those thinking that gun crime is new, for example, Day (1997, 11) recounts how in the 1940s a club member managed to shoot a club helper in the leg with a service rifle he had acquired. 'The police naturally intervened but all they could get from the helper was that a bullet had mysteriously come along and hit him in the leg' (Secretan quoted by Day *op. cit.*). Just about all of these writers have demonstrated elsewhere an ability to develop a sophisticated analysis of social issues and questions, but only Eagar (1953) set the work of the club in a broader context and developed a more detailed analysis of its significance.

Clearly, they had a different orientation to writing about club activities and personalities. Most studies 'start from the at least implicit premise that the organisation or practice under consideration was a "good thing" ' (Davies, 2001, 9).

Some of those engaged in writing local histories may well have got into it by accident e.g. by discovering papers and materials in a cupboard or skip, and then realising the significance of their finds. Many others have been involved with an institution or group for many years. Indeed, most of the historical accounts of youth work organisations have been written by people of more mature years. Looking at the dedications and introductions to these books, there is an important sense in which their efforts have been born of a sense of debt to those involved over the years, and of duty to those that follow.

Deepening understanding of contemporary practices, policies and relationships

A further, obvious, reason why people turn to history is an attempt to understand how things have come to be as they are. In our case – what actually has happened in youth work and work with young people – and why have changes and continuities occurred? The fact that many around the work experience or sense that there has been a significant shift in the orientation and nature of much practice has probably added to the turn to history. Attention to history allows us to lay down markers, 'guides to a better understanding of what we do and why we do it' (Gilchrist *et al.* 2001b, 2).

One of the great virtues of Davies' (1999a, 1999b and 2008) study of Youth Service history is that it reveals the incremental and not so incremental movements in policy and the organisation of state-sponsored youth work over the last seventy years. However, one of the most significant aspects of what is currently happening within state-sponsored work is the extent to which it is fast coming to resemble orientations to practice that were prevalent 150 years ago. There is an irony in this. It is not uncommon to hear workers who argue for more open and associational forms of work described as 'old school'. Yet the focus on the achievement of demonstrable outcomes, targeted provision and evangelical-like disposition to promote certain behaviours mirrors the work of ragged schools during the first half of the nine-teenth century. In other words, it represents a reversion to forms that are pre-youth work. Indeed, it was people like Tom Pelham (1889) and Maude Stanley (1878, 1890) who had experienced and understood the limitations of ragged schools that pioneered the development of the forms of work with boys and girls that later became known as youth work (Smith, 2001).

Looking to the future

We cannot 'read off' the future from past patterns. However, exploring the history of the ideas, commitments and practices of 'work among young people' does offer the chance to develop a repertoire of exemplars, ideas and images about how things may develop. For example, reflecting upon attempts to make attendance at youth provision compulsory during the Second World War, sensitises us to some of the issues around contemporary efforts to manage young people (Bradford, 2006). We can also identify longer term patterns and themes. One of the most important of these is the extent to which innovation and regeneration in youth work and social action has been, and continues to be, overwhelmingly located in the work of local organisations and animateurs that are part of civil society (see Mulgan *et al.*, 2007). Another concerns the constant need to ask the question 'In whose interests' does a particular policy or activity operate (Davies, 1979)?

Conclusion

From this review of the state of historical exploration and reflection in the field of 'work among young people' it is possible to conclude that there has been a turn to history – and that there are some important reasons why this has happened. A number of those involved with youth work have felt the need to examine what has gone before – some to sustain or develop their identities as youth workers, some to develop their understanding of how things have changed in the way they have. Others have sought to honour and record the contribution of previous generations, others to gain some insight into what could be done to build forms of work that might better meet the needs of young people and the communities of which they are a part.

The study of youth work history – as it has been practised – has helped to sustain and develop hope. In part this has happened because it has worked to combat what Halpin (2003, 18–30) has identified as the enemies of hope: cynicism, fatalism, relativism and fundamentalism. The study of history allows us to deepen our appreciation of current experiences and thinking, and to approach institutions and policies with a stronger understanding of how they function and respond to the environment. While a degree of cynicism and pessimism may be necessary in terms of developing our analysis, it has to be countered by a belief in the possibility of change and in the chance that people may live more fulfilling lives if we are to move on (Gramsci, 1971). When we reflect on the innovations that have happened around 'work amongst young people', it is clear that individuals and groups have been able to shape and reshape practice – often under very difficult circumstances – and that they have approached their task in hope and with a belief in agency. Things can be changed, events are not totally determined by factors outside our control. Engaging with history, learning from what has gone before, allows us to counter fatalism. As we have also seen, youth work history has not been significantly affected by the postmodern turn and relativism. It has avoided too strong an embrace with 'contingency, fragmentation, particularity and difference' (Halpin, 2003, 22). Last, while the study of youth work history can reveal some significant continuities or traditions in the work (see, for example Butters and Newell, 1978 and Smith, 1988), it also allows us to see some of the follies associated with an unquestioning adherence to tradition.

As has already been argued, attention to history does not allow us to read-off the future, but it does help us to see patterns and different ways of proceeding. Contemporary youth policy and the attempt by government to 'transform youth work' has been dominated by a concern to 'tackle' immediate appearances – and many state-sponsored workers have been caught up in this and have fallen in line in significant part because many have lacked a sound historical and theoretical understanding (Smith, 1988, 2003). To borrow from Gramsci, not only have they had no precise consciousness of their historical identity, they have not even been conscious of the historic identity or the exact limits of their adversaries (1971, 273).

Note

1 I have not explored what 'youth work' is in this piece but have worked within the parameters of what I have written elsewhere e.g. Smith (1988), Smith (1999, 2002), Jeffs and Smith (forthcoming).

References

Adolph, A. (2006) *Tracing Your Family History*. London, Collins.

Ancestry.co.uk (2008) *Discover your story*. [http://www.ancestry.co.uk/. Accessed 18 July 2008].

Aries, P. (1962) *Centuries of Childhood*. London, Jonathan Cape.

Baden-Powell, R. (2004) *Scouting for Boys* (edited by E. Boehmer). Oxford, Oxford University Press.

Bailey, P. (1987) *Leisure and Class in Victorian England. Rational Recreation and the Contest for Control 1830–1885* (2nd edn). London, Methuen.

Barnett, L.P. (1951) *The Church Youth Club*, London, Methodist Youth Department.

Barnett, L.P. (1953, 1962) *Adventure with Youth: a handbook for church club leaders*. London, Methodist Youth Department.

Baron, B.(1952) *The Doctor. The story of John Stansfeld of Oxford and Bermondsey*. London, Edward Arnold.

Barthes, R. (1968) 'The death of the author', Aspen 5 + 6. [http://www.ubu.com/aspen/aspen5and6/threeEssays.html#barthes. Accessed 17 July 2008.]

Beevor, A. (1999) *Stalingrad*. London, Penguin.

Binfield, C. (1973) *George Williams and the YMCA,* London: Heinemann.

Binfield, C. (1994) *George Williams in Context. A portrait of the founder of the YMCA*. Sheffield, Sheffield Academic Press.

Bishop, J. and Hoggett, P. (1986) *Organizing around Enthusiasm. Mutual aid in leisure*. London, Comedia.

Blatchford, R. and Blatchford, E. (2008) *The Family and Local History Handbook* 11e. York, Robert Blatchford Publishing Ltd.

Bolton, R. (2006) 'First for boys?' in (eds.) R. Gilchrist, T. Jeffs and J. Spence. *Drawing on the Past Studies in the history of youth and community work*. Leicester: The National Youth Agency.

Booth, D. and Corben, J. (2008) *DYA to Young Devon. A short history of a county youth association*. Ivybridge, Devon Youth Association.

Bradford, S. (2006) 'Practising the double doctrine of freedom: Managing young people in the context of war' in R. Gilchrist, T. Jeffs and J. Spence (eds.) *Drawing on the Past Studies in the history of youth and community work*. Leicester, The National Youth Agency.

Braudel, F. (1949) *The Mediterranean and the Mediterranean World in the Age of Philip* fl, Paris: Armand Colin.

Braudel, F. (1972) *The Mediterranean and the Mediterranean World in the Age of Philip II*. Volumes I and II. Translated by Sian Reynolds. London, Collins.

Brierley, D. (2003) *Joined Up. An introduction to youthwork and ministry*. London, Pasternoster Publishing.

Brierley, P. (2000) *The Tide is Running Out. What the English church attendance survey reveals*. London, Christian Research.

Brooks, P. (2008) *How to Research Local History: Find Out All About Your House, Village or Town*. Oxford: How To Books.

Buckland, L. (2006) 'The Aldershot Institute 1948–1956. "Our club" ' in R. Gilchrist, T. Jeffs and J. Spence (eds.) *Drawing on the Past Studies in the history of youth and community work*. Leicester, The National Youth Agency.

Bunt, S. (1990) *Years and Years of Youth*. Croydon, Pro Juventus.

Burgess, D. (1996) *My Life as a Youth Leader*. Drayton, T and A Publishing.

Butters, S. and Newell, 5. (1978) *Realities of Training*. Leicester, National Youth Bureau.

Butterworth, J. (1932) *Clubland*. London, Epworth Press.

Cannadine, D. (1992) *G.M. Trevelyan*. London, HarperCollins.

Carr, E.H. (1964) *What is History,* Harmondsworth: Penguin.

Cassidy, T. (2007) *Birth. A history*. London, Chatto and Windus.

Clarke, J. *et al.* (eds.) (1979) *Working Class Culture. Studies in History and Theory*. London, Hutchinson.

Corfield, P.J. (2007) *Time and the Shape of History*. New Haven Conn, Yale University Press.

Cowen, R.F.H. (2003) *Foundation of Faith. History of the Rank Foundation April 1953 to June 2000*. Lewes, The Book Guild.

Cranwell, K. (2001) 'Organised play and organised space for children and young people in London' in (eds.) R. Gilchrist, T. Jeffs and J. Spence. *Essays in the History of Community and Youth Work*. Leicester, The Youth Work Press.

Davies, B. (1979) *In Whose Interests? From Social Education to Social and Life Skills Training,* Leicester: NYB.

Davies, B. (1999a) *From Voluntaryism to Welfare State. A history of the Youth Service in England. Volume 1: 1939–1979*. Leicester, Youth Work Press.

Davies, B. (1999b) *From Thatcherism to New Labour. A history of the Youth Service in England. Volume 2: 1979–1999*. Leicester, Youth Work Press.

Davies, B. (2001) 'Struggling through the past: Writing youth service history' in (eds.) R. Gilchrist, T. Jeffs and J. Spence. *Essays in the History of Community and Youth Work*. Leicester, The Youth Work Press.

Davies, B. (2006) 'Extended Schooling: Some lessons for youth workers from Youth Service history' in (eds.) R. Gilchrist, T. Jeffs and J. Spence. *Drawing on the Past Studies in the history of youth and community work*. Leicester, The National Youth Agency.

Davies, B. (2008) *A History of the Youth Service in England. Volume 3 1997–2007 The New Labour Years*. Leicester, The National Youth Agency.

Davies, G. (1973) *The Story of the Urdd* (The Welsh League of Youth), Aberystwyth, Cwmni Urdd Gobaith Cymru.

Davies, N. (1996) *Europe. A history*. Oxford, Oxford University Press.

Davies, N. (1999) *The Isles. A history*. London: Macmillan.

Davies, R. (2006) 'Mission Impossible? Donald Hankey and youth work in the Oxford and Bermondsey Mission' in (eds.) R. Gilchrist, T. Jeffs, and J. Spence. *Drawing on the Past. Studies in the history of community and youth work*. Leicester, National Youth Agency.

Davin, A. (1996) *Growing up Poor: Home, School and Street in London 1870–1914,* London: Rivers of Oram Press.

Dyhouse, C. (1981). *Girls Growing Up in Late Victorian and Edwardian England*. London, Routledge and Kegan Paul.

Eagar, W.McG. (1953). *Making Men. A History of Boys' Clubs and Related Movements*. London, University of London Press.

Ermarth, E.D. (1992) *Sequel to History: Postmodernism and the Crisis of Representational Time*. Princeton NJ, Princeton University Press.

Evans, R.J. (1999) *In Defence of History,* New York: Norton.

Fabes, R. and Skinner, A. (2001) 'The Girls' Friendly Society an the development of rural youth work 1850–1900' in (eds.) R. Gilchrist, T. Jeffs and J. Spence. *Essays in the History of Community and Youth Work*. Leicester, The Youth Work Press.

Ferguson, N. (2004) *Empire: how Britain made the modern world*. London, Penguin.

Ferguson, N. (2005) *Colossus: the rise and fall of the American empire*. London, Penguin.

Ferguson, N. (2006) *The war of the world: history's age of hatred*. London, Allen Lane.

Fryer, P. (1984) *Staying Power. The History of Black People in Britain*. London, Pluto Press.

Gadamer, H-G. (1979) *Truth and Method* (2nd edn). London, Sheed & Ward.

Geertz, C. (1973) *The Interpretation of Cultures*. London, Hutchinson.

Gilchrist, R., Jeffs, T. and Spence, J. (eds.) (2001a) *Essays in the History of Community and Youth Work*. Leicester, Youth Work Press.

Gilchrist, R., Jeffs, T. and Spence, J. (2001b) 'Introduction' in (eds.) R. Gilchrist, T. Jeffs and J. Spence. *Essays in the History of Community and Youth Work*. Leicester, Youth Work Press.

Gilchrist, R., Jeffs, T. and Spence, J. (eds.) (2003) *Architects of Change. Studies in the history of community and youth work*. Leicester, National Youth Agency.

Gilchrist, R., Jeffs, T. and Spence, J. (eds.) (2006) *Drawing on the Past. Studies in the history of community and youth work*. Leicester, National Youth Agency.

Gillis, J.R. (1974, 1981) *Youth and History. Tradition and Change in European Age Relations 1770–Present*. New York, Academic Press.

Gramsci, A. (1971). *Selections from Prison Notebooks*. Edited and translated by Q. Hoare and C.N. Smith. London, Lawrence and Wishart.

Griffiths, S. (2007) *East End Youth Ministry 1880–1957*. London, YTC Press.

Griffiths, S. (2008) *East End Youth Ministry* 1880–1957, Cambridge: YTC Press.

Habermas, J. (1987) *The Philosophical Discourse of Modernity*, F. Lawrence (trans.). Cambridge, Cambridge University Press.

Halpin, D. (2003) *Hope and Education. The role of the utopian imagination*. London, RoutledgeFalmer.

Harris, O. (2004) 'Braudel: Historical Time and the Horror of Discontinuity', *History Workshop Journal* 57, 161–174. [http://muse.jhu.edu/demo/history_workshop_journal/v057/57.1harris.htm. Accessed 28 April 2008]

Harvey, D. (1990) *The Condition of Post-modernity. An enquiry into the origins of cultural change*. Oxford, Blackwell.

Heath-Stubbs, M. (1926) *Friendship's Highway. Being the history of the Girls' Friendly Society (1875–1925)*. London, Girls' Friendly Society.

Henriques, B. (1937) *The Indiscretions of a Warden*. London, Methuen.

Hobsbawm, E. (1984) 'Introduction. Inventing traditions', in E. Hobsbawm and T. Ranger (eds.). *The Invention of Tradition*. Cambridge, Cambridge University Press.

Hobsbawm, E.J. (1994) *Age of Extremes: The Short Twentieth Century 1914–1991*. London, Michael Joseph.

Holland, T. (2004) *Rubicon: The Triumph and Tragedy of the Roman Republic*. London, Abacus.

Holmes, J. (2001) ' "Youth and Community Work in the 70s": A missed opportunity?' in (eds.) R. Gilchrist, T. Jeffs and J. Spence. *Essays in the History of Community and Youth Work*. Leicester, The Youth Work Press.

Humphries, S. (1981) *Hooligans or Rebels? An Oral History of Working-class Childhood* 1889–1939, Oxford: OUP.

Hutcheon, L. (1988) *A Poetics of Postmodernism. History, theory, fiction*. London, Routledge.

Institute of Historical Research (undated) Discourse on postmodernism and history. [http://www.history.ac.uk/discourse/. Accessed 18 July 2008].

Jeal, T. (1989) *Baden-Powell*. London, Hutchinson.

Jeffs, A.J. (1979) *Young People and the Youth Service*. London, Routledge and Kegan Paul.

Jeffs, T. (2003) 'Basil Henriques and the "House of Friendship"' in (eds.) R. Gilchrist, T. Jeffs and J. Spence. *Architects of Change. Studies in the history of youth and community work*. Leicester, The National Youth Agency.

Jeffs, T. (2006) 'Oft referenced, never read? Report of the 1904 interdepartmental committee on physical deterioration' in (eds.) R. Gilchrist, T. Jeffs and J. Spence. *Drawing on the Past. Studies in the history of youth and community work*. Leicester, The National Youth Agency.

Jeffs, T. with Gilchrist, R.M. (2005) *150 Years of the Newcastle YMCA*. Leicester, National Youth Agency.

Jeffs, T. and Smith, M.K. (forthcoming) *Youth Work*. London, Palgrave.

Jenkins, K. (1997) (ed.) *The Postmodern History Reader*. London, Routledge.

Jenkins, K. (2006) 'New Ways Revisited', *Times Literary Supplement,* October 13th.

Kadish, S. (1995) *'A Good Jew and a Good Englishman'. The Jewish Lads' and Girls' Brigade 1895–1995*. London, Vallentine Mitchell.

Kennedy, P. (1988) T*he rise and fall of the great powers: economic change and military conflict from 1500 to 2000*. London, Unwin Hyman.

Lacquer, W. (1974) *Historians in Politics,* London: Sage.

Laqueur, T.W. (1976) *Religion and respectability: Sunday Schools and Working Class Culture*. New Haven, Yale University Press.

Lefebvre, G. (1939, 2005) *The Coming of the French Revolution*. Translated and with a preface by R.R. Palmer. Princeton NJ, Princeton University Press.

Lyotard, J-F. (1984) *The Postmodern Condition: A report on knowledge*. Manchester, Manchester University Press.

Marquand, D. (2004) *Decline of the Public. The hollowing-out of citizenship*. Cambridge, Polity.

Milson, F.W. (1963) *Social Group Method and Christian Education*. London, Chester House.

Milson, F.W. (1980) *Political education: A practical guide for Christian youth workers*. Exeter, Paternoster Press.

Montague, C.J. (1904) *Sixty Years in Waifdom. Or, the Ragged School Movement in English history*. London, Charles Murray and Co.

Mulgan, G., Rushanara, A., Halkett, R. and Saunders, B. (2007) *In and Out of Sync. The Challenge of Growing Social Innovations,* London: National Endowment for Science, Technology and the Arts.

Mulvagh, J. (2008) *Madresfield. The real Brideshead*. London, Doubleday.

Nicholls, D. (1997) *An Outline History of Youth and Community Work and the Union 1834–1997*. Birmingham, Pepar Publications.

Oldfield, S. (2008) *Jeanie, an 'Army of One': Mrs Nassau Senior, 1828–1877, the First Woman in Whitehall*. Brighton, Sussex Academic Press.

Passmore, R. (2003) *Meet them where they're at. Helping churches engage young people through detached youth work*. Bletchley, Scripture Union.

Paterson, A. (1910) *The Doctor and the OMM*. London, Oxford Medical Mission.

Paul, L. (1951) *Angry Young Man*. London, Faber and Faber.

Pelham, T.H.W. (1889) *Handbook to Youths' Institutes and Working Boys' Clubs . . .* With preface by . . . Archdeacon Farrar . . . With a list of Societies, institutes and clubs for young men and boys in the Diocese of London, London, London Diocesan Council for the Welfare of Young Men.

Percival, A.C. (1951) *Youth Will Be Led. The story of the voluntary youth organisations*. London, Collins.

Perkin, H. (1989) *The Rise of Professional Society: England since 1880*. London, Routledge.

Polayni, M. (1959) *The Study of Man,* Chicago: University of Chicago Press.

Porter, R. (1999) *The Greatest Benefit to Mankind: A Medical History of Humanity*. London, Fontana Press.

Porter, R. (2000) *London: A Social History,* London: Penguin.

Porter, R. (2002) *Madness: A Brief History*. Oxford, Oxford University Press.

Purkiss, D. (1996) *The Witch in History: Early Modern and Twentieth-century Representations*. London, Routledge.

Richardson, E. (2008) *DIY Community Action: Neighbourhood Problems and Community Self-help*. Bristol, Policy Press.

Riden, P. (1998) *Local History: A Handbook for Beginners* 2e. Chesterfield, Merton Priory Press.

Roberts, E. (1984) *A woman's place: an oral history of working-class women 1890–1940*. Oxford, Blackwell.

Roberts, R. (1973) *The Classic Slum. Salford Life in the First Quarter of the Century*. Harmondsworth, Penguin

Rose, C. (1998) *Touching Lives. A personal history of Clapton Jewish Youth Centre 1946–1973*. Leicester, Youth Work Press.

Rosenthal, M. (1986) *The Character Factory. Baden-Powell and the origins of the Boy Scout Movement*. London, Collins.

Rowbotham, S. (1973) *Hidden from History: 300 years of Women's Oppression and the Fight against it*. London, Pluto.

Samuel, R. (1992) 'Reading the Signs: II. Fact-grubbers and mind-readers', *History Workshop Journal* 33: 220–251.

Samuel, R. (1996) *Theatres of Memory: Past and Present in Contemporary Culture Volume 1*. London, Verso.

Say, M. (1997) *A Century of the OBC*. London, Deptford Forum Publishing.

Schama, S. (1987) *The embarrassment of riches: an interpretation of Dutch culture in the golden age*. London, Collins.

Schama, S. (2000) *A History of Britain. Vol. 1: At the edge of the world?: 3000BC–AD1603*. London, BBC Books.

Schama, S. (2001) *A History of Britain. Vol. 2: The British wars: 1603–1776*. London, BBC Books.

Schama, S. (2002) *A History of Britain. Vol. 3: The fate of empire, 1776–2000*. London, BBC Books.

Schama, S. (2005) *Rough crossings: Britain, the slaves and the American Revolution*. London, BBC Books.

Secretan, H. (1931) *London Below the Bridges. Its boys and future*. London, Geoffrey Bles.

Smith, M. (1988) *Developing Youth Work. Informal education, mutual aid and popular practice*. Milton Keynes, Open University Press.

Smith, M.K. (1996, 2008) 'Youth work history. A guide to the literature', *the encyclopaedia of informal education*. [http://www.infed.org/youthwork/b-yw-hist.htm. Accessed 23 July 2008].

Smith, M.K. (1999, 2002) 'Youth work: an introduction', *the encyclopedia of informal education*. [www.infed.org/youthwork/b-yw.htm. Accessed 23July 2008].

Smith, M.K. (2003) 'From youth work to youth development. The new government framework for English youth services', *Youth and Policy 79*. Available in *the informal education archives*: http://www.infed.org/archives/jeffs_and_smith/smith_youth_work_to_youth_development.htm

Sobel, D. (1998) *Longitude*. London, Fourth Estate.

Spence, J. (2001) 'The impact of the First World War on the development of youth work: The case of the Sunderland Waifs Rescue Agency and Street Vendors' Club' in (eds.) R. Gilchrist, T. Jeffs and J. Spence. *Essays in the History of Community and Youth Work*. Leicester, The Youth Work Press.

Spence, J. (2003) 'Frank Caws and the development of work with boys in Sunderland' in (eds.) R. Gilchrist, T. Jeffs and J. Spence. *Architects of Change. Studies in the history of youth and community work*. Leicester, The National Youth Agency.

Springhall, J. (1977) *Youth, Empire and Society. British Youth Movements 1883–1940*. Beckenham, Croom Helm.

Springhall, J., Fraser, B. and Hoare, M. (1983). *Sure and Stedfast. A History of the Boys Brigade 1883–1983*. London, Collins.

Stanley, M. (1878) *Work About the Five Dials*. London: Macmillan and Co. See extract in the *archives*.

Stanley, M. (1890) *Clubs for Working Girls*. London: Macmillan. (Reprinted in F. Booton (ed.) (1985) *Studies in Social Education 1860–1890*. Hove, Benfield Press.

Starkey, D. (2000) *Elizabeth*. London, Chatto and Windus.

Starkey, D. (2003) *Six wives: the queens of Henry VIII*. London, Chatto and Windus.

Starkey, D. (2004) *The Monarchy of England: The Beginnings*. London, Chatto and Windus.

Starkey, D. (2006) *Monarchy: From the Middle Ages to Modernity*. London, HarperPress.

Taylor, J. (1972) *From Self Help to Glamour. Working Men's Clubs 1860–1972*. Oxford, History Workshop.

Thomas, K. (2006) 'New ways revisited. How history's borders have expanded in the past forty years', *Times Literary Supplement*, 13 October.

Thompson, E.P. (1963) *The Making of the English Working Class*. London: Victor Gollancz. 2nd edition with new postscript, Harmondsworth, Penguin, 1968, third edition with new preface 1980.

Thompson, W. (2000) *What happened to history*. London, Pluto Press.

Tillyard, S. (2006) 'All our pasts. The rise of popular history', *Times Literary Supplement*, 13 October.

Times Literary Supplement (1995) 'The hundred most influential books since the war', 6 October 1995: 39. [http://tls.timesonline.co.uk/article/0,,25332-1999686,00.html. Accessed 3 July 2008].

Trevelyan, G.M. (1942) *English Social History: A Survey of Six Centuries from Chaucer to Queen Victoria*. London, Longmans Green and Co.

Wade, E.K. (1971) *Olave Baden-Powell. The authorised biography of the World Chief Guide*. London, Hodder and Stoughton.

Ward, P. (1996) *Growing Up Evangelical: youthwork and the making of a subculture*. London, SPCK.

Ward, P. (1997) *Youthwork and the Mission of God*. London, SPCK.

White, J. (1980) *Rothschild Buildings. Life in an East End Tenement Block 1887–1920*. London, Routledge and Kegan Paul.

White, H.V. (1973) *Metahistory: Historical Imagination in Nineteenth Century Europe*. Baltimore, Johns Hopkins University Press.

White, H.V. (1978) *Topics of Discourse: Essays in Cultural Criticism*. Baltimore, Johns Hopkins University Press.

White, H.V. (1987) *Content of the Form: Narrative Discourse and Historical Representation*. Baltimore, Johns Hopkins University Press.

CHAPTER 2

'The Playground of Today is the Republic of Tomorrow': Social Reform and Organised Recreation, 1890–1930s

Linnea M. Anderson

The development of organised recreation programmes in the American settlement and playground movements during the late 19th and early 20th centuries was part of the progressive reform response to industrialisation, urbanisation, and immigration and reflected concerns about the influence of the physical and social environment on the individual. This chapter offers a brief background on the settlement and playground movements in the United States and gives an overview of core themes surrounding recreation, as expressed by social reformers from 1890 to the 1930s. By current standards, some of the concerns and issues regarding recreation sound very earnest, and almost quaint. However, recreation activities, particularly recreation for youth, were a serious subject of social reform. Health, fitness, and physical activity for the individual were viewed as important national assets. Recreation was a means by which life in a urban industrial society could be made more tolerable, immigrant children moulded into Americans, and children of all classes protected from vice and prepared for citizenship. Equally important, reformers viewed organised recreation as a way to reconcile the needs of an industrial nation with the principles of democracy.

The American settlement and playground movements shared many of the same theories about the importance of recreation. The two movements evolved at essentially the same time and cross-pollinated both ideas and personnel. Recreation ideologies and programmes in both were influenced by turn of the century progressive reform spirit; belief in both public and private solutions to social problems; and emerging theories of psychology and child development, including the recognition of adolescence as a significant developmental period. Across the country, particularly in poor, urban areas, settlement houses and playground associations established some of the first playgrounds and fought for public funding for recreation. They developed core themes and methodologies that emphasised the relationship between organised play, health, character, and democracy.

The playground movement

Histories of the playground movement credit the Sand Gardens in Boston, established in 1886, with being the first supervised, public playground in the US. When Charlesbank Gymnasium opened in Boston in 1889, it became the first public, free, equipped outdoor playground. The first playground in New York City was opened in 1890 by University Settlement. In 1894, Hull House playground opened in Chicago. By 1905, 35 American cities had supervised playgrounds and the city of Chicago alone spent $5 million on 10 new playgrounds (National Recreation Association Records, 3; Curtis, 1907).

As the call for play space for children gained ground, the Playground Association of America (PAA) was established in 1906. The founding meeting of the Association was held at the YMCA in Washington DC on 12 April 1906. The delegates were eighteen men and women from playground associations, public school and municipal recreation departments, settlements, teachers' colleges, the kindergarten movement, and charity organisations. Luther H. Gulick, director of physical education in the New York City school system and founder of the Public School Physical Education Society and the Academy of Physical Education, was elected as the association's first president. Gulick brought a YMCA-influenced belief in the connection between physical and spiritual health to the PAA.[1] Henry S. Curtis, supervisor of playgrounds for Associated Charities of Washington, DC, became the secretary. President Theodore Roosevelt, who received the delegates at the White House, and reformer Jacob Riis were selected as honorary president and vice president, nicely symbolising the association's concern both for promoting health and character through exercise and organised sports and the improvement of conditions for the poor through supervised recreation. Among its founding principles, the fledgling association stated:

That inasmuch as play under proper conditions is essential to the health and the physical, social, and moral wellbeing of the child, playgrounds are a necessity for all children as much as schools.

(National Recreation Association Records, [NRAR] 1)

The association's first annual conference, called the Play Congress, was held in Chicago in 1907. The programme clearly illustrated important themes of democracy, citizenship and morality that continued to guide recreation through the mid 20th century. Speeches included 'Relation of Play to Juvenile Delinquency', 'Play as Training in Citizenship' and the 'Social Value of Playgrounds in Crowded Districts'. Jane Addams spoke on 'Public Recreation and Social Morality'. The convention concluded with a massive 'play festival' in Ogden Park, attended by 4,000 spectators. The programme included: marching, singing and circle games by 300 kindergarteners; eighty girls in gymnastic games and eighty boys on gym apparatus; 100 girls playing volley ball; relay races of 100 boys and girls, respectively; Swedish, Hungarian, Lithuanian, and Bulgarian national dances in costume; and 100 boys demonstrating six athletic events 'suitable for use in large or small playgrounds' (NRAR, Program of the first annual Play Congress, 20–22 June 1907). At PAA conferences, even the delegates were encouraged play games in order to experience the 'play spirit'.

The PAA, which became the National Recreation Association in 1930, lobbied for municipal funding of supervised public playgrounds, developed training programmes for 'play leaders', provided professional consultation and coordination services to fledgling local recreation departments, and facilitated community surveys and playground campaigns. It also offered lectures and a publication service. The association's journal, *Playground*, was a source of practical advice, programming ideas, and playground theory. During the PAA's early years, funding from the Russell Sage Foundation helped the organisation finance services and start-up costs.

From the earliest days, it was clear that recreation was not just about sports and physical fitness. In 1909, the PAA developed a curriculum for training playground and recreation directors. 'A Normal Course in Play' covered: child development, psychology, evolution, education, play theory, social and industrial conditions (including 'race history, tendencies and prejudices'), hygiene, eugenics, heredity, the playground movement in Europe and the US, playground facilities, playground management, games and activities, handicraft, nature study, playground planning, landscaping, record keeping, and fund raising. Texts included works by settlement movement leaders, such as Mary

Richmond and Jane Addams. Writings by educators, psychologists and reformers were also featured, including: Freiderich Froebel, German education theorist and inventor of Kindergarten; pioneer psychologist, G. Stanley Hall; Karl Groos, who introduced the idea that children's play was preparation for adult life; and journalist turned reformer, Jacob Riis.

Settlements in the United States

The first social settlement, Toynbee Hall, opened in 1884 in the East End of London. It was the inspiration for the American settlement movement. The social settlement was based on the idea that those who wanted to help the poor would 'settle' in the neighborhoods that they hoped to improve, often in a building purchased or donated by a benefactor. Many of these settlement workers were young, female graduates of education and nursing programmes or women's colleges. They endeavored to improve the lives of their working class, often immigrant, neighbours though social reform, educational programmes, health services, and friendly example (or 'uplift').

The first settlement in the United States, University Settlement on New York's Lower East Side, was founded by Stanton Coit in 1886. In 1889, Jane Addams founded Hull House in Chicago. Andover House in Boston and the Henry Street Settlement New York opened in 1891 and 1893, respectively. The National Federation of Settlements was formed in 1911, although associations of settlements in individual cities had been meeting since the 1890s.

Settlement houses, which existed on the 'front lines' of poverty and urbanisation, were logical sites for recreation programmes in working class, immigrant, urban neighbourhoods. They often provided the only recreation facilities and programmes available in these areas. Even prior to the formation of the PAA, settlements fought for public funding of playgrounds, often with mixed results when faced with disinterest or lack of funds on the part of municipal governments. In the face of government indifference or foot-dragging, many settlements formed their own recreational facilities and programmes.

Recreation was a natural component of the settlement programme, not only because it promoted the health of urban poor, but also because of its socialising effects: neighbourliness and neighbourhood action and cohesiveness being crucial to the settlement idea. The connection between sportsmanlike play and good citizenship, so often touted by recreation reformers, was also an attractive consideration for settlement workers, whose programmes and priorities were coloured with concerns about transforming the poor or foreign-born from a civic liability into a civic asset.

Recreation as social reform

Several core themes motivated settlement and playground reformers. Both movements drew on ideas about industrialisation, psychology, child development, and the effect of the environment on the individual to form a core argument that organised recreation was essential to the physical, mental and moral well being of the individual and critical to a modern, democratic, industrial society.

Not surprisingly, an important argument for recreation was the health and fitness of individuals. Physical exercise improved overall health, and benefited both mind and body. Recreation advocates cited toned muscles, improved circulation, increased vitality, better appetite, and improved co-ordination. Physical fitness was only one component of the recreation movement, however. Individuals were made fit, not only for their own sake, but for the good of democratic society, the industrial economy, and the future of American civilisation.

Reformers also argued that recreation promoted spiritual, moral, and character development. In 'Play and Democracy', written in 1907, PAA president, Luther Gulick, refers to the playground as 'our great ethical laboratory' (*Charities and The Commons*, [CTC] Vol. 18, 3 August 1907). PAA promotional literature touted the benefits of organised recreation and hinted at the dangers of negligence. 'Playgrounds develop[:] health, initiative, purity of mind, cooperation, ambition, honesty, imagination, self-confidence, obedience, and justice. Playgrounds diminish [:] idleness, delinquency, exclusiveness, unfairness, gang-spirit, selfishness, rowdyism, temptation, social barriers, reformatories' (NRAR, 'Playgrounds Develop, Playgrounds Diminish', ud). Recreation was described as an 'anti-vice, anti-saloon, anti-cigarette, anti-gambling influence and a positive training in morals' ('Schools for Play', *Survey*, 28, [17], 27 July 1912).

Biology, psychology, and evolution were used to support the argument that play was an essential part of the human character and that constructive, supervised recreation was necessary to positive character development. Humans, and children in particular, were described as having natural instincts and needs for play, outdoor activity, and group association. The very first sentence of the NRA philosophy describes play as a 'fundamental urge in human existence, scarcely less powerful and important than the urges of physical hunger and sex' (NRAR, 'Brief Summary National Recreation Association Philosophy', ud). Reformers argued that natural instincts lead youth to want play and fun, but could also mislead them. Recreation channeled and refined the play instinct.

Connecting recreation and character led some to draw links between physical and moral weakness. Citing physical studies of college students caught cheating or boys brought to juvenile court, Lee Hamner of the Russell Sage Foundation Child Hygiene Department and the PAA concluded that the physically inferior 'lack 'backbone' in both the physical and moral sense' and that 'The physically weak seem to be a prey to temptation' (Hamner, 1910).

Gendered concepts regarding natural abilities of boys and girls also influenced arguments about recreation and character. In particular, boys were portrayed as having instincts for camaraderie, leadership, war, hunting, and physicality that could be developed for citizenship or lead to crime, delinquency, and immorality. Athletics and recreation were promoted either as a natural antidote to, or training for, boys' war-like instincts, depending upon who was writing. Both boys' and girls' recreation emphasised fitness and health, leadership, self reliance, and courage, but promoters of recreation for girls also emphasised how sports added to beauty, grace, and friendships. Some recreation workers made the assumption that girls did not like competition.

Whereas boys were portrayed as training for leadership, girls recreation aimed to promote 'sturdy, normal womanhood', 'wise, efficient motherhood', and 'worthy citizenship' (National Federation of Settlements Records, [NFSR] *Study of Young Girls*, c. 1921). In some cases, girls were portrayed as needing more vitality and intelligence than their foremothers, presumably to offset the stresses of modern life or to survive their lives as urban shop girls or garment workers with their morals and reproductive ability intact (NFSR, 'Conference on Girl's work', c. 1920). Recreation for girls related to preserving and improving racial stock as well as to preparation for citizenship. 'The continuance of the race and its welfare, which is the main business of life, is left in the hands of careless children without any preparation or guidance whatever. The guardian of the future of race must herself be guarded from her own ignorance and folly and the selfishness or vice of others' (Kennard, 1912).

Some girls' recreation programmes were hampered by concerns for health and over exertion. At times, girls' recreation staff seemed unsure about how to reconcile physical activity for girls with assumptions about feminine characteristics. Participants in a United Neighborhood Houses of New York Girls' Workers meeting in 1924 concluded 'It is best to develop athletics for girls alone, since the ideals should be entirely different from the boys, stressing group work and the development of general physique instead of training individuals for record-breaking'. A 'Miss Wyman dwelt upon our moral responsibility in supervising athletics for girls' and 'pointed out that the question of jumping for girls is a mooted one, and that in no case should indoor jumping be allowed, nor out-door jumping without a soft sand jumping pit, on account of the jar' (United Neighborhood Houses Records, Scrapbook 4-94, 1924). At first glance, recreation advocates of the 1910s appear to have taken a more active, athletic approach to girls' recreation than their counterparts of the 1920s and 1930s. However, more research is needed to determine the existence and prevalence of such attitudes.

Building character on the playground benefited society as well as the individual. Citizenship and neighbourliness were touted as outgrowths of recreation. Speaking to the National Conference of Charities and Correction in 1910, Lee Hamner declared, 'The playground of today is the republic of tomorrow. If you want twenty years hence a nation of strong, efficient men and women, a nation in which there shall be justice and square dealing, work it out today with the boys and girls on the playground' (Hamner, 1910).

Settlement and playground advocates were eloquent on the subject of recreation as a foundation of citizenship. References to honour, loyalty, subjection to the rule of authority, fairness, honesty, and recognition of merit flowed freely (Gulick, 1909; Lies, 1926; Kennedy ca.1931; NRAR, 'A Constructive Creed', 1910). They emphasised the group as a means of socialisation and sports as an excellent source of group co-operation and loyalty. 'Playground National Song' states 'While playing we learn our duties, We owe to one and all, For with fair play and square deal, too, we are ready for our country's call' (NRAR, ud). 'People who play together find it easier to live together. Individuals enjoying a wholesome happy play life are more loyal as well as more efficient citizens', declared the PAA's 'A Constructive Creed' (NRAR, 1910).

Much has been written about the efforts of settlement workers and other early 20th Century reformers to Americanise immigrants. Teams of first and second generation immigrant children playing American sports, such as basketball or baseball, or participating in track and field events, with their classical Greek associations, were an important way that settlements fulfilled their role as socialisers and trainers of new citizens. 'Play as a school of The Citizen', written in 1907 by Joseph Lee (philanthropist, reformer and vice president and future president of the PAA), is a densely-packed exploration of child development, democracy, and recreation. In it, Lee expresses ideas about freedom and cooperation through sport that were an important theme of recreation reformers. Lee argues that recreation develops 'spiritual communication', 'bravery', a 'sense of organization', 'single minded determination', 'conscious participation', 'rhythmic instinct', 'loyalty' and a 'sense of membership'. Significantly, he contrasts these traits to 'the mechanical soldier of an autocracy', the 'hypnotic performance of a stereotyped part', or the primitive 'tribal consciousness' (CTC.(18), 3 August 1907). In this light, organised recreation was one of the building blocks of the republic. Properly equipped and run by a good leader of 'a high personal type' the playground was 'a school of all civic virtues' (Curtis, 1907).

But what about those who lived in poor urban areas or worked long hours in factories, shops and offices? What kind of citizens would they become? It is not an accident that the settlement and playground movements evolved along with the industrialisation and urbanisation trends of the later 19th early 20th centuries. Reformers in the settlement and playground movements expressed profound concern about industrialisation, urbanisation, and mechanisation – concern for how Americans could retain their health, individuality (as opposed to citizens of non democratic countries), and moral character in the modern world.

Settlement and recreation workers often used the phrase 'congested districts' to described poor, tenement neighbourhoods. The concern with congestion related not just to overcrowding. The impact of crowding on physical health, nerves, and character was a constant refrain of the recreation and settlement movements. Furthermore, reformers argued, the natural physical energies of children, especially boys, led them to want play and fun, but had no good outlet in the city. Speaking to the first Play Congress in 1907, Jane Addams noted 'We see all about us much vice which is merely a love for pleasure "gone wrong"' ('Public Recreation and Social Morality' 1907). Without space for supervised play, children played in streets, 'roamed' the city, or fell prey to commercial recreation places. Streets were described as a 'school of crime' (Curtis, 1907).

The urban environment made recreation more difficult, but even more necessary. The fresh air, sunlight, activity, and freedom of movement of the country were contrasted to the 'vitiated air', idleness, confinement, and overcrowding of city life. Lack of sunlight and pure air in cities was a constant refrain. Helene Ingram, Superintendent of Relief for the New York Association for Improving the Condition of the Poor cited '. . . small dark bedrooms, the damp, unwholesome basements, the tall, overcrowded houses, the narrow street, the scorching pavements, the airless atmosphere . . .' in her paper on 'fresh air' work at the National Conference of Charities and Correction ('The Value of the Fresh Air Movement', 1907).

Repeatedly, reformers expressed the fear that the nation's youth were unfit for citizenship and not prepared to defend the country and identified urban life as one cause of the crisis. During the 1920s the poor results of many World

War I era selective service exams, in which 25 per cent of inductees were supposedly found not fit for service, were cited repeatedly. '. . . [W]e have seen for the first time the nation's child, measured, weighed and found wanting', said the National Federation of Settlements ('Study of Young Girls', c 1921). Young men were described as 'incapable of effective service, and that at a time when civilisation hung in the balance' (Lies, 1926).

Reformers argued that urban life not only cut people off from the land, but also from each other and from beneficial traditions. This argument was applied to immigrants in particular, who were envisioned as uprooted, deprived of cultural background, and lacking in American traditions of liberty and individuality. Luther Gulick wrote how social pressures on the family and immigration, with its mixing of different cultures, lead to loss of traditions that were handed down from generation to generation. He believed that tradition had broken in the United States and deprived children of the guidance they needed to develop. 'Therefore', he wrote, 'we need tradition carriers, play leaders – and that's what the directors of the playground are' ('Doctrine of Hands off in Play', 1909).

Recreation advocates were conscious of living in the 'machine age'. The repetition of machine work and the increased pace of life that resulted from modern inventions were viewed as damaging to the nerves and body. Toil indoors with machinery and the drudgery of repetitive labour in a factory or office were portrayed as dehumanising and enervating, as opposed to the active, outdoor work of an idealised agrarian past. The NRA philosophy stated 'It is believed that even the most citified individual has remnants of biological hunger for the soil . . .' (NRAR, c. 1931). A recurring theme was the fear that industrial society would transform the individual into 'a mere robot, a clod' (Lies, 1926) who lacked the desire for individuality and freedom and, therefore, the desire to defend them. Urban dwellers and factory workers, especially immigrants who supposedly had no traditions of freedom of their own, were portrayed as especially vulnerable to this loss of individuality and vitality. Recreation literature sometimes contained an explicit or implied contrast between American workers and those in non-democratic countries and the fear that Americans would become 'cogs'.

Some recreation leaders cautioned against over-scheduled time or regimented play and urged an emphasis on play that led to spontaneity, joy, and exuberance, what reformers called 'Play Spirit'. Henry S. Curtis, Secretary of the PAA, stated 'Play is our education in the spirit of joyousness, but it has much to do, not merely with the joyousness of childhood, but with the joyousness and optimism of all after life [adulthood]' ('The Playground', 1907). The right combination of freedom and structure was necessary in order for recreation to successfully instill a desire for freedom alongside a willingness to work cooperatively and subordinate one's own will to the group. Mary Simkhovitch, founder of Greenwich House settlement, argued that:

> *Recreation, like education, has suffered from regimentation . . . To be done good to, to be planned for, to be cast into a mold, to be the victim of a program means the fixing of well defined patterns of thought and conduct according to a predetermined standard . . . Recreation then has to begin with the understanding of the individual . . . Recreational guidance, like vocational guidance, has its base in a psychology which takes into account native gifts, practical opportunity, the background of social experience and tradition in which the individual is placed.*
>
> ('Recreation in a Settlement Program', 1930)

How to pursue the benefits of organised play without over-regimentation was a tension running though much of the rhetoric of play. The NRA philosophy stated that leaders should not 'cramp initiative and resourcefulness'. If American children merely did what they were told on the playground, it defeated a crucial purpose of recreation: free association and energetic citizenship. They struggled to reconcile the need for structured play that would counteract the 'rough' or 'low' play of the streets and commercial recreation places with their concern that over-regimentation led to the loss of joy and vitality. Reformers looked at the regimentation of factory work and the grinding life in urban neighborhoods and worked to put the 'Play Spirit' back into the lives of children – not only for their own good, but for the good of democracy. Good citizens were not only fit, they enjoyed life.

Urban living in the machine age not only created problems for physical, moral and mental well being. Reformers argued that there was an increased need for leisure to counteract city and industrial life. Modern conveniences also produced increased leisure time. With time, however, came increased danger from the negative influence of commercialised amusements, such as movie theatres and dance halls: what reformers called 'low forms' of recreation.

Settlement workers believed firmly in the settlement as a positive influence and as a counterpoint to life at home or on the streets. They were particularly concerned for the development of the children of immigrants and the negative influences of poor neighbourhoods and 'old country' ways of immigrant parents. This fitted with theories about the benefits of 'wholesome', supervised activities and the dangers of unsupervised, commercial recreation. The 'tenement home was no longer a qualified place in which education, recreation and association could go on . . . many parents were so far out of relation with the actualities of life that they were not competent guides to their children in matters of health, education, recreation and vocation' (Kennedy, 'Settlement Method'). Bad homes and the lure of commercial leisure activities threatened these children. Louise de Koven Bowen, President of the Juvenile Protective Association of Chicago, speaking at National Conference of Charities and Correction in 1910, described with delicious horror the result of this situation. The '. . . girl living in tenements and working in the shop is nervously tired at end of day, home is unattractive . . '. 'She goes out onto the street and to the cheap theater, whose standard she possibly adopts because she has none of her own, or else she goes to the dance halls. *Her vitality is at a low ebb* [Author's emphasis]. She takes her first drink, which the boy in order to show his gallantry presses upon her, and so she takes her first downward step' ('The Need of Recreation', 1910).

Recreation programmes in the settlements and city playgrounds provided one counterbalance to the leisure-time problem, but an attack on commercialised recreation was essential to winning the fight for the character of the nation's future citizens. Motion picture houses, saloons, pool halls, vaudeville theatre, and even candy stores and ice cream parlors were portrayed as low, vicious, lustful, cheap, sordid, and dissipated (Bellamy, 1914; National Recreation Association, 1917; Thomas, 1910). Dance halls were the chief target of recreation reformers. Robert A. Woods of the Andover House settlement wrote in the 'Vice Problem in Boston', dated 1923, that 'The special evils which they present come of the free and indiscriminate mingling of young people who would ordinarily maintain quite a range of moral standards'. Woods suggested that social workers could combat 'objectionable forms of dancing' with 'attractive presentations of the better way' (Woods, 1923). Anti-dance hall advocates expressed tremendous concern for the protection of innocent girls who might enter a dance hall and the mingling of middle class girls with working class girls or even prostitutes. Dance halls were portrayed as scenes of predation and moral downfall.

It was not just commercial recreation that was viewed with suspicion. Unsupervised or unconstructive forms of play were also cause for alarm. George Bellamy of Hiram House settlement in Cleveland noted that a community recreation survey discovered children on the streets engaged in such activities as: 'chalking suggestive signs on buildings', 'throwing mud at street cars', 'telling bad stories', 'looking at pictures of women in tights on billboards', 'watching arrests', smoking, and drinking, among other unwholesome pursuits (Bellamy, 1914).

'Recreation is stronger than vice and recreation alone can stifle the lust for vice', wrote Jane Addams in *The Spirit of Youth and the City Streets* (1909). Settlement and playground reformers took these words to heart. Good recreation was described and contrasted to 'evil' recreation as wholesome, vigorous, manly, stimulating, joyous, free, organised, and co-operative. To settlement and playground reformers, good recreation meant supervised recreation. Their programmes focused on athletics (team games such as basketball, volley ball, and baseball), circle games for young children, gymnastics (or 'drill'), track and field games, play festivals or sports days, hikes and outings, and camping. Basketball was king of boy's recreation, especially in urban areas. *Boys Athletics in 33 Settlements in the City of New York* notes that, of the 33 settlements studied, all had basketball programmes and 32 had baseball teams. Handball, boxing, volleyball, track, swimming, and 'informal games' were also popular (Welfare Council of New York, 1931, in Albert Kennedy papers). Settlements fought for and then arranged to use city athletic fields. Most had indoor gyms and many had outdoor playgrounds. Some resourceful settlements that could scrape together funding even erected playgrounds on their roofs. There were at least 13 such playgrounds in New York City by 1931. In addition to sports, recreation also included settlement clubs, aesthetic or folk dances, handicrafts, pageants, dramatics, 'sings', stunts, and cheers.

Properly organised and filled with play spirit, recreation combated the temptations of commercial amusements and produced healthy citizens who were willing to be led by those who showed themselves to be worthy captains. PAA literature was full of stories of children saved from drudgery, delinquency, and squalor by recreation. 'Little thin hands and arms, flabby from inactivity, have become brown and firm. Pinched faces and dull eyes have taken on new light and expression. Coming from stuffy hot rooms, many of them have for the first time come into a real children's world and have been free' ('Six True Stories' ud.). Recreation not only benefited individual but also transformed a nation of alien immigrants, or downtrodden, unhealthy factory workers, into a cohesive, healthy, population of citizens working for common good or ready to defend their country.

Conclusion

Play was serious business for late 19th and early 20th century social reformers. Core themes surrounding recreation included the importance of physical, moral and social 'fitness' and the role of organised play in developing and preserving those traits. Play was viewed as a biological imperative that, if properly satisfied and directed, promoted a joyous attitude toward life; physical, mental, and moral health; and proper child development.

Settlement house workers and playground advocates often expressed concerns about the impact of the industrial, urban environment and modern working conditions on the individual. Recreation made life in the city, factory, and office tolerable and counterbalanced the stresses and demands of working in a modern economy. The urban environment was viewed as particularly threatening to the health and morals of children and youth. Positive forms of recreation diverted urban children, especially children of immigrants and working poor, from 'low' forms of commercialised amusements and vice.

Organised recreation was also a way to reconcile the needs of an industrial nation with the principles of democracy: training office and factory workers to function as a unit while maintaining the vitality and desire for independence essential to their personal investment in democracy. In particular, recreation was a means to acculturate children of immigrants and the poor and to prepare all children for citizenship.

These beliefs about fitness, democracy, citizenship and the environment informed the recreation programmes of settlement houses and playground societies, who viewed organised play as a means of socialisation and personal betterment as well as a source of amusement and health.

Note

1 In 1891, while head of the gymnasium department of the YMCA's training school in Springfield, Illinois, Gulick, along with James Naismith, developed the game of basketball.

References

Addams, J. (1909). *The Spirit of Youth and the City Streets*, New York: Macmillan; http://www.boondocksnet.com/editions/youth/, 6 July 2001.

Addams, J. (1907). 'Public Recreation and Social Morality' in *Charities and the Commons*, Vol. 18, 3 August 1907, 492–494.

Albert Kennedy Papers, Welfare Council of New York, 'Boys' Athletics in 33 Settlements in the City of New York', 1931, Box 5, folder 44, Social Welfare History Archives, University of Minnesota Libraries.

Bellamy, G. (1914). 'Recreation and Social Progress: The Settlement' in *Proceedings of the National Conference of Charities and Correction*, 1914, 376–377.

Bellamy, G. (1918). 'A Community Recreation Program for Juveniles' in *Proceedings of the National Conference of Charities and Correction*, 1918, 65–67.

Bowen, L. de Koven (1910). 'The Need of Recreation' in *Proceedings of the National Conference of Charities and Correction*, 102.

Bowen, L. de Koven (1914). *Safeguards for City Youth at Work and at Play*. New York: Macmillan.

Chapin, T.F. (1902) 'Play as a Reformative Agency' in *Proceedings of the National Conference of Charities and Correction*, 1914, 437–440.

Curtis, H.S. (1907). 'The Playground' in *Proceedings of the National Conference of Charities and Correction*, 285.

Daniels, H. McDoual (1914). *The Girl and Her Chance: A Study of Conditions Surrounding the Young Girl between Fourteen and Eighteen Years of Age in New York City*. New York: Fleming H. Revell

Forbush, W.B. (1907). *The Boy Problem*. Boston: Pilgrim Press.

Gillin, J.L. (1918) *Wholesome Citizens and Spare Time*. Cleveland, Ohio: The Cleveland Foundation Committee.

Gulick, L. (1907). 'Play and Democracy', in *Charities and the Commons*, Vol. 18, 3 August 1907, 481–486.

Gulick, L. (1909). 'Doctrine of Hands Off in Play', National Recreation Association records, Box 14.

Hamner, L.F. (1910). 'Health and Playgrounds' in *Proceedings of the National Conference of Charities and Correction*, 155–156.

Ingram, H. (1907). 'The Value of the Fresh Air Movement' in *Proceedings of the National Conference of Charities and Correction*, 288.

Kennard, B. (1912). 'Emotional Life of Girls' in *Proceedings of the National Conference of Charities and Correction*, 146–148.

Kennedy, A. (c. 1931). *The Settlement Method*, (manuscript) Albert Kennedy papers, Social Welfare History Archives, University of Minnesota Libraries.

Knapp, R.F. and Charles E.H. (1979). *Play for America: The National Recreation Association, 1906–1965*. Arlington: National Recreation and Park Association.

Lee, J. (1907). 'Play as a School of the Citizen' in *Charities and the Commons*, Vol.18, 3 August 1907, 486–491.

Lies, E.T. (1926). 'Community Recreation: Its Significance, Objectives, Machinery, and Standards' in *Proceedings of the National Conference of Social Work*, 493–500.

Moley, R. (1920). *Commercial Recreation*. Cleveland, Ohio: The Cleveland Foundation Committee.

National Federation of Settlements Records, [NFSR] Social Welfare History Archives, University of Minnesota Libraries. *Study of Young Girls*, c. 1921, 1921, 3.

National Federation of Settlements Records, [NFSR] Social Welfare History Archives, University of Minnesota Libraries. *Conference on Girl's work*, c. 1920, Box 5, folder 36.

National Recreation Association Records, [NRAR] Social Welfare History Archives, University of Minnesota Libraries. Historical material, *Early Days*, undated, Box 1, folder 1.

National Recreation Association Records, [NRAR] Social Welfare History Archives, University of Minnesota Libraries. *Program of the first annual Play Congress*, 20–22 June 1907.

National Recreation Association Records, [NRAR] Social Welfare History Archives, University of Minnesota Libraries. *Brief History of the Playground and Recreation Movement in America*, undated, Box 1, folder.

National Recreation Association Records, [NRAR] Social Welfare History Archives, University of Minnesota Libraries. *Playgrounds Develop, Playgrounds Diminish*, Box 1, folder 3.

National Recreation Association Records, [NRAR] Social Welfare History Archives, University of Minnesota Libraries. *Brief Summary National Recreation Association Philosophy*, undated, Box 2, 'Philosophy' file.

National Recreation Association Records, [NRAR] Social Welfare History Archives, University of Minnesota Libraries. Playground Association of America, *A Constructive Creed*, 1910, Box 1, folder 2.

National Recreation Association Records, [NRAR] Social Welfare History Archives, University of Minnesota Libraries. *Playground National Song*, ud, Box 2, 'Association Song' folder.

National Recreation Association Records, [NRAR] Social Welfare History Archives, University of Minnesota Libraries. *Brief Summary National Recreation Association Philosophy*, c. 1931, Box 2, 'Philosophy' folder, 3.

National Recreation Association Records, [NRAR] Social Welfare History Archives, University of Minnesota Libraries. Playground Association of America, *Six True Stories*, ud, Box 1, folder 3, 2.

National Recreation Association Records, [NRAR] Social Welfare History Archives, University of Minnesota Libraries. *Making a Recreation Survey*, 1917, Box 39, 'Forms, old' folder.

National Recreation Association. Committee on a Normal Course in Play (1910). *A Normal Course in Play for Professional Directors*. New York: Playground Association of America.

'Schools for Play' in *Survey*, Vol. 28 (17), 27 July 1912, 585.

Simkhovitch, M. (1930). 'Recreation in a Settlement Program' in *Proceedings of the National Conference of Social Work*, 373.

Thomas, W.I. (Mrs) (1910) 'The Five Cent Theatre' in *Proceedings of the National Conference of Charities and Correction*, 1910, 145–149.

United Neighborhood Houses of New York Records, Social Welfare History Archives, University of Minnesota Libraries. *Girls' Workers meeting minutes*, scrapbook page 4–94, 1924, Box 63, folder 17.

United Neighborhood Houses of New York Records, Social Welfare History Archives, University of Minnesota Libraries. *Minutes of the Round Table* on 'A City Plan for Settlement Athletics', 1928, Scrapbook 9–15, Box 66, folder 32.

Winter, T. (2004) 'Luther Halsey Gulick', *the Encyclopedia of Informal Education*, www.infed.org/thinkers/gulick.htm.

Woods, R.A. (1923) 'The Vice Problem in Boston', Reprint from *National Municipal Review*, Volume 12, December 1923, 710–711.

CHAPTER 3

From Knowledge of the World to Knowledge of Self: Perspectives on the Professional Training of Youth Leaders, 1942–1948

Simon Bradford

Context

During the early 1940s there was acute political concern about wartime disruption to family and neighbourhood life and about young people in particular (Ferguson and Fitzgerald, 1954, 4; Bradford, 2006, 134). The Board of Education (BoE) published a series of circulars that established and developed the Youth Service as a means of regulating and managing young people's leisure. The state's involvement in provision for the training of youth leaders also began at this time (Board of Education, 1942). Several universities became involved in this work from 1942, building on training programmes for leaders that had existed since the 1920s in the churches and voluntary organisations. These developments were important in mapping a framework of *professional* training for leaders from which courses for youth workers have developed in some 40 higher education institutions in the UK. This chapter draws on various published sources, including government circulars and reports, and material from the National Archive to explore some of the underlying assumptions of these early approaches to professional training. It discusses the form and content of the courses and identifies differing views of the nature of professional leadership. The chapter traces the growing conviction that professionals should gain not only subject knowledge but, perhaps more importantly, knowledge of self that would facilitate empathy between leaders and young people. The latter increasingly came to signify the emergence of a late modern professional identity that departed from earlier discourses of leadership.

In the nineteenth and early twentieth centuries the expertise of youth leadership was lodged in the cultural capital of leaders themselves, classed and gendered knowledge often embodied in notions of bourgeois duty and service (Mooney, 1998). By the 1920s the idea that youth work required more than the 'personality' and 'zeal, tact and energy' that had sustained its activities in the nineteenth and early twentieth centuries (Stanley, 1890, 269; Russell and Rigby, 1908, 690) was increasingly persuasive. The Church of England, for example, established courses for leaders in the 1920s which advocates considered equivalent to 'honours standard at the University' (Inter-Diocesan Council for Women's Church Work, 1925). During the 1930s the National Council for Girls Clubs added 'qualifications' to 'genius' through formal training courses (National Council of Girls Clubs, 1934, 8). Located in major cities in England and Scotland, 13 'certificates' were awarded in 1936–1937 and 20 in 1937–1938. Despite small numbers, the NCGC initiative re-imagined youth leaders who, as well as having 'birthright' and special 'gifts', would, through training, be able to deploy understanding '. . . of the problems with which they are likely to have to deal' (ibid.).

Pressure from the voluntary organisations (and some universities) to increase leader numbers at the beginning of the War and the anticipation of youth registration as part of wartime mobilisation (Bradford, 2007) persuaded the BoE to set up a committee to investigate the need for leadership training courses. The Informal Youth Training Committee (IYTC), consisting mainly of senior academics and representatives of the voluntary youth organisations, reported in November 1941 that the '. . . training of workers in this field is to be considered . . . as the training of workers for service in an integral part of the education and social work systems of this country' (IYTC, 1941, 1). It proposed that youth leaders should share some of the training received by social workers and teachers, arguing that these occupations shared a central core of competence. Situated in the universities and some voluntary organisations, training was to include theory and practice integrated in a minimum one year full-time course for students with existing qualifications (social science graduates, for example) and a three year 'full course' for others. Theory included the 'mental and physical characteristics of adolescents', sex education, 'principles and processes of instruction', club management, religious studies, 'social philosophy', 'social and educational administration' and 'social and industrial conditions' (ibid., 4–5). Up to half of the course was to be made up of assessed practice co-ordinated by a personal tutor.

The IYTC's broad model shaped the twenty-two full-time one-year 'emergency' courses which ran between 1942 and 1948 at five Universities and University Colleges (Bristol, Durham, Swansea, University College Nottingham, and Kings College Newcastle) and recognised under Circular 1598 (Board of Education, 1942). During this period 302 students completed these courses (Kuenstler, 1951, 24). In addition, full-time courses of six and three months respectively were organised by the NCGC, and at Homerton College Cambridge. Part-time courses also existed at Durham University (two years), Liverpool University (one year), and NCGC (eighteen months) (Evans, 1965, 194).

Emergency training for youth leaders, disciplined professionals

The importance of these courses cannot be underestimated. As the first university-based courses in youth leadership they anticipated future developments in the professional training and education of youth leaders (in terms of content, pedagogy, and assessment). They embodied an instrumental technical-rational training (emphasising rigorous problem solving through the deployment of specialised knowledge and technique) combined with elements of traditional (non-instrumental) liberal education that emphasised the cultivation of mind and character. The courses incorporated three principal elements. *First* was a relatively systematic body of knowledge deriving principally from the social sciences. The *second* element comprised the application of the body of knowledge to practice and included a developing repertoire of problem solving principles, skills, behaviours and values which seemed designed to guide the leader's broad outlook. These constituted an emergent 'theory of practice'. *Third*, technical-rational professional training typically incorporated a period in which the novice undertook supervised practice, testing out theory in a 'real' work situation. Importantly, technical-rationalism assumes that knowledge is an ahistorical commodity produced and disseminated in the academy and which can be acquired and deployed universally by practitioners. Although these courses were established on this model it was challenged in the 1940s by an incipient humanist discourse that viewed practice more as a social accomplishment and construed it as both indeterminate and uncertain (Schön, 1991, 40). The view emerged towards the end of this period that leader training required more than knowledge of the external world and that self-knowledge was necessary in order to develop a professional self able to empathise with young people and their circumstances. This, it was suggested, would come about through explicit work on the self rather than through the simple acquisition of the right knowledge.

A brief analysis of the Circular 1598 courses is offered drawing on data provided by Kuenstler[1] from courses at University College Swansea, University College Nottingham, the University of Durham, and the University of Bristol. These data show the Universities' understandings of what counted as professional competence in youth leadership and largely reflected the views of the BoE which approved these courses. Although Circular 1598 and the work of the IYTC gave guidelines for institutions establishing these courses (content, facilities, and certification, for example), there was variation in their content and the priority given to their component parts.[2] Data from documents surviving from the course run during the session 1942–1943 at Bristol University are also discussed but, inevitably, this chapter gives an incomplete account of these courses and must be seen as work in progress. All of the Circular 1598 courses had two separate elements, theory and practice. These marked an underlying division between broadly liberal and vocational dis- courses that represented competing views of the role of university education. Two further distinctions can be made between elements in the practice component. *First*, it entailed training in technical skills and, *second*, students were required to undertake varying amounts of sometimes supervised and assessed work in leadership settings. Together, these components formed one year's programme of training.

Disseminating knowledge, 'theory' in youth leadership training

Although little overall consensus existed between institutions on the time students should spend on studying particular subjects, there was apparent consensus on the *modes* of study thought appropriate. According to Kuenstler, the theoretical work was completed through attendance at formal lectures with supporting seminars and tutorials suggesting pedagogy based principally on a traditional *liberal* mode of university study. The areas of knowledge referred to in the four course syllabi are remarkably similar. They cover three broad areas, knowledge deriving from the social sciences; religious or philosophical knowledge concerned with broad ethical principles and knowl- edge focusing on young people's health.

First, psychology (and adolescent psychology in particular) was present in all courses yet was referred to in different ways in different institutions. For example, the Swansea syllabus referred to the 'Psychology of Adolescents with special reference to the development of personality and to the interests and needs of adolescents' and Bristol's syllabus included a 'developmental study of the growing child from birth to maturity, with particular emphasis on emotional needs, the development of interests, the growth of sentiments and the formation of ideals'. All four courses included the broad heading of 'social studies and sociology', covering a range of topics from 'the social background of adolescents' (Swansea), 'social and economic conditions' (Nottingham), 'economic history' (Bristol), and 'current affairs' (Durham). All courses, except Bristol, included studies in 'social administration'. Thus, in varying forms, the social sciences were common to all four courses. They (and indeed 'Landmarks of European Experience' and 'Aesthetics') identified a formal territory of objective knowledge whose empirical origins were the guarantor of its presumed neutrality and a universal status. As such, this is rational knowledge which became increasingly constitutive of the special expertise of the developing human service occupations.

Second, two of the syllabi included 'Religion' or 'Religious Education', the Durham syllabus referring to '. . . essentials of the Christian faith; its educational and social implications . . . (and) . . . religious problems arising in youth work', whilst at Bristol, 'Bible Study' was the only detail given of 'Religious Education'. Two of the four syllabi referred to 'principles of education' as a discrete area of theoretical study. In the Bristol syllabus, for example, this was combined with lectures on 'Landmarks in European Experience'. The latter, deeply embedded in a liberal mode of education and

> . . . *studied against the background of modern philosophers and in relation to contemporary educational, social and religious issues* . . . [was designed] . . . *to study the experience of some of the great minds who have contributed to the European tradition* . . .
>
> (Kuenstler, 1951, 23)

Third, each syllabus, except that of Swansea referred to studies which included a component concerned with young people's health. For example, at Nottingham a series of lectures on 'hygiene and philosophy' were an adjunct to the course in the 'psychology of the adolescent'. At Durham, the syllabus referred to a course in 'physiology', which includes '. . . physiology and anatomy of the human body; appreciation of social health', and at Bristol, 'Health Education; including both physical and mental aspects . . '. was included.

Kuenstler gives no information on the reading expected of students on these courses. However, the reading list for the Bristol course shows that the literature was borrowed almost exclusively from the social sciences, psychology, sociology, educational theory, 'hygiene' and 'health', 'civics', and a nascent literature on youth work which constructed increasingly complex discourses of an informal educational practice. An expanding practice-based literature on youth leadership was combined with formal course-based lectures to mark out a territory of professional knowledge and understanding, and emergent theory of practice. Much of the knowledge disseminated on these courses, especially in the form of the 'human sciences', is deeply implicated in the relations and networks of power which characterise modern societies (Foucault, 1976, 197). It has formed the basis of various technologies (a range of therapeutic and educational practices invariably based on the 'psy' disciplines, for example) whose object is the surveillance and discipline of population and its constitutive groups (Rose, 1996, 134). These forms of knowledge were calculated to inform the youth leader's work with young people at a time when youth was viewed as a social problem. Psychology, for example, was intended to provide appropriate insight into young people (construed as minds *as well as* bodies). Combined with knowledge centred on notions of 'hygiene', 'health', 'health education' and 'personal and social hygiene', it appears intended to enable the youth leader to engage with the management of the young person's body, and the regulation of their sexuality. This work was given considerable prominence in the IYTC's deliberations and was an issue around which extensive social and political concern continued to grow (Jephcott, 1942, 125; Board of Education, 1943). Anxieties had been expressed by the IYTC that 'sex education' in the past had been excessively preoccupied with the dissemination of merely 'technical' knowledge about sex, and had relied on warnings of the dangers 'immorality' and sexually transmitted diseases (IYTC, 1941, 4) It had been, the IYTC suggested, insufficiently concerned with the formation of the 'attitudes' and 'ideals' underlying the conduct of sexuality. The IYTC took the view that the youth worker should have a special place in the latter process, and would therefore require appropriate training:

> . . . *to see that not only is the knowledge on sex matters available to boys and girls when they need it, but also that their motives and attitudes of mind and their ideals are such as will lead to sex being used for the greatest benefit and happiness of themselves and of society . . . (the youth leader) . . . should have considered critically the accepted motives, ideals, taboos, and codes which regulate sex behaviour in this country and be aware of the degree to which social and racial welfare is involved as well as individual and personal happiness.*

> (ibid., 5)

This quotation provides a metaphor for youth leadership's concern to intervene in the intimacies of young people's lives and towards which professional training was increasingly directed. It contains an expression of the governance of adolescent sexuality, through the articulation of individual sexual behaviour (ideally managed by the young person themselves), the explicit role of the youth leader and the achievement of wider social harmony. This quote also suggests a philosophical view in which professional work is considerably more than the application of commodified liberal knowledge. Indeed, it suggests a strong *ethical* engagement in which young people are encouraged to consider themselves as responsible subjects and marks the leader's expanding role in encouraging responsible self-government (Rose, 1999, 259).

Applying knowledge to 'practice' in leadership training

All course syllabi identify practical areas in which youth leaders were required to achieve competence. The courses' practical components can be differentiated between areas of discrete skill and practice itself (students actually working in youth clubs and centres). Seven skill areas are referred to in Kuenstler's data, none of which are included in all four syllabi (discussion group work, vocational guidance, arts and crafts, music and drama, audio-visual aids, speech training and physical education including games training). According to Kuenstler, by 1947–1948 students at Bristol were invited to choose from a range of 'optional subjects' in the area of skills but it is not clear that students were formally assessed in any of these. Although in the 1942–1943 course at Bristol physical education and group discussion work were compulsory for all students, academic work appeared to have the highest priority for the course's organisers, reflecting the predominance of academic culture. For example, at Bristol essays were set in three course subjects through the year. Students were assessed on their ability to 'read papers', to 'act as discussion group leaders' and '. . . written evidence in the form of critical summaries of reading was required in several courses'. Examinations were set in 'General Principles, Economics, and Social Administration'. Practice was clearly less important than theoretical studies at Bristol. Referring to the eagerness of 'young Bristollians' to respond to students on work-placement, the Review Report of the 1942–1943 Bristol course lamented that some students

> . . . *were unable to resist these clamorous demands and became involved in too much outside work, to the detriment of theoretical studies. Yet in a short course of the two aspects, theory or practice, it is practice that*

should be sacrificed. Next year this work must be more closely watched and more severely rationed.

(University of Bristol, 1943, 21)

Clearly, liberal discourses of education were dominant at that stage.

The skills referred to in the syllabi provide a central core of practical know-how that forms the basis of intervention with young people. Youth leadership's practical content was, at that time, based largely on recreational activities although vocational guidance work was included on the Bristol syllabus. Superficially, little in this activity repertoire went beyond elementary skills reliant on a simple epistemology. It did not appear characteristic of complex professional work and would not, apparently, distinguish youth leadership from activities undertaken by the competent citizen or the caring parent. However, details of the Bristol curriculum demonstrate the degree to which even simple skills were transformed into relatively complex techniques, framed in the context of background knowledge and philosophy and requiring a high degree of proficiency from students. For example, the syllabus indicates that it is not sufficient for students to be proficient in '. . . coaching cricket, baseball, netball, hockey, and other team games'. They were also required to have an understanding of '. . . the place of physical education in youth work', and knowledge of '. . . physical recreation in relation to health work' (University of Bristol, 1943, 11). The Bristol syllabus also included 'discussion and democracy', 'the function of a discussion leader', 'the debate, the committee, and formal discussion' and 'the study group'. Group discussion work provides a good example of how a seemingly natural activity could be transformed to demonstrate its utility in reaching some of the wider political objectives with which youth work had been charged. Such work was expected to do much more than simply fill young people's time with wholesome activities and was designed to secure the individual's successful and responsible transition to adulthood. Circular 1598 gave some guidance on the nature of the practical work required on emergency courses.

A period, or periods of continuous full-time responsible work of various kinds with groups of young people. Such work should include participation in, and responsibility for, the organisation and direction of activities common to youth groups. Experience and training in the conduct of discussions on topics of interest and importance to young people should be provided.

(Board of Education, 1942, Appendix I)

All four syllabi refer to students committing themselves to 'regular attendance' at a youth club or organisation. Although having a longer tradition in the voluntary sector, the idea of the student placement emerged.

> In order that a student might come to know well the members of a particular group of young men and women it was decided to arrange a preliminary period of three weeks of visits to youth centres and then to ask each student to select some one centre with which he might be associated for the whole year.
>
> (University of Bristol, 1943, 7)

The Bristol review gives examples of the practice work undertaken during the first year of the course. Students '. . . took over and reorganised a new and difficult club', '. . . opened a new youth centre in a large housing estate . . .' and '. . . acted as liaison officer between a regional group of [Girls' Training Corps] units' (ibid., 7). As well as the continuous element of direct work in youth clubs and centres, 'visits of observation' formed part of the practical component of all four courses. The requirement for students to undertake practical placements in youth clubs and centres was important in their immersion in the everyday culture of youth leadership, sometimes 'under the guidance of an experienced Youth Leader' (ibid., 7) although many of the supervisors themselves would have been unlikely to have experienced substantial training in youth work. Little is recorded on the assessment procedures adopted for placements on these courses although, at Bristol, placement diaries and notebooks in which students were required to keep a record of their work were examined. Students were visited in their placements and '. . . assessments made of practical ability at a youth centre' (ibid., 15).

Although not originally intended to confer qualified status on their participants, the 1598 courses achieved some success in defining subsequent approaches to leadership training. They delineated a general syllabus which, in some ways, changed little over the subsequent fifty years or so. However, some of the practices deployed in the professional formation of youth workers changed radically.

Over-stimulation and mental indigestion, assessing the Circular 1598 courses

Towards the end of the war, Circular 1598 courses were assessed by the McNair Committee, which had been established to examine the training of teachers and youth leaders. Assessment was also undertaken (as a recommendation of McNair) by His Majesty's Inspectorate. Both were sharply critical.

Eileen Younghusband visited a number of the Circular 1598 courses in 1943 on behalf of McNair (she was co-opted to the Committee in her role as Training Officer for the NCGC). Younghusband's main criticism focused on pedagogy and learning. Students at Bristol University, for example:

> . . . *gave the impression of being in a continual state of breathlessly dashing from one thing to another. They said that when they had some responsibility in a club they had no time to do the necessary preparatory work. Neither had they enough time for reading. They gave the impression of being over stimulated and of suffering from mental indigestion, with too little opportunity to assimilate the various parts of the course*
>
> (Younghusband, 1943, 3)

Younghusband's criticism was partially acknowledged by the University (University of Bristol, 1943, 16). However, the courses' main problems were invariably expressed in terms of the students who had been recruited to them. In 1944 and 1945 HMI visited and assessed the courses as recommended by the McNair Committee (Board of Education 1944, 103). The Inspectors echoed Younghusband's earlier criticisms about course length and intensity and student learning. They indicated students' poor academic achievements, observing that the courses' assessment procedures 'vary greatly', and the '. . . quality of written work varies greatly. At its best it is equal to that of good WEA work, but it does not all reach this standard'. Inspectors pointed to diverse assessment practices ranging from written examination and assessment of 'practical competence' at Durham, Newcastle and Bristol to no assessment and the award of a 'certificate of satisfactory attendance' at Liverpool (HMI, 1945, 6). The Inspectorate was critical of the 'scantiness' of students' reading, the absence of 'authoritative' lecturers who could make appropriate links between theory and practical work (particularly in the field of psychology), the lack of available time to develop students' practical skills and the paucity of attention given to 'modern' educational technologies (e.g., radio and film). Although there was acceptance that the university offered the appropriate context for training youth leaders, HMI identified the '. . . scarcity and inadequacy . . .' of work placements in which students could complete the practical elements of their course work.

However, it is evident that the focus of criticism shifted from pedagogy and structural matters to the quality of the students themselves, who:

> . . . *can only be said to be fit to enter the Youth Service because the times have forced emergency measures on us. They have too poor resources of*

*background to last them through many years of youth work, and no
qualifications for entry into cognate services*

(HMI, 1945, 7)

There was little agreement over who should be admitted for training.
Younghusband suggested that one year courses were '. . . only suitable for
students with certain clearly defined past experience (e.g., having been
teachers, social workers or youth leaders) and of a reasonably good intellectual
level' (Younghusband, 1943, 3) but Bristol University suggested that previous
experience of that kind was an obstacle to learning. Bristol's own review of the
1942–1943 course suggested caution in recruiting students over the age of 35
or 40, particularly if they had been teachers or full-time youth leaders because
they '. . . are too set in their outlook to be influenced by a short course . . .
there is more emphasis on "remedial work" and "re-education" than is
desirable on so short a course' (University of Bristol, 1943, 17).

Some five years later, Kuenstler suggested that the '. . . acceptance of
unsuitable students' (1951, 43) was the main contributor to the 1598 courses'
limited success.[3] In Kuenstler's view more robust initial selection techniques
were necessary and he referred to the work of his colleague, Beverstock, who
was involved in the design and testing of selection techniques for youth
leadership training using 'group methods'. Beverstock's paper suggests that
these were based on the work of War Office Selection Boards and were used
in 1947 and 1948 at Bristol. They were intended to counter selection processes
that '. . . have failed to elicit adequately those qualities of personality which are
deemed necessary for success in this field' (Beverstock, 1949, 112).[4] Despite
these problems Kuenstler's view was that leadership training should combine
a liberal education with a theory of leadership practice.

> *. . . with an adequate experience of the practice of youth work, there can
> be no doubt that a course at University level is the most suitable means
> of establishing in the minds of future professional youth leaders an
> integrated philosophy of life, an understanding of the principles underlying
> human behaviour particularly at the adolescent stage, and an appreciation
> of the full, positive educational possibilities of the Youth Service*

(Kuenstler, 1951, 43)

But in relation to one year courses, HMI argued in contrast that

> *. . . courses of this length are necessarily almost entirely professionalised
> and, except in so far as the study and practice of professional subjects
> themselves educate the student, the courses can do little to provide a*

background of general culture and of personal interests. They are one and all overcrowded . . .

(HMI, 1945, 3)

This expresses a recurrent ambiguity about the precise identity of the professional youth leader and the nature and role of training (as well as the function of the universities). Was this identity to be constructed in terms of a vocational or technical model in which knowledge and skill enabled the leader to intervene in practical situations with young people? Was leadership necessarily something more than this, deriving from 'culture', 'background', and 'personal interests?' Kuenstler pursued this issue in his discussion of the nature and objectives of university-based training for youth leaders. He argued that training should enable the individual to develop a new 'philosophy'. This not only included the acquisition of abstract knowledge but the careful cultivation of liberal disposition '. . . a form of intellectual and social maturity which intrinsically is a matter of time and opportunity for reading, thought, discussion and reflection' (Kuenstler, 1951, 43). For Kuenstler, this 'philosophy' constituted a way of being, an orientation to the world to be meticulously developed through appropriate techniques of the self – through thought and reflection, as well as reading and discussion, for example – embedded in the institutional practices of the liberal university.

Both HMI and Kuenstler referred to a basic faculty which was beginning to be delineated as an indispensable component of professional identity in the emerging 'human service' occupations. This is the idea that the professional is characterised not only by the acquisition of commodified knowledge (drawn from the social sciences, for example) and technical skill but also by the degree to which he or she has achieved knowledge of self. In this sense, professional formation constituted a reflexivity that permitted the elaboration of an ethics of the self which required more than simple immersion in the right kind of knowledge in a university setting. Self-knowledge can be understood as being constituted by active processes of self-formation (and self-discipline) which became embodied in professional training in universities from the 1940s. By 1949, for example, Paul Halmos was suggesting that it was irrelevant to discuss university training for social work (and '. . . mutatis mutandis . . . youth work') in terms of practical or academic, liberal or vocational models. Anticipating Kuenstler's view and echoing Eileen Younghusband, the argument for Halmos was

. . . between the right and wrong sort of teaching. True academic instruction does not aim only at the broadening of critical thinking, at the

stimulation of abstract analysis and synthesis, but also at the deepening of
personal insight . . . the core of wisdom . . .

(Halmos, 1949, 254)

This would entail practitioners developing awareness of '. . . their own limitations (and) their own smug rationalisations or other ingrained defence mechanisms' (ibid.). Although the aim of extending 'insight' may have been indirectly present in some of the training discussed earlier, it seems so only implicitly. Lectures on 'aesthetics', or 'landmarks of European thought' may have encouraged insight in a liberal (and 'abstract') sense. However, it is difficult to imagine how such lectures alone could lead to the kind of insight – particular, personal and concrete – referred to by Halmos and Kuenstler and which later became such a central part of youth leader professionalism. The acquisition of insight was increasingly supported by various techniques and practices of the self in which students were engaged, personal tutorial work, recording, supervision and intensive group learning, for example. These were established to construct the professional self in a way that challenged liberal education's attempt to free the idealised and autonomous moral agent from the tyranny of the present and the particular (Bailey, 1984, 22).

Conclusions, the importance of the Circular 1598 courses

The early history of university-based training for youth leadership has been examined in this chapter. It has identified the broad historical background to 'emergency' training conducted under Circular 1598 in the 1940s and made largely in response to the social disruption that accompanied war. This signalled the state's first involvement in *professional* training for youth leadership. The wartime initiatives discussed here embodied a (sometimes implicit) view of the professions and what counted as professionalism, assuming that professionals were defined by expertise and authority. This authority, it was claimed, lay in professional access to knowledge that had been accredited by the universities and was considered superior to lay knowledge. Indeed, the significance of university involvement in training is precisely that it began the process through which such legitimacy was conferred on youth leadership.

The analysis of course curricula offered in the chapter suggested that these courses were broadly conceived on a model of liberal education that incorporated aspects of both abstract knowledge (largely from the social sciences) and a developing theory of leadership practice. The chapter indicated the broad criticisms that were made of the courses. Evaluations by Eileen Younghusband, Peter Kuenstler and HMI were critical of content, pedagogy, the students and the outcomes achieved. In its draft report (although not included in the final report) HMI indicated, 'None of these courses is recognised naturally as "qualifying" for as yet there is no standard or statement of what "qualifications" should be. Our general conclusion is that none of the existing courses in their present form should be so recognised' (HMI, 1945a, 4). By 1953 the only one of these courses still running was at University College Swansea. Perhaps inevitably, it would be easy to see the Circular 1598 courses as having been unsuccessful.

However, it is possible to take a different view. These courses established practices that, later, were influential in professional education for youth work (as in other helping occupations). As well as much of the content of the courses remaining largely unchanged over the years, the implicit model of the *ethical* youth leader that emerged through these courses was also important. Youth leadership was consistently recognised by policy-makers and practitioners as having an ethical dimension in three main ways. *First*, the micro-practices of leadership were always linked with a range of great 'moral questions' (e.g., service, fitness or the transmission of the right values). *Second*, leadership attempted to facilitate in young people a personal view of life, a personal ethics in which they would make good life choices. *Third*, leadership work was understood as contributing to the wider social good variously defined and broadly contingent upon political or religious ideology.

The emergence of university-based courses under Circular 1598 raised crucial questions about how leaders could best be prepared for this work and these continue to resonate. Broadly, as we have seen, two positions were taken in the 1940s. The *first*, reflecting a broad liberal perspective on education, assumed that the leader's character and judgement could best be formed through the acquisition of a body of universal knowledge exemplified, perhaps, by Bristol University's 'Landmarks in European Experience'. This would nurture the formation of the individual leader's character, powers of reason and judgement which would eventually shape their work with young people. This hegemonic position was deeply embedded in the cultures of the Board and Ministry of Education, the Inspectorate and the universities (largely because staff there had themselves experienced university-based liberal education). The *second* position entailed the novice leader engaging much more explicitly with technical and vocational aspects of leadership embodied in a repertoire of skills, practical capacities and values. This can best be understood as the development of a broad *theory of practice*, characteristic of a more instrumental technical-rationalism, which developed through the 1940s on the Circular 1598 courses. This theory of practice was further developed in the 1960s at the National College (Watkins, 1971) and in the higher education institutions that later became involved in youth work education.

However, there is another aspect to the discussions that occurred around the Circular 1598 courses. This concerns the view that training for youth leadership (as for social work, for example) should increasingly focus on the development of the professional self through increasing the novice's self-knowledge and personal insight. This perspective was an important departure from traditional liberal education that assumed that professional work was contingent on pure reason and that the power of mind was '. . . based on the nature of knowledge itself and not on the predilections of (individuals), the demands of society or the whims of politicians' (Hirst, 1965, 115). An implicit recognition was given of the importance of faculties beyond reason (e.g., feeling, spirituality, passion) as responses to the routine ethical dilemmas of practice with young people. Leadership training from the 1940s gradually conceded the particularity and contingency of knowledge and its location on the internal landscape of the individual self. This was partially a consequence of the growing influence of the 'psy' disciplines which, ironically, shaped practitioners as well as the targets of their practices. The leader's own ethical and emotional engagement was eventually acknowledged although professional training and education would entail the careful management of the professional's emotions. Youth leader training increasingly focused on the issue of empathy and 'other-directedness' that, it was thought, could only be enhanced by careful reflection on self. In common with other forms of professional training and education, youth work developed a range of often complex techniques of the self through which knowledge of the world could be articulated with knowledge of the self in the formation of the good professional.

Notes

1 Kuenstler's data apply to the courses which ran in 1947–1948. Where documents giving details of courses are still available, they show that these were substantially the same as those which were run in the preceding years (Bristol and Nottingham for example).

2 During the period 1942–1948, 80 students completed the course at Bristol, 74 at Swansea, 85 at Nottingham, 42 at Durham, and 21 at Newcastle (Kuenstler, 1951, 25).

3 Kuenstler's data show that the largest proportion of students on these courses between 1942 and 1948 from whom he collected data (167 out of a total 302 who undertook these courses) were from clerical and secretarial, HM Forces and industrial backgrounds. It is impossible to know the rank or position in the forces or industry these people came from, they do not seem typical members of the civic minded middle-classes (Kuenstler, 1951, 27).

4   Beverstock's approach entailed prospective students attending a two and a half day residential period at which they were required to undertake psychometric tests (Progressive Matrices and Group Test 33 of the NIIP) as well as essay writing, group discussion and 'problem solving'. Beverstock claimed significant correlations between test performances and later professional competence.

References

Bailey, C. (1984) *Beyond the present and particular, a theory of liberal education*. London, Routledge and Kegan Paul.

Beverstock, A.G. (1949) Group Methods Applied to Youth Leader Selection, in *British Journal of Educational Psychology*, Vol XIX, Part II, June 1949.

Board of Education (1942) *Emergency Courses of Training for Those Engaging in the Youth Service*, Circular 1598, London, HMSO.

Board of Education (1943) *Sex Education in Schools and Youth Organisations*, educational Pamphlet No. 119, London, HMSO.

Board of Education (1944) *Teachers and Youth Leaders. Report of the Committee Appointed by the President of the Board of Education to Consider the Supply, Recruitment and Training of Teachers and Youth Leaders*, London, HMSO.

Bradford, S. (2006) 'Practising the double doctrine of freedom, managing young people in the context of war', in R. Gilchrist, T. Jeffs, and J. Spence, (eds.) *Drawing on the Past. Studies in the History of Community and Youth Work*, Leicester, National Youth Agency.

Bradford, S. (2007, forthcoming) 'The Good Youth Leader, constructions of professionalism in English youth work, 1939–1945, *Ethics and Social Welfare*, 1, (2).

Evans, W.M. (1965) *Young People in Society*, Oxford, Basil Blackwell.

Ferguson, S. and Fitzgerald, H., (1954) *Studies in the Social Services*, London, HMSO and Longmans Green and Company.

Foucault, M. (1976) *The Birth of the Clinic, An Archaeology of Medical Perception*, London, Tavistock.

Halmos, P. (1949) The Training of Social Workers and the Teaching of Psychology, in *Social Work, a Quarterly Review of Family Casework*, Vol. 6, No. 1, January.

Hirst, P. (1965) 'Liberal Education and the Nature of Knowledge', in R. Archambault (ed) *Philosophical Analysis and Education*, London, Routledge.

HMI (1945) *Statement on Visits Paid to Emergency Courses Provided under Circular 1598*, June, 1945, PRO ED 124/16.

HMI (1945a) *Draft Report on the Emergency Courses Provided under Circular 1598*, June 1945, PRO ED 124/16.

Inter-Diocesan Council for Women's Church Work (1925) minutes of a meeting of the Inter-Diocesan Board, 29 April 1925.

IYTC (1941) *Informal Youth Training Committee, Report of the Working Sub-Committee, Paper No. 15*, 17 November, ED 124/16.

Jephcott, P. (1942) *Girls Growing Up*, London, Faber and Faber.

Kuenstler, P.H.K. (1951) *Training for Full-Time Youth Leadership, with special reference to the One-Year University Courses*, London, London University Press.

Mooney, G. (1998) 'Remoralizing the Poor? Gender, Class and Philanthropy in Victorian Britain', in G. Lewis (ed.) *Forming Nation, Framing Welfare*, London, Routledge.

National Council of Girls Clubs (1934) *Annual Report, 1933–1934*, London, NCGC.

Rose, N. (1996) 'Identity, Genealogy, History', in S. Hall and P. du Gay (eds.) *Questions of Cultural Identity*, London, Sage Publications.

Rose, N. (1999) *Powers of Freedom, Reframing Political Thought*, Cambridge, Cambridge University Press.

Russell, C. and Rigby, L. (1908) *Working Lads Clubs*, London, Macmillan and Company Ltd.

Schön, D.A. (1991) *The Reflective Practitioner, How Professionals Think in Action*, Aldershot, Ashgate Publishing Ltd.

Stanley, M. (1890) *Clubs for Working Girls*, London, Macmillan and Company Ltd.

University of Bristol (1943) *The Service of Youth. Memorandum on the Training of Leaders and Organisers in the Emergency Course of Training provided at the University of Bristol during the session 1942–1943 under Circular 1598*, PRO ED 124/16.

Watkins, O.C. (1971) *Professional Training for Youth Work, Educational Method at the National College for the Training of Youth Leaders, 1961–1970*, Leicester, Youth Service Information Centre.

Younghusband, E.L. (1943) *Report on the Bristol University One Year Course in Youth Leadership, visited February 24–25, 1943*, PRO ED 124/16.

CHAPTER 4

Chartism, Education and Community

Barry Burke

In the early part of the nineteenth century, only about three per cent of the people in the UK had the vote. Large towns such as Manchester, Birmingham and Leeds had no MPs, whilst 'rotten boroughs' such as Dunwich in Suffolk, which had a population of 32 in 1831, sent two MPs to Westminster. Parliament was effectively owned and controlled by the landed aristocracy and their cronies. There were many calls for parliamentary reform, particularly from the new manufacturing middle class supported by radical working men. Finally, the government was forced to produce a Reform Bill to increase the franchise and get rid of the 'rotten boroughs'. However, much to the dismay of many, all the subsequent 1832 Act did was increase the electorate to one in seven adult males whilst the constituencies remained remarkably unequal (35 constituencies had less than 300 electors whilst Liverpool had over 11,000!). Resentment built up, particularly amongst working people and it was out of this sense of resentment and a feeling of betrayal that Chartism was born.

Most people in England who, like me, studied nineteenth century history at school, came across the Chartists; this band of people who were dissatisfied with the results of the 1832 Reform Act, who campaigned for the Six Points, universal suffrage, annual parliaments, the abolition of property qualification for MPs, payment of MPs, secret ballots and equal constituencies. We were told that a number of petitions were put before parliament during the late 1830s and 1840s, all of which failed to gain support and finally the Chartists simply faded away. Eventually, we were almost certainly told, at least five of the six points were granted anyway. What we were not told was that the Chartist movement was probably the first mass movement of working people in Britain. It was 'a working class movement of a scope and magnitude that has not been approximated before or since' (Tholfsen, 1976, 23). Chartism mobilised millions of people from the south coast of England to the north of Scotland and was concerned with much more than parliamentary reform. It had a variety of aims, 'held together by a vision of an alternative social order . . . in which the values and practices of co-operation, mutuality, and individual and collective independence would occupy pride of place' (Kirk, 1985, 66). The Chartists had major concerns about the new Poor Law, about the huge inequalities between labour and capital, about free speech and assembly and a free press. And more importantly, they had a major concern for the need for education.

The Chartists had a number of objectives – political, social, educational and cultural. Chartist opinion was profoundly concerned with education in the broadest sense and adherents were deeply engaged in educational activities. There were a number of Chartist journals that advocated and provided intellectual enlightenment, and the principles of the movement were discussed in relation to the whole range of social and cultural experience – from teetotalism and temperance to Christianity and secularism, from the need for libraries to the desirability of currency reform. The sheer amount of experience brought about by the Chartist activity had the effect of increasing both the demand for and the necessity of what we might call 'popular education'. It also intensified individual efforts at self-education as well as collective attempts at mutual improvement by workers throughout the country.

Before and during the Chartist period, education of a kind did take place for some working men. This took the form of Mechanics' Institutes, which we *do* read about in our history books and which were quite often the subject of overt hostility from the Chartists. They were regarded by many as products of middle class patronage and simply a means of imposing a narrow technical education on susceptible sections of the working class. Jonathan Rose has described them as being 'founded and governed by paternalistic middle class reformers, where religious and political controversy was usually barred and the premises . . . uncomfortably genteel' (Rose, 2001, 65). Friedrich Engels, writing at the time, was more forthright. They were, according to him, 'organs for the dissemination of the sciences useful to the bourgeoisie . . . Here all education is tame, flabby, subservient to the ruling politics and religion, so that for the working man it is merely a constant sermon upon quiet obedience, passivity and resignation to his fate (Engels, 1845, 244). William Farish, a Carlisle weaver, who learned to read through sharing newspapers with his fellow weavers in their workshop, records in his autobiography that his local Mechanics' Institute,

> *though well maintained and liberally supported had failed somewhat in its mission, mainly as was thought through the reluctance of the weaver in*

his clogs and fustian jacket to meet in the same room with the better clad and possibly better mannered shop assistants and clerks of the city.

(Farish, 1889, 46)

For Farish and his colleagues, the Mechanics' Institute was an employer's organisation. What they wanted was an organisation that they managed and controlled themselves.

The Chartist Movement was never a united one. The working class itself was still in the stage of formation. Handloom weavers in Carlisle, agricultural labourers in Suffolk, factory operatives in the cotton mills of Lancashire, shoemakers in London, craftsmen of different kinds working in small workshops in Birmingham – they were all prominent in the movement and so there is no reason to believe that they would all have the same immediate needs or objectives. The industrialisation of Britain and the development of capitalism generally occurred in a haphazard and uneven way. As a result, there were local differences in both the ideas and activity of the Chartists. In his book *Chartist Studies*, Asa Briggs rightly reminded all students that 'a study of Chartism must begin with a proper appreciation of regional and local diversity'. He went on to point out that there were three main groups of workers involved in Chartist activity, there were what he called the 'superior craftsmen' which included printers, cobblers, tailors, cabinetmakers, booksellers and small shopkeepers. There were the factory operatives who were concentrated in the textile districts and there were domestic outworkers who were mainly handloom weavers, framework knitters and nailmakers (Briggs, 1960, 2, 4). It should also be noted that these were not all men and that women played a major part in the Chartist movement.

There were numerous strands within the movement, one of which, led by William Lovett, stressed the importance of working class education as a means towards working class emancipation. Prior to the publication of the People's Charter, an *Address on Education* was produced and it is claimed that this was 'the first statement on the theory and practice of education to be issued by a working-class organisation in Britain' (Simon, 1965, 243). The London Working Men's Association which produced it was born in 1836. Its educational programme proposed to fight for the removal of laws that 'prevent the free circulation of thought through the medium of a cheap and honest press' and to promote 'the education of the rising generation'. It proposed to collect information and statistics on labour conditions, hold meetings and publish material with a view to improving the workers' conditions and 'to form a library of reference and useful information' where members could 'associate for mental improvement' (Kelly, 1992, 139–140). The Association stressed the need for state provision of education for all classes. They made the point that,

> *poverty, inequality, and political injustice, are involved in giving to one portion of society the blessings of education, and leaving the other in ignorance . . . the working classes, who are in general the victims of this system of oppression and ignorance, have just cause of complaint against all partial systems of education.*

(quoted in Silver, 1975, 74)

The address put forward a plan in some detail. It called for an education system that was both publicly-funded as well as being locally administered by elected school committees. It proposed the erection of a whole range of schools and colleges. Buildings were to be open not just for the education of children but also in the evenings for adults. The programme was largely shaped by William Lovett. It was to form the basis of a later pamphlet written by Lovett and John Collins (1840) , in which they put forward 'the most far reaching programme of education to emerge out of the Chartist movement'. In addition to producing the address, the London Association appointed members to act as 'missionaries'. In 1837, there were associated organisations in Sheffield, Bath, Hull, Leeds, Halifax and elsewhere. By the end of 1838 there were 81 Working Men's Associations and 30 radical or other associations in correspondence with the London Association (Silver, 1975, 74–75).

Lovett and Collins's pamphlet (1840), written while they were in Warwick gaol was, like all of those emanating from the Chartists, a programme for obtaining both political and social rights. It was not a programme for education in the abstract. Their pamphlet rejected those systems of education that were exclusive to any particular segment of society. It proposed an unambiguous Chartist scheme for the education of everyone regardless of their class or gender. It proposed that a National Association be set up to work for the principles of the Peoples Charter, and to launch a nationwide scheme of education in the hands of the people. In addition, it discussed what in later years became the psychology and sociology of education and, what today has been a recurrent theme of current government education documents, the importance of education for 'citizenship'.

One of their most interesting ideas was their proposal that 'Public Halls' or 'Schools for the People' should be created. These were to take the form of day schools for infant, primary and secondary education whilst in the evenings they would be transformed into a space for adults to listen to public lectures on 'physical, moral and political science'. Their use would not stop there, however, as Lovett and Collins proposed that these halls should also be used for a variety of recreational pursuits – 'for readings, discussions, musical entertainments, dancing' (Kelly, 1992, 141). These far-reaching proposals for community halls and community education give us an indication that Chartism was not simply a movement to increase political representation but a movement for social transformation.

There was a dire need for places where Chartists could meet and discuss. In one meeting, reported in the Chartist journal *The Northern Star*, a speaker made a rousing speech in which he maintained that 'we are called ignorant ... but we will remove that ignorance by teaching one another, by discussing politics day after day, and by an interchange of thoughts and sympathy' (quoted in Simon, 1965, 244). Over the next ten years, Chartist Halls sprang up in both the large conurbations as well as in the smaller towns and villages. They were opened in many places to provide independent premises for political and educational activities as a result of town halls and other buildings which were owned or controlled by local 'worthies' often being refused to the Chartists. In the 1840s, these Chartist Halls appeared all over the country. There were differences in scale; some were financed by collections, some by subscription and some were financed by loans. Some of the halls were purpose built, whilst more often than not the members used an existing building such as a church or an inn. The main point was that they provided a meeting place where lectures could be given on a regular basis and visiting speakers could be invited. They frequently housed libraries and reading rooms. Chartists in Oldham, Leeds, Birmingham and Newcastle had their meeting places as well as those in London. There was a Chartist Hall in the Mile End Road in East London as well as in Skinner Lane in the heart of the City of London and later Chartist libraries were founded in Marylebone, Greenwich and Deptford. The *Northern Star* reported extensively on Chartist activities, particularly in Yorkshire and Lancashire where the main strength of the movement lay and we read of meetings near Huddersfield, in Dukinfeld, in Wakefield, Hyde, Preston, Macclesfield and Halifax and numerous other small towns. Without exception, education in one form or another took place in them all. In Keighley, we read that the Chartists had 'an excellent and substantial building' which was their own property and which housed a committee room and a library. They held a Sunday School, mutual instruction and reading classes, classes in grammar and logic and they had an orchestra as well. In Fig Tree Lane in Sheffield, discussion meetings took place on a weekly basis with speakers such as George Julian Harney, who edited the *Northern Star* for a time, lecturing on a range of topics. The walls of the meeting place were adorned with homemade banners depicting heroes of the movement from Wat Tyler to Byron and Shelley. They had a small library, dinners and teas were provided for members' families and the hall acted as both the centre of working class political activity and as a social centre.

One of the most successful halls used as an educational centre during the first few years of the Chartist movement was in Manchester. It was called Carpenters Hall as the local operative carpenters and joiners Union built it. The building, which was completed in 1838, was described by Feargus O'Connor as 'a glorious establishment' and 'a great intellectual hotbed'. It had a very large hall, which held up to 6,000 people as well as a library and later a Sunday School. The local Chartists met here on a regular basis and there was also a Carpenters Hall branch made up of joiners, painters and carpenters. A contemporary writer described the hall and something of its politically-charged atmosphere as 'the Sunday resort of the Chartists. They open and close their meetings with the singing of democratic hymns, and their sermons are political discourses on the justice of democracy and the necessity for obtaining a charter' (Simon, 1965, 244–249). Ten years after the opening of the Manchester building, O'Connor declared that besides that at Manchester, the most successful halls were in Oldham, Leeds and Birmingham.

The Chartist press made numerous references to the erection of new buildings or the establishment of local Chartist Halls. In 1839, in Stalybridge, the Chartists had a 'People's Institute' which provided both a Sunday and a day school. In Leeds, four years later, the 'New Chartists Hall' was opened which provided seating for 1,500, while a similar building was acquired by Birmingham Chartists and called 'Peoples Hall'. The hall at Oldham was built in 1845 because Chartists were refused the use of the local town hall. The £1,000 needed to finance this project came about through the issuing of shares which were taken up by 700 supporters. Educational activities were paramount here. There were lectures and discussions on literature, the fine arts, social and political economy as well as theology, ethics and scientific subjects. As well as a room seating 500, there was a school room for children of 'all parties and denominations' as well as newsrooms and a library. In 1845, Chartists in Hanley and Shelton put forward a proposal for the building of a 'Working Men's Hall'. Their intentions were that it should not only provide a meeting place for workmen to discuss their grievances but also allow them to listen to lectures in science, history and politics. They also proposed that an elementary day school be created. We read that at Huddersfield they had premises where readings and meetings were held on Mondays and discussions on Tuesday evenings. At Wakefield Working Men's Association, Chartists could listen to lectures on anatomy and physiology with the use of models and they also had use of a good library.

Chartist adult schools abounded although most had precarious existences. At times of economic crises with destitution and poverty the rule rather than the exception, many had to close their doors. Moreover, with long hours of work being the norm in good times, sheer exhaustion affected many workers at the end of the working day. Despite this, the educational work of the Chartists was phenomenal. After-work schools, Sunday Schools, mutual instruction, discussion groups, reading groups, libraries and reading rooms all contributed to the growth of adult education in the period. The topics discussed and the subjects taught were extremely eclectic. Basic education and politics was at the forefront but a whole host of cultural and scientific topics were prominent. The Sunday schools catered for adults, both men and women, as well as for children. We have a very good report of a Chartist Hall in Mottram in the North West which had a day school catering for 500 children who were taught reading and spelling as well as grammar and arithmetic. The school was clearly very popular which did not go down very well with the local clergy. The report in the *Northern Star* tells us that 'Our very amiable vicar . . . has been at no little trouble to denounce the whole fraternity as infidels'. Apparently, he went from house to house trying to get parents to withdraw their children from the school (quoted in Simon, 1965, 253).

It is clear that Chartist educational activity was extensive. By the end of 1830s political classes of various kinds had been organised on a wide basis and particularly in the Midlands and in the North with ten to twenty members in each class. The reasons for joining a class were often quite explicit. For example, in Sunderland, Chartists were urged to make their classes 'an important medium for the diffusion of intelligence'. There was a massive expansion in the number of classes in the following years. Towns and cities as far apart as London and Newcastle, Brighton and Liverpool, Plymouth and Durham reported that they had commenced classes. Not all of these classes were open to everyone. In Oldham, they held Female Chartist classes whilst in Dewsbury, as well as elsewhere, there were Chartist classes specifically for those who had gone down the road of teetotalism. All of these classes gave supporters an opportunity to participate in both political activity as well as adult education. Working people wanted to know more about their class situation, not only why they were in the state they were in but how to transcend it. In Durham, for instance, in organising classes, the local Chartists recommended that members should read 'works of history, and especially the history of our own country, discussing its events philosophically, not as mere matters of fact, but noting their bearing on our present state'. Also in the North East Newcastle-upon-Tyne working men were encouraged to participate in the classes not only as an educational ideal but also as a political one. They were urged to 'let each class constitute itself a fireside republic'. The classroom activities of the Chartists were part of a wide spectrum of educational activities and in Leicester we find that they had a fairly well-developed programme of lectures, reading rooms, discussions, schools, papers and pamphlets (Silver, 1975, 82–83).

Mutual Improvement Societies sprang up all over the country, many inspired by Chartism and its emphasis on education. In September 1848 a Chartist meeting held in Birmingham put forward a suggestion that the Chartist Executive establish 'mutual instruction societies throughout the Chartist ranks, as the dispelling of ignorance is the only means of obtaining the Charter' (Simon, 1965, 247). In Yeovil this was exactly what local Chartists did. They hired a big hay loft over a large barn, in a back lane of the town, and collected subscriptions mainly from their own members. They adapted the premises giving their time and skill freely, and fitted up the old loft for their purposes. One of the members, Henry Solly, the local minister, wrote in his autobiography that,

> our primary object was educational in the best and widest sense of the word. It was a bona fide attempt to work out Lovett's aims and principles by trying to educate those for whom we were striving to obtain the franchise, combined with the additional purpose of affording our members a pleasant and comfortable room for reading, games, conversation and entertainments.

> (Solly, 1893, 396)

However, much to his annoyance, the Mutual Improvement Society was represented to his employers as 'a very hot-bed of mischief'. The word 'sedition' was even mentioned. As a result, Solly was told that he could no longer be minister at the chapel in Yeovil and was dismissed from his post (Solly, 1893, Vol. 1, 397–400; see also Ashton and Pickering, 2002).

In addition to the schools and classes numerous libraries were also established. Bradford had the Bradford Chartist Library. In Derby, Heywood and Rochdale, Greenwich, Deptford and Marylebone reports were sent in to the *Northern Star* about the setting up of Chartist libraries. Christian Chartism had a very profound effect on the movement for education and 'the Chartist churches were everywhere associated with educational work'. The Chartist Church in Birmingham 'consisted of a political association which studied democratic thought as laid down in the works of Cobbett, Hunt, Paine and Cartwright, and a Church whose purpose was to further temperance, morality, and knowledge. It had schools for children and for young men, and a sick club' (Kelly, 1992, 141–142). In Deptford in South London there was a Working Men's Church and it was reported that the members there were studying the New Testament in Greek whilst the Nottingham Chartists met at what they called the Democratic Chapel.

I have mentioned the importance of the Chartist press. Chartist journals devoted an enormous amount of space to educational articles. The *Northern Star* would contain articles on political and economic theory next to poetry and reports from overseas. On a number of occasions the journal devoted a whole (broadsheet) page to literature, with Byron being particularly favoured as well as Burns, Shelley and a number of others. The main focal points of much of Chartist literature were the immediate political issues facing the emerging working class but Chartist journals also contained a considerable amount of both cultural and scientific material all of which provided matter for reflection and discussion. Newspapers such as the *Northern Star* were, in this way, clearly part of a tradition of earlier working class literature in devoting an enormous amount of column space to diverse educative articles on economic and cultural as well as scientific subjects. The political debates of the time were reported as were the religious and philosophical controversies. During the period 1842–1843, there was a series of 24 articles written by W.Gilpin on socialist theory and practice in the *Northern Star*, and in the *Red Republican*, in 1850, we find the first English translation of Marx and Engels' *Communist Manifesto*.

The influence of the Chartist Press was considerable. The *Northern Star* at one point had a circulation of 36,000 and the *Poor Man's Guardian* 20,000. Papers were passed from hand to hand and read in homes throughout the land. Imaginative literature was regularly mixed with politics and economics. The *Northern Star* published Captain Marryat, Fenimore Cooper and Charlotte Bronte. W.J.Linton's *National* had excerpts from Chaucer, Shelley, Keats, Spencer, Confucius, Robert Herrick, Izaac Walton, Socrates and Milton. The *Chartist Circular* introduced readers to Homer, Aesop, Socrates, Shakespeare, Milton, Defoe and Dr Johnson. The *Red Republican* made it clear to its readers that workers needed the 'Charter and something more'. Thomas Frost, the famous Welsh Chartist who suffered transportation to Tasmania, was later to make the point that the poetry of Coleridge and Shelley made him a Chartist (Rose, 2001, 36–37).

A special mention must be made of Chartist educational activity 'north of the border' as Scotland and the development of education seem to go hand in hand. There we find Chartist churches being associated with all manner of educational activity. There were libraries, debating and dramatic societies, evening classes and a number of schemes of what many described as 'liberal education'. A large number of them also established day schools. Chartists in Partick, on the western fringes of Glasgow, founded a Chartist Education Club where members met nightly for mutual instruction in reading, writing and arithmetic as well as grammar and geography. In Aberdeen there was a Chartist Mutual Instruction Society which worked on similar lines. The Scottish Chartist churches organised a variety of educational activities, including classes and schools for the children of Chartists. Chartist day schools for children were found in Leven, Arbroath, Aberdeen, Perth, Hamilton and elsewhere. Many of them had over 100 pupils and the one in Greenock had 300 (Kelly, 1992, 141–142; Silver, 1975, 83–84). Other Scottish Chartist organisations also developed educational work. Coupar Angus had a Mutual Improvement Society which also functioned as a co-operative group. At Dundee, on the other hand, politics was associated with poetry. There were at least two groups here. One met in the dark workshop of the weaver-poet James Gow and the other in a local coffee house.

It would not be right to speak about the link between Chartism and education and ignore the contribution made by Thomas Cooper. Cooper's autobiography, written in his old age, is a fascinating study of a fascinating man and tells of an almost unbelievable dedication to self-improvement. Cooper's Chartist work was carried out in Leicester and is one of the most interesting Chartist educational endeavours to be found. Cooper, a shoe-maker, was a remarkable individual. He could not be described as someone who was self-educated unlike many of the Chartist leaders as he was allowed to stay on at school until he was fifteen years old. This was undoubtedly as a result of the determination and self-sacrifice of his mother. However, once he left school he did not stop his efforts to increase his education. Cooper writes that

> *I thought it possible that by the time I reached the age of 24 I might be able to master the elements of Latin, Greek, Hebrew and French; might get well through Euclid, and through a course of Algebra; might commit the entire Paradise Lost and seven of the best plays of Shakespeare to memory; and might read a large and solid course of history and of religious evidences and be well acquainted also with the current literature of the day.*

(Cooper, 1872, 57)

On Sundays, he devoted his studying to Milton and theology but at weekdays he tells us that

> *Historical reading or the grammar of some language, or translation was my first employment on weekday mornings, whether I rose at three or four, until seven o'clock, when I sat down to the stall. A book or a periodical in my hand while I breakfasted, gave me another half hour's reading. I had another half hour, and sometimes an hour's reading, or study of language, at from one to two o'clock, the time of dinner – usually eating my food with a spoon, after I had cut it in pieces – and having my eyes on the book all the time. I sat at work until eight, and sometimes nine at night, and then either read or walked about our little room and committed Hamlet to memory, or the rhymes of some modern poet, until compelled to go to bed from sheer exhaustion – for it must be remembered that I was repeating something, audibly, as I sat at work, the greater part of the day – either declensions and conjugations, or rules of syntax, or propositions of Euclid, or Paradise Lost or Hamlet or poetry or some modern or living author.*

> (Cooper, 1872, 59)

Cooper carried out this punishing regime of self-education for about four years until, not surprisingly, he suffered a physical breakdown. Both his studies and his shoemaking came to an end and he became, in turn, a schoolmaster, a Methodist preacher and finally a journalist. In this capacity he came across the Leicester Chartists and his autobiography gives a vivid description of contemporary events in Leicester and in particular his educational efforts. He was a very active Chartist. In the early 1840s, he formed an adult Sunday School, for men and boys who were at work during the week. Some of the more literate members acted as teachers and were very willing to help their fellow members. The rooms they had acquired soon became full on Sunday mornings and afternoons. They used the Old and New Testaments as class books as well as Channing's *Self Culture* and many other tracts.

They formed themselves into classes but did not name them first, second, third etc but named them after famous literary and political figures. They had the Andrew Marvel class, the William Cobbett class, the George Washington class, the John Milton class, the William Tell class and the John Hampden class. Later on they extended their Sunday school to weekday evenings (Cooper, 1872, 164). In his autobiography, Cooper relates that

> *Unless there was some stirring local and political topics, I lectured on Milton, and repeated portions of Paradise Lost, or on Shakespeare and*

repeated portions of Hamlet, or on Burns and repeated Tam o' Shanter,
or I recited the history of England, and set the portraits of great
Englishmen before young Chartists, who listened with intense interest; or
I took up Geology, or even Phrenology, and made the young men
acquainted, elementally, with the knowledge of the time.

(Cooper, 1872, 69)

Although Cooper was not typical, it would be wrong to underestimate the degree of knowledge, scientific, cultural and political, made available to the Chartists in their Halls and lecture rooms, and in their class meetings. The influence of the Chartists and the effect they had on other educational endeavours was enormous.

In Carlisle, there was a movement for Workingmen's Reading Rooms, a movement of working class collective self-help which flourished between the late 1830s and the late 1850s. Brian Graham, in writing about this movement, maintains that 'the stimulus and impetus given to self-culture and self-reliance can be seen as the direct outcome and legacy of Chartism' and that 'the educative influence of the Chartist newspapers and journals would appear to be beyond question' (Graham, 1983, 17–18).

There is a major thread running throughout working class endeavours to educate themselves in the period from the 1780s to the second half of the 19th century. If radical men and women of the time asked themselves what could be done if they were dissatisfied with what was provided for them (or not provided for them), particularly in relation to education, the answer was overwhelmingly 'we must do it ourselves!' That way, they preserved their independence and won for themselves what they regarded as 'real knowledge' rather than the knowledge passed down from above (Johnson, 1979, 79). As the veteran Chartist George Jacob Holyoake put it many years later, 'Knowledge lies everywhere to hand for those who observe and think' (Holyoake, 1896, 4). Equally, the divorce of education from everyday life was something that was rejected totally. Knowledge was not seen as something outside of their experiences. The modern distinction between education (as represented by schooling) and life (everything outside the school grounds or the university campus) was not something working class radicals would accept. Radicals breached this distinction all the time, often quite self-consciously. Education was not only about everyday life, it was about *the struggles of everyday life*. It was also a co-operative effort based on fellowship. It was community education at its finest.

References

Ashton, O.R. and Pickering, P.A. (2002) *Friends of the People, Uneasy radicals in the age of the Chartists*, Nottingham, Merlin Press.

Briggs, A. (1960) *Chartist Studies*, London, Macmillan.

Cooper, T. (1872, 1971) *The Life of Thomas Cooper*, Leicester, Leicester University Press.

Engels, F. (1845, 1987) *The Condition of the Working Class in England*, Harmondsworth, Penguin Books.

Farish, W. (1889) *The Autobiography of William Farish*, Liverpool, privately printed.

Graham, T.B. (1983) *Nineteenth Century Self-Help in Education – Mutual Improvement Societies. Vol. 2 Case Study, The Carlisle Working Men's Reading Rooms*, Nottingham, Department of Education, University of Nottingham.

Holyoake, G.J. (1896) *Sixty Years of an Agitator's Life* (3rd ed.), London, Fisher Unwin.

Johnson, R. (1979) 'Really Useful Knowledge', Radical Education and Working-Class Culture in Clarke, J., Critcher, C. and Johnson, R. (eds.) *Working Class Culture, Studies in History and Theory*, London, Hutchinson.

Kelly, T. (1992) *A History of Adult Education in Great Britain* (3rd ed.), Liverpool, Liverpool University Press.

Kirk, N. (1985) *The Growth of Working Class Reformism in Mid-Victorian England*. London, Croom Helm.

Lovett, T. and Collins, J. (1840) *Chartism, A New Organisation of the People* (reprinted by the Victorian Library (1969), Leicester, Leicester University Press).

Rose, J. (2001) *The Intellectual Life of the British Working Classes*, London, Yale University Press.

Silver, H. (1975) *English Education and the Radicals 1780–1850*, London, Routledge and Kegan Paul.

Simon, B. (1965) *Education and the Labour Movement 1870–1920*, London, Lawrence and Wishart.

Solly, H. (1893) *These Eighty Years, or The Story of an Unfinished Life; Volumes 1 and 2*, London, Simpkin, Marshall and Co.

Tholfsen, T.R. (1976) *Working Class Radicalism in Mid-Victorian England*, London, Croom Helm.

CHAPTER 5

The Transition from Girls Clubs to Girls Clubs and Mixed Clubs: UK Youth, 1934–1944

Michael Butterfield and Jean Spence

UK Youth, which began its life as the National Organisation of Girls' Clubs in 1911, is fortunate in that the organisation's Minutes are virtually complete from that year onwards. Through nearly a hundred years these chart the deliberations of those involved in managing the organisation, and inevitably these reflect changes taking place in youth organisations and in the wider society. UK Youth has changed its name seven times in its history, which would seem to suggest that it has at least attempted to respond to the changes in society and in work with young people

1911
National Organisation of Girls Clubs
(Formed out of the Clubs' Industrial Association of the Women's Industrial Council)
1924: Commitment to industrial work marginalised.
1924–25: National Association of Boys' Clubs formed.

1926
National Council (Association) of Girls Clubs
(Emphasising the national character of the organisation in response to the success of National Association of Boys' Clubs and after the refusal of NABC to co-operate in forming one combined national youth organisation)

1944
National Association of Girls' Clubs and Mixed Clubs
(To enable affiliation to be extended to include mixed clubs)

1953
National Association of Mixed Clubs and Girls Clubs
(In recognition of the fact that most affiliated clubs were now mixed clubs)

1961
National Association of Youth Clubs

(Rationalisation of name: gender not really an issue any more)
1976: Feminist women youth workers' groups organising

1979
Appointment of Girls Work Officer

(Annual 'Feminist Women Youth Workers' conferences; development of a Girls Work Unit
and Newsletter; attempts to rediscover history of girls' work)

1987
Youth Clubs UK

(An equal opportunities approach; work with girls to be 'integrated')
Closure of Girls Work Unit and Newsletter
(Women workers in it dismissed; decline of movement for working with girls and young
women)

2000
UK Youth

(Recognising the broadening of youth work – beyond clubs)

An interrogation of some of these name changes, the reasoning behind them, and their timing can provide clues about both the internal debates of the organisation and the contemporary context in which it was attempting to maximise its reach and effectiveness. Nowhere is this more apparent in the minutes than in the name changes associated with the transformation from a girls' work organisation to one concerned with mixed gender work with young people.

In 1911, the National Organisation of Girls' Clubs (NOGC) was formed from the Clubs' Industrial Association (CIA) which had been a sub-committee of the Women's Industrial Council (WIC). The remit of the new NOGC derived largely from the concerns of the WIC, which was primarily a research and campaigning body concerned with the industrial conditions of female workers. Both the CIA, chaired by Lily Montagu and also the NOGC, which she chaired from its inception until her withdrawal to vice-president in 1924, were concerned with the relationship between industrial and social recreational matters in relation to girls and young women (Mappen, 1985; Spence, 2004; Turnbull, 2001).

Lily Montagu was unwavering in her commitment to single sex work (Montagu, [1944] 1954, 80). Nevertheless, the subject of 'mixing' was never far from the agenda of the NOGC. For example, as early as 1912 when a conference was being proposed, a Miss Nicholls 'was desirous of having a joint meeting for girls and boys'. The minutes record the predominant feeling of the members 'that the work of NOGC was solely among girls and it would not be advisable to include boys and men in the conference'[1] (Council Meeting, 5 June 1912). Yet by the end of 1913 there appeared to be some unanimity not so much about mixing clubs, but rather about co-operation with all-male youth organisations and the NOGC committee agreed that the Federation of Boys Clubs should be invited to join a delegation of NOGC to the Board of Education regarding grants for drill. The response they received was to prefigure future attempts to co-operate with men when the Federation of Boys' Clubs declined the invitation and 'advised the NOGC to act independently' (15/1/14). Shortly afterwards, in February 1914, a Delegates Conference was organised by the NOGC with the title 'Should the Factory Law be extended to men?' This time, delegates were invited to bring their 'boyfriends' (19/2/01). Again they were discouraged when only two men turned up to the event (19/3/14).

The question of cross-gender organisational co-operation was laid to rest with the outbreak of war in August 1914 when attention became focused more intensively upon conditions of female labour in a manner that resembled the earlier years of the WIC. The consolidation of the single sex focus was clearly associated with the conditions of war as increasing numbers of men joined the forces, as traditional female labour (such as the clothing trade) went into decline (Pankhurst, [1932] 1987; Spence, 2004) and as women moved into either specific war-related work (such as in munitions factories) or began to do jobs traditionally associated with men (Marwick, 1965, 1977). For example, the first item on the agenda for discussion at the first meeting of the Executive Committee in 1916 was the question of 'Rest and Sanitary Accommodation' for female tram conductors. However, the war also provoked a contradictory pull for the NOGC as it accelerated the tendency to consider 'youth' as a special and universal phase of life (Gillis, 1981) which required provision focused upon 'leisure' or 'training' rather than 'work' to meet its needs. Moreover, the state was becoming more involved in youth work, especially in relation to education and training and juvenile crime, matters which are reflected in the minutes after 1918. Whilst it was never explicitly debated, the question facing the NOGC after the First World War concerned whether it was to be predominantly a 'worker' organisation, or a 'youth' organisation and this had implications for its position on gender and mixing.

Changing times

The First World War had a considerable impact upon youth work. Not only did it encourage an emerging idealisation of 'youth' as a 'special' period of life

(Brittain, 1933), but in this idealisation, it re-emphasised virtues traditionally associated with masculinity, such as honour, duty, bravery. The sacrifices of young people and the loss of so many young men in particular through the war affirmed these tendencies and linked them with 'national character'. Ultimately they were to be manifest in the creation of the National Association of Boys' Clubs in 1924 (Dawes, 1975; Eager, 1953).

The war also exacerbated a divide, which had been growing before 1914, between the middle class activists who sponsored and managed clubs and organisations and those who actually undertook the face-to-face work with young people (Eager, 1953, 395; Spence, 2001). The new youth workers were increasingly individuals from respectable working class backgrounds, many of whom had benefited from club membership themselves. As such, their perspectives were responsive primarily to the sexual division of labour and role expectations which characterised working class life. The changes which were beginning to offer greater independence and freedom to professional middle class women were often of little relevance in this context (Todd, 2005; Williams, 2000).

This was a period when national politics were highly charged with the rhetoric of class conflict, with anxieties about the Russian revolution and its consequences never far from the agenda, culminating in a 'red scare' associated with the general election of 1924 (Mowat, 1955, 187). The NOGC inevitably suffered political tensions between its role campaigning for improved employment conditions for young women, its inherited belief in the benefits of cross-class 'friendship' (Montagu, 1904, [1944] 1954), and the new imperative to work a-politically with young people in relation to their personal development. This impacted upon the identities and roles of workers and committee members. Thus during a discussion about governance in 1919, one member, Miss Towers representing the YWCA, objected to the suggestion that a 'Workers' Council' be formed and suggested that this should be replaced with the words, 'Club Leaders' Council'. Seconded by Miss Nicholls, this suggestion was approved (2/6/1919). Although industrial work continued, involving research and campaigning, for example in relation to conditions suffered by hotel and restaurant workers (1923), political issues were never far from the surface and in 1924 it was recorded that Roehampton Club was 'Protesting against Miss Tuckwell's[2] address at the Annual Meeting, as likely to arouse feelings of antagonism towards employers' (Leaders' Council, 27/2/24).

The growing popularity of recreational and social educational work with young people specifically targeted at 'youth' rather than 'youth as workers' and characterised particularly in the phenomenal growth of scouting and guiding in the inter-war years, seemed to reflect the desire of young people for a more 'modern' approach to their leisure needs. The war had opened new work opportunities for women and their commitment and contribution to the war effort had been acknowledged in the granting of the franchise to those over the age of 30 in 1919. It seemed that a period of greater gender equality and freedom was dawning and that the gender-rigidities and patronising class-based voluntarism of the Victorian welfare system might be left behind to be replaced by centralised planning by the state in partnership with voluntary organisations (Woodroofe, 1962; Rooff, 1972; Thane, 1993).

Changes in the realities of class and gender relations inevitably manifested themselves in organisational politics and cultures. The origins of the NOGC in pre-war conditions meant that its industrial and campaigning concerns were out of harmony both with new views about youth and certainly with the politics of the new upper and middle class young women who were now associating themselves with voluntary organisations as a vehicle for entry into formal political life (Williams, 2000). Such women did not necessarily have a personal history of face-to-face practice in club work. Their focus was rather upon committee politics, upon matters of governmentality, purpose, structure and finance. Inevitably this precipitated tensions within NOGC and in 1924, there was a shift in the priorities and leadership of the organisation in which most of those who had been committed to the pre-war objectives resigned or quietly bowed out.

The crisis of 1924 was not specifically concerned with questions of mixing or relationships with men's organisations but rather with the financial circumstances, the focus and the structure of NOGC. The process of practical change began in January 1924 with the resignation of Miss McWilliams, the Industrial Organiser, which was followed by difficulties in finding a replacement and a corresponding set of issues about finance for such work and whether or not it was appropriate for the NOGC to continue to take responsibility for it. In May the Honorary Secretary Mrs Peel resigned, along with the Honorary Treasurer, Miss Lawrence Jones, who made reference in her letter of resignation to the parlous state of the general finances. Notably at this meeting, Lily Montagu, although present, was, for the first time, not in the chair. At the June meeting, chaired by Mrs Morgan, a letter of resignation was read from Nellie Levy, who had been paid secretary since the beginning of NOGC.[3] Later in this meeting it was noted that a bequest of £500 was forthcoming from the estate of a Mr Teichmann whose wife had been associated with the girls' club movement. Notwithstanding this unexpected legacy, there followed a debate at the various levels of the organisation in which not only its purpose and its relationship with its constituent organisations, but also its very being was called into question.

This culminated in the withdrawal of Lily Montagu firstly from the Chair and then from active participation in the work of the NOGC altogether. The minutes of an Emergency Joint Council (of Girls' Clubs) meeting of 21 July 1924 record her apologies and the contents of a letter in which she suggested that some of the proposed changes were unnecessary and that there were others with which she disagreed. In particular, she seems to have been in disagreement with the constitutional change which removed the executive functions from the NOGC, replacing them with advisory and co-ordinating functions. This of course involved a devolution of power towards the Federated clubs. From Montagu's perspective, such a move meant that there would be no organisation which could act on behalf of small, independent clubs. This perhaps had particular significance for Jewish clubs and it is notable in her letter that 'She urged the continuance of the Girls' council and hoped that the interdenominational outlook would always be retained.'

Throughout these changes the single sex nature of the organisation had been presumed and accepted. However, the nature of such single sex work was at stake in the process. In particular, industrial work was sidelined. The memorandum outlining the changes stated with regard to the 'Health Insurance Scheme and the Industrial Section' that 'It was felt that these were instances where another organisation – in these cases the Y.W.C.A. – was doing the work, and that it would be better for the N.O.G.C. to leave it to it' (Memorandum for consideration at the Joint Council Meeting, 21/7/1924).[4] The new priorities in addition to the general co-ordinating functions were to relate to the professionalisation (through training, salaries and status) of workers, the formation of local club unions, the development of a reference library, and significantly, 'the consolidation and development of the Games Council'. In these moves, the conditions were created in which concern with the question of 'mixing' in the clubs and collaboration with boys' clubs might find fertile ground. If Eager is correct in his comment that Lily Montagu 'more than anyone else gave definition to the term Girls' Clubs' (1953: 348), then her withdrawal from the organisation, and the loss of her view of girls' club work as a response to the working conditions of young women, meant that the re-formed organisation would be much more responsive to issues of youth in general. And so the stage was set to accommodate mixing.

From NOGC to NCGC

Although it was the crisis of 1924 which precipitated the changes which led to the change of name of the NOGC to the National Council of Girls Clubs

(NCGC) in 1926, the process of change can be traced back to 1916. In an effort to rationalise youth provision in the context of war, the Home Office had set up a Juvenile Organisations Committee (JOC) under the Chairmanship of Charles Russell, of the Manchester Boys' Club movement (Russell and Rigby, 1908). Lily Montagu had attended meetings of the JOC as the representative of NOGC and reported back that the women present 'had felt themselves to be of little service, as the work discussed was largely dealing with Boys'. In response to this, the Executive 'were strongly of the opinion that Miss Montagu should continue to attend the meetings on behalf of NOGC and endeavour to serve the Club movement whenever possible'. As a consequence of continuing participation the NOGC responded in 1919 to the desire of the JOC for national rationalisation of the club movement and agreed to implement a more co-ordinated national system. Girls' clubs would unite into local unions and the NOGC would become a 'Union of Unions' governed by two councils, one of representatives of Federations and Unions, and one of Club Members (15/5/19). This precipitated a debate about the name with Miss Nicholls indicating that she was in favour of a change of name to 'National Council for Working Girls Clubs'. However, at this stage, with one dissention, it was agreed not to change the name and continuity with the pre-war period was preserved for the time being.

Throughout the 1920s the single sex environment was increasingly associated with restrictions for women and Victorian prudery. There was a growing expectation amongst middle class women after the First World War that not only would they would not be 'protected' from men, but also that they could enter the same sphere as men in public life. This involved a rejection of the Victorian ideal of 'separate spheres'. In a climate which simultaneously encouraged rationalisation of organisation there thus began intermittent attempts by the NOGC to collaborate with boys' organisations. However, their efforts were persistently rebuffed. As the women became less wedded to single sex organisation, perceiving it as perhaps a 'bunker' in relation to their new ambitions, the men showed themselves to be less than enthusiastic about opening their single sex organisations to female participation and influence.

Writing about the beginnings of the NABC in 1924 Eager gives some insight into the mindset of the men involved:

An invitation from the National Organisation of Girls' Clubs to combine with it was unanimously refused, with compliments. That invitation, astonishing as it was to most of those present, did not seem so strange to the Londoners, for two years previously the London Federation had been approached by the London Union of Youth Clubs with a request that it – the Boys' Federation – should become one of its affiliated bodies. The Federation's sense of humour was aroused; but it was shocked by such a challenge to the essential masculinity of the Boys' Club idea, and it reacted towards alliance with other boys' organisations . . . Boys' Clubs were a distinct type of organisation needing a common link . . .

. . . Fads, fancies and fanaticisms – this queer feminism which would affiliate Boys' Clubs to Girls' Club Federations! It was evidently time that Boys' Clubs got together to stand for robust and wholesome boyhood!

(1953, 409–10)

Yet some boys' clubs had been happy to federate with the NOGC before the creation of the NABC. In the absence of any national co-ordinating male organisation, the Stepney Federation of Boys' Clubs had already been affiliated to the NOGC which recorded at its Executive Committee meeting of 14 February 1924:

Stepney Federation of Boys' Clubs: The Council had approved the resolution passed by the Executive proposing that they be affiliated for a further year pending any national movement for boys.

In seeking co-operation with the men, the women were hardly indulging in 'fads, fancies and fanaticisms' but following through the logic of previous developments. Before the creation of the NABC it appeared that relationships with boys' clubs had been cordial to the extent that it was proposed at the meeting of the NOGC Leaders' Council following the AGM of 1923 that a representative of the Boys' Federation be appointed to the Executive commit-tee. Exercising caution, this proposal was amended as follows:

That while in sympathy with the representation of the Boys' Federation on the Executive, such representation shall come later by co-option, and should not take a place among the three appointed members.

(28/11/23)

After the creation of the NABC one of its members was co-opted and during the 1930s their representative, Mr Piercy, was to play a prominent role in the discussions about mixing. It is not clear that the creation of a joint organisation with the Boys' Clubs would have helped the NOGC to resolve its internal tensions which were related in a complex manner to questions of finance, structure and identity. However, it is clear that the determination of the men to retain their singular approach to masculinity within club work could not be matched by a similar determination amongst women, and that the creation of NABC added to their weakness. Focusing upon femininity in a single sex setting did not carry powerful meanings of agency and control and the female organisation was left destabilised by the very changes which were thought to be improving women's circumstances.

It would have appeared to the men involved in the creation of NABC at this time that there was very little to be gained from active collaboration with NOGC. Drawing on the recollections of Lady Eleanor Keane, Eager says:

> *At the time when Boys' clubs were realising that their number and similarity of aim made it advisable for them to draw together in a national association, the NOGC was in low water; London defeatists were brought to reason by delegates from Lancashire and other provincial centres, who insisted that the movement must be national; the reformation of the NOGC and the subsequent vigour of the NAGC [sic] proved that in this matter, as in certain others, Lancashire was in the van.*
>
> (1953, 348)

Following the reformation, NOGC became a co-ordinating body for national societies and area federations or unions of girls clubs. The name was changed to National Council of Girls' Clubs (NCGC) at a National Council meeting on 12 July 1926 at University Hall, Fairfield, Liverpool with Miss Pilkington of the famous glass company chairing the meeting which made the decision. Nationally, the NCGC affiliated The Federation of Working Girls Clubs, the Girls' Friendly Society (GFS), the Girls' Guildry, the Girls' Life Brigade and the Young Women's Christian Association. The Girl Guides Association had representation on the Executive Council. Forty Unions in various parts of England and Wales, and some in Scotland were affiliated (Rooff, 1935).

Eager might be correct and the reformed organisation might have been structurally more 'vigorous', but, it is apparent that the changing perception of the meaning of 'youth' was becoming ever more insistent during the inter-war years. The fetishisation and socialisation of youth which became such a feature of the growth of fascism in Germany, had its corollary in Britain as pathological questions of healthy development of body, mind and spirit became increasingly dominant in the discourse associated with adolescence during the 1930s (Gillis, 1981; Turnbull, 2001). In both ideal terms and with reference to questions of control and fear of disorder (Dawes, 1975), this notion of youth, conflated with questions about adolescence, had strong masculine connotations (Spence, 2005). However, its expression in the successful development of mass organisations and youth movements included the free association of young men and women from which young women in particular would be likely to benefit as the restrictions on their social lives were lifted.

Increasing numbers of pre-existing girls' clubs were admitting boys to membership and increasing numbers of new clubs and organisations, such as the Youth Hostel Association, and the Woodcraft Folk, were mixed in character from the outset. The women in involved in the NCGC could not but be aware of this trend; it had implications for their affiliated clubs and it brought to their attention the fact that there was no national body to represent mixed clubs. Thus began the journey which was eventually to lead the NCGC to become the National Association of Girls Clubs and Mixed clubs.

Towards mixing

Given that the First World War precipitated the social and cultural changes which were to lead to the emergence of tensions relating to purpose and crises of identity in the NOGC, it is perhaps no accident of history that it was the Second World War which created the conditions in which the organisation eventually ceased to be a single sex, female controlled venture by encompassing Mixed Clubs in 1944.

However, the detailed story of this second change essentially begins in December 1934 when the Executive Committee Minutes report that

> The National Council for Social Welfare of Women and Girls in London held an informal conference on the demand for mixed clubs. Of 400 applications for assistance 158 had been club enquiries and of these 27 had asked for girls clubs, 75 for mixed clubs and 56 for social clubs. It had been agreed that mixed clubs meet a much felt need and that all channels of possible expansion must be explored. Representatives of the YWCA and YMCA had spoken of their experiences.[5]

(10/12/1934)

This extract indicates awareness within the NCGC of the need for adjustment in response to the realities of grass-roots developments. At one level the figures suggested that girls were losing out in terms of provision to address their specific needs. It was perhaps in recognition of this that the Executive Committee commissioned an enquiry, undertaken by Madeline Rooff and funded by the Carnegie UK Trust, 'To survey the recreational facilities available for girls and young women in England and Wales with a view to determining their leisure-time needs' (Rooff, 1935). NABC 'were also making a survey' according to Rooff, but as the minutes later showed, NABC were less committed and undertook their side of the work with less vigour (3/2/1936).

Meanwhile, the mixed clubs were beginning to organise independently and during 1935 a 'National Association of Social Clubs for Young People' was formed. This clearly had implications for the strength of both and NCGC and NABC, but it was NCGC which was most likely to be weakened by such a venture.

The women of the NCGC seemed unaware of the power of the commitment to separation and to the pursuit of a masculinity free of female encumbrance which Eager claims characterised the ideas of the NABC. The first reaction of the women to their acknowledgement that there was a demand for mixed clubs had been to return to the question of co-operation with NABC. Although it was the women taking the initiative, the men did not totally refuse to communicate over the matter this time. In February 1935 the minutes record, in relation to a grant application to the London Parochial Charity,

> *special efforts to be made to co-operate with NABC in giving help to clubs accommodating boys and girls.*

The same meeting records:

> *Mixed Clubs – possibility of co-operation with NABC on the question of mixed clubs. Appointed a Sub-committee to meet with the NABC and National Association of Social Clubs for Young People (recently formed).*

In May 1935 the Executive of NCGC reported on an informal meeting with the NABC to discuss the newly formed National Association of Clubs for Young People. Both organisations had received a letter from the Executive Committee of the British Association of Residential Settlements (BARS) expressing concern about the formation of the new body and suggesting that there was a danger that the work of the new Association would overlap with that of the two older bodies. BARS offered to support NCGC and NABC if they would take joint steps to cater for the growing demand for mixed activities in clubs.

The chair of NOGC, who by this time was Lady Eleanor Keane, was conscious of the need for schemes for joint activities and it was agreed that representatives from NCGC, the Federation of Working Girls Clubs and the YWCA should serve on a Mixed Clubs Joint Committee with NABC. A constitution for such a committee had been drawn up and sent to NABC which agreed to its creation.

In February 1936 the Joint Committee received a memo from Madeline Rooff prepared from recent material collected by the BARS, the YWCA, local unions of NCGC, and information drawn from her survey questionnaires. Although they had agreed to do so, NABC had collected comparatively little material and at the annual Secretaries Conference of NCGC in April 1936 a report from the Mixed Clubs Joint Committee suggested that the contribution from NABC was limited.

The position of the NABC was clarified in early May 1936 when the Executive Committee of NCGC considered a resolution from NABC which read:

> *The formation of entirely mixed clubs containing boy members under 18 shall be discouraged and that normally such clubs shall only be eligible for affiliation to NABC in so far as they conform to the rules laid down by the Association.*

> (7/5/1936)

Here the significance given to the period of adolescence in the formation of character and its relevance in the construction of masculinity can be read into the position taken by the NABC, and so too can it be deduced that for them, mixing was only relevant to the question of boys meeting girls in order to form sexual relationships. Once again, Eager explains the reasoning of the men of the NABC:

> *Boys' Clubs were a man's job – if only because, if anything so obvious needed to be argued, boys needed manly pursuits and manly ideals to complete their manhood before they thought of mating.*

> (1953, 411)

Despite such limited support from NABC, the secretaries of the affiliated clubs re-emphasised the great need for mixed clubs and activities and worked on the small window of opportunity offered by the NABC's concession to boys over 18 and girls over 16. Accordingly, it was suggested that a proposal should be made to Boys' Unions to set up local joint committees for mixed clubs and to authorise a Joint Committee to prepare and implement conditions for the affiliation to special sections of NCGC and NABC. However, once again, the position was modified. At the next meeting (18/5/1936) it was suggested that instead of joint committees being set up by local Unions, the Girls' Club Unions should establish Committees to deal with mixed clubs and invite representatives of Boys Clubs to serve on them. Referring to the particular difficulties of boys in mixed clubs who could not affiliate to NABC and were ineligible for grants from NCGC, the NCGC committee clearly thought there was some urgency in the situation and that they could not afford to wait for the local Boys Unions to act jointly. Simultaneously they continued their efforts to collaborate with NABC. At this stage NCGC stated their belief that useful work might be done by a Standing Committee of NABC and NCGC (18/5/1936). Such a Joint Committee would enable both organisations to retain freedom and independence whilst pursuing opportunities for collaboration and the Mixed Clubs Joint Committee seems to have become the National Joint Committee at this stage.

The National Joint Committee reported in December 1936 that a representative of the National Association of Clubs for Young People had attended a meeting. It appears that this new organisation was mainly doing propaganda work and compiling a directory of mixed clubs. A leaflet had been drawn up on activities in mixed clubs which had been approved by NABC and was put before the NCGC Committee for approval which was agreed. There is no further reference to 'Clubs for Young People' in the minutes. This organisation presumably lost its relevance as NCGC took increasing responsibility for mixed work.

In December 1937 it was reported that a pamphlet had been prepared on mixed activities. Albeit within restricted terms, it seemed that NABC had shifted slightly over the year, and by December 1937 it was hoped that the Joint Committee would be able to report progress to the next NCGC Executive. However, the discussion at the next meeting of the Joint Committee seems never to have happened. There are no references to it in the minutes in 1938, and in May 1939 it was reported that the Joint Committee 'having completed the exploratory work which had been reported from time to time to its parent bodies recommends to NCGC and NABC that it should be dissolved.' The efforts of the committee and its difficulties in bridging the gap between the NCGC and the NABC were acknowledged in a resolution which sought a way forward in relation to the continuing question of mixed clubs:

> *Being fully alive to the many problems its parent bodies have in common, the Committee appreciates steps which have been taken to promote co-operation between them and recommends that every effort be made to ensure active encouragement of close working arrangements between its parent bodies, their representative area organisations and between individual boys and girls clubs.*

> *The resolution suggested that the NCGC should invite the National Council of Social Service to: call a conference of persons and organisations interested in the question of mixed activities for the purpose of considering how their organisations and directors ... and the pooling of information on the subject can best be achieved.*

> *Miss Macalister Brew proposed acceptance.[6] (19/5/1939).*

Before the proposed conference could be organised, the outbreak of war in September 1939 added new dimensions to the work. The influence of the state was brought to bear directly upon the voluntary organisations via Circular 1486. This required youth organisations and Local Authorities to work in closer partnership on local Youth Committees in order to make provision for the leisure time of all young people. Both NABC and NCGC were to be represented on the these Youth Committees along with 12 other organisations (Bradford, 2006; Davies, 1999). To deal with the emerging situation NCGC set up a War Time Executive Committee comprising Chairman (Mrs Walter Elliot), Hon Treasurer, Organising Secretary and four other members who were elected through a postal ballot. These were: Miss Batten (British Association of Settlements), Miss Colm, (Scottish Association), Miss Henly (London Union) and Miss Rippe (Birmingham Union).

The first meeting of the War-time Executive was held on 11 October 1939. An active reading of the minutes at this point suggests that although there was an increased level of communication between NCGC and NABC, there was no significant shift in the position of NABC regarding the place of their own clubs in encouraging mixed activities. Working together within the Youth Committees might lead to a softening around the role of mixed clubs in general, but these were not to be allowed to impact in any way upon the single sex dimensions of the boys' clubs. Thus, for example, the NCGC meeting of 7 November discussed as a 'matter arising' an issue relating to mixing two boys clubs in Stoke-on-Trent. Mr Piercy (Secretary NABC) stated that he thought NABC would be unwilling to turn the two boys clubs in Stoke into mixed clubs but they would welcome co-operation in mixed activities between boys clubs and girls clubs.

Clearly there was some pressure from the ground for clubs to mix. At a Conference of National Juvenile Organisations (9/10/1939) a memo on Mixed Clubs had been considered and it had been agreed that a sub-committee of reps from NABC, NCGC, YMCA, YWCA, GFS and Welsh Youth Organisations should be appointed to explore the possibilities of mixed activities. NCGC appeared to be the organisation most prepared to take responsibility but in the context of the recalcitrance of NABC, they could not afford to lose their focus on young women. They therefore attempted to provide for both girls clubs and mixed clubs and the War Time Executive Committee on 5 March 1940 agreed that NCGC should form a Mixed Section to which mixed clubs should be affiliated at the same rate as members of girls clubs. The way was now open for the further development of mixed sex youth clubs.

At the Executive meeting of 14 October 1940, Miss Batten, representing the Settlement Movement (BARS), outlined a scheme for an organisation to promote the organisation of mixed groups of young people aged 18–30. The Chairman (Mrs Elliot) responded that the Carnegie Trust might give finance for the movement. She indicated that she had already discussed the scheme in detail with Miss Drysdale, Chair of BARS. It was hoped that Miss Batten might give half her time as organising secretary of the new organisation. Carnegie responded by the next meeting on 12 November 1940 requesting that the applicants should form one body (not NCGC and BARS). It was suggested that the application might be sent in the name of NCGC with the co-operation of BARS. The application was successful – £1,000 for organising mixed 18 plus groups in 1941. The extent of collaboration and the speed of this development would suggest that personal networks of like-minded individuals were as important as formal co-operation in moving progress. However it was effected, it moved NCGC even further onward towards becoming the principal co-ordinating and development body for mixed sex work.

Towards the National Association of Girls' Clubs and Mixed Clubs

In November 1941 there was another significant moment which was to culminate in the National Council of Girls' Clubs finally changing its name and constitution to incorporate mixed clubs. Mr Beloe, Chief Education Officer for Surrey wrote to NABC and NCGC requesting the formation of a Surrey Association of Clubs. Following this request, a suggested 'code' for Youth Centres and Mixed Clubs was formulated by NCGC and by Sir Robert Llewellyn and Mr Piercy of the Boys Clubs. A subsequent minute indicates that this was based on an original code drawn up by Mr Beloe. However, the revised code was not accepted by NABC Policy Committee and Council and at the Executive meeting of February 1942, Miss Honoria Harford, Miss Lesley Sewell, Sir Herbert Llewellyn Smith and Mr Piercy of NABC, prepared a revised statement for NABC. It was also reported during this meeting that NABC had appointed a sub-committee to consider the question of a Joint Committee. Mrs Elliot, Miss Sewell, Miss Ross and Miss Harford were elected to sit on the proposed joint committee.

The March 1942 Executive reported a further meeting with Sir Herbert Llewellyn Smith and Mr Piercy where a further draft of the code and resolution was prepared and agreed after amendment. In July 1942 it was reported that the Code and Resolution had been adopted by NABC after an amendment which read:

To keep a register of Mixed Clubs and Youth Centres, whose aim in general is in accordance with the Code, and to encourage the development in those which will be eligible for affiliation according to the respective constitutions and machinery of NCGC and NABC.

This amendment fell far short of Beloe's original suggestion which would have led to a Surrey 'Association of Clubs'. However, it was unanimously agreed to accept the Declaration with the proviso that the scope and membership of the Committee should be reviewed in two years' time.

In March 1943 it was reported at the NCGC meeting that three meetings had been held of the Joint NABC/NCGC Committee. A document on the Code plus conditions of affiliation had been prepared, a register of clubs had been partially drawn up, to be completed as soon as NABC Federations supplied the information, and the lines of approach to clubs affiliated to one or another of the national organisations were clarified. There was a difficulty over questions of common policy. Raising questions policy appeared to be indefinitely shelved. NABC were not allowed to bring such discussions to the Joint Committee as the NABC Council would not agree to this in its terms of reference. Moreover, questions could not be referred back to the NABC Council as they must be 'left in peace'. After discussion it was agreed that a letter outlining the difficulties should be sent by NCGC to the Joint Committee and if necessary the matter should be referred to the NABC Council.

The Executive meeting of NCGC in May 1943 received a report from Miss Sewell of a meeting between 24 NABC and 28 NCGC representatives. After discussion it was agreed that members of NCGC who sat on the Joint Committee should be free to say how unsatisfactory this meeting had been, and to ask for a full discussion as to the fundamental differences between the two organisations over mixed work. Apparently, the women could not understand the difficulties put in their way by the NABC Council. They were uniformed about the implacable hostility of the men to anything which might divert their attention from the masculine focus of their work to which Eager alludes so unselfconsciously.

Whilst efforts were underway to keep NABC in the frame of decision-making about mixed clubs, a group from NCGC had been independently considering the constitutional position of mixed clubs and NCGC. In August the Executive reported that the recommendations of this group had been circulated. This same meeting agreed to write a letter to NABC, the purpose of which was to ask whether they were prepared to consider and take such action, constitutional or otherwise, as was necessary to set up a National Association of Clubs, and to indicate that the NCGC was prepared to recommend constitutional alterations to the Council of NCGC. Meanwhile, an informal meeting with representatives of NABC would take place in September. It was further agreed that if the negotiations with NABC were not satisfactory NCGC should implement the proposal to become the National Association of Mixed Clubs and Girls Clubs (10/8/1943).

Negotiations were not satisfactory. For at the Executive meeting in September the Secretary (Honoria Harford), outlined the stages covering a period of nine months which might lead to the NCGC becoming the National Association of Mixed and Girls Clubs. To begin the process it was decided to set up a Committee of Enquiry to receive evidence from Associations and make recommendations to the Executive and the Council. The Committee of Enquiry was set up with the following terms of reference:

> To investigate, consider and advise upon the actions that NCGC should become NAYC (Girls and Mixed) with reference to:
> (a) the necessary revised constitutions of the Association and local organisation and administration
> (b) the services required by mixed clubs. (14/9/1943)

Before this Enquiry was able to report, Associations had been responding to a memo drawn up by NABC on the subject of mixed clubs. Their comments were summarised:

> (a) regarding the principle of affiliating mixed clubs – all 22 replies had agreed with some stressing the need for a single national association, whereas others said the main concern should remain with Girls Clubs and
> (b) the suggested title of National Association of Mixed and Girls Clubs was not satisfactory and suggestions were made of Association of Youth Clubs or National Association of Youth Clubs, (a title which was not adopted until 1961). It was also pointed out that the word 'Mixed' was not used by young people themselves who referred to Mixed Clubs as Youth Clubs.

The Executive Committee resolved that the title should be the National Association of Youth Clubs (Girls and Mixed).

At an all-day meeting of the Executive Committee on 9 November 1943, itemised under the heading 'Mixed Clubs' it was pointed out by a delegate that possibly the NABC did not realise the demand for the affiliation of Mixed Clubs which was coming to NCGC and it was thought important to try and convey to them some idea of its intensity and urgency. Mr Piercy, General Secretary of

NABC, joined the meeting at this point. He was subjected to a number of questions including one about the title. Mr Piercy said that it appeared that NCGC were going wholeheartedly for Mixed Clubs and were not so interested in co-operation with NABC. Mr Piercy felt that the title Youth Clubs was deemed undesirable as this was a generic title to which many other clubs were entitled. With regard to the title National Association of Youth (Girls and Mixed) he alleged that the public could not be bothered with a long title and brackets and NCGC would inevitably become NAYC. The Chair emphasised the serious view NCGC took in undertaking the new responsibility for mixed clubs and how real was the demand from all areas of the country for services for mixed clubs. Mr Piercy responded that Boys Clubs and Girls Clubs covered a very large part of the field and as much energy must be given to Boys and Girls Clubs as Mixed Clubs. The Chair again referred to the great demand from the country for an Association to deal with Mixed Youth Clubs (not Boys and Girls Clubs) and wondered whether NABC had in fact realised the nation-wide extent of this demand. In the afternoon session it was agreed to amend the Resolution to be put to the November Council regarding the new name – National Association of Girls and Mixed Youth Clubs.The same meeting heard of an offer of accommodation in three houses in Devonshire Street. This was to become the HQ of the organisation for the next 32 years.

The Council meeting later in the month reported that the choice of name had upset NABC, that the men believed Girls Clubs were taking advantage of the circumstances when many of NABC's 'best people' were away on other work. NABC were of the opinion that with a little persuasion Mixed Clubs might become clubs with separate (single sex) activities and had suggested that 'those who remained obstinate should be ignored' (Minute 18/11/1943). Despite these objections from NABC, the Council agreed to move a name change with two suggestions to be put to an Extraordinary General Meeting: National Association of Girls Clubs and Mixed Clubs *or* National Association of Girls and Mixed Clubs. Before the final decision was made in July 1944 there was a great deal of continuing discussion. At the Executive meeting in January 1944, in response to replies from local Associations it was agreed to recommend a name change to 'National Association of Girls Clubs and Mixed Clubs and that Local Associations were free to choose their own name'.

The Committee of Enquiry reported to the Executive on 14 March 1944 with the suggestion that a separate committee should be set up to support mixed clubs. Responding to the Report, Mr Robert Beloe said it was a brilliant document but went on to say that there could not be any satisfactory arrangement unless boys, girls and mixed sections had some sort of central authority. He believed something should be done at once, but whatever was done now should not prevent a much better arrangement coming about. That could be possible if girls and mixed clubs were in one association and boys in another. He said that it would be a mistake to do anything to prejudice the future of a 'National Association of Clubs'.

At the Executive on 18 April 1944, NABC representatives who were present pleaded that they should not be left out of any developments in the matter of Mixed Clubs, but at the same time made it clear they were chiefly concerned with the boys who were members of mixed clubs. NABC had meanwhile decided to circulate the Committee of Enquiry Report amongst themselves, but in May they declined to accept it. By this time, whatever the views of NABC, it was clear that NCGC were committed to changing their own organisation in order to support mixed work. As an indication of their seriousness, an interview committee for the appointment of an officer to support mixed clubs was approved.

On 10 May 1944 it was reported that NABC were unlikely to support the formation of a National Association of Clubs. However, the Executive Committee had received information that thirteen local associations had already considered changing their title to Girls and Mixed Clubs. Many Associations spoke in favour of the resolution suggested by the Committee of Enquiry to set up a committee under the auspices of NCGC to support mixed clubs. The resolution was passed 41 to 1.

Incredibly, and despite all setbacks, at the next Executive in June 1944 it was reported that a further attempt had been made to secure the active co-operation of NABC with a letter offering it four places on the new Mixed Clubs Committee, the same numbers to be allocated to NCGC representatives. NABC were also informed that the idea of a National Association of Clubs would not go ahead. It was announced that H.T. Longland, then Director of Education for Dorset, later of Derbyshire was to chair the Mixed Clubs Committee – the first time that someone from a local authority had been invited to work with NCGC and the first man to be appointed to any position (apart from the Honorary Treasurer). Perhaps not insignificantly this corresponded with the move to mixed clubs and a desire to ensure that the needs of boys in them would not be ignored.

An Extra-ordinary General Meeting held on 15 July 1944 resolved to change the name of the Association to National Association of Girls Clubs and Mixed Clubs.

A New Era

The first meeting of the Mixed Clubs Committee was held on 10 October 1944 with the following terms of reference:

> to encourage mixed clubs to develop on sound lines;
>   to investigate the present and future services they need, with special reference to the type of club programmes;
>   to assist in the training of leaders and members of mixed clubs;
>   to co-operate with statutory and voluntary organisations;
>   to take the action necessary to supply these needs.

At a meeting of the Executive on 12 December 1944 the terms were modified and an addition made:

> to supply the needs of mixed clubs and to consider what form of central organisation is required to carry out these purposes.

A process which began in 1934 finally reached a resolution. Overwhelmingly it was pressure from local associations and clubs which drove the changes. Young people mainly wanted to associate in mixed clubs and it was necessary for the relevant organisations to adapt to changing realities.

The adjustments to the organisation which had started life as the National Organisation of Girls Clubs came about at time when the national body was led by an impressive team of women – Mrs Walter Elliot in the Chair, with Miss Honoria Harford as Organising Secretary (from 1939) supported Miss Lesley Sewell as Deputy Organising Secretary from December 1939. Eileen Younghusband became Principal Officer for Training, Employment and Public Relations in 1939 until1944 and Josephine Macalister Brew joined the staff as Education Secretary in 1942. This team attempted to maintain the integrity of an organisation set up to meet the needs of girls at the same time as providing the conditions within which mixed work could flourish. To achieve the best results for young people, the girls' clubs workers maintained a dialogue with representatives of the NABC long after the boys' clubs workers were apparently retrenching into male-only clubs. In the end the refusal of the NABC to take constructive action meant that the NCGC had to go forward without them. This was not without consequence for work with girls and young women.

Acknowledging the controversy surrounding mixed clubs, in 1943 Brew admitted that,

> I myself am not really happy about the establishment of any new club except on a mixed basis unless there are difficulties either of premises or

of leaders.; since it seems to me that the mixed club can can make by far the best contribution to adolescent welfare.

(1943, 56)

Perhaps in a swipe at the difficulties which had been put forward by the NABC, she goes on to suggest that

Broadly speaking there appear to be two sections who oppose mixed clubs and activities – the lazy and the fearful, and both of them reach the same conclusion, that such clubs are impossible, or that they are so difficult as to be almost impossible. The fact that for the last ten years at least there have been mixed youth Community Centres on housing estates and that for the past few years a crop of mixed Youth Centres has grown up, avails little as an argument since all these valiant efforts are dismissed and disregarded as not being 'really clubs'.

(ibid.)

Yet despite her support for such work, and in defence of its virtues she indicates that in 1943 that

One of the most noticeable features is that the boys, in addition to retaining their manliness, superimpose on it a few manners and the girls, in addition to retaining their feminine qualities tend to emphasise their purely feminine occupations.

(ibid., 57)

Over a decade later, she acknowledged that in the process of 'mixing' there was a tendency for the numbers of girls attending clubs to decline (Brew, 1957, 157). This tendency, has been explained in relation to the ways in which young men tend to dominate public space (eg. Nava, 1984). In the post 1945 period, the mixing of clubs corresponded with the development of specifically teenage sub-cultures, some of which emphasised dominant working class masculinities, provoking scares about social order and teenage boys (Pearson, 1983). This inevitably impacted upon the priorities of youth work and addressing the needs and interests of girls gradually became less urgent in club work. Perhaps reflecting these developments, the Association changed its name again in 1953 by reversing the order to National Association of Mixed Clubs and Girls Clubs.

The subsequent change in 1961 to National Association of Youth Clubs (NAYC), was probably an inevitably outcome of the inexorable movement away from girls' clubs, towards generic youth work with both young men and young women. By the 1960s, single sex work with girls hardly seemed relevant to contemporary conditions. This change also coincided with the post Albemarle development of statutory 'youth work'.

A return to single sex work with girls in generic youth club settings did not occur until the feminist movement of the 1970s began to impact upon the youth work sector. As women became more conscious of the limits of their equal status, so too it became apparent that girls themselves had become 'unknown' in generic youth work practice. More than this, they had become a problem which youth workers no longer felt able to address adequately (Hanmer, 1964). Ironically, in the process of developing a responsive youth work organisation the specific interests and needs of girls and young women had been overshadowed by those of boys and young men within NAYC. It is impossible to say whether the outcome would have been any better for girls had the NABC co-operated more fully with the NOGC. However, it is apparent that the refusal of NABC to countenance mixing or to co-operate in the creation of a joint organisation with NOGC created the conditions in which the work of the girls' organisation would eventually come to be monopolised by male concerns, eclipsing for a while its history of single sex work with girls.

Notes

1   Unless otherwise stated, dates refer to minutes of Executive Committee.
2   Gertrude Tuckwell (1861–1951) was an active trade unionist and campaigner for women's rights. She was a member of the Labour Party and until 1918 had been involved in the Women's Trade Union League and the National Federation of Women Workers.
3   Nellie Levy had been a member of the West Central Jewish Girls' Club, developed by Lily Montagu. After her resignation from NOGC, she went back to West Central as a paid worker.
4   Of course as a Christian organisation it is unlikely that the YWCA would be centrally concerned with the specific industrial and social circumstances of Jewish young women. Lily Montagu's reference to inter-denominational work possibly alludes to this but might also signify some Christian-Jewish tensions emerging in the NOGC at the time.
5   There had been continuous debate about the possibility of merger and of mixed sex work between the YWCA and the YMCA since at least 1884. See 'The Women's Signal' *Should the Y.M.C.A. and the Y.W.C.A. be Amalgamated?* And article by Frederick A. Atkins, 1 February 1884, p71, col. 1.
6   Macalister Brew later became a very influential member of the staff – together with Honoria Harford who was introduced as the new Organising Secretary at the same meeting. Lesley Sewell joined the team later that year, in December 1939.

References

Bradford, S. (2006) 'Practising the Double Doctrine of Freedom: Managing Young People in the Context of War' in R. Gilchrist, T. Jeffs and J. Spence (eds.) *Drawing on the Past: Studies in the History of Community and Youth Work*, Leicester, NYA.

Brew, J. Macalister (1943) *In the Service of Youth*, London, Faber and Faber.

Brew, J. Macalister (1957) *Youth and Youth Groups*, London, Faber and Faber.

Brittain, V. (1933) *Testament of Youth*, London, Victor Gollancz.

Davies, B. (1999) *From Voluntaryism to Welfare State: A History of the Youth Service in England, Volume 1, 1939–1979*, Leicester, Youth Work Press.

Dawes, F. (1975) *A Cry From the Streets: The Boys' Club Movement from the 1850s to the Present Day*, Hove, Wayland Publishers.

Eager, W.McG. (1953) *Making Men: Being a History of Boys' Clubs and Related Movements in Great Britain*, London, University of London Press.

Gillis, J.R. (1981) *Youth and History: Tradition and Change in European Age Relations, 1770–Present*, London, Academic Press.

Hanmer, J. (1964) *Girls at Leisure*, London Union of Youth Clubs and London YWCA.

Mappen, E. (1985) *Helping Women at Work: The Women's Industrial Council 1889–1914*, London, Hutchinson in association with the Explorations in Feminism Collective.

Marwick, A. (1965) *The Deluge: British Society and the First World War*, London: Macmillan.

Marwick, A. (1977) *Women at War, 1914–1918*, London, Fontana.

Montagu, L.H. ([1944]1954) *My Club and I*, London, Neville Spearman and Herbert Joseph.

Montague, C.J. (1904) *Sixty Years of Waifdom: Or the Ragged School Movement in English History*, London: Charles Murray.

Mowat, C.L. (1955) *Britain Between the Wars*, London, Methuen.

Nava, M. (1984) 'Youth Service Provision, Social Order and the Question of Girls' in A. McRobbie and M. Nava (eds.) *Gender and Generation*, London, Macmillan.

Pankhurst, E.S. ([1932] 1987) *The Home Front*, London, The Cresset Library, Hutchinson.

Pearson, G. (1983) *Hooligan: A History of Respectable Fears*, Basingstoke, Macmillan.

Rooff, M. (1935) *Youth and Leisure: A Survey of Girls' Organisations in England and Wales*, Prepared at the request of the Trustees of the Carnegie United Kingdom Trust under the auspices of the National Council of Girls Clubs, Edinburgh.

Rooff, M. (1972) *A Hundred Years of Family Welfare*, London, Michael Joseph.

Russell, C. and Rigby, L.M. (1908) *Working Lads' Clubs*, London, Macmillan.

Smith, M.K. (2001) 'Josephine Macalister Brew: Youth Work and Informal Education' in R. Gilchrist, T. Jeffs and J. Spence (eds.) *Essays in the History of Community and Youth Work*, Leicester, Youth Work Press.

Spence, J. (2001) 'The Impact of the First World War on the Development of Youth Work: The Case of the Sunderland Waifs' Rescue Agency and Street Vendors' Club' in R. Gilchrist, T. Jeffs and J. Spence (eds.) *Essays in the History of Community and Youth Work*, Leicester, Youth Work Press.

Spence, J. (2004) 'Working for Jewish Girls: Lily Montagu, girls' clubs and industrial reform', *Women's History Review*, 13 (3), 491 – 509.

Spence, J. (2005) 'Concepts of Youth', in R. Harrison and C. Wise (eds.) *Working With Young People*, London: Sage.

Thane, P. (1993) 'Women in the British Labour Party and the Construction of State Welfare, 1906–1939' in S. Koven and S. Michel (eds.) *Mothers of a New World: Maternalist Politics and the Origins of Welfare States*, London, Routledge, 343–377.

Todd, S. (2005) *Young Women, Work and Family in England, 1918–1950*, Oxford University Press.

Turnbull, A. (2001) 'Gendering Young People – Work, Leisure and Girls' clubs: The Work of the National Organisation of Girls' Clubs and its successors 1911–1961' in R. Gilchrist, T. Jeffs, and J. Spence (eds.) *Essays in the History of Community and Youth Work*, Leicester, Youth Work Press.

Williams, A.S. (2000) *Ladies of Influence: Women of the Elite in Interwar Britain*, London, Allen Lane, The Penguin Press.

Woodroofe, K. (1962) *From Charity to Social Work in England and the United States*, London, Routledge and Kegan Paul.

CHAPTER 6

'Why Did They Take That Game Away From Us?' The Rise and Fall of Girls' Basketball in the US

Dan Conrad

Basketball was invented in 1891 by James Naismith who taught the game to his male students at the International Young Men's Christian Association (YMCA) in Springfield, Massachusetts. A few weeks later a group of women teachers from a nearby elementary school came to watch and asked if they could also play – and they did, in their high button shoes, corsets and long dresses.

From these beginnings the game spread across the United States at a dizzying rate. By the turn of the century it was being played in nearly every town and hamlet in the country. The game was popular with both boys and girls, but for girls it was the best-loved sport of all and came to be labelled the New Game for the New Woman.

Girls' basketball flourished for just over three decades and then disappeared. By the late 1930s there was hardly a school in the country that allowed girls to play basketball. By the time equal opportunity in school activities was mandated by law, in the 1970s, few remembered that girls had ever played the game at all.

What follows is the story of how this drama played out in a small rural village of mostly Swedish immigrant farmers in the Midwest of the United States: Cokato, Minnesota.

Prologue

In November of 1931 prospects were bright for the Cokato High School girls' basketball team. They would miss high-scoring Hazel Dahlin, but they had Miss

Adeline Lundin back as coach, four seasoned veterans, and a group of highly promising newcomers. The girls were certain they would improve on the 500 record of the year before – but we shall never know. Only days before the opening of practice, they were told that girls' basketball was being eliminated from the school's athletic programme. The headline in the *Cokato Enterprise* (CE) put it bluntly: BASKET BALL PRACTICE OPENS; GIRLS' TEAM DROPPED THIS YEAR. And so it was – for more than forty years.

In November of 2005, seventy four years later almost to the day, I visited Mrs Lorraine Lee in her room in the Cokato Manor nursing home. In 1931, as Lorraine Kvam, she was one of those 'promising newcomers'. When I explained that I wished to talk with her about girls' basketball, a doleful look spread across her face. She looked at me intently, took one of my hands in both of hers and exclaimed more than asked: 'Why did they take that game away from us?' She added that she couldn't tell me any more about it: 'because I never got a chance to play'. More than seven decades had passed, but the pain of a thwarted dream had not.

This article will suggest an answer to Lorraine Lee's question but tell another important story too – that of pioneering young women who brought basketball to Cokato and played it with passion in the early years of the last century. They did so in defiance of a belief that participation in competitive sports was harmful to girls and that to do so was 'unladylike'. It is the story of superintendents who encouraged them, women who coached them and townspeople who cheered them on; a tale of determination, triumph, defeat, and pluck as these young women played with fervour a game they loved. Their story should not be lost.

1903–1904: basketball comes to Cokato

In March of 1903, the Cokato High School Lyceum met to debate the relative greatness of Hannibal and Alexander. When this had been decided, a resolution was passed that, 'The pupils and teachers of Cokato High School regard it as an insult to have young men who attend the literary meetings spit tobacco juice on the floor' (CE). Then came the final order of business, which was to appoint a 'Yell Committee' to come up with recommendations for school colours and a school cheer.

Six weeks later the 30 members of the student body met to vote on the choices presented them. Cardinal and white were overwhelmingly approved as the school colours. The school yell was more controversial but the students finally decided on:

Ching a lacka ching ching
Boom a lacka baa
   Cokato High School
Ran! Rah! Rah!

Armed with colours and a cheer, Cokato High School was ready to take on any foe. The problem was they didn't have a team these whom these accoutrements could inspire. Hopes were raised for a time when the boys collected enough money to purchase a football and organised a football club. They adopted a constitution, titled themselves 'the Roughs' and boasted in the town's newspaper: 'Prospects are very bright this year . . . We have received a challenge from our Howard Lake rivals and will no doubt give them a "rubbing" ere long'.

(CE)

That 'rubbing' would have to wait: it was another twenty-three years before Cokato finally got a football team. For now, it was up to the girls to put the school colours and cheer to good use.

In mid October of 1903 this modest notice appeared in the *Cokato Enterprise*: 'There has been talk of organising a Basket Ball Team in the High School Department'.[1] That simple statement masked some imposing difficulties. There was no coach, no gym, no uniforms, no league to join nor any schedule of games. Worse yet, they didn't even know for sure how the game was played since it is unlikely that any of them had ever seen one. What the girls did have was one basketball and a lot of determination. By the end of the month the *Enterprise* could announce: 'A Basket Ball team has been organised by the high school girls and we may now look for some interesting games. This is a pastime that should be given the proper support by all our citizens' (CE). In two more weeks the girls had raised money for equipment, secured the upstairs of Stevenson's Hall to play in, got baskets installed, ordered uniforms, and had begun to practise in earnest.

Two of the girls, Mathilda Love and Julia Larson, travelled to nearby Howard Lake to watch their girls take on Litchfield in the first basketball game ever played by those schools. The little gym upstairs in the old Town Hall was crammed with spectators from surrounding towns as well as from the contesting schools. The Litchfield girls were handicapped by never having played indoors before, but this proved easier to overcome than having the baskets inexplicably placed two feet higher than the Howard Lake girls were used to. With the latter's shots consistently falling short, the Litchfield girls gained the victory, 13 to 7.

The game was followed by music and speeches and then the crowd drifted off to their horses and wagons or to the train depot for the trip home. The players were then treated to a 'sumptuous supper' in the Degree of Honor Hall and afterward the Litchfield players went to the homes of their opponents to spend the night. They returned home by train the following day. This custom, of the game being part of a larger social event, with the players eating and partying together afterward, and the visitors staying overnight in the homes of the host players, was one that characterised girls' basketball throughout this era.

Back in Cokato, and armed with first hand knowledge of what a basketball game was like, the girls resumed practice with even greater determination. By early 1904 they were ready to challenge another school and they invited neighbouring Dassel to come to Cokato for a game. The Dassel girls accepted, and the stage was set for Cokato's first inter-school athletic event of any kind: a girls' basketball game, to take place on Saturday, 26 March 1904, at 2:30 p.m., at Stevenson's Hall.

The second floor ballroom of Stevenson's Hall could not have been more festively adorned for the occasion. Tables from the Episcopal Ladies' church supper had been pushed to the side, lines drawn to mark the court, benches and chairs placed along the walls and red and white streamers were everywhere! The air was charged with electricity as the girls scrambled up the stairs and onto the court in their new black bloomers and smart middy blouses. One can readily imagine how their hearts were pounding as they heard the cheers of the crowd and the rhythmic *Ching a lacka, Ching Ching/Boom a lacka baa* from their classmates. The noise became almost deafening as the voices from the sizable Dassel contingent rose in support of their own girls.

The account of the game on page one of the *Enterprise* described the tenseness of the moment: 'It was the first match game either team had played and the players on both sides were nervous as they took their places on the field . . .' (CE). But it was now time for the opening jump between Clara Osterberg of Cokato and Dassel's Grace Desmond. The referee tossed the ball in the air – and history was made!

There is no record of the rules under which the game was played, but the fact that there were five on a side suggests it was played under 'boys rules' meaning players could run the full court. There would have been a jump ball after every basket and each time the ball went out of bounds or there was a foul. There may also have been a limit on the number of dribbles but with a ball four to six inches larger than the modern ball, with exposed laces and uncertain roundness, dribbling would not have been an effective means of advancing the ball in any case.

In the early going the Dassel girls had the clear advantage. They were quicker and less bothered by the free throw line being drawn a full foot off the mark. Thus, 'When the whistle blew at the end of the first half Dassel was feeling jubilant' (CE). The second half was a different story. The Cokato girls came out with heightened determination and began to take advantage of their familiarity with the slippery dance floor. Moreover, 'They put science into the game and the team work was excellent' (CE).

In the end, it was a *happy victory* for Cokato. In a larger sense it was a triumph for the girls on both teams. In a still larger sense it was one more victory for young women everywhere in the struggle to counter stereotypes, break out of fixed and confining roles, to stretch limiting definitions of the 'feminine' and to work toward a full and equal place in society.

After the game, the girls celebrated their joint triumph at a luncheon and social hour and then the Dassel girls were entertained by the Cokato players in their homes and it was reported to be 'a pleasure for them to open their homes to such congenial company' (CE). There was one more triumph. The gate receipts of $17.65 proved more than enough to pay the balance owing on the players' uniforms.

A few weeks later, on a Saturday, the girls and their rooters boarded the noon train for a return match at Dassel. And that was it. There was not to be another Cokato girls' basketball game for fifteen years.

1904–1919: a fifteen year hiatus

The boys take over

The Cokato girls organised another team in the fall, but having lost access to Stevenson's Hall they were forced to play outside. They went ahead anyway and scheduled a match but, as the Cokato Enterprise reported: 'The game between Cokato and Dassel scheduled for last Saturday could not take place on account of the muddy conditions of the grounds'. By the time things dried out it was too cold and they gave it up for a lost cause.

The school's sole basketball was now available to the boys and they decided they would organise a boys' team and a week later they played a game at Howard Lake. The Howard Lake Town Hall had burned down so the game was played outdoors and Howard Lake won 19 to 13. It was not an auspicious beginning, but it marked a turning point. For the next fifteen years there was only a boys' basketball team, only a boys' track team, and only a boys' baseball team. Even the High School Athletic Association was exclusively a boys' association. Even for them, however, basketball amounted to little more than playing a few games each year with poor equipment under difficult conditions. Reports to the local newspaper suggest as much:

> *Basketball practice has been neglected this week because the ball was out of order. It is hoped that it will be speedily repaired.*
>
> (CE, 5 November 1908)

> *It was a very loosely played game* [at Howard Lake] *and part of it was played in the dark.*
>
> (CE, 3 November 1910)

> *Basket ball practice has been abandoned on account of the fresh snowfall.*
>
> [CE, 17 November 1910]

Sport takes a back seat

It was not sport that dominated the calendar in the first quarter of the century but an array of cultural and academic activities in which girls were equal participants. The monthly meetings of the Literary Society combined vocal and instrumental music, readings, speeches, and dramatic presentations (with a social hour to follow) and drew large numbers of both students and townspeople. The high school also sponsored regular Lyceums featuring visiting lecturers and musicians. These were community events and held outside the school to accommodate the numbers who attended. The high school had both boys' and girls' debate teams that were consistently successful. Thus it was with some pride, even a little smugness, that Superintendent Hargrave wrote, in 1909, 'Cokato never has been crazed over athletics but her school is none the worse for that . . . The crowds that come out to hear the school literary programmes prove that there is a genuine interest in things that are worthwhile' (CE).

The biggest event of these years was the County Declamation Contest. The contest was the brainchild of Superintendent Hargrave who, in 1908, sent out a challenge to all schools in the county to meet Cokato in a declamation (oratory) contest. Each school was to send one girl and one boy. Four schools accepted the initial challenge: and Mr Hargrave crowed, 'There have been Basket Ball contests and Base Ball contests and Field Day contests in the county for several years; this is the first year that we have had a contest of brains' (CE). These were not stodgy, vapid affairs but spirited contests played before packed houses. Orchestras performed, spectators sang their school songs and lustily cheered the efforts of their champions. In the end, however, the winners were applauded by all, and rivalry melted into camaraderie during the social hour that followed.

Basketball thrives amid controversy

Meanwhile, girls' basketball was spreading rapidly across the state. Basketball was first played in Minnesota in 1892 by the young women (not the men) at prestigious Carleton College. Soon afterward it was being played by women in every college and teacher training school in Minnesota. These young women, such as the 1897 Winona Normal College players (pictured on page x), carried their knowledge and love of the new game to the communities where they taught. Their pose in the picture suggests they were bringing a new attitude as well. The winds of change were in the air. Elizabeth Cady Stanton, Susan B. Anthony and the Suffragettes were not only demanding voting rights but proclaiming a new vision of what was appropriate for women socially, healthy for them physically and possible for them economically.

And just as the tight-laced corsets of the day were an apt symbol of the restrictive social rules confining women within narrow boundaries, so the loose fitting bloomers of young women playing basketball were an apt symbol of a new sense of freedom, of women's insistence on defining for themselves what was 'ladylike' and 'appropriate'. Besides, playing basketball was fun.

It was not a universally popular message and women's basketball became a lightning rod for competing beliefs about what women should be and do. It triggered passionate opposition as well as support. In 1908, the University of Minnesota dropped its women's team and soon afterward other colleges and most urban high schools followed suit. But in the small towns of rural America, the game was thriving – for the girls who played and for the crowds who came to watch. By the 1917–1918 school year, girls' basketball teams were competing almost everywhere in Minnesota. But not in Cokato. That was just about to change.

1918–1921: girls' basketball returns to Cokato

In the fall of 1918, Mr N.N. Stevenson took over as superintendent of the Cokato schools. With him came new opportunities for girls. One of his first acts was to decree that from now on, 'Both boys *and* girls are eligible to membership in the [athletic] association' (CE). With everybody now allowed to join, virtually the whole student body did and they promptly elected a girl to its slate of officers. Mr Stevenson was particularly supportive of girls' basketball and that fall he concluded, 'This is a form of girls' athletics which furnishes healthy invigorating exercise and should be encouraged as much as possible' (CE).

The Cokato girls could recognise a green light when they saw one and within a few days had formed a team, elected Ruth Johnson captain, arranged for practices, scheduled a game and persuaded Miss Myron, a grade school teacher, and Miss Thompson, the principal's assistant, to be their coaches. They boldly declared they would now 'challenge any team in the county!' Mr Stevenson was pleased and to make sure no one doubted where he stood, added, 'We hope that the parents will give the girls the support they desire in this school activity. *If athletics are good for the boys why should not the girls derive equal benefit by participating in sports*' (CE) [emphasis added].

And then disaster struck! The infamous influenza epidemic of 1918 hit Cokato full force in early October. People of all ages were ill and every *Enterprise* featured stories of those who had died. Public gatherings were cancelled, shopping was discouraged and the schools were closed. On Sunday mornings even the churches stood empty and cold. By early December Cokato had counted 17 deaths with many more seriously ill and expected to die. It was not until late December that any break came and the churches announced they would hold Christmas services after all.

School reopened in January 1919, to a longer school day, a six day week – and the determination to return things to normal. The basketball game that was cancelled in October was rescheduled and, at long last, on 10 January 1919, Cokato girls' stood poised at centre court for the start of the first girls' basketball game in Cokato since 1904. Girls' basketball was back! Sadly, however, so was the flu. The school closed again and when they reopened all sports were cancelled for the rest of the year. There was too much else to do. When school opened in the fall the girls (and boys) discovered they had still another disappointment to face. Stevenson's Hall was no longer available for basketball and there was no other place in Cokato to play. Things just had to get better! And during the next school year (1920–1921) they finally did.

In January of 1921, the Athletic Association was reactivated and this time half the officers were girls. Better yet, the Village Hall was remodelled to accommodate basketball and bleachers were installed for the spectators. The girls' had a place to play, a new coach and a full schedule of games. They lost every game, but were happy just to be playing. Best of all, girls' basketball was now an established part of the fabric of life at Cokato High School. The girls, and their superintendent, had won the day. Mr Stevenson summarised his thoughts about the value of sports for boys *and* girls in an Enterprise column that spring:

One of the most essential things in school life and in the upbuilding of the youth is to create enough enthusiasm and push, so that when they get out of school they will be ready to tackle the problems of life. By encouraging athletics, we can help to show that we are interested in the welfare of our school girls and boys . . . Get behind your girls and boys, parents.

Mr Stevenson left Cokato at the end of the 1920–1921 school year. The inclusion of girls in areas previously closed to them, was no small part of his legacy.

1921–1924: girls' basketball 'the biggest show in town'

The fall of 1921 was a good time to be a young woman in Cokato. The war was over; women had won the right to vote; the mayor of Cokato, was a woman – Ida Sparks Clarke; the publisher of the *Cokato Enterprise* was a woman – Maude Donahue; dresses had inched up past the ankle; the new superintendent, Ernst Jacobson, was a fan of girls' basketball; and a sophomore player named Mildred Olson showed promise of being something special.

Accordingly, the basketball season opened with high interest that year. Girls' basketball had become so popular that no less than three women teachers signed on to be coaches and almost half the girls in the school tried out for the team. Before the first game, the whole student body turned out in grand assembly for the school's first pep rally. Superintendent Jacobson, in what would remain his custom throughout his tenure, began the festivities by leading the students is a Swedish cheer:

Va Ska vi ha? (or 'What do we want?')
Va Ska vi ha?
Basket, Basket
Ja! Ja! Ja!

A report of the event added: 'Who says we have no pep? Now watch our teams play basketball!' (CE).

Girls' basketball in that era was played differently than it is today. The girls played in improvised 'gyms' that were primarily designed to be dance halls or community meeting rooms and varied widely in size, height of baskets, condition of floor and more, all of which gave literal meaning to the term 'home court advantage'. To complicate things further, the rules and format of the game, even to the number of players on a side, were not standardised. The custom was that you played the game as played by the home team. The format used by Cokato was a six-player, half court game with no more than three dribbles allowed. There were three guards positioned on one end of the court and three forwards on the other. No one could cross over the centre line, and only forwards could shoot the ball. The girls' and boys' teams typically played 'double headers' with the girls playing the first game. After the games, the host school would hold a 'social' for all the players. A trip to Atwater, for instance, resulted in losses for both the boys and girls teams in basketball, but wins in friendship. The *Enterprise* writer reported: 'After the game the Home Economics department served substantial and appetizing refreshments. All around we were treated well and did not really mind losing to our generous and sportsmanlike opponents.'

The season had begun with little expected of a team that had lost all its games the year before. But that was because people didn't yet know about Mildred Olson. She was, like most Cokato girls, the daughter of immigrant farmers from Sweden. Unlike them, she was six feet tall, athletic and an honor student – the kind that today would have college coaches camped at her front door. As the season started, the girls had only modest success until their coach/maths teacher, Miss Madigan, switched Mildred to forward. They lost only two games the rest of the season, had the best record (500) in school history and found their star of the future. And it was about to get better.

As the 1922–1923 season approached, involvement of girls' in athletics was greater than ever. More than three quarters of the student body belonged to the athletic association and again half the officers were girls. Superintendent Jacobson, meanwhile, was working to shore up community support for girls' athletics and to hold off the opposition to girls' basketball that was rumbling through the state and causing some schools to drop their programmes. Just before the season began he placed an item in a November *Enterprise* that was entitled 'Girls Should Play More' in which he quoted the Chief Medical Officer of the London schools to the effect that:

> *Girls require more opportunities for play than they get and boys should share domestic tasks with girls . . . Girls have too much work to do and in consequence they suffer more than boys from defective vision, heart disease, anemia and spinal curvature. These can all be traced to the same causes: less opportunity to play than boys, less time spent in the open air, the performance of household duties and in regard to school a different curriculum.*

(quoted in CE)

You can almost hear Mr Jacobson murmuring: 'That'll hold 'em off for awhile.'

The season opened with a game at Maple Lake in a contest billed as 'The Swedes against the Irish'. The 'Irish' won in a close game and also took the rematch at Cokato on their way to an undefeated season. The Cokato girls, for their part, would lose only one more game that season. They had become 'the Biggest Show in Town'.

The boys team was having a rough time of it, so it was the girls' team, and Mildred Olson in particular, that pulled in the crowds that packed Village Hall for every contest. When the girls went on the road, scores of Cokato fans followed by car, train, sleigh or buggy to spur them on to another victory.

Girls' basketball in this era was not a game of demure young ladies daintily tossing a ball to and fro. It was fast-paced, exciting and sometimes rough as evidenced by the need, in 1919, to add kicking, shouldering, tackling and hair pulling to the official list of 'fouls'. The excitement of the games is captured in a story one of the players related to her children many years later. Ruby Johnson was the last of nine children born to a rural Lutheran pastor who still delivered his Sunday sermons in Swedish. A 5foot 4inch speedster, Ruby was the defensive star of the team and this is the story she told.

> *Cokato was playing at Dassel and the place was so packed and noisy you could hardly hear yourself think. Dassel was ahead the whole game and we just couldn't catch up. With only a few seconds left they were still ahead by a point and were playing keep-a-way to run out the clock. But then one pass came my direction and I jumped, I think higher than I ever have in my life, and intercepted the ball and threw it as hard as I could to a forward. She put it in at the last second and we won the game by one point. The Cokato people went crazy and so did we.*

In its account of the game, the town newspaper added: 'The goodly delegation of high school students who braved 25 degree below zero temperatures in an open sleigh to attend the game were well-rewarded and should be decorated for bravery' (CE).

When the season ended, Cokato had won six games in a row, finished second in the county and Mildred Olson had scored in double figures in every game. As she headed into her senior year she was then, and ever afterward, stuck with the moniker of 'Johnny' Olson.

The 1923–1924 season featured continued success by the team and even greater accomplishments for its star, 'Johnny' Olson. Her point totals that year would be impressive in any era, but at a time when a typical basketball score, for boys or girls, was on the order of 13 to 9, Mildred Olson's numbers are astounding: 24 points in one game, 26 in another; 32 points, then 36 and 40. In the final game of the regular season she set her all time personal record by scoring 49 points in a 63 to 3 victory. When the regular season came to a close, the Cokato girls had won 15 of their last 16 games by a combined score of 340 to 98.

The stage was set for the season's final contest, the County championship, against powerful Annandale. That the Annandale and Cokato boys would play first in what was dubbed a 'preliminary game' provides insight into the relative interest in girls' as opposed to boys' basketball that year.

People came from all over the county and filled the gym with tension and noise. They were rewarded by a game that was close from beginning to end. When the final gun sounded Annandale had won its sixth championship in seven years. Mildred Olson, as sports editor of the yearbook, later characterised the game as follows: 'Our opponents deserved to win, but the Cokato girls played well and lost to a superior team.'

The Mildred 'Johnny' Olson era was over. In her last two seasons the Cokato girls had won 20 games and lost only 5. She had, as the *Enterprise* reported: 'made more baskets than any other girl in seven counties'. Her 49 point game still stands, after 82 years, as Cokato's single-game scoring record.

The one thing that eluded her and the Cokato girls' team was the county championship. That would have to wait for another star, and another group of girls.

1924–1925: Adalyn Wright remembers her playing days

The most remarkable feature of the 1924–1925 season is not what happened on the court but that 81 years later a member of that team, Adalyn (Eckstrom) Wright was still living in Cokato. At 97 years of age she was still active and she still loved to reminisce about her basketball-playing days.

What follows are excerpts from taped interviews held in late 2005 and early 2006.

I see you are in the 1925 team picture. Did you play other years also?
Oh yes. I started when I was in seventh grade; and I'd go along and sometimes, you know, you wouldn't get to play; just the older ones. But they'd let you play if they were ahead you know, the way they do now.

Did you practice with them?
Oh yes. I'd have to hurry up and do the dishes and clear the table so I could run up to the hall and practice. We had practice in the evening.

[And on the way home . . .] *Sometimes we'd stop at Akerlunds. You know about Akerlund? He had the first radio in town; we'd stop in there and listen to the radio, you know, after practice.*

What about the country girls (like Ruby Johnson) would they stay late . . .?
Oh yes. She [and the other country girls] *would stay in town a lot of times, especially when we had a game or something like that.*
  We'd cook together in home economics; and, you see, what we cooked we could bring home and then Ruby would come and we'd have supper and then Ruby would stay all night. We had such good fun. We'd giggle and laugh together and my father would holler up: 'Aren't you two ever going to stop laughing and go to sleep?' Of course you had your homework and everything too.

Where did you play your games in Cokato?
Well, that was upstairs at the old town hall. That's where they had their meetings and stuff.

Did many people come to the games?
Oh, the whole town would come. You see, there wasn't as much going on years ago so people came to the games. They were really good supporters.

Was it a good place to play basketball?
Oh, the floor was terrible. Some weekends they'd have the chicken show and it'd still be chicken feathers and straw on the floor.

Sounds like it could be dangerous.
Well it was. One time we were playing a game and I slid and got a sliver in my back and I run up to Dr Peterson's office up over the drug store. He took it out and give me a shot and I got back and played in the game.
  And there was a stove in the corner to heat it up. You had to watch out for that.
  And now look at the nice places they got to play in.

Would Cokato fans follow the team – to towns like Dassel and Howard Lake?
Oh yes. Oh yes.
  We were rivals; we played our hardest you know. It was dog eat dog. We were very happy to beat Dassel and Howard Lake. That was our goal.

Did it ever get rough?

Well, I shouldn't tell you this but when we played Howard Lake one time we played in the town hall and we had no showers, we had no dressing room; and while we were playing basketball they threw our clothes out the window.

Who did?
Howard Lake; I don't know who. So we had to pick our clothes off the street. That's how rivals we were.

What about after the game?
Oh, we always had a social hour, and it'd be hot chocolate, something like that . . . and we met, you know, boy friends, you know, because you see if you were a forward you'd have lunch with the forward on their boys team. That's the way they paired us up. We had a lot of fun. It got to be real social.

How did you get to the out-of-town games?
We went in cars, you know; there wasn't busses or anything. Our superintendent, Mr Jacobson, would drive us and he'd get somebody else. He had a coupe so he could only take 2 or 3 people but sometimes we'd squeeze in more.

Did you ever take the train to those games?
Oh yes. Like we took the train to Delano and stayed overnight and come back the next day. I know we took the train to Atwater.

Where would you stay?
Well, like I was a forward, and then I'd stay with a forward from their team. I remember meeting this girl from Atwater; I stayed with her and then when she came to Cokato she stayed with me. And we got to be real good friends. Her name was Lund. We wrote to each other for many years. And, you know, it was a really good social thing besides the fun of playing sports. It's been lost.

Tell me a little about your uniforms.
We wore bloomers and we had to buy our own. I think some girls might have made theirs. They were black serge [and] they were pleated so they looked, well, like skirts. They called 'em bloomers. They were awfully warm, but that's what we had.

They [the school] ordered our jerseys. They were white and had a red 'C' on the front. The other girls used to wear middies. They were navy blue. I think we were the first to get jerseys.

You got a letter too, by playing real well. I still have one that I won. I know I have it someplace, 'cause I treasured that. I sewed that on my sweater. I still have my sweater. That's, you know, a long time ago.

Tell me about Mildred Olson.
She was big and tall, and so was the rest of the family. I think she was about six feet tall. They called her 'Johnny'. Oh, she was just outstanding. She was a forward and we'd always try to get her the ball.

Did she live in town?
She was a country girl. She lived three miles out at the first place past the Baptist cemetery.

What do you remember most fondly about playing basketball?
Well, we had such a wonderful coach, Miss Madigan; she had a very good way of working with girls; and we all got along so good together. It takes that to make a good team; you have to have, you know, good relationships.

Are you still interested in basketball?
I get a big kick out of watching basketball on TV now because it was such a great game for me. They play awfully fast now. We didn't play that fast. But we did pretty good.
   And then, you see, for many years they did not have girls' basketball. They quit, you know, I think shortly after we graduated.

Would you mind telling me your age?
I'm 97.

Excuse me for laughing, but I just never would have guessed it. What's your secret?
Loving people, and working hard, and enjoying life.

1925–1929: 'The Cokato miracle'

By the mid 1920s, opposition to girls' basketball was gaining ground, particularly in urban centres. There they took seriously such 'findings' as reported in the prestigious *Scientific American* that: 'It may be a good thing that women are not as interested in athletics for feminine muscular development interferes with motherhood',[2] and believed assertions by experts such as that 'under prolonged and intense physical stress a girl goes to pieces nervously'.[3] As a result, girls' basketball was rapidly becoming a phenomenon of small town America. In places like Cokato people were not as easily swayed by such opinions. When the Director of Physical Education for women at the University of Minnesota claimed 'It is a well known fact that basketball . . . is too strenuous a game for girls'[4] it brought only smiles among folks used to seeing their girls driving teams of horses, pitching hay and tossing milk pails about.

So the Cokato girls kept on playing and that was a kind of victory in itself. Sadly, it was the only kind of victory they could claim. During the 1925–1926 season they not only lost every game but were humiliated by scores like 52–10, 61–1 and 89–3. Still, if you are going to have a miracle it must be unexpected – and not much was expected of these girls.

The opening of the 1926–1927 season was heralded by the less than rosy prediction that 'the girls should make a fair showing this year' (CE). That turned out to be optimistic. Once again they lost every game and people gradually stopped paying attention to their efforts. As a result, they didn't notice the emerging heroine in their midst. Anna Niemala was a sturdy, broad shouldered daughter of Finnish immigrant farmers. Eighty years later Adalyn Wright would describe her like this: 'Oh, she was a *wonderful* player, something like "Johnny" Olson. She wasn't that tall, but she was very strong. Oh, she was powerful!' By the middle of her sophomore, season, Anna was scoring most of the team's points and several times ALL of them such as in the season-ending loss of 42–26. Still, it was a loss, like all the others, and there was not much reason to hope for better things next year.

By the fall of 1927, the Twenties, if not exactly 'Roaring' through Cokato were at least chipping away at its Scandinavian reserve. Temperance rallies were still a sure-fire draw, but the town voted (narrowly) to allow Sunday movies, and the ads for the 'Big Store' showed hemlines had jumped a good six inches from the year before and now barely covered the knee. If that wasn't scandalous enough, the girls' basketball team had traded their bulky black bloomers for bright red tops and flashy white shorts that showed ALL the knee—and a bit more. It is surely no coincidence that newspaper accounts of the girls' games began to include phrases like 'Cokato's good looking basketball sextet and an aggregation of fair athletes' and 'Miss Eppel, as well as being the best looking athlete on the floor . . .' (CE). No such reference to appearance was ever used in accounts of boys' games.

The big event of that season was to be the unveiling of the school's new auditorium in January. It was the town's pride and joy and every person who could secure a ticket jammed into it for the festive occasion. Orations by dignitaries and selections by the orchestra preceded the scheduled basketball double header. There was one problem. The first game ever played in the new gym, before the biggest crowd in the town's history, would feature the Cokato girls' team that had not won a game in over two and one-half years.

What happened that day is best conveyed by quoting a little of what was reported about the event on page one of the next *Cokato Enterprise.*

GIRLS WIN FIRST GAME IN NEW AUDITORIUM

Twas a grand and glorious occasion, that opening game in Cokato's splendid new gymnasium last Friday evening. The six hundred spectators . . . were elated to see the elegant commodious auditorium-gymnasium and thrilled to watch the excellent exhibition of America's most popular indoor sport . . . To the classy, well-coached girls' team belongs the honor and distinction of having won the first game played in the new gymnasium. And the girls chose to make the aforesaid victory emphatic enough to be both convincing and easily remembered, to wit 48 to 11. The victory was double sweet to the players because it was their first success in two and a half years of endeavor. They began as Freshmen, utterly inexperienced even in handling the ball, and were obliged to play seasoned teams with defeat their inevitable lot. But they refused to be discouraged . . . The individual star of this aggregation of fair athletes is the adroit Anna Niemala whose 14 field goals and four free throws make a total of 32 points . . .

For an encore the best team in the county was given a similarly rude introduction to the new gym the following week. Anna Niemala scored 31 points en route to a 43 to 16 victory. But, alas, midnight arrived quickly for these Cinderellas and the girls lost all of their remaining games.

The reader might well expect the next item to be an account of the deep depression that now enveloped these hapless young women. However, even a casual glance at their yearbook picture, taken at the close of their third consecutive losing season suggests that would be to misjudge and underestimate them. The picture suggests instead a group of young women who appear to feel pretty good about themselves and who don't seem to think losing a few basketball games is the end of the world.

Their pose – crossed ankles, rolled down socks and twinkling eyes depict girls who are having a whole lot of fun and were perhaps not that offended by being called an 'aggregation of fair athletes' and 'a good looking basketball sextet'. A closer look shows something else; something more like pride, self-confidence, and determination. They, and Anna Niemala in particular look all the world like they have 'something up their sleeves' and can't wait to spring it on an unsuspecting world. That's just what Anna and her teammates were about to do.

The 1928–1929 season began with little public fanfare and no hope for success. However, it turns out the girls really did have something up their sleeves. The four returning players improved over the summer and they added three new sophomores who were pretty good players. Most of all they had a huge incentive. The county championship game was going to be played in the Cokato gym and the Cokato girls were determined to be in that game!

Still, this was a team that had won only two games in three and a half years and had pretty much disappeared from public notice. Their games were seen primarily by fans who had come early to watch the boys' game. Thus it garnered only passing notice when Anna Niemala, scoring most of her 16 points in the fourth quarter, led Cokato to a come-from-behind victory over a strong Maple Lake team. And the girls continued to win, always against favored opponents and always by the narrowest of margins. Two games even ended in a tie since there was no provision for overtime in those days. People finally began to take notice and once again were packing the gym to see the Cokato girls enter game after game as underdogs and emerge as victors. When the regular season ended they were, almost unbelievably, 'The Undefeated Cokato Cardinals'.

There was one game left to play, the one they had fought so hard to be in: the County Championship. The game was scheduled for 15 February 1929, in the Cokato auditorium and was proclaimed to be 'the most auspicious athletic attraction that has been staged at Cokato'. The opponent would be mighty Annandale, winners of eight of the last nine county championships and a team that had lost but one game in three years.

The game was scheduled to start at 8 p.m., but festivities began early in the afternoon and included concerts by both the Cokato and Annandale orchestras. The town was alive with excitement and the Cokato stores were closed from 2 o'clock on that day. By 8 p.m. the auditorium was packed and the atmosphere electric.

Annandle took the lead from the opening tip and held it throughout the first half. In the third quarter the Cokato girls began to cut into the margin and by the final quarter it was down to two. The auditorium exploded and the Cokato fans began chanting their meaningless but nonetheless menacing-sounding Swedish cheer:

Rockar, stockar
Thor och hans bockar

Kör igenom!
Kör igenom![5]

With less than a minute left, Annandale still clung to its two-point lead. But the never-say-die Cokato girls, with years of frustration driving them, were not about to quit. With five seconds left they stole the ball and got it to Anna Niemala who muscled it into the basket to tie the game at the final horn.

The fans and players went wild. The county officials, on the basis of Annandale having one defeat and Cokato none, awarded the championship trophy to Cokato. But Annandale did not accept defeat so easily. They were, after all, mighty Annandale, perennial county champions and could not stomach losing the title to these Cokato girls who had hardly won a game in years! They argued vehemently, contending that since the game ended in a tie neither team had won, or, alternatively, that they both had and should both be awarded trophies. Cokato then offered to play an overtime period to settle the matter. Annandale refused, on the grounds that it was against the rules of girls' basketball and demanded instead that a second game be played. At this point the county officials stepped in and said: 'No, *this* was the championship game'. The Cokato High School Girls' were now: **Champions of Wright County**!

The 1929 Cokato yearbook would include these words as their legacy:

The 1928–1929 basketball season will long be remembered as the year when the Cokato girls won the long coveted Wright County championship trophy, the only one of its kind thus far placed in our roomy trophy case.

It was, indeed: **'The Cokato Miracle'**.

1929–1931: the last hurrah

The 1929–1930 season was characterised in the school's yearbook as 'up and down'. They proved no more able to replace Anna Niemala than their predecessors had been able to replace Mildred Olson and they finished the season with as many losses as wins.

The biggest loss of the year was not on the basketball court however. In May it was announced that Cokato girls' basketball would lose its most avid supporter, the person who for nine years had led the cheers, made sure the girls got their uniforms and the equipment they needed and who had seen to it they got to out-of-town games even if he had to drive them himself. Ernst T. Jacobson, ('Jake') resigned as superintendent of the Cokato schools. His send off was one of the biggest events in Cokato history and concluded with a rousing cheer for Mr Jacobson by the students and townspeople. His replacement was to be a man more attuned to modern educational thought.

There was one season to go, and it began with the same mixture of excitement and optimism as any other. It is only with hindsight that one sees the irony in the *Enterprise* prognosis that 'The future of the girls' basketball club . . . appears bright' (CE). The girls had no way of knowing that the sword of Damocles had already begun its descent.

When the season ended the girls had rallied to achieve a 500 record. In May they played a prominent role in the last co-educational Spring Athletic Banquet. Lollie Harkman gave a speech on behalf of the girls and then joined teammates Hazel Dahlin and Victoria Ekstrand in an instrumental trio that supplied the music for the occasion. The senior girls received their letters and then walked off the stage. They were **'The Last Cokato Cardinals' Girls' Basketball Team'**.

Later that spring, a columnist for the Cokato newspaper penned the following:

> *A branch of athletics which is likely to become passé within a few years is the participation of high school girls in public exhibitions of basket ball. There are several good reasons for this situation. For one thing it is proved that such activity for girls of high school age is not beneficial from either the physical or mental standpoint. Educators will testify to the correctness of that statement. Girls' basket ball is being dropped all over the state, and therefore it can be said that its passing generally will soon be true.*

In retrospect, what he averred had been 'proved' about girls' basketball turned out to be wrong. What he predicted as its future was exactly correct. Cokato dropped girls' basketball the next fall, as did three neighbouring towns. A few more communities held on another year or so and then dropped it also. The game that had been played so enthusiastically by girls in every town and hamlet in Minnesota was now virtually extinct. A few scattered Minnesota towns held on stubbornly until told to desist by the state's Department of Education in a 1938 letter that said, in part:

> *In those few remaining schools still sponsoring a program of girls' interscholastic athletics, it is recommended that the interscholastic program be dropped and that a Girls' Athletic Association be installed in its place.[6]*

Cokato had already replaced its Athletic Association with separate ones for boys and girls. It was not long afterward that the new the role for girls in

Cokato athletic events was noted. 'The Girls' Athletic Association gave a pep fest on Thursday, October 20, for the boys' football team' (CE). One year later the girls formed a cheerleading squad. An era had ended.

Conclusion: *Why did they take that game away from us?*

The announcement in the *Enterprise* that girls' basketball was being dropped included nothing, then or later, about why. There was no explanation in the school yearbook and no mention of it in the school board minutes. The two former players interviewed for this project still didn't know, 75 years afterward, why girls' basketball was dropped. Adalyn Wright's response was: 'No, I don't. I was disappointed because I enjoyed it so much and I thought it was such a clean sport for the girls to enjoy'. Lorraine Lee responded with a hint of impatience at the naïveté of the questioner: 'They didn't give reasons. They didn't ask. They told. And, in those days you did what they said'.

An item written in 1995 for the Cokato Historical Society stated that girls' basketball was dropped to save money during the Great Depression. But an examination of school board records revealed that the only expenditures from general funds for athletics from 1927 to 1931 were for boys' teams. Money needed for girls' basketball came from gate receipts and from fund raising efforts of the Athletic Association or by the girls themselves.

The most reasonable conclusion is that Cokato dropped girls' basketball for the same reasons as everybody else. The view finally prevailed that playing basketball was 'inappropriate' and 'unwomanly' and harmful to the physical and emotional health of young women. It was accepted by those in authority that the harmfulness of the sport to girls had, as the *Enterprise* writer put it, been 'proved'. In short, girls' were forbidden to play basketball for their own good.

With the benefit of 75 years hindsight, the arguments and assertions that led Cokato and other schools to eliminate girls' basketball have been shown to be mistaken and even a bit ludicrous, based more on myth and prejudice than scientific investigation. By the late 1960s, more objective research into women's health had clearly demonstrated that girls had more than sufficient strength and stamina to play basketball; their hearts would not collapse from the strain; their reproductive organs would not be displaced by running and jumping; their interest in child rearing not be diminished by sport; their psyches were not in danger from 'over stimulation'; and their endocrine systems would not be thrown out of kilter by loud bands and cheering crowds.

By the late 1960s, other myths about women were being challenged as well. Women were carrying on the tradition of their suffragette sisters and going beyond them to demand equal rights and equal opportunities for women in all aspects of life. They were challenging old assumptions and long standing prejudices about women, and enunciating a new vision of what it was appropriate for women to do, and possible for them to be. It is hard to believe it is mere coincidence that women's basketball arose in concert with the suffrage movement of the early 1900s, and then faded to near extinction, only to re-emerge with the women's movement of the late 1960s and early 1970s.

Girls' basketball has now returned and appears to be here to stay. It is being played by today's young women with a zest and at a level of skill that would make their predecessors proud. Perhaps these pioneers of Cokato basketball are even now looking down from somewhere, and smiling, as their grand-daughters and great grand-daughters play once again the game they loved and lost. Conversely, as today's girls take the court for the start of yet another game, they can draw strength from knowing that they are, in some indefinable yet unmistakable way, standing upon the sturdy shoulders of pioneering women who played the game first, in the early years of the last century.

Notes

1   It was the convention until the 1940s to write basketball as two words: basket ball.
2   Dr Donald Laird, quoted in Beran (see 'Sources') p. 48.
3   Agnes Wayman, President of the American Physical Education Association, quoted in Johnson and McIntyre (see 'Sources') p. 75.
4   Dr Anna Norris, Physical Director for Women, University of Minnesota, quoted in the *Cokato Enterprise*, 12 February 1925, p. 4.
5   Roughly translates as: *Rocks, Logs, Thor and his steeds, Drive on through, Drive on through.*
6   26 October 1938, letter to school superintendents from Harold Jack, Supervisor of Health and Physical Education, Minnesota Department of Education. Quoted in Johnson and McIntyre (see 'Sources') p. 76.

References

Beran, J.A. (1993) *From Six on Six to Full Court Press: A Century of Iowa Girls' Basketball.* Ames, Iowa: Iowa University Press.

Dosch, N.C. (1991)'The Sacrifice of Maidens or Healthy Sportswomen? The Medical Debate over Women's Basketball' in J.S. Hult and M. Trekell (eds.) *A Century of Women's Basketball: From Frailty to Final Four*, Reston, Virginia: American Alliance for Health, Physical Education, Recreation and Dance: 125–136.

Grundy, P. and Shackleford,S. (2005) *Shattering the Glass: the Remarkable History of Women's Basketball.* New York, The New Press.

Johnson, M.B. and McIntyre, D.E. (2005) *Daughters of the Game: the First Era of Minnesota Girls High School Basketball 1891–1942*. Minnesota: McJohn Publishing.

Lanin, J. (2000) *A History of Basketball for Girls and Women: From Bloomers to Big Leagues*. Minneapolis, Lerner Sports.

Primary sources:

Interviews with former players:

Lorraine (Kvam) Lee, Cokato; November 2005.

Adalyn (Eckstrom) Wright, Cokato; December 2005, January 2006.

Contemporary accounts:

Cokato Enterprise, issues from 1902 to 1933, 1969–1975. Available in microfilm at the Minnesota Historical Society, St. Paul, MN.

The Aurora. Yearbook of Cokato High School: 1922, 1923, 1924, 1928, 1929, 1930. Available at The Cokato Museum.

Various events were also checked out in the *Annandale Advocate, Delano Eagle*, and the *Howard Lake Herald*. In microfilm at the Minnesota Historical Society, St. Paul, MN.

School Board minutes for Cokato, Minnesota, 1925–1931. Available at the Minnesota Historical Society, St. Paul, MN.

Photographs:

Photo of 1897 Winona Normal Women's Basketball Team used by permission of Winona State University.

All other photographs from the collection of the Cokato Museum.

1922 Basketball Team

CHAPTER 7

Cardijn Versus Baden-Powell: The Methodical Turn in Youth Work History

Filip Coussée

In 2007 Scouting celebrated its hundredth birthday. Baden-Powell's Brownsea experiment is an important moment in the context of youth work history. But 2007 was important for yet another reason. It was the international Cardijn year, celebrating the 125th anniversary of his birth and commemorating the 40th anniversary of his death. Jozef Cardijn and Robert Baden-Powell met almost hundred years ago in London. The discussion between them is significant for youth work developments to this very day.

From youth work to positive youth development

'This is a service, I am tempted to conclude, without a history and therefore, if it is not very careful, without an identity' (Davies, 1999: ix). This finding seems valid for youth work in Flanders too. Flanders, the Dutch speaking region of Belgium, probably has the highest youth work index in the world. There is a youth work initiative for every 250 inhabitants below the age of 25. However, this should not be taken to imply a clear understanding in Flanders of what youth work essentially is. A focus on numbers and participation rates does not indicate any engagement with pedagogical questions. However, policymakers and youth workers do have a lot to say about the positive outcomes of youth work for its participants, and academic research in Flanders as in many other western countries, underpins their belief in its efficacy. Following North American hype around 'positive youth development' researchers are keen to prove that participation in structured youth activities contributes positively in a number of areas – relating to: academic results (Quane and Rankin, 2006); the development of social and cultural capital (Dworkin, Larson and Hansen, 2003); mental health (Mahoney, Schweder and Stattin, 2002); a sense of citizenship

(Williamson, 1997); the prevention of all kinds of risk behaviour (Mahoney, Stattin and Lord, 2004); gaining a stronger position in the labour market (Jarret, Sullivan and Watkins, 2005); and to the nurturing of democratic skills and attitudes (Eccles *et al.*, 2003). This is not new. Since the very beginnings of youth work similar positive outcomes have been described as the results of 'good youth work'.

An outcome related youth work identity

This seems to be a good thing for youth work. Notwithstanding the somewhat overblown headings that accompany the positive youth development paradigm (see for instance Lerner, 1995), at least the actual youth agenda seems to have development rather than deterrence as its base. But at the end of the day this new paradigm does not seem able to unveil the pedagogical identity of youth work. How does youth work contribute to youth development? And why does it appear that the best developed young people are likely to profit most from the youth work on offer? Moreover, the 'outcome related identity' invites policymakers and academics to evaluate different youth work forms according to their contribution to the aforementioned appreciated outcomes. The introduction of best value performance indicators in the UK illustrates this (Flint, 2005). In Flanders youth workers are not yet confronted to the same degree with these restrictive, a-historical and a-pedagogical *Best Value Performance Indicators* (*BVPIs*), but in essence the state of youth work affairs seems not very different from that in the UK.

The legacy of Baden-Powell

In Flanders the uniformed youth organisations – although in many cases not uniformed anymore – are still very popular. In most western countries this kind of youth work has experienced a dramatic decrease in numbers (Hart, 2006). This is not the case in Flanders. One in three young people participate in Catholic Student Action, Scouting, Chiro or other so called 'youth movements'. These organisations are also called 'traditional' youth work as their roots can be traced back to Baden-Powell's Scouting Movement and beyond. This common understanding of youth work history does not show the full picture. Nevertheless, in Flanders Scouting and alike organisations are seen as the 'real and original' youth work. Such youth movements have evolved from self-government under adult supervision to an ideal of self-organised work, intended to be run by young people for young people, without changing much in their external manifestations – as a youth work approach these have stood the test of time. As Jephcott (1954) observed more than half a century ago, youth organisations still can be trusted 'to provide guidance without dictation'. Since the beginning of youth policy in Belgium a central place has been given to youth movements (Van der Bruggen and Picalausa, 1946). Today the youth movement model is still considered the educational instrument *par excellence*.

There is however another recurrent observation to be made. Participation in youth movements is not equally spread amongst the young population. The creation of new, 'less demanding' youth work forms and methods, seems to be the perennial answer to this observation. The introduction of youth clubs in the 1960s for instance was organised with the explicit intention of lowering the threshold for non-involved youth to participate in 'traditional', more structured youth work. Although, originally aimed at the so called 'ordinary youth' who did not feel attracted to the different youth movements, in Flanders many of them evolved – especially in the 1980s and early 1990s – in the direction of provision for vulnerable youth. Given the gulf between the habits and culture of these young people and the world of policymakers, the calling in of professional expertise was from the start considered indispensable. These new youth work organisations set up varied programmes ranging from individual help, through group work, to social action. All these were glued together by the infinitely large and elastic concepts of prevention and participation. In some countries, such as the UK, this form of youth work achieved statutory status. In Flanders youth work organisations working with vulnerable young people are organised through private organisations, but nevertheless the fast growing gap between 'traditional' youth work and professional youth work has been obscured and largely ignored.

On income and outcome: a youth work paradox

The burgeoning paradigm of positive youth development returns our attention to this gap. Recent studies state that professional youth work succeeds in attracting 'hard-to-reach' young people, but cannot always produce the highly appreciated results noted earlier. Set against this, just saving young people from boredom (Furlong *et al.*, 1997) is hardly a high ambition. Even worse, some other studies show that professional youth work has counter-productive effects. Open youth centres, some claim, bring with them drugs, consumerism, aggression and troubles in the neighbourhood (Mahoney, Stattin and Lord, 2004; Feinstein *et al.*, 2006). Such evaluation studies on the effect of UK youth work, tempted the British Minister of Youth to say that 'it is better to stay at home and watch TV than to attend a youth club' (Williamson, 2006). These studies contrast sharply with voices that applaud the contribution of 'traditional' youth work (MacDonald, 2000; Merton et al., 2004) and voluntary work in general, to the acquisition of social skills and the development of appropriate attitudes (Eccles and Barber, 1999). Unfortunately such organisations do not generally reach the young people who seem to need them most. Concerns about this 'Matthew effect'[1] were reiterated in the work of the Russell Commission, asking for special attention for the young people who are 'historically less likely to volunteer'. We seem to stand before a strange youth work paradox: 'the work that works is not accessible, the accessible work does not work'.

Imposing solutions, reinforcing the paradox

Youth work contributes to the acquisition of various social skills and the gaining of self-confidence, but it is only accessible for those who have already to some degree achieved such skills and confidence. The professionalised attempts to overcome this 'Matthew effect' seem to have counterproductive effects. Of course both positive and counterproductive effects can be traced predominantly to a 'selection' effect (see Fredricks and Eccles, 2006), but then this is an avenue of enquiry that inevitably raises the uncomfortable question of whether youth work has anything at all to contribute. What might be the raison d'être of youth work? And particularly: why should we need professional youth work? The youth work paradox condemns professional youth work to drift between an efficiency crisis and an identity crisis. A thorough analysis of youth work policy in Flanders reveals two strategies to go beyond this youth work paradox (Coosée, 2008): a policy of moving up and a policy of upgrading.

In the first strategy professional youth workers try to move their members little by little towards so called 'regular' youth work because this has proven to be more successful. This is the strategy that has been followed in Flanders since the adoption of the youth movement model as the best form of youth provision just after World War II. It echoes the old social work adage that professionals should seek to make themselves superfluous and not make others dependent on their intervention.

The second strategy is less popular in Flanders, but more so in the UK. According to this strategy professional youth work attempts to produce the same results as 'regular' youth work. In doing this the 'work that doesn't work' is replaced by short term targeted programmes with very specific purposes, for example the acquisition of identified skills, increased employability, or drug prevention. Thus, in form and content youth workers are encouraged to narrow the scope of their work and to set straight and measurable goals (Smith, 2003). The introduction of *BVPIs* in the UK is an outstanding example of this strategy. Unfortunately both strategies seem to end up with the same drawbacks that led to the creation of professionalised youth work in the first place, namely a heightened threshold in terms of access, cherry-picking and a relative high drop-out rate.

An a-historical search for a youth work identity

Both approaches, 'moving young people on' and 'targeting deficiencies', do attempt to forge a youth work identity. They start from the point that youth work (there is a tendency to speak more generally of youth work as 'positive activities') contributes to the acquisition of certain social skills and the development of positive attitudes. But these seem to be things that evolve pre-eminently and most fruitfully in informal educational settings (Brew, 1946; Jeffs and Smith, 2005). What happens is that both strategies try to overcome the youth work paradox, but in a critical and contrary sense they pursue these goals of informal learning by formalising the work. In the first approach, informal learning is grafted onto a certain youth work form, the youth movement, or more broadly regular, traditional youth work.

In the second approach some potentially broadening elements are (re)introduced: for example, the value of youth-adult partnerships is rediscovered; the learning process is put at the heart of the work; youth workers go beyond recreational activities; and the work bridges the gap between school and workplace. These are elements that are potentially appealing to young people. They echo the findings of Marczak *et al.* (2006) that 'youth and families want more connections between people and age groups . . .' The problem is not that these elements are improper to 'real' youth work, this could be doubted on historical grounds anyway (Davies, 1999; Williamson, 2006, Coussée, 2008). But the problem in this second approach is that individualised and methodical thinking pushes 'informal' learning into the background, '. . . as well as more of the free-spirited, organic activities likely to emerge in neighbourhoods and communities' (Marczak *et al.*, 2006). There is a belief in the superior value of informal learning, but if the informal climate in which young people grow up does not reveal itself as a positive, stimulating environment it seems as if formalisation is the only option left. The process of youth work itself is becoming formalised, provoking the question – including among the young – 'Is this still youth work?'

Both strategies are so obsessed with imposing solutions that they seem to ignore some unintended but counter-productive consequences. First of all, in formalising the informal the most important aspect of youth work is threatened: the pedagogical and thus open and dialogical relation between youth worker and young people. Second, in being implicitly labelled as 'irregular', youth work with vulnerable young people becomes as vulnerable as its clients. It gets a derived, diluted identity and is forced into a position that leads inevitably to a crisis of professionalism in youth work (Banks, 1996). And third, the dividing lines between non-vulnerable and vulnerable young people are reinforced and extended from school-time to leisure time. In focusing on positive, but individual, youth development, actual youth work policy neglects these structural, counter-productive consequences and keeps on running into the deadlock of the youth work paradox.

An historical perspective

A social-pedagogical and thus more historicised perspective could help us to go beyond the youth work paradox. History cannot show us the one and only, universal and eternal fixed youth work identity. 'Youth work histories' however can show us the richness of different youth work shapes. They can throw a light on previous discussions in youth work, that may be parallel to contemporary discussions. In other words: youth work history does not serve present evolutions and policy objectives, but has the power to frame them in a broader context, thus feeding and inspiring the present discussion on youth work identity. Therefore it is important to analyse which views on youth work and young people are underpinning youth work debates.

Youth work *avant-la-lettre*: cultural renewal, social action and prevention

Flemish youth work histories take as their starting point the emancipatory movement of students in the Flemish colleges at the end of the nineteenth century. This youth work history is a history of the youth movement model, and especially of the boys' movement. It is also the case that student actions protesting discrimination against the Flemish language in schools and the threatening laicisation of society were an important condition for the growth of a youth movement. By means of study, play and poetry this played an important role in the Flemish fight for emancipation. As the Flemish student movement was there before the German Wandervögel some authors identify this as the first real youth movement in the world (Cammaer, 1962; Gevers and Vos, 2004). This is a somewhat romanticised view as the Flemish youth movement was supported to a significant degree by adult teachers and priests who fought the same fight. But more important is that this youth movement was not the direct predecessor of contemporary youth movements, nor was it the only movement or initiative that worked with and for young people. The Young Socialist Guards for instance were young workers united in their fight for their particular interests including better working conditions, abolition of conscription law, and paid holidays. Given their background, it is not surprising that their aims were focused on social change, unlike the students' middle class concerns around cultural renewal. Like the students the Young Guards fought side by side with adults sharing the same concerns.

Younger children were at school or were looked after in so called 'patronages' or playground organisations. Most of them were Catholic and modelled on the Italian oratorio of Don Bosco. In the 1840s Don Bosco took care of hundreds of street children. He was convinced that a warm and safe home, a positive approach and a focus on learning could save most of them from criminality and degeneration. Up to World War II Flemish pedagogues praised Don Bosco for installing 'the preventative method' and revealing that the social problem was in essence a pedagogical problem (De Hovre, 1935).

In many places there were still other attempts to bring young people together trying to give them some additional education or saving them from the street or from 'poor parenting'. So in the second half of the nineteenth century we see a highly differentiated youth work field. Attempts to co-ordinate all these initiatives were rather marginal. After World War I this situation would come to an end.

The psychological turn: adolescence as a crucial phase in life

Some major changes heralded a new youth work era around the Great War. The so-called 'children laws' prohibited child labour, and compulsory education was introduced. This established a sharper distinction between adults and young people and between school or working hours and leisure time. Through French psychologists such as Mendousse and Compayré the ideas of Stanley Hall on adolescence as a phase of life, with typical characteristics and its own needs, became known in the lowlands and influenced the existing youth field. Also influential were other developmental theorists, the German Americans Charlotte Bühler and Edouard Spranger, and much later Erik Erikson, who based their ideas on observations of the middle class students in the Wandervögel-movement. Thus a 'single concept of boyhood' was firmly established (Selten, 1991, 1993).

After the International Socialist Youth Conference in Stuttgart (1907) the socialists started to redirect their Young Guards as a kind of preparatory unit for 'the real work'. The Catholic Flemish Student Movement evolved in the same direction. Direct social action became less important. Study and preparation for a future as adult leaders came to the fore. This institutionalisation of the youth phase and the corresponding psychologisation of youth work became definitely established at the first Pedagogical Congress in the Netherlands (1919). The Great War had provoked some moral panics about the education of youth. Adolescence was reshaped as the most crucial phase for the healthy development of young people into good citizens. Leisure was defined as youth's own sphere where young peoples' activities had to be put on the right road by means of the well-considered steering of adults (De Graaf, 1989). At this conference the Scouting method attracted considerable attention.

Some years earlier Baden-Powell had developed his method driven by concerns about the physical and moral deterioration of the nation's younger generation. He found his inspiration in the public school system, his army experiences in India and Africa and the experiments of American contemporaries such as Ernest Seton and Dan Beard. Thanks to the efforts of newspaper magnate Pearson, and existing youth work organisations like the YMCA, the Boys' and Church Lads' Brigades, Baden-Powell's method grew into a movement (Wilkinson, 1970) which quickly gained ground outside the UK. Numerous Flemish patronage leaders thought that the Scouting method could help them to modernise their pedagogical system. Like the Boys' Brigade, Flemish patronages lost popularity, especially amongst older working class young people after the war. Young workers in particular were no longer attracted by the gentle but often boring climate. Over and above that, the patronages lost members to a new organisation: the Young Catholic Workers established by the priest Jozef Cardijn. He founded Katholieke Arbeiders Jeugd (KAJ) as an antidote to the demoralising effects of factory life and to keep young workers away from the socialists. He was a charismatic leader who felt the need for a positive and respectful approach to working class youth (De La Bedoyere, 1958; Launay, 1985). 'You are worth as much as the princess of Laken' was his message to factory girls. Cardijn had travelled extensively and was inspired by the English labour movement, the German Gesellenbund and French Sillon. Based on his well known enquiry method 'judge, see and act',

Cardijn found a way to work actively with young people. Many of the old members still give testimony of the emotions Cardijn created at the time. He gave young working men and women the feeling that they were a significant part of society and things could change if they took responsibility. Not inappropriately he has been called the first Flemish youth work pedagogue, but he soon came into collision with the structures in his own Catholic hierarchy.

Of extreme importance for youth work developments in Flanders was the inauguration of Catholic Action by Pope Pius XI after World War I. To reinforce the weakening Catholic influence on society, church leaders initiated and stimulated an extensive system of societies and clubs aimed at the mass organisation of the population. Youth Union for Catholic Action (JVKA) was set up to coordinate Catholic Action interventions focused on young people.

The methodical turn: from youth movement to best method of youth work

Scouting was increasingly seen as the ideal method to glue together youthful enthusiasm and adult concerns. Its methodical character made it easily adaptable to various purposes and ideologies. As a consequence of their participation in the 1907 International Socialist Youth Conference in Stuttgart, under the presidency of Hendrik De Man, the socialists increasingly picked up aspects of German youth work transformations. From 1908 on it was forbidden in Germany for young people under the age of eighteen to participate in political activities. Therefore the programme of the Socialist Youth Movement was focused on cultural activities, inspired by the romantic Wandervögel tradition. Besides that, the social situation had become less precarious and the Socialist Party obtained a more or less acceptable place in the political sphere, so the need for participation of young people in the social struggle became less critical. The youth movement programme, until then characterised primarily by hiking, camping and an aversion to obscene language, tobacco and alcohol, was increasingly popular in Flanders, and the 'youth movement method' became in no time the ideal model of spending leisure time. Inspired by the evolutions in Germany and Austria the Socialists established the Red Falcons, and in doing so reshaped their youth work as a variant of Scouting (Tesarek, 1929).

Under the impulse of Catholic Action the existing youth work field however was increasingly occupied by Catholic organisations. The Student Movement (KSA), was reshaped with the apostolic Catholic Action as the guiding principle for KSA. Members had to renounce Flemish activism for the JVKA leaders wanted one big Catholic youth organisation but Cardijn threw a spanner in the works. His KAJ had grown into a mass movement in a short time. He refused to help establish a single Catholic youth work organisation. Cardijn even called in the help of the Pope and he won the argument. Instead of one youth work organisation, several class and gender specific youth organisations were established: besides the KAJ and the KSA, there were the BJB (farmers' youth) and KBMJ (merchants' youth), each with their female counterparts. Scouting was found too militaristic and not religious enough; with the patronages they were relegated to the status of 'auxiliary work'.

Cardijn's victory could not hide the fact that he was under increasing pressure from his own clerical hierarchy and the Catholic trade union. His superiors were not amused with his firm statements on the nature and conditions of working life. The unionists from their side were anxious that Cardijn would start a separate youth trade union. Ultimately Cardijn was pushed into the direction of a more depoliticised youth work and he too adopted the burgeoning youth movement method. So, the ideological and pedagogical fundaments of De Man's cultural socialism (Pels, 2003) and Cardijns Catholic personalism finally came together in one a-political youth work method. This was an adapted form of Scouting finished with some typical romantic Flemish-Catholic flavours. Youth work was still emancipation, but emancipation had been 'decontextualised' (Lewin, 1947). The concept was now detached from poor working conditions, poor schooling, general poverty, and discrimination of language, and had become attached to 'the status of youth'.

Purifying the youth work method: making abstraction of context

Before Cardijn started the KAJ he had spent a couple of days with Baden-Powell in London. Baden-Powell suggested that he become the Scouts' commissioner for Belgium. The difference in their view on youth work is obvious:

Cardijn: *do you know that there are young workers with their very own problems?*
B-P: *I do not know young workers, I only know citizens and I want to shape strong-willed men.*
Cardijn: *do you realize how young workers have to survive in factories and*

how they are influenced by the workers' milieu? How could we help them, not just to stay good, but even to have a positive influence in their milieu?
B-P: *I don't know the workers' milieu!*

(Cardijn, 1948, 137, my translation)

Both men had clear youth work purposes before their eyes. Baden-Powell defined the identity of youth work detached from the potential participants and was not too critical in his vision of the prevailing social order, while Cardijn took the living conditions of working-class youth as his point of departure. Both organisations were flourishing at that time. In spite of its founders' original intentions Scout troops recruited mainly from the middle and higher classes (Scheidlinger, 1948). Scouts often needed a bike, and the cost of a uniform was 62 francs when the price for bread was 2 francs and 20 cents. In terms of membership KAJ left the other youth movements far behind. In 1933 they were three times as big as Scouting and reached over 36,000 young workers (Alaerts, 2004: 159). Nevertheless the KAJ did not succeed in reaching the lower blue-collar class. Cardijn often used the metaphor of the yeast in the dough. Other youth movement leaders after World War II would use similar images.

It appears that the youth movement method was becoming more and more purified. Some 'traditional' elements had been thrown overboard in this evolution. The students' and workers' actions, in their interests in the second milieu (school and workplace), were replaced by additional education in the third milieu (leisure time) and the semi-professionalised youth workers (including priests) were gradually making way for young volunteers. It was this purified youth work format that was adopted as the youth work standard when Belgium established for the first time an official youth work policy and set up a National Service for Youth in 1945.

Re-differentiating youth work: where have all the working class kids gone?

Just like the British Kibbo Kift Kindred and the Woodcraft Folk leftist youth movements in Belgium never succeeded in attracting large numbers of young people. But whereas all youth movements in neighbouring countries knew hard times, the membership numbers of the Flemish Catholic youth movements kept on climbing. Cleymans, the chaplain of the JVKA, transformed the patronages in Chiro, yet another youth movement (today the largest in Flanders) that was modelled on the Scouting method and German youth movements like Quickborn and the Bund Neudeutschland.

The decade after 1945 was the heyday of the Flemish youth movements, with grand mass spectacles and glorious pilgrimages to Lourdes or Rome. This is the main reason why initiatives like Albemarle and similar in other countries seem to have passed unnoticed in Belgium. Nevertheless the problem of non-organised youth cropped up again. The National Service for Youth defined the problem as a passing thing:

> *The youth movement remains the ideal for a child's education in the third milieu. Some forms of open youth work are gaining ground. The main point is that affiliation to the youth movement remains the final aim, so that the youth club is a temporary solution for youth that is not noble enough for the youth movement, but has to be brought to that point.*
>
> (Totté, 1961, 17, *my translation*)

We recognise in the above the strategy of moving young people on from a less demanding youth work form to the youth movement model. The new methods fall back on what we could call traditional youth work (like the patronages), but they are defined as a renewing differentiation (not a pure methodical re-differentiating) departing from the standard of youth work and reaching out to the 'non-engaged'. The faith and confidence in the youth movement method was very strong: the ambitions were correspondingly high as illustrated in the next quote.

> *The foreign observer is struck by the great diversity of youth movements in Belgium, and, if he has been in the country before, by their immensely increased importance in national life since the recent war . . . Through governmental measures and through their own initiative, the leaders of the youth movements are now taking a definitive responsibility towards the needs of youth in this changed world: physical health and fitness, moral and character education, vocational guidance and apprenticeship, education toward family responsibility, and an adequate civic education adapted to the technical and moral needs of democracy. The youth movements are firmly decided to help solve all these problems by the influencing of the public opinion and of the government, by a close co-operation with one another, by the extension of their action to the mass of youth, and by the complete and well-integrated education they aim to give to their members, alongside the family and the school, so as to enrich their personality and equip them to accomplish the great task of rebuilding their country and helping to make a better world.*
>
> (Van der Bruggen and Picalausa, 1946, 112–113)

The 'traditional' youth work forms have largely disappeared. The KAJ is transforming itself from a movement focussed on study and action into a youth movement. The KSA and the Socialist Young Guards underwent the same transformation. Most patronages did not survive; those who did were rapidly transformed into Chiro. Even the programmes of preventative health financed from health insurance funding, were reshaped with reference to the models of Baden-Powell and Cardijn (Jongen, 1997: 21). And soon they all started to ask the same question, 'Where have all the working class kids gone?' It seems as if the standardisation to the supposed highest youth work form had to a large extent ruled out working class youth.

The emancipatory turn

From the 1970s on the youth movement model started to lose appeal. A consciousness was growing that one size doesn't fit all. A two track policy was acquiring a definite shape. The organised and the non-organised became the main categories for youth work policy. The same happened in other countries. In the UK the effects of the Albemarle and Fairbairn-Milson reports faded away as soon as Thatcher appeared on stage. The gap between 'youth work' and 'the youth service' was growing there too (see Eggleston, 1976), a situation we recognise to this very day. It even seems as if this unfruitful categorisation is experiencing a revival with the support of the European Commission: 'Tackling the problem of becoming accessible to non-organised or marginalized young people is now felt by all key players to be essential to increasing participation by young people' (Commission of the European Communities, 2006: 9). Note that being 'non-organised' is made almost synonymous with being marginalised. This is a legacy from the 1980s. The concerns for so-called vulnerable youth were a typical crisis phenomenon and can be interpreted as a reaction to the 1970s emancipatory wave. The youth movements had liberated themselves from church, parents, schools and political parties. For a short moment, social action and critical reflection on the social context had returned to the fore. Unfortunately those who could have profited the most from this emancipatory wave had already left the building. They were left to their own devices (Te Poel, 1987). Paradoxically the young people from lower social classes who had not yet left, did so now. The youth movement model had nothing to offer to them, so it seemed. But the grand Freirian narratives of the professional youth workers were not immensely appealing to them either. On the rebound and under the influence of CCCS theories on educational moralising, pedagogical and political theoretical underpinnings were further eliminated from youth work. Youth work was restricted to the organisation of young people's leisure time. Lacey (1987) describes this as an evolution from 'enabling to providing'.

Back to basics: a new psychological turn?

The advantage of hindsight is getting smaller as we are reaching the end of our history, but it does not demand too much from our imagination to see a sociological turn in the 1990s. Faith in youth work – although mainly because of its supposed preventative effects (Jeffs and Smith, 1999) – was quickly coming back. The first Minister of Youth Affairs in Flanders even spoke of the 'definitive recognition of youth work'.

What we are experiencing today looks suspiciously like a new psychological turn. The differentiated methodical approach to young people is – as it always was – partly a response and attempted answer to different needs and cultures. Learning to cope with these differences is a real challenge for youth policy, but the dominant youth work strategies described above seem to tackle the problem of diversity by trying to wipe out the differences on an individualised basis. However youth work doesn't work as an equaliser. On the contrary, the setting of standardising goals seems to exaggerate and even create differences. To go beyond the youth work paradox we need to leave behind a youth work concept that is methodically differentiated but theoretically too one-sided (individual developmental psychology). Thus the main question is whether the youth work theory that we still have to construct, has to focus on youth workers' delivery of an additional contribution to individual development or rather on the contribution of youth work to community development. As we illustrated above traditional youth work (eg. the student movement and Socialist Young Guards) could easily be seen as enabling young people to contribute to community development. It seems as if England, in line with the concept of the 'social investment state' (Giddens, 1998) has chosen for youth work a role that contributes to individual development. Reading the 'Ten Year Strategy' (HM Treasury, 2007) that is designed to shape England's youth policy for the next ten years, it seems that G. Stanley Hall is very much alive.

Note

1   The term Matthew effect was first coined by Merton describing how rewards and appreciation in the world of science disproportionately go to researchers who are already famous, even if their work is not any better than that of their less known colleagues (Merton, 1965). The name refers to a passage in the Christian Bible's book of Matthew (25: 29): *For unto every one that*

nhath shall be given, and he shall have abundance: but from him that hath not shall be taken away even that which he hath. This effect was applied to social policy by the Flemish researcher Herman Deleeck indicating that most advantages of social policy measures goes to middle and higher classes even if they are targeted at the more disadvantaged people (Deleeck *et al.*, 1992).

References

Alaerts, L. (2004) *Door eigen werk sterk. Geschiedenis van de kajotters en kajotsters in Vlaanderen. 1924–1967.* Leuven, Kadoc – Kajottershuis vzw.

Banks, S. (1996) 'Youth Work, Informal Education and Professionalisation: The issues in the 1990's', *Youth and Policy* 7 (54), 28–39.

Brew, J.M. (1946) *Informal Education. Adventures and reflections.* London: Faber.

Cammaer, H. (1962) 'Het jeugdwerk in Vlaanderen: Geschiedenis en huidige vorm', *Dux. Katholiek Maandblad voor Vrije jeugdvorming* 29 (3/4), 108–129.

Cardijn, J. (s.d.) *En nu vooruit!* Merchtem, Kajottersbeweging.

Coussée, F. (forthcoming 2008) *A century of youth work policy history.* Ghent, Academia Press, Brussels, Flemish Community.

Davies, B. (1999) *From Voluntaryism to Welfare State. A History of the Youth Service in England Volume 1: 1939–1979,* Leicester, Youth Work Press.

De Graaf W. (1989) *De zaaitijd bij uitnemendheid: jeugd en puberteit in Nederland 1900–1940,* Leiden, De Lier.

De Hovre, F. (1935) *Paedagogische denkers van onzen tijd,* Antwerpen, Standaard Boekhandel.

De La Bedoyere, M. (1958) *The Cardijn Story: A Study of the Life of Mgr. Joseph Cardijn and the Young Christian Workers' Movement Which He Founded,* London, Catholic Book Club.

Deleeck, H., Van Dan Bosch, K. and De Lathouwer, L. (1992) *Poverty and the Adequacy of Social Security in the EC,* Aldershot: Avebury.

Dworkin, J., Larson, R., and Hansen, D. (2003) 'Adolescents' Accounts of Growth Experiences in Youth Activities', *Journal of Youth and Adolescence* 32 (1), 17–26.

Eccles, J. and Barber, B. (1999) 'Student Council, Volunteering, Basketball, or Marching Band. What Kind of Extracurricular Involvement Matters?' *Journal of Adolescent Research* 14 (1), 10–43.

Eccles, J., Barber, B., Stone, M. and Hunt, J. (2003) 'Extracurricular activities and adolescent development', *Journal of Social Issues* 59 (4), 865–889.

Eggleston, J. (1976) *Adolescence and Community. The Youth Service in Britain.* London, Edward Arnold.

Feinstein, L., Bynner, J. and Duckworth, K. (2006) 'Young People's Leisure Contexts and their Relation to Adult Outcomes', *Journal of Youth Studies* 9 (3), 305–327.

Flint, W. (2005) *Recording Young People's Progress and Accreditation in Youth Work.* Leicester, National Youth Agency.

Fredricks, J. and Eccles, J. (2006) 'Is Extracurricular Participation Associated with Beneficial Outcomes? Concurrent and Longitudinal Relations' *Developmental Psychology* 42 (4), 698–713.

Furlong, A., Cartmel, F., Powney, J. and Hall, S. (1997) *Evaluating youth work with vulnerable young people.* Glasgow, Scottisch Council for Research in Education.

Gevers L. en L. Vos (2004) 'Jeugdbewegingen in Vlaanderen: een historisch overzicht' in M.

D'hoker en M. Depaepe (eds.) *Op eigen vleugels. Liber Amoricum Prof. dr. An Hermans (59–70)* Antwerpen/Apeldoorn, Garant.

Giddens, A. (1998) *The Third Way: the renewal of social democracy*, Cambridge, Polity Press.

Jongen, M. (1997) *Ma, met ons gaat alles goed. Preventieve luchtkuren – Jeugd and Gezondheid. 50 jaar jongeren in beweging in de Christelijke Mutualiteit, 1947–1997.* s.l.: Jeugd en Gezondheid.

Hart, R. (2006) *Participation in What?: The changing boundaries of children's roles, responsibilities and opportunities*. Keynote paper presented at the international conference 'Childhood and Youth: Choice and Participation', University of Sheffield, 4–6 July 2006.

HM Treasury (2007) *Aiming high for young people: a ten year strategy for positive activities*. London, HM Treasury/Department for Children, Schools and Families.

Jarret, R., Sullivan, P. and Watkins, N. (2005) 'Developing Social Capital through Participation in Organized Youth Programs: Qualitative Insights from Three Programs', *Journal of Community Psychology* 33 (1), 41–55.

Jeffs T. and Smith, M. (1999) 'Resourcing Youth Work. Dirty hands and tainted money',in S. Banks (ed.) *Ethical Issues in Youth Work*. London: Routledge.

Jeffs, T. and Smith, M. (2005) *Informal Education*, Ticknall, Education Heretics Books.

Jephcott, P. (1954) *Some Young People*, London, Allen and Unwin.

Jongen, M. (1997) *Ma, met ons gaat alles goed. Prentieve luchtkuren – Jeugd & Gezondheid. 50 jaar jongeren in beweging in de Christelijke Mutualiteit, 1947–1997.* s.l.: Jeugd en Gezondheid.

Lacey, F. (1987) 'Youth Workers as Community Workers', in T. Jeffs, and M. Smith (eds.) *Youth Work*, London, Macmillan Education.

Launay, M. (1985) 'Réflexions sur les origines de la JOC', in Cholvy, G. (ed.) *Mouvements de Jeunesse Chrétiens et Juifs. Sociabilité juvénile dans un cadre européen 1799–1968* (223–231), Paris, Editions du Cerf.

Lerner, R.M. (1995) *America's Youth in Crisis. Challenges and Options for Programs and Policies*, Thousand Oaks-London-New Delhi, Sage Publications.

Lewin, H.S. (1947) 'The Way of the Boy Scouts', *Journal of Educational Sociology* 21 (3), 169–176.

MacDonald, H. (2000) 'Why the boy scouts work', *City Journal*, Winter, Accessed, 30.08.2006, http://www.city-journal.org/html/10 1_why_the_boy.html .

Mahoney, J., Schweder, A.E. and Stattin, H. (2002) 'Structured after-school activities as a moderator of depressed mood for adolescents with detached relations to their parents', *Journal of Community Psychology* 30, 69–86.

Mahoney, J., Stattin, L. and Lord, H. (2004) 'Unstructured youth recreation centre participation and antisocial behaviour development: Selection influences and the moderating role of antisocial peers', *International Journal of Behavioral Development* 28, 553–560.

Marczak, M., Dworkin, J., Skuza, J. and Beyer, J. (2006) 'What young teens and parents want from youth programs' *New Directions for Youth Development*, Special Issue 2006 (112), 45–56.

Merton, B., Payne, M. and Smith, D. (2004) *An Evaluation of the Impact of Youth Work in England*. London, DfES.

Merton, R.K. (1968) 'The Matthew Effect in Science. The reward and communication systems of science are considered', *Science* 159 (3810), 56–63.

Pels, D. (2002) 'Socialism between fact and value: from Tony Blair to Hendrik de Man and back', *Journal of Political Ideologies*, 7 (3), 281–299.

Quane, J. and Rankin, B. (2006) 'Does it pay to participate? Neighborhood-based organisations and the social development of urban adolescents', *Children and Youth Services Review* 28, 1229–1250.

Scheidlinger, S. (1948) 'A comparative study of the Boy Scout Movement in Different National and Social Groups', *American Sociological Review* 13 (6), 739–750.

Selten, P. (1991) *Het apostolaat der jeugd. Katholieke jeugdbewegingen in Nederland. 1900–1941*, Leuven/Apeldoorn, Acco.

Selten, P. (1993) 'The religious formation of youth. Catholic youth movements in the Netherlands from 1900–1994', *Paedagogica Historica* 1, 165–187.

Smith, M. (2003) 'From youth work to youth development: the new government framework for English Youth Services', *Youth and Policy*, 14 (79), 46–59.

Te Poel, Y. (1987) 'The subcultural paradigm and youth work in the Netherlands' in E. Meijer (ed.) *Alledaags leven; vrije tijd en cultuur. Conferentieverslag*, Volume 2 (565–578) Tilburg, Centrum voor Vrijetijdskunde.

Tesarek, A. (1929) *Das Buch der Roten Falken*, Wien, Verlag Jungbrunnen.

Totté, R (1961) 'Jeugdvorming in de vrije tijd in België. Ontwikkeling, huidige situatie, toekomstver-wachting', *Clubhuiswerk* 13 (3), 15–17.

Van der Bruggen, C. and Picalausa, L. (1946) 'Belgian Youth Movements and Problems', *Annals of the American Academy of Political and Social Science*, 247, 111–116.

Vermandere, M. (2001) 'Door gelijke drang bewogen? De socialistische partij en haar jeugdbeweg-ing, 1886–1944', in R. Van Doorslaer e.a. (ed.) *Bijdragen tot de Eigentijdse Geschiedenis/Cahiers d'Histoire du Temps Present*, 8, 225–256.

Wilkinson, P. (1969) 'English Youth Movements', *Journal of Contemporary History* 4 (2), 3–23.

Williamson, H. (1997) 'Youth Work and Citizenship' in J. Bynner, L. Chisholm and A. Furlong (eds.) *Youth, Citizenship and Social Change in a European Context* (196–213) Aldershot, Ashgate.

Williamson, H. (2006) *Spending Wisely. Youth Work and the Changing Policy Environment for Young People*, Leicester, NYA.

CHAPTER 8

The Rise and Fall of Community and Youth Work Courses at Westhill College

John Holmes

Westhill College would have celebrated its centenary in 2007, but instead tutors and students faced the closure of courses for community, play and youth work by the University of Birmingham, who took over the college and its courses in 1999. The decision to end recruitment has been made and the proposal is to move the courses to the University of Central England, Birmingham with the remaining three tutors. Four tutors had already left to take up other jobs, and five agreed to take severance in July 2007. Students who have not yet completed their studies have been told they can continue at the University of Birmingham but concerns are being expressed both locally and by the National Youth Agency about the quality of their remaining educational experience. A proud history of educating community and youth workers in Selly Oak, Birmingham is coming to an end. The training of youth workers can be traced back to the original purpose of Westhill College and it is the intention of this chapter to explain why this tradition was so central to Westhill. A full history cannot be attempted here but is hoped by a series of snapshots to show how this area of work at Westhill developed to be a key influence on community and youth work policy in Britain. It is also hoped to understand some of the reasons for the fall of Community and Youth Work at Westhill, and whether this was inevitable in the changing nature of British higher education at the beginning of the twenty-first century.

The current plans are a matter of considerable concern to those previously involved as tutors and students, but current staff and students are facing the greatest uncertainty. It is impossible to be objective at such a time when feelings are running high and people have taken different views on how best to respond. Tutors and students were initially divided about whether and how strongly to challenge the University when in early 2005 it decided to end recruitment to the full-time courses. At this time it was argued that the part-time courses could continue and some tutors felt that to challenge the University too strongly, eg. to go to the press, would be counter productive. Others, including myself, felt this was the beginning of the end and it was better to make a stand at this point. The result was that staff and students were divided and it became impossible to maintain collective solidarity in the face of the threat posed by our employers. As such this is offered as one interpretation of recent events from somebody who came to Westhill in 1991, was a tutor for 15 years, head of department for 10 years, but left in 2006 to set up a JNC qualifying course at nearby Newman College in Birmingham. Since I left, and the University announced that all Community, Play and Youth Work courses would close tutors have challenged the University through the University and Colleges Union on the basis of institutional racism in that their actions would disproportionately target black and minority ethnic staff for redundancy, and disproportionately affect provision for black and minority ethnic community students. It seems unlikely (THES, 6 July 2007) that this challenge will affect the outcome even though it is recognised that there is a case to be answered and the proper procedures were not followed by the University.

The following analysis is an attempt to record and celebrate the Westhill tradition, to try to identify the challenges to this tradition that have occurred over the last century and how these were dealt with. The Westhill tradition is rooted in liberal Christian education and had strong foundations by building a strong sense of community and identity in Westhill students and with the local community in Birmingham. This strong identification with Westhill approaches was then taken into a wide range of work settings in Britain and elsewhere in the world. All of these strands of the Westhill tradition – liberal education, Christianity, a community of scholars, links to the local community and further a field – came under threat during the twentieth century, yet Westhill adapted to survive. My argument is that Westhill could have continued to adapt and survive in the 1990s, and community and youth work courses could have continued but there was a failure to be aware of and recognise the strength within the Westhill tradition. The result was allowing the takeover by the University, and a further weakening of the Westhill tradition with the disastrous consequence that when the University moved to close community and youth work courses tutors and students were unclear on what they should be defending and became divided and weakened.

Origins 1907–11

The origins of Westhill College are in Christian benevolent philanthropy, and in paternalism. The two leading players were the successful businessmen George Hamilton Archibald and George Cadbury. The last but one Principal of Westhill, Jack Priestley, has written about them as 'The Lumber Merchant and the Chocolate King' (Priestley, 2003). Archibald came to Birmingham in 1905 at the invitation of Cadbury as part of a nation wide lecture tour to promote the development of Sunday schools. Archibald was at this time the Provincial Secretary to the Protestant Sunday School Union in Quebec, Canada and was a leading member of the Sunday School movement, aiming to modernise the practice of Sunday schools. His family background, three generations back, were Ulster Presbyterians, but Archibald had reacted against the strict controls placed on children, particularly on Sundays. He wished to promote Christianity and to do this by drawing on the freedom loving experiences of children and young people. He was a near contemporary of John Dewey and as with others in America, much influenced by Dewey's child centred philosophy. As a lumber merchant he had made enough money to pursue his educational interests, and his experiences of life, including the tragic early death of his brother, had taught him that there were more important things than making money.

In George Cadbury Archibald met somebody open to this thinking. Cadbury was also a successful businessman. With his brother Richard, he had developed a highly successful cocoa business from an inherited risky tea business and was manufacturing chocolate in nearby Bournville. Like Archibald, Cadbury had struggled against adversity, was a committed Christian but in the Quaker tradition, and saw money as a means to develop higher ends. He was involved in Sunday school work in Birmingham and was a strong advocate of providing a better life style for his workers at Bournville. The benevolent paternalism included having substantial gardens in the Bournville Village area in which workers were required to have fruit trees, and short Christian services at the Bournville factory. Priestley (2003, 6) notes that the 2,200 women workers attended a service every day whilst the 1,000 men attended only once a week. Cadbury did not see Christianity as something only happening on Sunday and linked it to the education and personal development of his workers. Both he and Archibald had gone directly into business rather than studying at university, but both believed in the central importance of Christian education. Whilst clearly paternalistic, Cadbury worked in the Quaker tradition and his Sunday Schools were advertised as, 'A Chat with George Cadbury' (Priestley, 2003, 7).

Cadbury already recognised in 1901 that the British had much to learn about developing Sunday Schools stating that, 'America is ahead of us in treating the Sunday School as an educational institution while perhaps we are ahead in the stress we lay upon the need for the deep silent work of God in our heart' (quoted in Priestley, 2003, 8). So when he heard Archibald speak in Birmingham in 1905 he challenged him to turn his ideas into practice. Archibald accepted the challenge and became the first Principal of Westhill College. The college opened in 1907 with buildings and a site in Selly Oak largely provided by Cadbury money. Westhill was an independent college, Archibald was unpaid, and initially a small group of residential students (mainly women) undertook training over a term or two in order to improve the educational basis of Sunday school work, recognising that such work extended beyond both young children and Sundays. Archibald argued for 'activity work' on different nights of the week for different age groups, which in effect constituted an argument for a type of youth work training.

In addition to John Dewey the educational philosophy at Westhill was much influenced by the German, Friedrich Froebel, best known as the originator of the kindergarten system (Parker, 1982, 6). Froebel emphasised the importance of play, play materials and activities (Smith, 1997, www.infed.org). This has much relevance for informal educators but at Westhill the Froebel Certificate (lasting 3 years) was developed mainly for schoolteachers. This introduction of teacher education prior to 1914 (Parker, 1982, 6) was an extension of the notion that Christian education was more than just Sunday School work and in this context there were few divisions between ideas about the nature of formal and informal education at Westhill. Pictures from Westhill at the time (Westhill Training College, 1937, 2) show teachers sitting on the floor with young children and there was even experimentation at local schools to teach without timetables.

Early Westhill can be understood best as a fairly small group of tutors and students living as a community, but before the First World War staff were identified with reference to three discrete areas – church education, teacher education, and youth work. All were in the Christian tradition and had close links to the wider community in other Selly Oak colleges.

Westhill was only one of the Selly Oak Colleges, five of which had been formed by 1914 (Mole, c. 1970, 6). Archibald had spoken in 1905 at Woodbrooke College which had been formed in 1903 by the Society of Friends. To Westhill and Woodbrooke were later added Kingsmead in 1905 originally owned and supported by the Friends' Foreign Mission Association but later to become predominantly Methodist, and Fircroft College, (1909) also

Quaker inspired but linked to the Settlement and Adult Schools Movement (Mole, c. 1970, 3–5).The fifth was Carey Hall founded in 1912 by three missionary agencies to train women missionaries. Although a loose federation of Selly Oak colleges emerged post World War 1, it is hard to generalise about these colleges. As Mole comments:

> *The general aim has been the provision of education for the ordinary person, free from the constraints of and temptations of examinations and professional advancement, yet from early years, teachers and social workers have been trained for professional qualifications. Throughout the years two theological emphases have been in counterpoint – a dominant liberalism and a vigorous evangelicalism, joined in the 1920s by liberal catholicism and later by neo-orthodoxy. Even on such a basic issue as the Christian character of the federation there is a qualification to be made: the federation is undoubtedly a Christian institution, yet there are parts of it which are not Christian. Perhaps only the Quaker ethos could have enabled such a body to grow and flourish.*
>
> (Mole, c. 1970, 1)

To this might be added that the failure of Westhill College to survive the century can be linked to the contradictions and tensions exposed by this diversity, but more on this later.

International work was important in Westhill College as well as the wider Selly Oak colleges. Before the Second World War, Westhill was involved in work in 33 countries, and five continents (Westhill Training College, c. 1939, 17). The link to evangelical missionary work was clearly there but so was building links to other countries through international friendship. One hundred and three students from 28 countries studied at Westhill before 1939 and this reflected that Christian evangelism was not just about the spread of the British Empire. The educational philosophy of the Froebel approach to 'set the child in the midst' was also reflected in the Westhill motto of *Docere est Dicere* (roughly, *To Teach is To Learn*) and this demanded some recognition of cultural differences. The international reputation of Westhill grew and famous international visitors spoke at Westhill, including Rabindranath Tagore in the 1920s and later Paulo Freire who came to the youth work department in the 1970s.

1939–57 moves to specialist youth work training

Youth work was largely part of the wider work up until 1943. However, in the 1920s the college had introduced training for YMCA workers well before a specialist training section was developed in the UK YMCA. In addition Westhill students ran a youth club on the campus for boys (the 'Cave') and women students ran a girls' club in Selly Oak from 1919. (Parker, 1982, 9). This reflected the wider Westhill tradition of building links to the local community, the main evidence of this being a primary school on the campus, which lasted from the 1920s to the 1960s.

Westhill College was faced with a dilemma with the rise of State interest in Youth work from 1939 onwards. The wartime circulars 1486 and 1516 provided an opportunity to develop general youth work training, but Westhill was an independent Christian college linked to the 'free' churches. The training of youth leaders was promoted by the government mainly in the secular universities (Bradford, 2007). Nevertheless, Westhill did respond by running short courses for youth leaders between 1940 and 1943. Weekend courses for the growing number of local leaders started in 1943–4 when a Youth Tutor was appointed. It was not until 1947 that a two-year Certificate in Children and Youth Work, with age group options, was established and this became University of Birmingham endorsed in 1951. These two-year endorsed courses had the advantage of attracting State funding for students, although the college remained independent, relying on private fund raising. With the help of youth work students, the Rev. Bryan Reed, the Youth Tutor in 1947, was able to pursue research into the state of young people and youth work in post war Birmingham that led to the publication *Eighty Thousand Adolescents* (Reed, 1950).

The independent nature of Westhill College meant that tutors were relatively poorly paid compared to university tutors, or even voluntary college tutors, but Westhill tutors were often provided with housing on site or nearby. Whilst such 'tied' housing can lead to significant problems it did help to create a strong sense of community with most tutors and students living and worshipping as well as studying together. Youth work tutors encouraged extra-curricular activities and wove them into the curriculum to simulate the kinds of programmes then operative in youth work. Students organised a social half-hour after supper for all in college. The strong sense of community was demonstrated in the 1957 Jubilee celebrations, aimed both to celebrate 50 years and raise money for the college. Ambitious events took place including making a film (*Vision and Opportunity*) which Mary Burnie, the Warden, took around the country (Parker, 1982, 28). An article written to promote the Jubilee stated:

> *The peculiar and significant value of Westhill as a training institution is in its community life. Men and women drawn from many lands, with greatly*

differing social backgrounds, seeking various kinds of training, come here with one uniting factor: the desire to prepare for a life of service . . .

(quoted in Parker, 1982, 29)

Such a statement can appear rather self denying but it is clear that the community life was one that included much fun and even irreverence. For example, the students took the off-cuts from the official Westhill Jubilee film and deliberately misinterpreted college life as a bit of fun. Even the ambitious and serious production of Purcell's *Faerie Queen* appears to have turned into a bit of a farce in that, following wet weather, the opening entry by a fairy was sliding down the grassy slope rapidly after slipping in the mud. Other fairies were plagued by frogs brought out by the wet weather. This was all treated as good fun, due to what Connie Parker describes as the 'enthusiasm and exuberance' that pervaded the college. This was my own memory of Westhill in the early 1990s when students and staff put much energy and imagination into extra curricular activities (more than into their studies in some cases) and there was a strong feeling of community.

1960–65 responding to Albemarle

When the government became serious about developing youth work in the late 1950s, which led to the Albemarle Report (Ministry of Education, 1960), Westhill was well placed to respond to the professionalisation of the work. The college already had a two year full time training course and training was going to be the key to professionalisation. The government wanted the NABC and the YMCA to join with Westhill as the leading voluntary sector players to develop training at Westhill. However, the voluntary sector could not agree, partly because of the single sex nature of their youth work, and partly because the YMCA and NABC wanted to maintain their own traditions (from interview with John Parr). Westhill College was also nervous about a development that could lead to specialising in youth work at the cost of other developing areas, such as teacher education. So the National College to promote emergency training of youth leaders was set up in Leicester with one year full time courses, and Westhill carried on with its own two year course.

At this time Westhill had just moved from an independent to a voluntary college. This meant that staff had to be paid on national Burnham scales, and although state funding considerably increased 10 per cent of income still needed to be found privately and costs were increasing fast. At the same time, although Westhill courses were still strongly practice based the tradition of combining training with practice was reduced when the Westhill school was closed due to financial costs. There was also a community cost to this closure in that young people and adults were part of Westhill, meeting and learning from each other, often in social contexts, and this was much reduced by the closure of the school. The much closer links to the state resulting from the acceptance of government money in becoming a voluntary college, and the priority given to teacher education was symbolised by Anthony Crosland (then Minister of Education) coming to open new government funded buildings in 1965. It also led to concerns in other Selly Oak colleges that Westhill was becoming too big, losing its roots, and worst of all 'empire building' in a federal structure (Parker, 1982, 35). Youth Work also benefited from the state funded expansion in terms of the purpose built Mary Burnie House, a headquarters for the Community and Youth Department, opened by Denis Howell.

By then the department had become the Community and Youth Work Department, preceding the *Youth and Community Work in the 70s* Report, published in 1969, and co-authored by Fred Milson who had been head of department since 1960. Community Centre Warden training had been developed by John Parr, initially as a distinct course, since 1963, but the commonality with youth work of an academic base in sociology, psychology and education drew the college-based parts of the courses together. By 1963 Christian education, once integral, had become an option, although links to the 'free' churches remained strong.

Whilst growth and development was central to the 1960s, student numbers remained fairly small compared to today with the normal limit being two year groups of 15 full time students on the youth work course. These were older than other Westhill students, they were mainly men, and often much involved in the Student Union, reflecting their leadership roles and commitment to social education. These students were placed in local clubs for placements and attended a three week residential as part of their course.

The Principal of Westhill College at this time was Ralph Newman (1954–71). He was famous for saying that 'Westhill is not a normal college' (Parker, 1982, 36). Whilst this is true, doubts about its identity, especially in relation to its Christian origins were growing amongst governors, the chaplains, the staff and the students (Parker, 1982, 36). The issue at the time seems to have been to what extent should Westhill adapt to survive?

1970s–1980s Diversification from Youth work

The closer link with the state, in particular the DES, presented problems for Westhill, in particular the Church education department for whom there was little role in this development. Yet it also presented opportunities. In the case of community and youth work this involved trying to influence government policy on the direction of youth work. Although the Fairbairn-Milson Report, *Youth and Community Work in the 70s* (DES, 1969) was rejected by the Conservative government, it did help to promote a closer link between youth work and community development in practice for many years. One of the recommendations of this report was for a graduate profession – an aspiration due to be implemented in 2010! Westhill's Community and Youth Work Department also helped to build links with the related professions of teacher education and social work. The B.Ed degree offered a youth work option that enabled students to have both qualified teacher status and specialist knowledge of youth and community work (qualifying them as youth and community workers under JNC conditions as teachers, but recognising the separate specialism). This was particularly relevant for the youth tutor posts, based in schools. Some of these students went onto to do innovative work in the community schools, which at this time were trying to break down some of the barriers between communities and schools (e.g. Countesthorpe School in Leicestershire). This work went alongside the development of post qualifying courses in community education for JNC qualified workers and other professionals such as teachers and social workers. The tutors involved in both these schooling-related initiatives added to the staffing of the Department but also created distinct sub areas with differing interests. (Inga Bulman – teacher education link, and David Clark – community education link, were the tutors most closely identified with these developments.)

The gaining of the CQSW professional qualification (at the time the professional qualification for social workers) for students studying the Community and Youth Studies JNC qualifying course was a bold move that in retrospect seems surprising. Students did the same two-year full time course but came out with a dual qualification. This followed a successful bid to CCETSW (Central Council for Education and Training in Social Work) that they were equally fitted for social work as youth and community work. It appears that the case was made in relation to the importance of social group work in both areas and the link to preventative measures proposed by the Seebohm Report (HMSO, 1968) (in particular Intermediate Treatment, which involved intervening with young people at risk of becoming involved in criminal activity).

The only other JNC qualifying course to gain this double qualification was Goldsmiths in London. For both it was short lived, with CCETSW withdrawing it because of the limited study of law, but by this time social work, with its increased emphasis on individual case work, was moving away from youth and community work.

These developments in community and youth work might be seen to have protected the position of this area of work in Westhill, but they occurred in the context of the growing centrality of teacher education at the college, and wider concerns about the viability of small specialist colleges in the future of higher education generally. The democratic tradition at Westhill did mean that a wide range of staff were involved in decision making, even crucial decisions such as the appointment of Principals of the college. However with the increasing reliance on state funding for teacher education it is not surprising that new Principals came from teacher education backgrounds. Alan Bamford was no exception, arriving as the new Principal in 1971. As with all other Principals he was also a Christian, although his adherence to Plymouth Brethren beliefs, albeit not of the exclusive variety, did raise some doubts with more liberal Christians. For community and youth work staff the problem was as much how to convince this new Principal that their area of work should remain central to the Westhill mission. This had been less of a problem when Principals, such as Basil Yeaxlee in the 1930s, were appointed linked to the original purposes of Westhill. The appointment of Alan Bamford took place in Westhill fashion with applicants meeting a wide range of staff and students, and John Parr, by then Deputy Head of Community and Youth Work, recounts how surprised he was that Alan Bamford approached him and greeted him as a long lost friend. It emerged that John had been his patrol leader in the Scouts in Liverpool, and this had clearly been a formative experience, which helped to establish good working relationships despite Alan Bamford now being appointed mainly because of his knowledge of teacher education. Alan was proposed by the community and youth work tutors to be Chairman of Birmingham Association of Youth Clubs, and through this role came to understand the importance of youth work. It may seem odd to stress these personal links and semi-private roles but my experience in the 1990s, when as the first non-Christian head of department trying not very successfully to work with another Principal with strong teacher education links, would suggest they can be critical.

With the election of the Conservative government in 1979, the wider context was threatening; small specialist colleges were out of favour with government. It was the next Principal of Westhill, Gordon Benfield (recognised for his contributions to teacher education with a CBE) who was appointed in 1984, who took the controversial step of forming a partnership with Newman College in nearby Bartley Green to try to protect the future of Westhill. This was particularly controversial because although Newman was, and is, a Christian College in its origins, it comes from the Roman Catholic tradition. Newman was also under threat as relying at that time wholly on teacher education and to some extent the partnership appears to have been a marriage of convenience on both sides. The fact that Gordon Benfield came from a high Anglican tradition made it easier to achieve and develop. However this move did have serious repercussions for relations with the other Selly Oak colleges, coming from a range of Protestant traditions but with few if any links to Roman Catholicism.

1990–1997 growth, development (and decline?)

This section will have a different style as it relates to the period when I was a tutor at Westhill College relying more on my personal memories than written texts. When I took up my post as Head of Department in 1991, I remember feeling how different the atmosphere was from that I had experienced at a higher education institution in Wales. It did feel a little like moving back in time with the strong sense of community at Westhill, the level of autonomy in the Community and Youth Work Department, and the amount of debate in the college generally. As somebody who does not always believe that modernisation is progress, I remember been pleasantly surprised but wondering how long it would last. There were changes to the programme that needed undertaking and my focus turned inwards rather than looking at the wider Westhill context. In retrospect this was a mistake. Compared to other HE institutions community and youth work had a greater influence in the wider governance partly because of its significant size in a small college but also because of its links alongside church education to the origins of Westhill. This was reflected in membership of Academic Board and in a Heads of Departments group that met regularly with the Principal. In addition to the influence of my role, Inga Bulman who started as a youth tutor, had a number of senior management roles including Deputy Principal. The potential to influence Westhill policy as Head of Community and Youth Studies was weakened in status terms (in that I was appointed on Principal Lecturer scale rather than the Head of Department scale that John Parr had been on) but it was still possible.

The move from Certificate to Dip.HE for the full time JNC qualifying course had already been agreed by the University of Birmingham. As with other JNC qualifying courses this had the advantage that the discretionary awards to students (which meant that receipt of a grant depended upon local authority policies and circumstances) were replaced by mandatory awards. Westhill managed to achieve this transition without any change to the curriculum (based on a matrix at this time) but whereas previously there had been no examinations, reflecting the student-centred approach, an end of course 'seen' exam was now required for University of Birmingham validation. This change coincided with the development of a three year full time degree, enabling the first cohort to undertake the Dip. HE to have the option of moving to degree level studies, which the majority decided to do. The move to a degree coincided with a major revision of the curriculum, including modularisation in line with what was happening elsewhere, especially in the new universities. Student numbers on community and youth work were increasing in the 1990s (approaching 200 by the late 1990s) but staff numbers remained static as occurred elsewhere in higher education. In 1999 Westhill, with an annual intake of 60 students, was similar to St. Martins Lancaster, Bradford College, Huddersfield University, and the new Centre for Youth Ministry, Oxford. This meant Westhill was one of the largest courses in the country with only courses that recruited for distance learning (YMCA George Williams College, London and De Montfort University, Leicester) having larger student intakes (NYA, 1999).

This growth in the Dip.HE and B.Phil courses (the University of Birmingham required this degree title at the time whereas other programmes opted for BA Hons.) was added to by the development of a post qualifying Masters course which mainly attracted ex-qualifying students but also some students from related professions. Also links were built with related areas of work in both a new Sports, PE and Community Studies degree, and a short-lived Race and Ethnic Studies Degree. In terms of the curriculum, play work was added to community and youth work in 1997. These additions were in some ways replacements for the wider links to teacher education and schools lost with the B.Ed Youth Option course which the government ended in the late 1980s and the Dip/B.Phil in Community Education which did not outlast the retirement of David Clark in the late 1990s.

Maybe the most significant change was in the make up of the student group in the early 1990s. Although Westhill had always wanted to attract a diverse student group including international students, and had done so particularly in areas like community and youth studies where working class students were the majority, it remained a largely white, middle class institution. In the 1990s black and then Asian British students applied in large numbers to study at Westhill.

This better reflected the multi-cultural composition of the West Midlands and the increasing emphasis on targeting black and Asian communities. In community and youth studies white students were in a minority by the mid-1990s. A number of black and Asian staff were also recruited at this time so ensuring greater balance within the staff team. This growth in student numbers and diversity of both the backgrounds of students and staff was a strong basis to explore the many issues arising from our divided and unequal society and the role of community, play and youth work. Yet sometimes it felt as if Westhill College was struggling to adapt, even resisting the changes, and was unable to sufficiently respond to the needs of these students and staff. It is one thing to attract new students and staff: it is another to ensure they are really included in the curriculum and structures.

As elsewhere in higher education there was an increasing reliance on part time students by 2000, primarily as a result of reduced funding during the 1990s for full-time adult students and the preference of employers to train their workers 'on the job'. Whilst Westhill responded to both employer and worker demand for more flexible ways of training, starting part time routes in 1997, and these part-time students usually came with considerable experience, they were often under considerable pressure to fulfil the competing demands of work, study and personal life. As a result drop-out and non-completion rates rose and the numbers of students staying on for the degree decreased (as students often needed a break after three years of study part time). Unfortunately this occurred at the same time as there was increasing pressure for staff to research, write, and complete higher degrees. The potential to combine teaching in Level 3 or Masters level specialist options with the staff's own development activities was limited. As a result staff often came to see research and teaching as competing demands rather than as mutually complementary activities. The result of staff and students juggling competing demands was less a loss of quality in itself, as most did succeed in completing albeit taking longer than originally planned, it was rather expressed in a fragmentation of interests and consequent loss of community. The contrast was clear between the early 1990s (and before) when the majority of full time students lived on campus, and when both students and staff developed their thinking together outside as well as inside the time-tabled sessions, and the turn of the century when it seemed impossible to arrange meetings between staff and most students dashed off after sessions. The price of this fragmentation became clear a few years later.

Whilst I saw my role as HOD primarily within the department, the most significant developments for the future were happening in the wider Westhill

College. When I came to Westhill it was part of Newman and Westhill College, following the partnership set up by the previous Westhill Principal, Gordon Benfield and his Newman equivalent. One part of my role was to liaise with Newman and examine the potential for joint working around community and youth studies. I found Newman to be receptive but within two years the atmosphere between the two colleges had soured and an acrimonious divorce occurred. The reasons for this I remain unsure of. At the time it was explained in terms of control of finance but in retrospect it would seem likely that religion also played a part. The new Westhill Principal, Jack Priestley, as a Methodist, was keen to ensure the 'free' Church tradition continued at Westhill, and turned to similar minded people rather than the Catholics at Newman. He seemed to think that colleagues in the universities, in particular Birmingham where academic validation derived from, in conjunction with modern business approaches would mean that Westhill could return to its roots in the Selly Oak colleges. My observations were that although my contacts at Birmingham University had been helpful in developing and validating new degrees, the modern business approaches seemed to be killing the Westhill community spirit. Services were being contracted out or non-academic staff being put on worse conditions of service, academic staff were going to be charged for use of rooms and other resources, yet no budgets seemed to be forthcoming and income seemed unrelated to HEFCE allocations for subject areas. Although it can be argued that the new managerialism was rampant across HE generally, the specific issue for Westhill, as a small college, was could it survive if it shifted its partnership back to the Selly Oak colleges from Newman College? My experience of the Selly Oak college people was that they were even more suspicious of Westhill than Newman, that they felt Westhill was too close to government and that Westhill had imperialistic ambitions. The long term viability of the Federation of Selly Oak Colleges remained uncertain in that it was a loose grouping with meetings and planning partnership arrangements but funding was largely down to individual colleges. The effect, if not the intention, of the split with Newman College would seem to have made Westhill dependent on the University of Birmingham, who proved to have different interests to Westhill. At the time in the early 1990s I was initially glad to be able to focus on departmental matters rather than college politics and in any case my voice was not one influencing the bigger picture in the new managerial structures nor, as I suspected but could not prove, in the discussions held within local Church contact networks of which I was not a part. When in 1999 it was clear that Westhill in conjunction with the Selly Oak colleges was not seem by government funders as viable, the decision about the future of

Westhill was put to the staff. Options included partnerships with Oxford Brookes, University of Central England or the University of Birmingham. Academic staff already had links with the University of Birmingham this not only being local but also through validation procedures, and it was clearly attractive in status terms to be university staff. So it was not surprising that staff voted this way. At the time the 'strategic alliance' was presented by the university as a coming together of different but mutually beneficial groups.

> *In Selly Oak, we are forming what is described as a strategic alliance with Westhill College. Working together we shall be able to increase access to university study for more students from a great diversity of backgrounds including those groups which are, at present, under-represented. We shall be offering more continuing studies programmes and more part-time courses. This, of course, is all part of the new higher education agenda which seeks to broaden the opportunities available to people and to facilitate their access to higher education.*
>
> (Irvine, 1998)

Whilst Professor Irvine, the Vice Chancellor, may have been sincere when stating this, those at the time who saw it more in terms of asset stripping might have cause subsequently to feel that they were right.

1999–2007 university take-over and closure

The 'strategic alliance' proved to be a take-over and Westhill College staff should have realised at the time that is what it was. All the signs were that the university managers wanted to distance themselves from the Westhill tradition. 'University of Birmingham, Westhill' quickly became the Selly Oak campus of the university and the academic programmes were incorporated within the activities of the School of Education. There were plans at one point that this school was to be re-located from the main Edgbaston site to Selly Oak but this was resisted and key staff were either moved to Edgbaston or ex-Westhill staff found it in their interests to move up the road. It was not surprising that academic staff in the School of Education at Edgbaston were wary of Selly Oak staff as academic standing and funding depended on doing well in the Research Assessment Exercise and Selly Oak staff did not have the level or number of academic publications, nor the amount of Ph.Ds to ensure a high ranking for the School of Education. Community, play and youth studies tutors were set targets for achieving the award of their Ph.Ds that in my view, were unrealistic in terms of the time in which they were expected to complete, and became meaningless when the goalposts shifted to publications. The university's membership of the 'Russell group' of universities, that defined themselves primarily in terms of research and competing in global higher education markets, did not bode well for academic programmes based on British professions and local links to the local authority and voluntary sectors. Crucially Westhill had traditionally recruited students who had proved themselves in work rather than in traditional academic terms such as high A levels grades, and although 'widening participation' was supposed to be required in higher education this clearly meant something different in the Russell group universities compared to other universities, particularly the 'new' post 1992 universities.

There were, however, some early signs of encouragement with staffing levels in community, play and youth studies actually increasing in the early years of the new century. The higher number of hours Selly Oak staff were expected to teach, compared to Edgbaston staff had led to feelings of inequity and maybe this alongside continuing high levels of student recruitment helped to achieve some additional staffing.

Yet disputes about income levels and budget deficits continued with the university management as they had with Westhill management. The way these figures were calculated were certainly open to dispute, and it was not hard to draw the conclusion that even when income increased the goalposts would be shifted to show a deficit for community, play and youth studies. The first indication that the university wanted to close this area of work was in the latter part of the 2004–5 academic year when staff were told that recruitment for full-time students would end in 2005. This was presented as a consequence of over recruitment elsewhere in the university, leading to a loss of funding, and the need to cutback in areas that had low A level entry scores. This related to the introduction of £3,000 fees per annum for undergraduates in 2006 and the intention of the university to ensure it was high on entry score league tables-with the longer-term intention to increase fees to £7,000 or even £10,000 per annum. We were told that part-time students could continue to be recruited, as these were not measured in the same way. A decision had to be made about how much we should protest about the loss of full-time students. When it became clear that the Vice Chancellor's office had already contacted Newman College about transferring the whole community, play and youth studies programme the writing seemed clearly on the wall. However this action was taken without the knowledge of the School of Education which resulted in a rearguard action to defend this area of work by the School and resistance to any move elsewhere. In 2006–7, with a new Head of School in place within Education it was announced that the original plan was to be implemented with no recruitment to any community, play and youth studies programme from 2007 onwards. The rationale for this was keeping within budgets, and more important that too many 'non-traditional' students were being recruited.

It is easy to cast the university as the villains of the piece, ignorant of the tradition they were ending and uninterested in meeting the needs of people in Birmingham to have properly trained and qualified youth workers working with their young people. Certainly the elitist traditions of the university do not fit with 'widening participation' as practised in community, play and youth studies, but it was government policy on student fees that gave validity to the new Vice Chancellor's policies of Birmingham competing as a global player at the cost of local interests. The way the closure was announced, in stages and without any transparency, made it difficult for staff and students to respond effectively to the challenge but by then the divisions between staff and the lack of community between staff and students would have made this difficult in any case.

The ethos of acting collectively to achieve political ends is a lesson drawn from community work but clearly was not achieved in this situation. Almost certainly staff and students could not have achieved this on their own but a mixture of strong support from the local youth and community work field plus timely media pronouncements might have made the university think again. The importance of community was also part of the Westhill tradition but as has been noted above this had been much diminished even before the end of Westhill College. It appeared to me that tutors were torn between their original commitment to being community, play and youth work tutors and their new roles as university academics that required research and publications even if students had to pay the cost of insufficient support. The growth of individualism in our society has consequences even in areas that are there to promote community.

Conclusion

Jack Priestley, Principal of Westhill College from 1991 to 1997, has written

> *From the late 1950s onward, as the college expanded and diversified, the influence of individual Principals inevitably declined as they increasingly became administrators of policies increasingly determined by government*

agencies. By the mid eighties those policies began to take on a form which was in complete defiance of Westhill's founding principle of child centredness. It was perhaps at this time that the death of Westhill College as an institution became inevitable . . .

(Priestley, 2002, 169–170)

Government education policy has clearly turned away from 'the child in the midst' and this has affected youth work as much as teacher education but my reading of the history of Westhill is of an institution that was struggling to keep to its ethos *and* be viable from early in the twentieth century. The history of the Community, Play and Youth Work Department was one of grasping opportunities and making compromises and this reflected a wider Westhill tradition. Maybe the closure of Westhill was inevitable, and community, play and youth studies cannot survive within pre 1992 universities (the Durham University undergraduate course is another casualty). Yet it is possible, with the benefit of hindsight, to identify possible points when different decisions could have made a difference.

The greatest irony is that the Westhill youth work tradition, based as it was in the Christian liberal education tradition, ended just as youth ministry has revived. As was noted above, the Centre for Youth Ministry had similar intake numbers to Westhill in 1999, and has grown considerably since then, partly helped by financial support from the Westhill Endowment Trust, set up to promote Christian education since the closure of Westhill. The University of Birmingham as a secular university has always been resistant to courses that are faith based, and maybe this is why George Archibald was wary of getting too close to the university at the start of Westhill. But at the time of the 'strategic alliance' would it have not been possible for the Westhill tradition to be carried on in youth work and youth ministry, outside of the university? Before this, was the point in the early 1990s, not mentioned by Jack Priestley, when Westhill, with Priestley as Principal, decided to end the partnership with Newman College. Newman survives and is developing youth work and youth ministry courses but Westhill has closed. Maybe if I, with others, had been more pro-active in resisting the split with Newman there would have been a different outcome, or maybe if I could have achieved greater unity within the staff team we could have resisted the university plans following the merger. There will be a number of 'if onlys', but most important is to recognise the importance of this Westhill tradition and ethos.

Thanks

My thanks to John Parr, who as student, lecturer, head of department, governor and neighbour to Westhill College from 1949 onwards shared his considerable experience with me. The views expressed are my own.

Dedication

This article is dedicated to the memory of Anne Flinn who died in 2006. Anne was a student and tutor in the Community and Youth Studies Department, and for me represented the enthusiasm and exuberance that characterised the best of Westhill College, and led many students to learning and personal development.

References

Bradford, S. (2007) 'Practices, policies and professionals, emerging discourses of expertise in English youth work, 1939–1951' *Youth and Policy*, 97/98, 13–28.

DES (1969) Youth and Community Work in the 70s (The Milson-Fairbairn Report) London, HMSO.

HMSO (1968) Report of the Committee on Local Authority and Allied Personal Social Services (The 'Seebohm Report'), London, HMSO.

Irvine, M. (1998) *Birmingham Magazine*, Birmingham, University of Birmingham.

Ministry of Education (1960) *The Youth Service in England and Wales* (Albemarle Report). London, HMSO.

Mole, D.E.H. (c. 1970) *The Selly Oak Tradition*, Birmingham, Selly Oak Colleges.

National Youth Agency (1999) *Youth and Community Work Training Institutions – Location Map and Student intake*, Leicester, NYA/ETS.

Parker, C.M. (1982) *Westhill, An Informal History of Seventy Five Years*, Birmingham, Westhill College.

Priestley, J. (2002) 'Westhill College, the embodiment of a Religious and educational ideal' in *Panorama, International Journal of Comparitive Religious Education and Values*, Vol 14, 2.

Priestley, J. (2003) 'The Lumber Merchant and the Chocolate King' in S. Orchard and J.H.Y. Briggs (eds.) (2007) *The Sunday Movement: Studies in the Growth and Decline of Sunday Schools*, Milton Keynes: Paternoster Press.

Priestley, J. (2007) 'The Lumber Merchant and the Chocolate King', in S. Orchard and J.H.Y. Briggs (eds.) *The Sunday Movement, Studies in the Growth and Decline of Sunday Schools*, Milton Keynes, Paternoster Press.

Reed, B. (1950) Eighty Thousand Adolescents, London, George Allen and Unwin.

THES (Times Higher Education Supplement), 6 July 2007.

Westhill Training College (1937) *A Record of Achievement and Challenge – A brief history and 30th Annual Report*, Birmingham, Westhill College.

Westhill Training College (c. 1939) *Westhill's World-Wide Work*, Birmingham, Westhill College.

Smith M.K. (1997) on Friedrich Froebel and Basil Yeaxlee in Encyclopaedia in www.infed.org.

CHAPTER 9

Starting Out: Origins of Newcastle YMCA

Tony Jeffs

It is always a risky business making claims regarding the longevity of youth organisations. However with over 150 years of almost continuous existence behind it, Newcastle-upon-Tyne YMCA can claim, with good grounds, to being one of the oldest youth work agencies operating anywhere in the world. This chapter will tell something of the history of that organisation up to the end of the nineteenth century.

In the decades before and after the YMCA opened, Newcastle – where almost half the population was under 25 years – was a young person's town and a community experiencing its most rapid period of expansion. At the beginning of the nineteenth century Newcastle was still largely confined within medieval walls but it soon expanded northwards into the fields beyond as well as along the banks of the Tyne. Prosperity facilitated the development of elegant residential areas to house a burgeoning new middle class. These avenues, terraces and squares dramatically contrasted with the overcrowded dwellings of the Close, the Quayside and Sandgate. But in terms of physical distance the gap separating squalor and prosperity was slight. These two communities collided in the crowded streets. Poor, under-developed transportation, helped to ensure rich and poor alike walked the same thoroughfares to work, worship, shop and visit. Indeed such was the lack of 'public' transport, that the large gathering organised to celebrate the first anniversary of the Young Men's Christian Institute at the Westgate Road Assembly Rooms in 1852 assured potential participants, 'carriages to be in waiting at half-past nine o'clock' – maybe for comfort, but also no doubt to guarantee the respectable participants a swift, safe exit from a venue ominously close to what were then some of the most disreputable dwellings in town.

In the first half of the nineteenth century Newcastle's population almost trebled. In the next fifty years it virtually doubled reaching 215,000 in 1901. A flourishing industrial environment sustained growth as steam engines enabled yet deeper pits to be sunk and ever greater quantities of 'King Coal' to be shipped from the port. Iron, lead, glass and soap works grew apace as did roperies, shipyards and potteries. Alongside the expansion of 'traditional industries' modern enterprises emerged such as chemicals and food processing. Simultaneously, new service employers appeared, notably the railway and postal services. In tandem, retailing, banking and insurance activity expanded, resulting in the transformation of the centre of the city to accommodate commercial enterprises servicing the larger population and industrial base. This was the age of great North Eastern architecture when John Grainger, David Stephenson, David Newton and, above all, John Dobson indelibly stamped their respective visions upon the centre of a Newcastle that was by then firmly established as the commercial and economic capital of a region stretching from the Scottish Border to North Yorkshire.

Economic expansion incurred social costs. Industrial pollution, inadequate housing and a willful failure to invest in the civic infrastructure of drains, water supply and cleansing, ensured that Newcastle, for most of the nineteenth century, had death rates, infant mortality and overcrowding which ranked amongst the nation's worst. Not surprisingly, the cholera epidemic of 1853 extracted a dreadful revenge for the incompetence and indifference of the town fathers – 1,533 fatalities amongst a population of 122,000. Nor did expansion transpire without other forms of social and economic disruption. Riots, strikes and disorder occurred at regular intervals and street crime made some parts of Newcastle dangerous for 'respectable folk'. Local newspapers invariably contained numerous, often lurid, accounts of violent crime. For many throughout the nineteenth century, Newcastle was neither a healthy nor an especially tranquil place. Over-crowded, insanitary dwellings teeming with the ills of poverty multiplied in the low-lying areas adjacent to the river. Houses once occupied by some of the town's wealthiest citizens, were 'parcelled into tenements becoming the foulest shelters of the poor' (Reid, 1845, 89). These communities were barely a stone's throw away from where the Newcastle and Gateshead YMCA established itself. Yet, as one contemporary commentator observed, the adjacent slum was a dreadful enclosure that 'respectable people, having no occasion to visit scarcely know anything about' (Anon. cited in Long, 1999, 35).

Then, as now, youth work and youth provision was commonly viewed as a means of diverting some young people from involvement in criminal and 'anti-social' activity and of helping others born into 'respectable' and 'God fearing households' to follow the route mapped out for them by their parents. Young people, whatever their background, were perceived as being particularly vulnerable to temptation, especially in the industrial towns where ties of family and community were loosened, and temptations in the form of public house, music hall and worse proliferated. The years spanning late childhood to early adulthood were held to be an interlude during which, for good or ill, the die was cast. Youth work sought to positively influence the process of maturation. The theory underwriting practice was clear-cut. It set out to bring young people into regular and close contact with wise, morally sound adults; men and women judged fit to serve as superior role models with a talent for establishing groups and clubs offering educative and enjoyable activities capable of out-competing the dubious temptations of the street and public house. It was educative, in the sense that members not only learnt through 'instruction', i.e. from lectures and classes, but more significantly through association; learning how to live and behave in the wider community by observing the demeanor of those with whom they associated in the micro community of the group and club. Guided activity, sporting and cultural pursuits initiated the process and through this an understanding of service to the club or group, and the world beyond, was taught. Service to others, as Lord Shaftesbury explained to one of the earliest YMCA groups, lay at the heart of youth work for:

> Nothing is more likely to keep you from mischief of all kinds, from mischief of action, of speculation – from every mischief that you can devise, than to be everlastingly engaged in some great, practical work of good.
>
> (Hodder, 1886, 327)

If the theory was simple the practice was not. In urban areas such as Newcastle, where often the needs of the young people were most acute, funding and staff were the most difficult to come by for an activity viewed as challenging, arduous and, with regards to exposure to disease and illness, frequently dangerous.

The earliest youth clubs and organisations established in Newcastle were Sunday Schools, modeled on those founded by the 'cheery, talkative, flamboyant, and warm-hearted' Robert Raikes in Gloucester in 1780 (Kelly, 1970, 75). So successful were these in attracting members that within a decade replicas existed in every town and city in the country. Churches of all denominations set up Sunday Schools, as did Co-operators and Chartists before 1850 and later, socialist and anarchist groups. Sunday schools varied enormously in size and content. Those affiliated to churches habitually provided religious instruction but many were ambitious undertakings offering young people, and some adults, a basic education in literacy and numeracy; access to a library and workshop; clothing; food; rudimentary medical care; and various forms of entertainment. Alongside Sunday Schools, for the better educated of all classes were reading rooms, the 'intellectual seminaries of men' as Hudson called them (1851, ix) which served as social centres as well as libraries. Many were attached to churches, others to Chartist Halls. By 1850, in addition to reading rooms, Newcastle had a Literary and Philosophical Society, with a library containing over 8,000 volumes, and two 'flourishing' Mechanics Institutes (Hudson, 1851, 142; Callcott, 2005). In the social and religious firmament of the early nineteenth century countless long forgotten study and reading groups surfaced, many affiliated to national bodies. Some were political in orientation, some religious and others social. One such group deserves special attention with reference to the antecedents of the YMCA. Established by Thomas Binney in Newcastle in 1817 it was possibly the most direct precursor of the YMCA amongst a number claiming that honour. Binney, a bookseller's apprentice and influential member of the Presbyterian Church in Newcastle, recruited a dozen young men, mostly committed members of his own denomination, to meet on Sunday evenings for prayer, Bible study, and the reading of essays and sermons as 'a means of spiritual improvement'. What makes this especially noteworthy was that in 1829 Binney became the pastor of the Weigh House Domestic Mission attached to King's Weigh House Chapel, Fish Street Hill, London: the Chapel that George Williams attended before and after he founded the YMCA in 1844. Williams and Binney remained close until the latter's death in 1874. According to Williams' official biographer it was Binney that 'taught him to draw men to Christ with cords of love' (Williams, 1906, 41).

Early beginnings

The YMCA was not the first organisation to undertake youth work in Newcastle though it was the first national and international body to do so. George Williams, a London draper's assistant founded the YMCA in 1844 (Binfield, 1973). Deeply religious and active in the life of his church he managed, despite working a 60 hour week, to teach in a Ragged School and energetically raise money for the London Missionary Society. One of over 120,000 drapers then employed in the city, he viewed his colleagues as a distinct class:

> *untouched by any agency of philanthropy, whose need is as deep as any in London. These men of the middle class, of shop and warehouse, of stool and counter, make no loud appeal for help, scorn to advertise their*

wrongs, suffer silently and in loneliness, for such is the way of 'respectability'.

(Williams, 1906, 107)

Determined to respond to what he perceived as the needs of this group he invited a small number of like-minded young men to a meeting at his lodgings to discuss the formation of a Christian association to work amongst drapers and their social equivalents.[1] All were committed Christians but they were intentionally recruited from numerous denominations. Within six months the number involved had grown to 161. These assembled at Radley's Hotel (Blackfriars), a building chosen because it was a religiously neutral venue, to receive a report on progress made. Before dispersing those present agreed on 12 rules defining the Association's aims and the lines upon which it should develop. These included the following:

> *That the object of this Association be the improvement of the spiritual condition of young men engaged in the drapery and other trades, by the introduction of religious services among them.*
>
> *That two social tea meetings be held in the year at which a report of the society's proceedings shall be read.*
>
> *That a general meeting be held once a fortnight (or oftener if required) for the purpose of hearing reports from members of the progress of the work of God in the various establishments, and for such and other purposes as the Committee shall see fit to determine; and that all meetings shall be open for members and those friends whom they may consider proper persons to bring, and to those who shall receive invitations from the Committee.*
>
> *That no person shall be considered a member of this Association unless he be a member of a Christian Church, or there be sufficient evidence of his being a converted character.*
>
> *That all persons desirous of becoming members shall be proposed at a general meeting, and a deputation be appointed to inquire into their moral character, upon whose report the Committee shall decide whether they be eligible or not*

(quoted Williams, 1906, 131)

The essentials were now in place. First the democratic structure of the YMCA was established. Associations controlled their budgets, membership and affairs, thereby ensuring national and international structures would be federalist. Second was the requirement that Associations avoid becoming the handmaiden of a given denomination. In ensuring this did not remain a pious hope Williams and his colleagues displayed prodigious skill. Such was the antagonism between Anglicans and non-conformists that even Lord Shaftesbury was able to persuade only one Bishop to sit on 'Ragged School' platforms. All the others were, at that time, afraid of meeting Nonconformists' (Hodder, 1893, 350). By careful attention to administrative detail and by focusing upon what united rather than divided Christians, Williams largely circumvented the type of adversarial disputes that bedeviled virtually all charities working with young people during his lifetime. It is a measure of its success that whereas, apart from the Army Cadets, all the uniformed youth organisations founded in the nineteenth century fragmented into sectarian rivalry, the YMCA did not. The point is well illustrated by the fact that the 28 full-time general secretaries attending the Edinburgh Conference in 1892 comprised 10 Anglicans, five Presbyterians, four Methodists, four Baptists, three Quakers and one Congregationalist (Binfield, 1973, 264).

Williams and his unfaltering supporter, and incidentally, employer George Hitchcock took inordinate care to cultivate wealthy and influential patrons. Most notably Saul Morley and Lord Shaftesbury, who like Hitchcock, provided the funding to enable Williams and others to ceaselessly travel in order to establish and support Associations. By any measure the rate of growth was remarkable. Within 11 years of the initial meeting the first international gathering of delegates from Belgium, Britain, France, Germany, Holland, Switzerland and North America was held in Paris. Crucially it agreed a declaration that provided a raison d'être for an international movement. Known as the 'Paris Basis' this affirmed

> The Young Men's Christian Associations seek to unite those young men who, regarding Jesus Christ as their God and Saviour according to the Holy Scriptures, desire to be His disciples in their doctrine and in their life, and to associate their efforts for the extension of His Kingdom among young men.

This afforded the 'Basis' upon which the affiliation of an individual Association was accepted or rejected. For example, when the North East YMCAs came together in 1866 to form a Federation, the starting point was that all present agreed to abide by the 'Paris Basis'. It was sufficiently unambiguous to spell out who might or might not wish to join, yet devoid of the detail and clarification that could inhibit the expansion of a federal organisation, thus bestowing core aims and purposes whilst gifting almost unlimited autonomy to individual Associations. Furthermore, the 'Paris Basis' meant the YMCA could avoid damaging splits within and between its own national Associations. It has also helped sustain a structure allowing branches to adjust, grow and contract in ways that minimised the potential for damage to the well-being of other Associations or the organisation as a whole.

YMCA arrives in Newcastle

It is not known who convened the first meeting to discuss setting up the Newcastle and Gateshead YMCA Institute, nor when or where it took place. However we know that in 1846 deputations from London began visiting major centres of population to persuade sympathetic individuals to establish YMCAs based on the London model. By 1847 Associations were functioning in Liverpool, Manchester, Taunton, Exeter, Leeds, Hull, Oxford, Derby and Bath (Chamberlain, 1944, 15).[2] All that is known for certain is that by 1849 *The Newcastle and Gateshead Young Men's Christian Association* branch was operating on the first floor of 32 Grainger Street, above Mr Blaney's grocer shop. The front portion of the room was used as a Reading Room, with a good stock of books and the rear portion served as a classroom. A folding partition allowed the whole room to be utilised for larger meetings. Prior to being launched the organisers adroitly secured the public endorsement of prominent individuals linked to the main protestant denominations, as well as eminent civic and political figures. They appear to have meticulously abided by the 'modus operandi' for establishing an Association outlined in the widely circulated *The YMCA – What it is and how to Begin It*. This recommends that once someone indicates a willingness to serve as an Honorary Secretary, then he:

> Will first seek the counsel of God, and then invite, as far as he can, twelve to fourteen laymen from 18 to 30 years of age, converted men of all denominations, securing, if in England, if possible, both those of the Established Church and Nonconformists, to a meeting in a public room, but not if it can be avoided in a chapel, chapel school-room, or vestry, sooner meet in a hotel. An almshouse or Freemason's lodge are suitable, but we must be clear, especially now of all sectarian taint.
>
> (Anon, ud., 5)

The Newcastle and Gateshead Association seemed to have followed these strictures to the letter in its 'endeavor' to promote amongst the 'younger portion' of the populace 'by moral means, the culture and elevation of the mind'.

The organisers prevailed upon the Earl of Carlisle to serve as President. Both he and Lady Carlisle were celebrated supporters of the Temperance Movement – fêted for having created 'drink free zones' by closing the pubs on their estates; some of which they transformed into temperance clubs. Carlisle was also strongly committed to the reform of the legal system that incarcerated young offenders in the forbidding and often brutal adult prisons of the period. To this end he established and funded one of the earliest 'reformatories for young offenders' to operate in England. In addition to the President, a total of 26 Vice Presidents were recruited, 13 were clergymen and two were local MPs – Thomas Headlam and W.M. Hutt. Others included George Hitchcock, George Williams' employer and close friend; John Benson, founder of the Prudhoe Street Chapel and prominent temperance campaigner; Emerson Muschamp Bainbridge, a director of Consett Iron Company; Swan, Hunter and Wigham Richards (shipbuilders); Cairn Line and the department store he established; and John Hunter Rutherford. The latter was an Anglican clergyman and temperance campaigner who, to assist the elucidation of his temperance principles qualified as a medical practitioner. As friend of Joseph Cowen and supporter of numerous radical causes, Rutherford is also best remembered as an educational reformer who instituted within Newcastle a system of education offering working and middle class men access to a college education at minimal cost. The college he established in 1877 was named after him and the lineage of Northumbria University can be traced directly to it. George Hitchcock's involvement clearly signaled a link with Associations operational elsewhere as he was already the treasurer of the London YMCA. The connection is evident in an attachment which further spelt out in the *Prospectus* that

> *During the Winter Season, CLASSES will be formed for instruction in various departments of useful and edifying knowledge, similar to those established in the London and other Associations.*

(Prospectus, Newcastle YMCA archive)

The post of secretary was shared between J.B. Falconar and George Luckley. Falconar was a Methodist who later, alongside Thomas the son of Emerson Bainbridge, worked at the Children's Mission which Thomas had opened in Jesmond on the outskirts of Newcastle. Falconar maintained this YMCA Association and records show that he was still actively involved 25 years later. The day-to-day running of the Association was left to an elected committee comprising the secretaries, the treasurer Mr A. Stringer, and 12 other members. In addition nine other members sat on a separate Library and Reading Room Committee.

Not long after opening, the Association moved from number 32 to 53 Grainger Street where the Association Institute was opened on 10 April 1851. Meetings took place each Monday evening at 8 o'clock in the Association Rooms. The Library and Reading Room was opened every weekday evening from 7 p.m. until 10 o'clock, except Thursday when the room was used for lectures. The Monday programme adhered to a four-weekly cycle. The first and third were 'Biblical and Devotional' meetings. The second a 'Conversational' at which members reported on their religious activities and planned with each other the 'taking advantage of any opportunities for usefulness which occur to any of them'. The fourth involved a member delivering an essay that served as a basis for general discussion. The first five essays, all written by committee members, were entitled: *The Ancient Cities of Scripture*; *Christmas*; *Festus*; *Eternal Life* and *The Missionary Aspect of Christianity*. In addition to attendance at Association meetings members were expected to be involved in Sunday School duties and to undertake outreach work with the Association's *Tract Society*. This entailed members in twos or threes visiting on Sundays the 'spiritually neglected localities of the Town . . . to bring the inhabitants of such neighbourhoods under the influence of the Gospel'. Each pairing called at a number of dwellings over a period of weeks 'for religious conversation', the intention being to persuade sufficient residents from the 'neglected areas' to make it practical for the Association to establish in the locality 'meetings for Prayer, Scripture Reading, or Cottage Preaching'.

Within weeks of opening in 1849 the membership reached 157. Besides these full members, Sunday School Teachers were urged to pay 2s 6d, half the full membership fee, to 'enroll such *elder Sunday Scholars* as may be recommended by their respective superintendents or secretaries'. The Association also offered these 'youths' classes in

> Reading, Writing, and Arithmetic, gratis; and they may retain these privileges so long as they remain attached to their several Sunday Schools, and their nominators consider it proper.

The *Prospectus* promised members access to an array of standard and recent works on Christian, scientific, philosophical and historical topics. The selective list of the texts available and journals subscribed to indicate this was a serious library, far more so than the list of the 869 books comprising the 1878 stock. The collection was largely made up of improving texts, sermons, superficial biographies and popular travel and scientific books. The *Prospectus* described the rooms 'as the more comfortable and suitable than any in the town' emphasising the superior quality of the facilities.

To commemorate the first anniversary of the Newcastle and Gateshead YMCA, a three hour celebratory gathering was held in the opulent surroundings of the Westgate Road Assembly Rooms. In the presence of the President, the Earl of Carlisle, the audience listened to speeches from Thomas Headlam MP, one of the vice presidents, and from various dignitaries. Two musical interludes and refreshments prepared by a Committee of Ladies added to the grandeur of the occasion. The dessert according to the poster advertising the event was

> Strawberries, Grapes, Red and White Currants, Biscuits, Dried Fruits, Oranges, Pines, and Ice Creams.

It was not a cheap evening by contemporary standards. Tickets cost 1s 6d (approximately £18 at today's prices). The choice of venue, the price of the tickets, the status of those in attendance, and even the quality of menu speaks of an organisation of good standing and order, one that had made rapid and healthy progress and was clearly worthy of support. By association with it, a public figure or religious body might well enhance its reputation.

Unfortunately for reasons unrecorded, the Newcastle and Gateshead YMCA collapsed shortly after this celebration. All that is known is that Thomas Cairns, who was involved in the 1858 re-launch, and may have been a member of the original Association, tells us:

> of this Branch it may be said that 'Misfortune marked it for its own', for after a struggling existence of a few years it collapsed, involving some of its friends in the payment of 'smart money'.
>
> (*Newcastle Daily Journal*, 24 July 1896)

That comment and a subsequent one by Stephens at the meeting held in 1858 suggests the first Association closed leaving a trail of debt, but this remains conjecture.

Starting again

Within a short period, an initiative to re-establish a Newcastle branch of the YMCA surfaced. The invitation to an inaugural meeting was sent by Reverend George Bell, secretary of the Union of Evangelical Ministers, addressed to all those belonging to the Union and urging them to attend along with members of their churches. Reverend J.C. Bruce, one of the previous 26 vice-presidents under Carlisle's presidency, chaired the meeting held at the St James' Congregational Chapel, Blackett Street on 11 November 1858. The intention was to form 'a Young Men's Christian Association on the model of associations under the same name which have been established in London' (*Northern Times*, 12 November 1858). Bruce was a renowned scholar, founder of the Percy Academy and author of the celebrated *Handbook to the Roman Wall*. His likeness is now preserved by a substantial marble sarcophagus located in Newcastle Cathedral. The report of the meeting mentions the presence of only one other vice-president from the original list, a D.H. Goddard. However the willingness of E.M. Bainbridge to subsequently serve as a vice-president indicates his support for this venture even if he was absent that evening. The chair, the Reverend F. Stevens, who had been responsible for setting up the first Irish YMCA in Dublin in 1849 and was now resident in Newcastle, moved the following resolution after his opening address:

> *That the association shall consist of young men of Christian character, irrespective of denominational distinction, and such other persons as shall lend their aid in promoting the interests of the association.*
>
> (*Northern Times*, 12 November 1858)

Mr Alexander seconded the motion stressing the benefits that would accrue from being linked to the 'London Association of that name' not least for those young men from Newcastle who travelled to that city. It was passed unanimously after which a Mr George Lucas caused something of a commotion by suggesting that if the new Association was to truly embrace the spirit of the resolution then it

> *Would open their embrace not only to Churchmen, Methodists, and Dissenters generally, but to Roman Catholics, Unitarians, to Arians, Socinians,[3] and the young men of Christian character who might have fallen into the errors of Mormonism.*
>
> (ibid.)

A Mr Campbell from Leeds supported Lucas. Comments by the Reverend Brown censuring the principles outlined by Campbell and Lucas 'elicited marks of disapprobation from a portion of the audience'. Nevertheless, the meeting unanimously voted in favour of Brown's resolution:

> *That the means by which the objects of the Association shall be promoted shall be the opening of a reading room, the formation of classes for instruction in various branches of knowledge, the delivery of lectures, and the establishment of meetings for conference and prayer.*
>
> (ibid.)

So Newcastle once again had a YMCA and a certain Mr Johnson accepted the post of Honorary Secretary.

Where Newcastle led, others followed. By 1866 other Associations had formed in Alnwick, Berwick, Bishop Auckland, Consett, Darlington, Durham, Hartlepool, Hexham, Middlesborough, Morpeth, Pocklington, Redcar, Ryton, Seaham Harbour, Spennymoor, Stockton, West Hartlepool, Whitby, Yarm and York.[4] Sunderland followed five years later but Gateshead did not break with Newcastle until October 1885 when a separate Association acquired premises in Catherine Terrace, Gateshead. In 1866 the existing Associations formed a North Eastern Confederation of YMCAs. Earlier, in 1864, the Stockton Association, whose Honorary Secretary Thomas Whitwell served as the District Secretary, introduced a rule that all wishing to be received into membership must serve a probationary period as Associates. This procedure was adopted at the first meeting of the Confederation, then nationally where it soon became known as the 'Stockton Rule'. At the same meeting the Confederation embraced an imaginative system of what might nowadays be termed 'peer evaluation'. This entailed an annual visit to each YMCA in the Confederation by a team of delegates drawn from three neighbouring Associations. It was the responsibility of the visiting team to advise their hosts on possible improvements and ensure the Association was operating in ways that complied with the spirit and letter of the 'Paris Basis'.

Consolidation and expansion

The new Association first rented rooms in 36 Clayton Street West, Newcastle and shortly after transferred to shared accommodation at 13 Hood Street. But lack of space eventually obliged them to rent additional rooms at 16 New Bridge Street until the YMCA acquired exclusive use of the Hood Street premises in 1876. There it remained until Blackett Street Chapel, the venue used for the 1858 meeting, was purchased in 1884. Despite periodic downturns in trade, Newcastle YMCA appears to have sustained itself between 1858 and 1880. Membership at the 1858 opening stood at 20, but it never rose above 30 young men at any time in the decade to 1868. However records show that one member who joined in 1858, William Murray, remained affiliated in various capacities to Newcastle YMCA until his death in 1920. During the early period, Thomas Cairns notifies us that it 'was entirely a spiritual or religious bond which kept the members together and gave life to their meetings' (*Newcastle Daily Journal*, 24 July 1896). By 1876 the Library was open every evening from 7.00 to 10.00, the Reading Room every day, except Sunday from 9 a.m. to 10 p.m. and the Coffee Room every evening 5 p.m. through to 10 p.m.. Prayer Meetings and Bible Classes were held on Fridays and Sundays; Mutual Improvement Classes on a Tuesday; and a Singing Class on Mondays (Annual Report, 1876). In May 1876, Alex Hoddle was appointed the first General Secretary at an annual salary of £100. Hoddle's appointment coincided with a significant extension of the Association's activities. A West End Branch in the working class neighbourhood of Scotswood was established by renting two rooms from a body called the *British Workmen*, and 100 books, one eighth of the central stock, was transferred to provide the bare bones of a library. Members also ran a Saturday night Devotional Meeting; an Open Air Meeting was held at Grey's Monument every Sunday at 5.30 p.m.; and a Cottage Meeting on Thursdays in 'one of the lowest parts of the town'. In addition on Friday evenings the YMCA organised the *United Sunday School Teacher's Preparation Class* taught by Ministers from various denominations. Open to both 'ladies and gentlemen' this class attracted 39 students. To help pay for these activities Lord and Lady Armstrong were persuaded to open their home in Jesmond for an 'at home' and later a fund-raising bazaar was held in their Banqueting Hall. The bazaar was a longstanding annual event.

The *Report of the Committee* published in September 1879 informed the members that 'feeling the necessity of strict economy in the finances of the Association' they 'were compelled early in the year to dispense with the services' of the General Secretary. However one suspects that funding was not the sole issue. Hoddle remained at the YMCA for a short while after as Librarian but within a year a Thomas Moffett took up the General Secretary post with the appreciably improved salary of £150. Where Hoddle worked in the intervening years is unknown. We do know however that in August 1887 along with J.O. Curnow, another member of the Newcastle YMCA, he sailed to join the China Mission (*Daily Leader*, 25 July 1885). According to Thomas Cairns, Hoddle was something of a disaster. Cairns recalled that by the autumn of 1878 the Association was in the Doldrums:

> *Nominally the roll-book showed a fair membership when patrons and well-wishers were included, but the active workers could be counted upon the fingers . . . I can well remember the 'day of small things'. I can recall being in the rooms at Hood Street upon secretarial work some nights without a single visitor to the reading room. But in 1879 a change came over the scene. The young men gathered up by whom its destinies were to direct during the year that witnessed its most rapid progress.*

(*Newcastle Daily Journal*, 24 July 1896)

Hoddle's replacement, Thomas Moffett was 'a man of quiet manner' (*Newcastle Evening Chronicle*, 6 August 1896) whose secret of success, Cairns tells us, lay 'in his brotherliness and his manifest ingenuousness' (*Newcastle Daily Journal*, 24 July 1896).

Meetings and activities now took place every evening. For example, the weekly programme in 1879, apart from Prayer and Business meetings, incorporated string band rehearsals; choir practices; a choral society; French; German; Greek; shorthand classes; weekly lectures; and a Sunday School Teacher Preparation Class that produced 12 successful graduates that year. A cricket club operated during the summer and an annual camp was held during Race Week – a date selected, one assumes, to protect members from the 'debauchery' and over-indulgence reputed to occur during that week. The 123 members and 72 associates also ran 'cottage meetings' in the 'neglected districts of Newcastle'. One Mission operated in Queen's Lane, where according to the 1880 Annual Report, 'attendance is usually to over-crowding' and a second in Concord Court 'in the midst of a district where the lowest degradation exists'. A Mutual Improvement Society was organised for full members of the Association, wherein each participant took turns to prepare a paper for discussion by the group. The Rules of Membership of this Society stated that 'All Religious Questions of a Doctrinal Character to be Excluded' (capitals in original). Not every initiative worked. For example, the West End Branch closed after 18 months. The building was judged to be unsuitable and attendance at Sunday Bible Class so meagre it was decided that members' time would be better spent on evangelistic work visiting dwellings in the winter and holding open-air meetings in the summer. Judged by any criteria the number of meetings and scope of the programme was impressive. As shown by the syllabus for the Winter Session 1881 this had become an incredibly active organisation with 176 members and 220 Associates on the roll in that year. The syllabus for 1881 was:

Sunday:
7.15–8.0 a.m.	PRAYER MEETING
9.30–10.15 a.m.	PRAYER MEETING
10.30 a.m.	TRACT DISTRIBUTION & VISITATION
2.45 p.m.	TRACT DISTRIBUTION MEET
3.0–4.0 p.m.	CONVERSATIONAL BIBLE CLASS
5.0–6.0 p.m.	CHILDREN'S SERVICE at Queen's Lane
6.0 p.m.	OPEN-AIR SERVICE at Queen's Lane
6.30–7.30 p.m.	MISSION SERVICE at Queen's Lane

8.0 p.m.	TRACT DISTRIBUTION MEET
8.15–9.15 p.m.	EVANGELISTIC SERVICE

Monday

7.30–9.0 p.m.	WORKING MEN'S NIGHT SCHOOL
7.30–9.0 p.m.	SINGING CLASS at Queen's Lane
7.30–9.0 p.m.	HARMONIC SOCIETY (Rehearsals at C of E Institute)
8.0–9.0 p.m.	BOOK KEEPING CLASS

Tuesday

7.30–9.0 p.m.	CHESS & DRAUGHTS
7.30–9.0 p.m.	WORKING MEN'S NIGHT SCHOOL
6.0–9.0 p.m.	FELLOWSHIP MEETING

Wednesday

7.30–9.0 p.m.	GOSPEL TEMPERANCE MEETING (Byker School)
7.30–9.0 p.m.	SHORTHAND WRITER'S ASSOCIATION
8.0–9.0 p.m.	DANISH CLASS
8.0–9.0 p.m.	ITALIAN CLASS

Thursday

7.30–8.30 p.m.	MISSION SERVICE at Queen's Lane
7.30–8.30 p.m.	FRENCH CLASS (elementary)
8.30–9.30 p.m.	FRENCH CLASS (advanced)

Friday

7.0–8.0 p.m.	SHORTHAND CLASS (advanced)
8.0–9.0 p.m.	SHORTHAND CLASS (elementary)
8.0–9.0 p.m.	ARITHMETIC CLASS
7.30–9.0 p.m.	GOSPEL TEMPERANCE MEETING, Princess Street Mission
8.0–9.0 p.m.	SUNDAY SCHOOL TEACHER'S PREPARATION BIBLE CLASS (open to both Ladies and Gentlemen)

Saturday

5.0–6.0 p.m.	SAVINGS' BANK at Queen's Street Mission
7.30–9.0 p.m.	GOSPEL TEMPERANCE MEETING, Nelson Street Hall
8.0–9.0 p.m.	DEVOTIONAL MEETING

The Reading Room and Lavatory are open Daily (Sundays excepted) from 9.0 a.m. to 10 p.m. Library every evening (Wednesdays excepted) from 6.30 p.m. to 10 p.m.

General Secretary in attendance at the Rooms daily from 9.0 to 10.0 a.m. and 2.0 to 3.0 p.m. and every evening during the week (Wednesdays excepted) from 6.0 p.m. to 10 p.m.

The following year Moffett reported that Newcastle YMCA had organised and hosted the equivalent of a youth parliament, the *Newcastle House of Commons*, attended by delegates from the different debating societies and clubs. Hood Street also provided the venue for the newly established *Working Men's Night School*. Most years the list of activities offered was augmented: A *Literary Society* and *Sacred Harmonic Society* in 1880; Sunday breakfasts and *Swimming* and *Bi-cycling Clubs* in 1882. An *Orchestral Society* and *Rambling Club* were founded in 1883. A *Vigilance Corps* was established in 1886 in collaboration with a number of sympathetic local churches and businesses. The Corps visited places of work and 'toured' city centre streets hoping to draw

> *young men (especially strangers) to the Association, and thereby assisting them to resist the many temptations which unhappily beset the course of every young man in a City like this.*
>
> (Annual Report, 1885, 7)

The Corps may well have been the first outreach and detached youth work project to operate in Newcastle. The same year a Gymnasium was fitted out, made possible by the acquisition of a new building in December 1885.

Another focus of activity for members was organising religious meetings. Moffett reports over 375 of these in 1880, attended by 20,000 souls. At times members organised evangelistic work with specific occupational groups, for example among showmen during the Hoppings,[5] at other times with railway-men, cab drivers and policemen. Over and above all these activities members regularly planned regional campaigns to be undertaken by leading evangelists and preachers. These men, now largely forgotten, were in their time celebrated figures capable of attracting crowds numbering thousands to open-air meetings and gatherings in places such as the Cathedral. For example, a Canon Hay Aitken came for a fortnight speaking at as many as three meetings daily in 1878 and 1908. Miss Watts of Stowmarket and the Reverend W.B. Cullis of Philadelphia (USA) both undertook two weeks' of meetings in 1880. The Gospel Temperance Campaign headed-up by the American preacher R.T. Booth lasted from 2 to 17 March 1881 filling the Royal Circus, Percy Street every evening and motivating 15,000 to sign the pledge. Between 9 October to 13 November of the same year the YMCA brought Dwight L. Moody and Ira D. Sankey to the city. Described as the 'most famous American twin performers of the nineteenth century' the verve of their style was, according to Binfield (1973, 212), 'without parallel' in a way that was strongly appealing to 'the half-converted, intelligent, busy young', men the YMCA sought to attract. After each meeting the young men and women in the audience were invited for tea at the Association rooms. Subsequently members made home visits to those who responded to this invitation to encourage them to join the YMCA or YWCA.

During the final two decades of the century there was an expansion in the level of welfare provision offered members. The Association was functioning much more as Friendly Society than previously. For example The *Pleasant Sunday Afternoon* gathering between 3 p.m. and 4 p.m. had comprised a talk of a religious nature, the singing of hymns and a musical interlude. After 1890 those who attended aged 18 to 50, were invited to join the *Pleasant Sunday Afternoon Benefit Society*. In return for a down payment of a shilling and a weekly subscription, members unable to work due to sickness received six shillings per week for the first 13 weeks, four for the next 13, three for the next and two for the final quarter. Any members who died had their funeral expenses met. However strict conditions of membership were laid down. For example Rule 6 states:

> That no sick Member be out of the house between the hours of 9 p.m. and 6 a.m., from the 1st of April to 30th of September; or between the hours of 6 p.m. and 8 a.m., from 1st October to the 31st March. Should any Member bring trouble on himself by irregular conduct, or in any way impose upon the Society, or being on the sick list, be found intoxicated, or doing any kind of work, he shall be excluded from benefits of the Society for the remainder of the year, and from participation in the dividend at the year's end.

A similar *Benefit Society*, but only for full members of the YMCA, set contributions at six pence per week and paid more generous benefits. Other initiatives included a *Thrift Club* and an *Emigration Service* that assisted young men planning to work abroad. A *Visiting Service* was established to ensure regular contact with members who were unwell. An *Apartment Register* inspected and arranged accommodation for members and young men moving to Newcastle. An *Employment Register* supplied details of posts with approved employers, and gave employers seeking staff details of members looking for work. Furthermore via the Department of the Association of General Secretaries of the YMCAs of Great Britain and Ireland members were able to gain access to Convalescent Homes and the opportunity to take low cost holidays organised by the *Holiday Bureau*.

Members

The decision to develop welfare provision alongside the traditional emphasis upon self- and mutual-improvement and evangelical work was significant. It reflected a need to attract new members and retain them once recruited by locking them into a web of services and benefits. It might also be seen as a natural progression for an organisation that was responsive to the needs of its membership but it also represents the YMCA 'catching-up' – it had initially neglected this crucial aspect of the lives of its members and left such activities to secular bodies such as trade unions. Certainly by 1880 between 75–80 per cent of male workers belonged to at least one friendly society (Hopkins 1995, 51). Whatever the reason for its development, welfare intervention led to an upward shift in the age profile of the membership – a trend apparent to both the British and International Committee of YMCA as the organisation reached its half century (Muukkonen, 2002).

Press cuttings, reports and papers help piece together a history of Newcastle YMCA during these early years. But these sources fail to covey a coherent picture of the 'types' who joined the Association. Although membership was restricted to young men it is clear that as the years unfolded women intruded into the life of the Association with increasing frequency. In 1852 a Committee of Ladies was on hand to prepare the refreshments, but serving food remained a task of the male stewards. By 1876 ladies were attending the Sunday School Teachers' classes put on by the Association and six years later they were allowed to become members of the Library. Women were also clearly active in shaping some of the evangelistic work. It was the 'Lady Friends of the Association' who suggested the Mission to railwaymen and the subsequent one to policemen, whilst Miss Watson, from the Prudhoe Street Mission, helped to run the Cottage Meetings in Liverpool Street and Mackford's Entry alongside other ladies. Already by 1878 women had become invaluable in sustaining the desired level of activity. By the turn of the century, they were playing a central role in the work needed to raise the funds to pay for a new building.

Almost certainly every Association member once belonged to a Sunday School. A survey conducted in 1852 found that among Manchester mill workers 91.8 per cent had at one time been members; and an 1881 study recorded no less than 19 per cent of the entire population were either scholars or teachers (Laqueur, 1976, 88–9). They were most certainly respectable. The membership procedures were meticulously systematised to ensure no 'wrong 'un or cad' wormed their way in with the condition of eligibility for membership according to Rule IV requiring:

A Belief in the Lord Jesus Christ as God and Saviour, as set forth in the Holy Scriptures, a personal acceptance of Him, a desire to be His disciple in doctrine and life, and a willingness to unite with the Association for the extension of His Kingdom amongst young men. Candidates for Membership are only eligible for election after having been Associate Members for three months . . . All those desirous of entering the Association must be nominated by Associate Members or Members.

As a failsafe mechanism the elected General Committee retained the prerogative:

To suspend or expel any Member, Associate Member, or Honorary Member, whose conduct is, in its opinion, hurtful to the character of the Association.

With few, if any exceptions, members were employed in retail or commerce. This was no accident. It was to cater for the needs of such young men that George Williams had created the YMCA as an organisation that would strive to recruit the petty bourgeoisie. With regards to the poor however the aim was merely to evangelise them. Thus the establishment of Bible Classes were, as Williams explained in 1870:

in order to instruct young men of the artisan class whom it might not be convenient or desirable to introduce into existing meetings, and for whom rooms in suitable localities might be provided.

(Williams, 1906, 162)

Membership was neither sought nor encouraged from certain sections of the working population. The young men enlisted were earnest, educated and hard working. They were different from those who possessed similar characteristics but who joined instead the Chartist Institute in Nun Street; different too from those gravitating to the reading rooms attached to 19 out of the 54 pits operating in Northumberland and Durham in 1850 (Benson, 1989, 152–4). Likewise those who joined the Mechanics Institutes; the men and the fewer women able to spare the time, to attend the frequent lectures at Co-operative and Miner's Association Halls; formed Literary and Debating Societies; flocked to hear Joseph Cowen, Kropotkin and William Morris lecture; and supported organisations like the Northern Reform Union (Todd, 1991; Hugman, 2001). As the books in the YMCA Library indicate, and the activities confirm, Association members were not drawn from this segment of the working and lower middle class. Some members were undoubtedly Philistines, likely to concur with the opinion of Mr Collins, General Secretary of Yeovil YMCA, who told the delegates to 1900 Newcastle Conference that 'theatre going and novel reading were the greatest curses of the nation' (YMCA. British Conference, 1900, 125). Probably the majority fitted the description Virginia Woolf unkindly styled as middlebrow men uncomfortable with high culture (Woolf, 1967, 196–203). Judging by the reports of the meetings here were young men certain of their faith, not far removed from those described by Rose as 'accustomed to accepting dogmas handed down by churches, chapels, teachers, politicians, and employers' (2002, 5). They were certain, yes, but with the added virtue of respect for religious tolerance and acceptance of other Christian sects and denominations. A large number among them would have been teetotal. The *YMCA Literary and Debating Society* cancelled its meeting when Sir Wilfrid Lawson was speaking to a temperance gathering on the same evening and the majority of the members expressed a wish to attend (*Newcastle YMCA Magazine*, February 1896, 5). Politically they were Liberals and Conservatives, but tolerant towards each other. The YMCA was an organisation that supporters of both these parties attended and upon whose committees leading members of each side of the political divide served without apparent animosity. However they were less sympathetic to the outlook of the growing number of socialist and trade unionist activists in the region; this was not the club for such people. Irrespective of political stance they were the sort of young men readily given to patriotic fervor as they demonstrated at the meeting organised by the YMCA to raise money for the Reservist Fund during the Boer War. At this meeting, the speaker aided by 'beautiful lantern pictures and racy verbal description' secured 'prolonged and hearty cheers' from the large audience 'for a picture of "Jameson's dash into the Transvaal"' (*Newcastle Evening Chronicle*, 1 December 1899). Leading members of both the main parties in Newcastle were willing patrons of the YMCA, as were paternalistic employers, such as T.H. Bainbridge who sought to extend the Christian stewardship that lay at the heart of the YMCA to his company. As he explained in a letter to staff

> *We have a good many Christian salesmen in the house, and I should like some of them to take a personal interest in some one apprentice by gaining his confidence, becoming his friend and counsellor, and some-times inviting him to tea on Sunday afternoon or supper on Sunday night, and having a talk with him after the Sunday evening service.*
>
> (quoted, France, 1913, 19)

Association members were the respectable, industrious and deferential young men Bainbridge and his ilk admired, and sought to employ. A high proportion, as even the most cursory reading of the Annual Reports will show, were enormously hard working and committed to the welfare of others and the work of the Association. They were young men for whom 'service' involved sacrificing what little spare time they had left over from a working week of around 60 hours. Most appear to have made that sacrifice willingly.

W.M. Richardson resigned from his post as General Secretary of Newcastle YMCA in 1892 to undertake a similar role at the Borough Polytechnic, London. When Lord Rosebery opened the Polytechnic in the same year, he bluffly informed his audience, which included Richardson, 'I do not know much about instruction, but I can claim to be an authority on recreation' (quoted, Hogg, 1904, 241). He then proceeded to tell them that any institution desirous of keeping young men out of public houses was on a hiding-to-nothing if it prohibited smoking, dramatic entertainment and dancing. Poor Rosebery, what he failed to grasp was that excluding such activities would deter the habitue of the public house; but that doing so was essential to ensure the attendance of the young men Mr Richardson knew and loved, the genus whom Richardson spent his life working alongside in Newcastle and elsewhere, and whom he knew so much better than Rosebery.

Conclusion

Membership of Newcastle YMCA grew steadily until it peaked at 812 in 1895. By this time the Association had acquired its own building located at the centre of the city facing Grey's Monument. This was demolished and in 1900 the Association opened a magnificent four storey building on the same site. Equipped with a gymnasium, reading rooms, lounges, restaurant, theatre and a variety of offices and meeting rooms it was in scope and size probably the equal of any non-metropolitan youth facility then operating in Britain, and one suspects now. However despite an enormous expenditure of effort during the years that followed the membership was never sufficient to either justify, or financially sustain, the new premises. During the next century affiliation steadily declined until by the early 1970s the numbers had become so low it was no longer feasible to operate as a membership organisation. Henceforth it ran as a quasi-independent youth agency funded by grants and income generated from rental income provided by the properties it owned. It would be only partially accurate to say that the Association was eventually brought to its knees by the cost of maintaining and financing the building, but that expense did play a major part in bringing about the demise of Newcastle YMCA as a membership organisation, one in which the members determined policy and priorities, rather than funders. In this respect it was not the first, and will certainly not be the last, youth agency to have fallen the victim of an overly ambitious desire to acquire lavish premises.

During the early years of the twentieth century YMCAs around the country increasingly focused attention on work with boys. Indeed both the YMCA nationally and World Alliance did much to encourage such work. Newcastle ignored this trend until after the end of the First World War. At that point members decided to offer a redundant hut they had opened in 1915 for servicemen adjacent to the Central Station as a home for a boys' club. This club was for the younger age group and for those living in the poorer parts of Newcastle. It was a new departure for these two groups had never previously been sought as members by the respectable young men of the Association. As in the past they were to be kept at a physical, as well as a metaphorical, distance. Contact between the YMCA Boys' Club located down by the station, and the Association situated in the heart of the city was minimal. And in that respect the relationship reflected what had gone before and predicated what was to follow. The first fifty years and the second were equally marked by a design to foster a style of youth work that would relate to the experiences of a particular class of young men. At no point did the Association seek to break down class barriers in the way it sought to erode religious ones. However before we become overly judgmental it is perhaps important to remember that in that respect in reflects the history of almost all youth groups and agencies not merely its own.

Notes

1   The date of the meeting was 6 June 1844 the number attending remains a matter of dispute.
2   At the time of writing all those mentioned still operate apart from Oxford and Hull.
3   Arians were followers of Arius, a theologian of the fourth century, who denied the doctrine of consubstantiality, that taught that Christ, although the son of God, was not equal to or of one substance with God. Socinians were followers of the religious doctrines of Laelius Socinus (1525–1562) and Faustus Socinus (1539–1604), two Italian theologians who denied the divinity of Christ and expressed disbelief in the Trinity, in eternal punishment and the personality of the Devil.
4   Of the original 20, apart from Newcastle, only Consett, Darlington and Morpeth still operate in 2009.
5   The Hoppings are a large fair held annually on Newcastle Town Moor. Similar to Goose Fairs held elsewhere and like them historically viewed as being somewhat riotous and boisterous events.

References

Anon. (undated) *The YMCA – What it is and how to Begin It*, London, YMCA.

Barker, E. (1943) 'The YMCA and Adult Education' in *World Association for Adult Education Bulletin* 2nd Series No. 32 (February).

Benson, J. (1989) *British Coalminers in the Nineteenth Century*, London, Longman.

Binfield, C. (1973) *George Williams and the YMCA*, London, Heinemann.

Callcott, M. (2004) 'The Campaign for Public Libraries in Victorian Newcastle', *North East History* (35).

Chamberlain, F.J. (1944) *A Century Not Out, 100 years of YMCA Work in London*, London, YMCA.

Dimmock, F. Hayden (1937) *Bare Knee Days*, London, Boriswood.

France, G. (1913) 'Life and Character' in T.H. Bainbridge *Reminiscences*, Charles H. Kelly.

Hodder, E. (1886) *The Life and Work of the Seventh Earl of Shaftesbury vol. 1*, London, Cassell.

Hodder, E. (1893) *The Life and Work of the Seventh Earl of Shaftesbury*, London, Cassell.

Hogg, E.M. (1904) *Quintin Hogg, A Biography*, London, Archibald, Constable.

Hopkins, E. (1995) *Working-Class Self-Help in Nineteenth Century England*, London, UCL Press.

Hudson, J.W. (1851) *The History of Adult Education*, London, Longman, Brown, Green and Longman [reprinted Woburn Press 1969].

Hugman, J. (2001) 'Print and Preach, The Entrepreneurial Spirit of Nineteenth Century Newcastle' in R. Colls and B. Lancaster (eds.) *Newcastle Upon Tyne, A Modern History*, Chichester, Phillimore.

Jeffs, T. (2005) *Newcastle YMCA 150 Years*, Newcastle, Newcastle YMCA.

Kelly, T. (1970) *A History of Adult Education in Great Britain*, Liverpool, University of Liverpool Press.

Laqueur, T.W. (1976) *Religion and Respectability, Sunday Schools and Working Class Culture 1780–1850*, New Haven, Yale University Press.

Long, J. (1999) *Conversations in a Cold Room: Women, Work and Poverty in Nineteenth Century Northumberland*, Woodbridge, Suffolk, Royal Historical Society/Boydell Press.

Muukkonen, M. (2002) *Ecumenism of the Laity: Continuity and Change in the Mission View of the World's Alliance of YMCAs, 1855–1955*, Helsinki, Joensuu.

Reid, D.B. (1845) 'Appendix on the sanatory (sic) condition of Newcastle' in *Report of the Commissioners for Inquiring into the State of Large Towns and Populous Districts (second report)*.

Rose, J. (2002) *The Intellectual Life of the British Working Classes*, New Haven, Yale University Press.

Todd, N. (1991) *The Militant Democrat, Joseph Cowen and Victorian Radicalism*, Whitley Bay, Berwick Press.

Williams, J.E. Hodder (1906) *The Life of Sir George Williams*, London, Hodder and Stoughton.

Woolf, V. (1967) 'Middlebrow' in *Collected Essays Vol. 2*, New York, Harcourt, Brace.

Primary sources:

Annual Reports of Newcastle YMCA 1864–1900

Minute Books of Newcastle YMCA (incomplete) and ephemera retained in the Association archive such as posters, programmes, photographs and advertisements

Minutes of the YMCA British Conferences

Newcastle YMCA Magazine 1895–1896
Northern Times 12 November 1858
Daily Leader 25 July 1885
Newcastle Daily Journal 24 July 1896
Newcastle Evening Chronicle 6 August 1896
Newcastle Evening Chronicle 1 December 1899

YMCA Blackett Street, 1881

CHAPTER 10

Familiar Rooms in Foreign Fields: Placing the 'BB Atmosphere' in The Boys' Brigade's Recreation Hut, Rouen, France, 1915–1919

Richard G. Kyle

When I'm among a Blaze of Lights,
With tawdry music and cigars
And women dawdling through delights,
And officers in cocktail bars,
Sometimes I think of garden nights
And elm trees nodding at the stars.

I dream of a small firelit room
With yellow candles burning straight,
And glowing pictures in the gloom,
And kindly books that hold me late.
Of these things I choose to think
When I can never be alone,
Then someone says 'Another drink?'
And turns my living heart to stone.

(Siegfried Sassoon (1886–1967) *When I'm among a Blaze of Lights*)

The Great War began for Britain on 4 August 1914 when war was declared on Germany. A few days later, Field Marshal Lord Kitchener became Minister of War. Taking a position contrary to popular opinion, that famously suggested the war would be over by Christmas, Kitchener forecast a conflict lasting at least three years and calculated that a larger army was required. To this end, he proposed to build a 'New Army' from the civilian population to augment the professional full-time regulars and part-time Territorials that was the sum of the British Army at the time. Thus, a Bill sanctioning Kitchener's plan to raise half a million men forming 18 new divisions was promptly passed by Parliament and by the end of the month Kitchener had made his appeal for the 'First Hundred Thousand' (Middlebrook, 1984, 5).

Seven months after Kitchener's appeal for men, the Executive Committee of the Boys' Brigade (BB) launched their own. As 'an opportunity of showing in a practical way their appreciation of the splendid services which such a vast number of their old Comrades are rendering their country and the cause of humanity and righteousness at the present time' (*BB Gazette* 1 March 1915, 98) the Executive proposed to establish a BB Recreation Hut in co-operation with the YMCA, 'for the benefit of the troops generally and Old Boys of The Boys' Brigade in particular' (*ibid.*, 99), roughly 100,000 of whom would enlist during the first year of the war (Springhall *et al.*, 1983, 106). Estimating the cost of the Hut to be £500, an appeal for funds was launched through the pages of the BB's monthly publication for Officers, the *Gazette*, on 1 March 1915.[1] By 16 April, £1,232 had been raised from about a seventh of all BB Companies – all were expected (and reminded monthly) to contribute (*BB Gazette* 1 May 1915, 130).[2] The target was met almost three times over and on 1 May the *Gazette* proudly reported that 'the scheme [had become] an accomplished fact' (*ibid.*); a BB Recreation Hut had been established at a base infantry camp (Peacock, 1915, 132) about four miles from Rouen – an important stopping point both for troops arriving from home and those returning from the front.

Although military restrictions prevented the opening of a second hut on the continent at Havre (*BB Gazette* 1 September 1915, 2) contributions to the appeal continued to rise. On 1 September 1915, £2,719 – over five times the original target – had been raised. This allowed the Executive to proceed with plans to open a Hut in Britain. Thus, and again in co-operation with the YMCA, a second Recreation Hut in Edinburgh was officially opened on 1 February 1916 (*BB Gazette* 1 February 1916, 82). Located adjacent to Princes Street (*BB Gazette* 1 January 1916, 66), the city's main thoroughfare, between, and within a few minutes of, the two railway stations (*BB Gazette* 1 November 1916, 33), the Hut provided reasonably priced accommodation and refreshment to the many soldiers and sailors passing through the city and its stations (Springhall *et al.*, 1983, 108).[3]

At the same time as the initial call for funds was made, a call for staff was also issued:

An important feature of the scheme is the personnel of the Staff at the Hut. It is hoped that it will be entirely manned by present and past Officers of the Brigade, and offers of such service for periods of not less than one month will be gladly received. No more splendid or more useful field of service could be conceived, and no one ought to be better suited to it than the experienced and efficient BB Officer.

Those offering their services should state their age, any past experience of similar work, and any accomplishments, such as singing, playing, or other form of entertaining. Even ability to cook will be taken into account in selecting staff.

(BB Gazette 1 March 1915, 98)

By September the military insisted the service period be extended to a minimum of three months (*BB Gazette* 1 September 1915, 2) and that BB Officers should be above military age (*ibid.*) or disqualified from active service – a point made clear the following month. Reflecting the opinion of many soldiers who believed that some at home were 'slacking' from their duty or profiting from their absence, an author writing in the *Gazette* notes '[t]he soldier is inclined to look askance at physically fit men, other than ministers, between the ages of 20 and 35' (*BB Gazette* 1 October 1915, 21). Appeals for staff continued in the pages of the *Gazette* throughout the War yet on 1 January 1916 the constant changing of personnel disliked by the military (*BB Gazette* 1 September 1915, 2) was, at least in part, abated by Rev. A.H.H. Organ's decision to leave his Church in Pontypridd to take permanent charge of the Recreation Hut in Rouen (*BB Gazette* 1 January 1916, 66). Organ, previously Captain of the 2nd Pontypridd Company and secretary of Pontypridd District Battalion, clearly fits the staff profile repeatedly outlined in the pages of the *Gazette*.

Having raised £2,820 through the first appeal (*BB Gazette* 1 November 1916a, 31) a decision was taken by October of 1916 that a second appeal was required (*BB Gazette* 1 October 1916, 22) in order to extend and maintain both the Hut in Rouen and that in Edinburgh (*BB Gazette* 1 November 1916a, 32). The following month this appeal was launched and once again every company was encouraged to co-operate. Indeed, in January 1917 the *Gazette* put this in no uncertain terms when it stated that '[i]f a Company fails to support heartily such a scheme as this the failure is not the Boys', it is the Officer's failure in not placing it before his boys in the right way – or in omitting to do so at all' (*BB Gazette* 1 January 1917, 54). By the time a third appeal was sanctioned by the Brigade Council meeting in Birmingham in the autumn of

1918 approximately the same sum of money, as had been elicited by the first appeal, had been raised for the second (*BB Gazette* 1 November 1918, 26).[4]

Although the procedure for the redistribution of funds in the event of the cessation of conflict had been put in place at the launch of the second appeal (*ibid.* 1 November 1916a, 32) it was hoped that this third appeal would be the last (*ibid.* 1 November 1918, 26). It was. The Armistice was signed on 11 November 1918, just ten days after the *Gazette* reported the launch of the third appeal, yet the appeal for men and money continued. Despite being informed that the Rouen Hut would have to close in April the following year the BB was requested to carry on its work with the army of occupation (*BB Gazette* 1 March 1919, 80). Deciding to accept the YMCA's invitation, the BB duly 'follow[ed] the boys into one of the Rhine towns' (*BB Gazette* 1 April 1919, 87); it transpired that their new 'home' was to be Cologne (Wilson, 1919, 12).

Placing the 'BB atmosphere'

Brief mentions of the story of the BB Recreation Hut can be found in several documented histories of the BB (see Birch, 1959, 54–55; Peacock, 1954, 138; Springhall *et al.*, 1983, 108) and, on one level, by delving further into the archive this chapter is an attempt to deepen and enliven these accounts. Indeed, it is an intriguing line following one description of the Hut that serves as this chapter's springboard. Springhall *et al.* in their comprehensive history of the BB's first century write that the hut in France was, 'intended to be as similar as possible to the club rooms which so many companies ran' (1983, 108). On the surface, this is an innocuous statement, to be sure, but one which becomes curious when two questions are asked of it: why was this important, and more crucially, how was this effected? Arguably what Springhall *et al.* are hinting towards is a process of *translation*, translation not only over space, but also across time; the folding of past ordinary events in familiar rooms into extraordinary lifecourses that had led, through war, to individuals finding themselves in foreign fields.

Through sharing answers to these questions this essay aims to make explicit the implied process Springhall *et al.* pinpoint. It contends that this translation was effected through the re-creation of that which is a constant presence in the various tellings of the story of the life of the Hut through the pages of the *Gazette*, the 'BB Atmosphere'. I argue, though, that far from being something ethereal – 'just there' – the 'BB Atmosphere' was *materially* re-created in this place through the purposive manipulation of the Hut itself and more specifically the objects and bodies present. By doing so I suggest that the 'BB

Atmosphere' played a distinct role, through relocation; taking 'Old Boys' back to those familiar rooms, at home and in their past, memory rekindled does the work of engendering anew the influence infused within those Club Rooms, re-equipping them to meet the temptations of a large camp which are, as it will be discovered, perceived to be not too dissimilar to those of the city upon which the provision of Club Rooms first rested.

On another level, then, thinking through this episode in the BB's history from a different, *geographical*, perspective provides a lens through which to start teasing out the distinct and various spatialities in the histories of youth work in Britain and abroad; broader aims that seek to make strides in a nascent field of research enquiry. First steps towards this, though, are taken by returning to Rouen, and crossing the Hut's threshold.

Returning to Rouen

Roger Peacock, reporting his visit to Rouen in the *Gazette*, provides a first glimpse inside the Recreation Hut:

> [T]he B.B. Hut [. . .] consists of two large separate halls, connected by a short passage. The halls measure about 120 feet by 50 feet, and there are also a number of other rooms for the Staff – a kitchen, lavatories etc. All these are lighted by electric light, with which the whole of the Camps are illuminated. The larger of the halls is the club room, open most of the day. It is provided with tables and chairs for reading and writing, and at one end there is a long counter at which refreshments are served and the various needs of the men catered for . . . The adjoining hall is a concert hall, where the nightly entertainment and services on Sunday are held. It is provided with a platform and a piano, and every evening there is an entertainment of some sort.
>
> (1 May 1915, 132; added emphasis)

As accurate as this description of the internal geography of the Hut may be, it remains lifeless. Later in Peacock's own report, and especially in subsequent *Gazette* articles, life is breathed into the Hut through the recollection of small episodes in its history; Christmas celebrations are reported (*BB Gazette* 1 February 1916, 85), pen portraits of those passing through its doors are drawn (Organ, 1917, 55), and meetings of 'Old Boys' over tea recorded (*BB Gazette* 1 September 1917, 9). Some episodes are tragic:

> Then there was Sergeant Rice from 1st Stoke-under-Ham Company. Though only nineteen, and boyish for that, he had already won his

Sergeant's stripes in the army as well. A letter from his BB Captain told me he was lying seriously wounded at a hospital a few miles away. Twice I was able to get over to see him, where I found he had been lying on his back for two months. While spending an hour together over cups of tea, he would tell me, as far as his strength would allow him, of his old Company and how he longed to get on crutches and come to see the BB Hut of which he had heard so much. Not one murmur of complaint all the time. Once he spoke of some day getting back to the old home in Blighty and helping his Captain with the old Company; but God in His mercy had prepared for him a better country and a higher service, and the BB has another sacred grave-spot in France.

(Organ, 1917, 55)

Others are mildly comedic:

On one occasion a newly-arrived Scottie handed me a five franc note and demanded two penny [refreshment] tickets. As change he received a franc note on the Ville de Rouen, a half-franc note on the Ville de Boulogne, an English shilling, a postal order for 6d., a Swiss half-franc piece, two penny stamps, a 25c. nickel, two French pennies, and seven sous of assorted nationalities. He stared indignantly at the change and demanded English money. I invited him to 'search me', and as he grasped the situation the suspicious frown slowly melted into a pleasant smile.

As a rule the English and Irish lads take their change with the casual nonchalance that distinguishes them, and sometimes move away before they have received the half of what is due to them, and have to be called back. But Jock blocks the way until he has counted his twice over!

(*BB Gazette* 1 September 1915, 5)

The playing out of national stereotypes within the Hut aside, what shines through all writing on the Hut is the emphasis on the 'BB Atmosphere'. Repeatedly this is perceived to be something that sets the BB Hut apart within the camp as a unique space within which individual soldiers, such as Sergeant Rice, 'long' to spend time. Yet, as already hinted towards, arguably this is something that the space itself makes; or, more accurately, the 'BB Atmosphere' is (re)created through the manipulation of space.

(Re)creating 'atmosphere'

In an article entitled 'An Old Boys' testimony to the BB Hut at Rouen' an unnamed 'Old Boy'[5] writes:

I was in the billiard room last night, and I soon spotted the BB photographs which decorate the walls. It did me a world of good to see those happy faces again. 'Cheero', we too are trying to 'keep smiling', but it would be a trifle easier if our tents were away back on the familiar old camp field, and we dwelt again in that sweet-scented meadow by the sea instead of in the mud of France.

(*BB Gazette* 1 May 1917, 104)

Display of 'things BB' was central to this manipulation. And not only photographs. A portrait of the Founder – Sir William Alexander Smith – found its way onto the walls (Peacock, 1915, 133) and from early in the Hut's life a list of Companies contributing funds to the hut was displayed (*BB Gazette* 1 April 1915, 114). At Old Boys' teas held on Sunday afternoons:

The annual report, with the Boys in BB Uniform on the cover, was of great interest. Men were glad to see the names of their old Companies there. Some were delighted to find that the man who had been Captain in their time was still in command; and others found, with regret, that their old Company was extinct or that the same number was now that of a different Company, connected with another Church.

(*BB Gazette* 1 September 1917, 9)

Although at the outset the division served by the camp in which the Hut was situated did not include any Territorials or 'New Army' troops (see above; *BB Gazette* 1 October 1915, 21) over time the Visitor's book, to be signed by Old Boys (Peacock, 1915, 133), slowly filled and by November 1916 it held over 1,000 names (Organ, 1916, 32). Two months earlier, Territorials and New Army troops began to pass through the Recreation Hut and the proportion of Old Boys began to increase and the Old Boys' tea instituted (*ibid.*).[6] Yet, where the aforementioned displays could be said to *reconnect* the ex-BB member with the BB back home, Old Boys' teas were concerned also with *relocation*; quite literally 'taking them back' to another time and place:

On a recent Sunday no fewer than twenty-five ex-members crowded into our new writing room, and were welcomed by Mr Organ, who acted as host. After grace, sung in true camp fashion, each man was asked to name his old BB Company. [. . .] During the next half-hour the war, which in one or other of its many aspects, usually occupies all our minds, was absolutely forgotten. Some went back two years, some twenty years, to their old BB days, old camp experiences, old picnics, old drills, and old Bible-Classes were brought to our minds once more. Long-forgotten scenes were revived and vivid accounts were given of how the — th — Company had for the — th time won the — Cup.

(*BB Gazette* 1 September 1917, 9)

Two cards were given to each 'Old Boy' at the close of the tea. Emblazoned with the BB anchor the first headed 'To Old Boys serving in the Forces' expressed the gratitude of boys at home for the service of those in France before paragraphs expressing bravery, determination, mercy, chivalry, patience and cheerfulness.[7] It ended 'May you at all times be true to the best which is in you and loyal to the King of Kings' (*BB Gazette* 1 September 1917, 9). The second contained the message; 'Greetings from Officers and Boys of the BB to their old comrades in admiration of their devotion and self-sacrifice, and in glorious memory of those who have fallen' (*ibid.*). Both cards served to reconnect the Old Boys to home but also to the Hut and their time spent there somewhere else.

Yet, the Hut itself was about more than reconnection and relocation, it fulfilled its name fully, its mission was also recreation, or rather, re-creation. It was, to trace the etymology of the word from its Latin roots (*recreatio*) through its Old French incarnation (*recreare*), about 'creating again and renewing' (Pearsall, 2001, 1198). And not simply connections, but character,

> *The BB Atmosphere and the renewal of old associations meant a deal to them, and during their stay the Hut became their own club room. The brotherhood of the BB, the friendships formed and cemented at Brigade Council meetings between Officers from all parts of the kingdom, proved their value here. During the less busy periods, when handing a cup of tea, say, to a lad wearing the badge of the Blankshires, we would ask, 'Do you come from A —, or B —, or C —' naming the chief towns of the county. 'From C —, sir' might be the reply. We then mentioned some of the best-known officers of the C — Battalion, and in many cases they would be recognised. A kind of introduction being thus effected, the lads would be only too happy to talk of their towns and homes, would appreciate the interest shown, and would be linked to the life of the Hut, so that they and their chums would henceforth spend all their spare time within its influence.*

(*BB Gazette* 1 October 1915, 21; added emphasis)

In being modelled as closely as possible on the club room (see also Springhall *et al.*, 1983, 108) and, in fact, becoming it (see also Peacock 1915, 132), it could be speculated that it was hoped the values imbued in that space – values designed to influence character – would be re-created in France through its transportation. Yet, in order to understand this further we must ourselves take leave of the Hut in France, and turn our attention to the Club Room itself, and, particularly, the construction of the city upon which its existence is founded.

Club rooms

Also known as the 'Boys' Room', the 'Club Room' was first introduced as a feature of the BB's work during the second session of the 1st Glasgow Company (Shaw, 1983, 24). An 1884 report of the Free College Church, to which the North Woodside Mission Hall the home of the 1st in Glasgow's West End was connected, records the motivation behind its introduction. On that occasion the founder noted:

> *The Officers had long been conscious of the demoralising effect upon the boys of hanging about at night, for want of any better place to go. They accordingly made application to the Deacon's Court and were cordially granted the sole use of a large room in the Mission buildings. This room is now brightly and tastefully, though plainly, furnished; is supplied with games, papers and attractive periodicals and books and is open every night in the week. It really forms the 'home' of the Company and very pleasing it is to drop in of an evening and find the boys taking full advantage of it, some sitting quietly reading, others playing games and others sitting around the fire discussing matters in which they may be interested.*

> (Smith, quoted Springhall *et al.*, 1983, 58)

That this somewhat romantic and peaceful portrait was replicated throughout the BB is perhaps doubtful. Springhall *et al.* go on to suggest that the scene at the 26th Edinburgh Company may have been more typical:

> *We are occasionally treated to a musical 'turn' by Jock Stewart who plays on his wooden crackers, the noise of which annoys the boys studying a game of draughts.*

> (quoted Springhall *et al.*, 1983, 58)

Club Rooms quickly became an important, and popular, feature of the BB's work in Glasgow prior to the Great War. Inaugurated in 1899, the Recreation Committee of Glasgow Battalion fostered their development by encouraging Companies to participate in team and individual draughts competitions (Shaw, 1983, 24). Over time the popularity of the competitions waned, yet the future of the Boys' Room as a 'helpful adjunct to the ordinary work of a Company' was secured (McClure, 1911, 15). A similar story presents itself within the BB nationally. Between 1907 (the year when statistics on Boys' Rooms started to be reported) and the outbreak of conflict between 37 per cent and 41 per cent of all Companies operated such rooms. While statistics evidence the popularity of this branch of the BB's work they cannot reach the underpinning imagined geography of the city upon which its provision rests. Uncovering this construction requires one to delve into the archives once more.

Imagining the city

Smith notes of Boys' Rooms:

> *Acting on the principle that 'Satan finds some mischief still for idle hands to do', the Brigade seeks so to occupy the time and interest of its Boys, that there shall be no room for the entry of that evil spirit who is ever on the alert to take possession of the empty heart and life. And, so, on the nights that are not occupied by Drill, Ambulance,[8] gymnastics, or anything of a definite nature, it is becoming increasingly common to open a 'Boys' Room' which is made as bright and attractive as possible, and is furnished with games, books, papers and periodicals, where the Boys may spend the winter nights with pleasure and profit under the influence of their Officers, instead of running wild about the street.*
>
> (1893, 15–16)

The rhetoric of evil, particularly in relation to idleness, is no surprise to the scholar of the late-Victorian era, yet, in this, and subsequent reports in later years, personified evil is *placed*; Satan lurks in the busy (McClure, 1912, 15), crowded (Smith, 1898, 18) urban[9] streets and particularly on street-corners from where 'he' tempts young men (Smith, 1894, 18), leading them astray (Smith, 1896, 20). The Boys' Room, then, served as a 'counter-attraction to the evils of the streets' (Smith, 1892, 59) yet not only as a 'space' to keep young men off the streets temporarily but one in which, through influence, Satan's temptation outwith the space was rendered ineffective. In other words, provision of Boys' Rooms was concerned not only with the containment of bodies in one space rather than another, but was also motivated by a desire to influence minds. As Smith suggests:

> *Acting on the principle that the best way to keep evil out of a Boy's life is to fill his thoughts and interests with all that is good and pure and true, the Brigade is not content with stated meetings for various purposes on particular nights of the week, but in a great many Companies seek to*

provide something profitable for the spare evenings as well, by opening what is known as the Boys' Room.

(Smith, 1895, 17–18)

Control of time was therefore crucial. At no point should 'the Boy' be outside the influence, a point made clear the following year:

Officers of the Brigade are realising more and more that much of the work they endeavour to do will be nullified by adverse influences, unless they can provide a continual counter-attraction to the evils of the streets.

(Smith, 1896, 19)

Boys' Rooms, then, were perhaps more than a useful adjunct to the BB Company. Instead, Smith considered them to be a crucial keystone which, if removed, allowed all other building blocks to fall, or at very least significantly reduced their efficacy. Questions remain, however, regarding exactly how positive influences seeped into the boys spending time within their walls.

Influence infused

The Boys' Room was set up to be 'the most wholesome surroundings, where every influence for good may be brought to bear upon them' (Smith, 1898, 18). Literature as a good wholesome influence was central. In 1901 the Boys' Room was first referred to as a Reading and Recreation Room and by 1906 Boys' Libraries as 'a useful and helpful adjunct to the Boys' Room' (Smith, 1906, 16) were first mentioned, under a separate heading in the annual report of Brigade Executive, in the following quote 'small Library of well-selected Boys' Books' (*ibid.*) was designed to '[play] an important role in regulating and guiding their reading' (*ibid.*). One could imagine the contents of the book-shelves. Perhaps, though, we need not, because a similar library was set up in the Recreation Hut in Rouen. When a call for 'wholesome literature' was made by Rev. Walter Mursell on 1 November 1917 after a visit to the Hut, in addition to a case of books he himself sent out, 'a set of Dickens' and Thackeray's novels, three volumes of Shakespeare, Green's *History of the English People* [and] Macauley's *Essays* had been sent' (*BB Gazette* 1 March 1918, 85). This gives an indication of the type of literature designed to 'encourage the Boys to read, and cultivate among them a taste for good healthy literature' (Smith, 1912, 19) within the Boys' Rooms. Yet, literature and games such as draughts, were not the only tactics employed to achieve influence over the Boys; central also was knowledge of the individual.

The belief that knowledge *of* the individual equated with influence *over* the individual is most clearly set out by Smith in 1899. Here he notes:

> As a means of getting to know their Boys more thoroughly, and, consequently having more opportunity of influencing their lives and characters, Officers are finding that there is no more helpful agency than the 'Boys' Room' which has become almost a sine qua non in a well-organised Company.

(Smith, 1899, 16)

Although following the death of William Smith in 1914 this equation was played down (perhaps saying more about the role of the annual report's author, the Brigade Secretary, than a change in underpinning motivation) at its inception it was central, as repeated statements in the report echoing that above testify.[10]

In short, Club Rooms were designed not simply as a diversion *from* the streets but, through the manipulation of the space (i.e., the presence/absence of objects [eg., books] or bodies [eg., Officers]) as a tactic in the influence of character, a direct challenge *to* the streets and the evil perceived to be contained therein; the space served to create young men able to resist the 'evil city's' temptations. And, so, just as the body must be taken away from immoral spaces the mind must be purged of any desire to enter them in the first place; the Boys Room – *as a discipline* – is not only corporal but also carceral.

Conclusion: familiar rooms in foreign fields

This essay's starting point was a simple proposition, that in order to fully understand the underpinning motivation behind the BB's provision of a Recreation Hut in Rouen during the Great War one cannot simply explore the life of the Hut in its foreign field. Instead, acknowledging that such provision rests upon a process of translation, the familiar rooms upon which the Hut was modelled need also to be explicated. By carefully carrying out such an unfolding of the operation of Club Rooms and their *raison d'etre*, this chapter has argued that from the first Club Rooms were not only conceived as a temporary counter-attraction to the streets but a direct, continual, and ideally permanent, challenge to the temptation perceived to reside there through the subtle exertion of influence over the boys spending time within them. Arguably, what infuses these Rooms is the 'BB Atmosphere' that later becomes a constant presence in writings about the life of the Hut in France. The 'BB atmosphere' is not, therefore, unique to the Hut. Instead, it has already been known, experienced and 'felt' by those 'Old Boys' in their Club Rooms. It is re-created through the purposive manipulation of the Hut itself, a space made in the Club Rooms' image.

Though shedding light on this process of translation, that in turn stresses the importance of supplementing accounts of episodes in the history of youth work with those exhibiting a spatial sensibility, one of the two questions posed at the chapter's outset remains unanswered, why was ensuring the Hut was 'as similar as possible to the Club Room' (Springhall *et al.*, 1983, 108) so important? The answer is arrived at through an excavation of the imagined geographies of the city and camp upon which the provision of Club Room and Recreation Hut respectively rest. Put simply, ensuring this similarity assisted the aforementioned process of overcoming temptation. As outlined above, Club Rooms are constructed not only *through* a discourse of 'evil as temptation', but against a placed 'evil other', Satan lurking on city streets. In France, however, it is not the temptations of the city but those of a large camp which are to be allayed. George Barclay, in a report to Roger Peacock of 5 October 1915, writes:

> At a time when the fierce and cruel temptations of a large camp are making themselves felt; it is no small service to remind Old Boys of the things that they were once taught in The Old Company.
>
> (quoted Springhall *et al.*, 1983, 108)

That this was indeed the express purpose of the Hut in France should not be downplayed. It is worth recalling that shortly after the establishment of the Hut at Rouen a second in France at Havre was planned, yet prevented by military restrictions. Clearly, combating such 'cruel' temptations of large military camps on the continent was considered desirable. It is however, in the decision to follow the YMCA into Cologne after the Armistice that this rationale becomes clear. In a report of the decision in the *Gazette* it is noted:

> Now that the fighting is over, the Boys have much more spare time on their hands, and there are many temptations all around, so we must get there quickly to help them. Funds are urgently required if the work which has been so well done during the past four years is to be continued, so do not let us think that because there is no fighting there is no need to trouble. Our Boys were safer from many of the temptations during the four years of war than they will be now, away from home with little to occupy their time.
>
> (*BB Gazette* 1 April 1919, 87)

And, so, we are back in the Club Room of a city Company; productively occupying free time to save idle hands from turning to the devil's work. Before drawing the chapter to a close, though, there is time for one final reflection. Perhaps what Sassoon sought in the poem with which the chapter began, the BB, in a roundabout fashion, aimed to provide. When among a blaze of lights, Sassoon dreams of a personal heaven, or at the very least something that takes him to a haven far from the setting in which he finds himself. Snapped out of his reverie, the reality of the world – a personal Hell – closes in around him once more. But he is left with a memory of having been momentarily elsewhere. And it is this which sustains, strengthens, and renews. So amidst talk of influence, control even, within the BB's Recreation Hut we must strike a balance between this and an acute need to escape, if only for a short while, the Hell of warfare.

Notes

1   At this time *The Boys' Brigade Gazette* was published on the first day of each month between September and June, the BB session.
2   The Gazette of 1 May 1915 records that just over 200 companies had contributed by this date (*BB Gazette* 1 May 1915, 130). At the close of the previous session (i.e., 31 May 1914) the Annual Report of The BB records 1,360 companies in operation (Wilson, 1914).
3   Trains were met by staff from the Hut and troops encouraged to make use of the Hut before making their onward journey (*BB Gazette* 1 November 1916b, 33). Indeed, William Hudson recounting his experience of a night's service at the Hut in the *Gazette* a year after its opening details the instructions he was given before conducting this task, 'It is now time to meet the London Train. Mr —— goes with you and two boys in uniform. Here is a badge that will be your warrant. Don't be shy. Ask any men in khaki who seems to be all at sea if he wishes supper and bed. You'll do all right' (Hudson, 1917, 67). He did, picking up ten men that night yet, on occasion, 50 were 'recruited' for the Hut in this manner (*ibid.*).
4   Brigade Council is an annual peripatetic gathering and decision-making forum for BB Officers.
5   The anonymous nature of this letter may suggest possible fabrication. This possibility must be weighed, however, against the perception within a Christian organisation that such a manoeuvre would be regarded as unethical. The protection of identity may therefore be a more plausible explanation. Yet, this ambiguity highlights that all such articles quoted herein are, of course, only one side of the BB Recreation Hut and are particularly, and admittedly somewhat cynically, presented to ensure continued support for the Hut at home.
6   In an address given to Brigade Council, meeting in Glasgow, Rev. A.H.H. Organ notes that Old Boys' Teas were experimented with just prior to his leave (Organ, 1916, 32).
7   Since its founding in 1883 the anchor has been the emblem of The BB and excepting the addition of the Geneva Cross at the amalgamation of The BB with The Boys' Life Brigade in 1926 and a more recent change in the spelling of the word 'Stedfast' the image remains largely unaltered. The use of both this symbol, and the motto 'Sure & Stedfast', derives from Hebrews 6, 19 in the King James Bible; 'Which hope we have as an anchor of the soul both sure and

stedfast'. Note the emblem's prominence on the Recreation Hut in Rouen and its presence alongside the YMCA's 'Triangle' in Edinburgh.

8 Ambulance is an early name for First Aid.

9 The 'evils of the streets' (Smith, 1896, 19) of cities are usually referred to, yet in 1899, Smith remarks of Boys' Rooms; 'It would be difficult to imagine a better counter-attraction to the temptations of the streets in our large cities *and even in our country villages*' (Smith, 1899, 16; added emphasis).

10 For example, in 1915 Smith's son Douglas Pearson Smith, interim Brigade Secretary, notes that the Boys' Room 'is found to be a very helpful agency in counteracting the influences of the streets, and gives the Officers the opportunity of getting alongside their Boys in an informal way, and consequently getting to know them more thoroughly' (Smith, 1915, 21). H. Arnold Wilson five years later remarks that it 'affords a valuable opportunity for informal intercourse between Officers and Boys' (Wilson, 1920, 12) whereas Charles Guthrie and J.A. Roxburgh note that 'Officers find that it gives them an opportunity of understanding Boys who they might otherwise never get to know well' going on to note that 'apart from everything else, the Boys' Room provides an effective counter-attraction to the streets' (Guthrie and Roxburgh, 1916, 19).

References

Articles quoted from the *Boys' Brigade Gazette* no author cited:

[1 March] 1915 'A Boys' Brigade Recreation Hut in France' vol. 23 (7), 98–99.

[1 April] 1915 'The Boys' Brigade Recreation Hut in France' vol. 23 (8), 114.

[1 May] 1915 'The B.B. Recreation Huts in France' vol. 23 (9), 130–131.

[1 September] 1915 'The Boys' Brigade Recreation Hut in Rouen' vol. 24 (1), 2.

[1 October] 1915 'The Boys' Brigade Recreation Hut in Rouen' vol. 24 (1), 21.

[1 January] 1916 'B.B. Recreation Huts' vol. 24 (5), 66–67.

[1 February] 1916 'B.B. Recreation Huts' vol. 24 (6), 82.

[1 October] 1916 'B.B. Huts' vol. 25 (2), 22.

[1 November] 1916a 'BB Recreation Huts, Second Appeal to the Boys' vol. 25 (3), 1–32.

[1 November] 1916b 'The Boys' Brigade Rest Hut, Edinburgh' vol. 25 (3), 33.

[1 January] 1917 'BB Recreation Huts' vol. 25 (1), 54.

[1 May] 1917 'An Old Boys' testimony to the B.B. Hut at Rouen' vol. 25 (9), 104.

[1 September] 1917 'Ex-members in France, An "Old Boys" Tea at the B.B. Hut' vol. 26 (1), 9.

[1 March] 1918 'The Boys' Brigade Hut at Rouen' vol. 26 (7), 85.

[1 November] 1918 'Boys' Brigade Recreation Huts, Third Appeal to the Boys' vol. 27 (3), 26.

[1 March] 1919 'The Boys' Brigade Hut at Rouen' vol. 27 (7), 80.

[1 April] 1919 'The Boys' Brigade Hut at Rouen' vol. 27 (8), 87.

Birch, A. (1959) *The Story of The Boys' Brigade*, London, Frederick Muller.

Guthrie, C.J. and Roxburgh, J.A. (1922) 'Report of Brigade Executive' *The Boys' Brigade Annual Report 33rd Year, 1915–16*, London, The Boys' Brigade.

Hudson, W. (1917) 'War-Time Duty, A Night at the Mound in Edinburgh' *The Boys' Brigade Gazette* vol. 25 (6), 66–67.

McClure, A. (1911) 'Report of the Executive' *The Boys' Brigade Glasgow Battalion Twenty-sixth Annual Report, 1910–1911*, Glasgow, The Boys' Brigade Glasgow Battalion.

McClure, A. (1912) 'Report of the Executive' *The Boys' Brigade Glasgow Battalion Twenty-seventh Annual Report, 1911–1912*, Glasgow, The Boys' Brigade Glasgow Battalion.

Middlebrook, M. (1984) *The First Day on the Somme, 1 July 1916* Harmondsworth, Penguin.

Organ, A.H.H. (1916) 'The Boys' Brigade Hut at Rouen, Address delivered at Brigade Council Meeting in Glasgow' *The Boys' Brigade Gazette* vol. 25 (3), 32–33.

Organ, A.H.H. (1917a) 'The Boys' Brigade Recreation Hut at Rouen, A letter from Mr Organ, 17th December 1917' *The Boys' Brigade Gazette* vol. 25 (5), 55.

Peacock, R.S. (1915) 'With the Expeditionary Force, The First B.B. Recreation Hut in France' *The Boys' Brigade Gazette* Vol. 23 (9), 132–3.

Peacock, R.S. (1919) 'Report of Brigade Executive' *The Boys' Brigade Annual Report 36th Year, 1918–9*, London, The Boys' Brigade.

Peacock, R.S. (1954) *Pioneer of Boyhood, Story of Sir William A. Smith, Founder of The Boys' Brigade*, London, The Boys' Brigade.

Pearsall, J. (2001) *The Concise Oxford Dictionary (10th edition)*, Oxford, Oxford University Press.

Sassoon, S. (1961) *Collected Poems 1908–1956*, London, Faber and Faber.

Shaw, J.B. (1983) *The Glasgow Battalion of The Boys' Brigade, 1883–1983*, Edinburgh, St. Andrew Press.

Smith, D.P. (1915) 'Report of Brigade Executive' *The Boys' Brigade Annual Report 32nd Year, 1914–15*, London, The Boys' Brigade.

Smith, W.A. (1892) 'Report of Executive Committee' *The Boys' Brigade Eighth Annual Report, 1891–92*, Glasgow, The Boys' Brigade.

Smith, W.A. (1893) 'Report of Executive Committee' *The Boys' Brigade Ninth Annual Report, 1892–1893*, Glasgow, The Boys' Brigade.

Smith, W.A. (1894) 'Report of Executive Committee' *The Boys' Brigade Tenth Annual Report, 1893–94*, Glasgow, The Boys' Brigade.

Smith, W.A. (1895) 'Report of Executive Committee' *The Boys' Brigade Eleventh Annual Report, 1894–95*, Glasgow, The Boys' Brigade.

Smith, W.A. (1896) 'Report of Executive Committee' *The Boys' Brigade Twelfth Annual Report, 1895–96*, Glasgow, The Boys' Brigade.

Smith, W.A. (1898) 'Report of Brigade Executive' *The Boys' Brigade Fourteenth Annual Report, 1897–88*, Glasgow, The Boys' Brigade.

Smith, W.A. (1899) 'Report of Brigade Executive' *The Boys' Brigade Fifteenth Annual Report, 1898–99*, Glasgow, The Boys' Brigade.

Smith, W.A. (1906) 'Report of Brigade Executive' *The Boys' Brigade Annual Report 23rd Year, 1905–06*, Glasgow, The Boys' Brigade.

Smith, W.A. (1912) 'Report of Brigade Executive' *The Boys' Brigade Annual Report 29th Year, 1911–12*, Glasgow, The Boys' Brigade.

Springhall, J., Fraser, B. and Hoare, M. (1983) *Sure and Stedfast, A History of The Boys' Brigade, 1883–1983*, Glasgow, Collins.

Wilson, H.A. (1914) 'Report of Brigade Executive' *The Boys' Brigade Annual Report 31st Year, 1913–14*, London, The Boys' Brigade.

Wilson, H.A. (1919) 'Report of Brigade Executive' *The Boys' Brigade Annual Report 36th Year, 1918–19*, London, The Boys' Brigade.

Wilson, H.A. (1920) 'Report of Brigade Executive' *The Boys' Brigade Annual Report 37th Year, 1919–20*, London, The Boys' Brigade.

CHAPTER 11

T.R. Batten's Life and Work

George Lovell

Dr Thomas Reginald Batten was a rare individual who discerned revolutionary ways of approaching, educating and working with ordinary people for betterment. He practised those ways extensively in many countries of the world and profoundly influenced the praxis of educationalists, community development and youth workers and academics internationally. For over thirty years I was closely associated with Reg, as he was affectionately known, and Madge, his wife and colleague. They were my tutors and mentors. I attended their twelve-week 'Community Development and Extension Work' course with a group of international students in 1967. Reg supervised my doctoral studies (Lovell, 1973) and became a consultant partner and colleague in my subsequent work up to the mid 1990s. In this chapter I draw upon this privileged experience and his many writings to sketch out his life and work.

Batten's life spanned most of the twentieth century. He was born in Wimbledon on the 30 November 1904 and died in a local hospital on the 27 January 1999 at the age of 94 years (see Craig and Mayo, 1999 for an appreciation of his life and work). His brilliant mind and his deeply compassionate and truly humble nature infused his life long commitment to the holistic development of underprivileged and under educated people and communities the world over. He followed a first in history at Oxford with a Diploma in Education. Subsequently his career had three major phases.

Africa and education, 1927–1949

From 1927 to 1943, Batten served in the Education Department of Nigeria first as Superintendent and then Senior Superintendent of Education. As an undergraduate he was inspired to undertake this career following a talk by a missionary working in Africa. For four years he taught in a Nigerian Secondary School. He was fluent in the local language. During this period of work with children and young people he wrote: *Handbook on the Teaching of History and*

Geography in Nigeria (1933); *Koyaar Labarin Kasa da Tarihi* (1934); *Tropical Africa in World History* (1939/40); *The British Empire and the Modern World* (1941); *Africa Past and Present* (1943). This work at the outset of his career established his life-long commitment to combining fieldwork and training with research and writing-books, chapters for books and articles (some thirty in all). His published output was original and prolific.

In 1943 he became Vice-Principal of Makerere College, Uganda and inaugurated and headed up a Social Studies Department. During this period (1943–49) he wrote, *Thoughts on African Citizenship* (1944) and *Problems of African Development* (1947 and 1948). The significance of this book is indicated by the conclusion of a review by Thomas S. Donohugh:

> *The book should be required reading for all missionaries, educators or others engaged in government, trade, mining or large scale agriculture in Africa. Many of the difficulties would be overcome by such understanding of the African point of view and [action taken] to secure . . . active co-operation.*
>
> (The copy of the review in Batten's files had been torn from what I think was a missionary publication and dated September 1948 without naming it)

In a note about his books published prior to 1949 found in his private papers, probably written in the mid-fifties for a publisher's blurb, Batten wrote:

> *These books were each . . . a product of several years work on some aspect of African education which had previously been neglected, and each has had a marked influence on subsequent educational practice in its particular field. The teaching of history and geography in Nigerian elementary schools is still largely based on the ideas and methods worked out in the [earlier] . . . books, and most junior secondary school history syllabuses in most parts of British tropical Africa are still influenced by the approach adopted in Tropical Africa in World History, and Africa Past and Present. Problems of African Development is used by numbers of university extra-mural classes.*
>
> (Private papers, c. 1955)

London and worldwide community development, 1949–1972

From 1949 until his retirement in 1972, he was first a Senior Lecturer and then Reader in Community Development Studies, University of London, Institute of

Education. It was there that he met Mrs Madge Gill (nee Bailey), his research assistant. They became work partners; they married and became life long collaborators. In this period Batten, with the help of Madge, first formulated the notion of 'non-directive' community development work. They put the material to the test at the Institute by developing a long series of courses for national and international groups of people widely experienced and influential in community development as well as for youth and community workers engaged with secular and religious groups in the UK. They also undertook an ambitious and far reaching fieldwork programme. Through these extensive interactive courses and projects the Battens promulgated their ideas about non-directivity, inducted people into its praxis and got them to consider it critically against their experience. Thus they tested and refined their theory as they went.

Batten wrote seven books in this period, the last three in collaboration with Madge Batten: *Communities and Their Development* (1957);[1] *Schools and Community in the Tropics* (1959); *Africa Past and Present* (1959, 1963);*Training for Community Development* (1962); *The Human Factor in Community Work* (1965); *The Non-Directive Approach in Group and Community Work* (1967); *The Human Factor in Youth Work* (1970). He was also one of the prime movers in establishing in 1966, what became an Oxford University Press publication, the *Community Development Journal: An International Forum (CDJ)*, as a successor to the *Community Development Bulletin*. He chaired the Editorial Board of the *CDJ* until 1981. By then the *Journal* was well established, prestigious and widely influential. Lochhead, in a tribute to Batten at the end of this phase said:

> *His retirement* [from the University] . . . *ends nearly a quarter of a century of quite remarkable pioneering effort. Not only did Reg Batten . . . introduce community development courses as a subject to be taught in universities, but the method of teaching was as novel as the subject itself. He drew from the students their experience and their difficulties as a kind of continuous group discussion and exploration. In the process the members, including Dr Batten himself, gained insight and confidence and knowledge which no amount of didactic teaching could have given. Community Development method was demonstrated in the classroom. It is appropriate that his account of this teaching method, published as* Training for Community Development *(1962), should have gained him his Doctorate.*

(Lochhead, 1972, 194)

Retirement, consultant and mentor, 1972–1994

During his active retirement from 1972 to 1994 Batten's mind was clear and sharp and he could concentrate for long periods until the onset of Alzheimer's in his early 90s. Apart from five short overseas projects, he concentrated on two long-term consultancy commitments in the UK. For several years he acted as a non-directive consultant to members of a team of avant-garde YWCA detached field workers engaged in pioneering community development projects, which involved unstructured, face-to-face work with individuals and small groups of young people variously alienated from society. Batten threw himself into this programme with young workers significantly different from him in age, culture and politics. Meticulously, he wrote up records of the consultancy sessions and notes about emergent practice theory but later destroyed his copies because they did not come up to his high professional standards. The second commitment was to an extensive consultancy arrangement with Catherine Widdicombe and me.

Throughout his career he undertook an impressive sequence of consultative and training field work/research assignments, which, *inter alia*, complemented, earthed, contextualised and informed his London-based central training programmes. From 1954 to 1972 there were sixteen of these assignments, seven in collaboration with Madge Batten. They varied in length from one to six weeks. Most of them were conferences or seminars for senior people and government departments and ministries in national community development work and training programmes. Variously they involved lectures and training sessions and several involved Batten submitting reports and recommendations to governments and their departments. The list of the extant reports presented after the Bibliography shows the geographic scope and indicates the range of his first hand experience of world-wide community development in: Nigeria, Ghana, India, Guyana, Trinidad, Jamaica, Canada, Rhodesia (twice), Nepal (three times), Thailand (twice), USA (twice), Liberia, Nepal (twice), Saudi Arabia, Finland – and all this in addition to twenty-two years in West and East Africa!

Alongside this, Batten was a member and President of the Wimbledon Society and Chairman of its Museum and Education Committee. He classified, annotated and catalogued the contents of the museum and commissioned historical essays. He and Madge were active members of the Wimbledon Horticultural Society and, surprisingly, the Modern Sequence Dancing Club!

In 1974 he published an important article in the *Community Development Journal*, 'Major Issues and Future Direction of Community Development'. It was based on a lecture he had given to the Peace Corps in the USA in which he concluded:

> *As I look back over my years of research, study and fieldwork, my overall feeling is one of sadness that so much community development effort has, on the whole, resulted in relatively so little actual betterment and more especially for the poor and under privileged people who need betterment most. I know, of course, that powerful minorities in every country often succeed in influencing development policies in their own interests at the expense of the mass of ordinary people, and I accept that as a fact of life we have to live with. What concerns me much more is that the well-intentioned efforts of so many planners, administrators and field workers who really want to promote betterment have, on the whole, so often fallen so far short of realising their full potential.*

(Batten, 1974a, 96)

This was his last publication.

Before 1985 Batten was actively researching and outlining two books. He wrote copious notes on the chapters but he never got them into manuscript form. One, entitled *Principles of Extension Work*, I knew nothing about until I went through the papers he left. This draft outline drew heavily upon the Community Development Courses at the University of London and had sections on: purpose and people; finding, planning and presenting the 'message'; working in groups; and the worker and his aids. Why he abandoned it is a mystery. Given all the thoroughly documented work he and Madge had done with international seminar groups of very able and widely experienced people, he had the necessary materials for what could have been a useful book.

The second, entitled *Development and People: A Critical Study* is quite a different matter. An earlier subtitle was, *A Critical Study of Principles and Practice*. This book was meant to make a fundamental contribution to overcoming a problem, which he said he had encountered throughout his career from his earliest days in Nigeria. It was that all forms of secular and religious programmes and projects designed and intended to contribute to the common good failed to achieve their potential, to a greater or lesser extent, because, he argued, of inadequate understandings and definitions of 'develop-ment' and 'betterment'. (Clearly he was grappling with the implications of the statement quoted above.) Starting with a multiplicity of understandings of these two concepts, he set out to establish a generic philosophical and theoretical basis and framework, which would inform holistic developmental programmes. The detailed outlines had sections on: purposes; basic approaches to the development of environment and people; promoting the development of environment and people; problems; training; and evaluating work.

Reading through his papers I realised, with deep empathic feelings and sadness, that he simply could not conceptualise the issues with sufficient clarity to describe the philosophical and theoretical framework he saw to be so necessary. Attempts to discuss things with him did not get very far and an offer that we, Catherine Widdicombe and I, made to organise and record a seminar group on his thinking was not taken up. It was disconcerting that, although he had promoted so much creative group discussion on all kinds of subjects, he was not open to such help on this difficulty. As I reflected on this, I realised he had done all his research and writing either on his own or, during the later phases in collaboration with Madge. They worked on things separately and together. He drafted; they discussed what he had written and then he re-drafted until they got an agreed text. Eventually he abandoned the book in the early eighties for health reasons: he could not write without smoking his beloved pipe. Smoking was having a deleterious effect on his health and life expectancy and he very much wanted to live on particularly for the sake of Madge who was ten years his junior and unwell. (In the event she outlived him by some three years.) So he gave up smoking and with it writing. Reg was bitterly and lastingly disappointed, and so was I.

Emerging principles for education and development

Batten's vocationally operative life spanned sixty-seven years of focussed, independent, original thought and intensive creative action. During the second half of the twentieth century the Battens were best known for their work, courses and writings on the non-directive approach to community development. Consequently the last half of his career eclipsed the early years, which had formative influences upon his philosophy and praxis of education and development and the evolution of the non-directive approach. As I muse on his awesome life I see him, especially during the African years, as a thoroughly professional and dedicated 'secular missionary' with a passion for education and development of those most deprived and in greatest need. In this section, I attempt to describe the principles related to education and development that I have discerned through researching Batten's work on Africa. Later I indicate how these principles influenced the evolution of the non-directive approach.

Principle 1. Belief in human equality and potential

Batten believed firmly 'that black men [*sic*] are capable of equality with white men' at a time when such a view was not common among white people (Batten, 1944, iii). He argued:

> The ideal of human equality does not deny that differences and inequalities exist, but it does refuse to label any men or group of men as innately inferior to others – and therefore less right-worthy – on a priori grounds. The ideal stands for equality of opportunity and equality of rights, including political rights, as the best means of securing a healthy development of society and each individual in it.
>
> (Batten, 1948, 162)

> Africans appear to be as capable as men of other races of applying their labour with intelligence and skill.
>
> (Batten, 1947, 135 cf. 1948: viii)

Most of his work in tropical Africa was done in educationally 'backward' areas and it had left him with a 'sense of tragic waste' (Batten, 1948: vii).

Principle 2. Respectful attention to historical perspectives and world-views

Batten saw that well composed historical perspectives and world-views[2] have positive effects on the education and development of people and upon their personal and corporate sense of identity. A working principle for him, therefore, was that serious attention be given to identifying, articulating, modelling and reflecting on them critically and, as necessary, attempting to get them revised or adjusted. Aware of this principle very early in his career and its implications, Batten identified a cardinal mistake in the education of Africans, which he expressed as follows: 'Education in Europe had the right aim, that of fitting the child to take his place in the adult community. But what Europeans taught in Africa was intended to fit *European* children to live under *European* conditions (Batten's italics, Batten, 1944, 47, cf. Batten 1948, 66 *et al.*).

To correct this he undertook the enormous task of recasting world history *from the perspective* of Africans living in tropical Africa. For three or four years he tested out how to do this at Government College, Ibadan (cf. Batten, 1953). Then he wrote a series of four textbooks for a four-year course of study for middle and junior secondary schools, *Tropical Africa in World History* (1939–1940). Sub-titles of the books indicate the comprehensive scope of this work:

The Foundations of Modern History; *The Growth of Europe and the British Empire*; *Africa in Modern History after 1800*; *The Modern World*. These books made a significant contribution to correcting the previous dysfunctional orientation to education. In the general preface he writes:

> *Interest throughout is firmly centred on tropical Africa, and no aspect of world history is included unless it is in some way directly relevant to understanding what has happened in tropical Africa or is happening there today.*

> (Batten, 1939–40, first page in all volumes)

His knowledge of history was encyclopaedic; he dealt with each subject comprehensively albeit briefly (the books vary in length from 140 to 240 pages). He gave good, balanced, sympathetic, interconnected, incisive interpretations of events in Africa and the world in a vocabulary likely to be familiar to those who had been studying English as a second language for three years. (Glossaries and pictorial vocabularies were included of words considered outside that range.) These books demonstrate that he was a serious professional academic historian and an avant-garde educationalist deeply concerned about and affected by human sufferings and injustice, as demonstrated, for instance, in his writings about slavery. Unaided, African people, indoctrinated and seduced by a British world-view, were unable themselves to correct their historical perspectives and write such books. Batten provided African people with textbooks, which enabled them to centre themselves on *their* own historical perspectives and world-views. The books were widely used for many years.

   In the 1930s this was an enormous shift in world-view orientation. Not surprisingly, a parallel series was produced in China (Goodban *et al.*, 1958–1961). When he wrote *Problems of African Development* (1947, 1948) he used the same principle: 'Throughout, I have tried to assess the situation from the standpoint of educated Africans' (1947, viii). Thus, early in his career, Batten had discerned and introduced as good educational and developmental praxis the principle of helping people to establish their own historical world-views and to think constructively and act creatively with proper respect to them.

Principle 3. Commitment to conceptualising, factorising and contextualising

Batten's working principle in promoting and contributing to the holistic development of complex systems is to engage repeatedly in conceptualising, factorising and contextualising. This is what he did in two major works under the general title of *Problems of African Development*. Part I was *Land and Labour* (1946) and Part II *Government and People* (1948). Their scope is breath-taking as is readily seen from the chapter headings.[3] First, he *conceptualises* and *factorises* all the problems that influence development, and then, as he analyses the problems related to each factor he *conceptualises and contextualises* them in relation to each other and the whole. Without naming it as such, he carried out a comprehensive systemic analysis of development issues in tropical Africa. He told me that he was helped to do this by what he considered to be a great work by Lord Hailey (1938). The revised edition, 1956, had over 1600 densely packed pages. Batten's copy was still on his bookshelves when he died. Two extracts from reviews of the 3rd edition of Batten's *Problems of African Development* (1960) indicate that he too had made a masterly survey of social and economic problems.

> *Few other introductions – on any subject much less, on problems of development – achieve such concreteness, lucidity and precision. Mr Batten is equally at home in methods of animal husbandry or the uses of foreign capital or the operation of local government.*
>
> (Glickman, 1961, 14)

And a Polish Marxist's critique of the same edition concluded:

> *Notwithstanding many reservations concerning the author's general assessment of British rule in Africa as well as particular policies adopted by the colonial administration, Batten's book is outstanding for the wealth of statistical and factological [sic] material it provides.*
>
> (Letocha, 1961)

Principle 4. Commitment to qualitative autonomy

A recurrent theme throughout all Batten's work on African development was that qualitative autonomy, not simply independence, must be a conscious aim of development programmes. It emerged in *Tropical Africa in World History*, was further developed in *Thoughts on African Citizenship* and worked out more fully in *Problems of African Development*. At one point he gathered his thinking in this way:

> *Throughout . . . we have assumed that we are aiming at something more than independence. We are interested not only in the fact of independence but also in its quality. Self-government should mean representative*

and preferably democratic self-government, and not government by any
small minority enjoying special economic and political privileges. Self-
government should also mean efficient government. If these two condi-
tions are not met there is a danger of perpetuating for many of the people
their present unsatisfactory way of life, and on these terms self-
government might well be bought at too high a price.

(Batten, 1948, 156 *et al.*)

Batten's deep and passionate commitment to qualitative democratic self-
government and the independence, autonomy and responsibility that goes
with it, did not blind him to the danger that granting independence 'too early
might lead to serious trouble and possible civil war' and to the handing over
to privileged minorities (black and/or white) and to autocratic rule (Batten,
1940, Book 4, 226 and 1944, 12 *et al.*). Manifestly the conditions for
qualitative democratic autonomy were not achieved before self-government
was granted. Understandably, people who had suffered injustice, repression
and exploitation wanted their freedom as soon as possible. Sadly much that
Batten foresaw and feared in the 1930s and 40s has happened and is still
happening with tragic consequences. Notwithstanding, Batten worked assidu-
ously to establish the cultural, developmental, economic, educational, financial
and governmental conditions necessary to constructive self-government (see
above, Batten, 1944, 1947 and 1948; cf. Batten 1959).

Principle 5. Focus on education

For Batten education was a substantive factor in achieving qualitative
autonomy. He saw the need for greatly extended and improved standards of
educational provision through formal programmes at primary, secondary and
higher levels and, concurrently, through programmes of community and 'mass
education' or, as it became known, community development (Batten, 1948,
31–91 cf. Batten, 1939/1940, 1959). The aims of these programmes must be,
he argued, to fit people to live under African conditions in a modern world
context and not, as previously, to fit them to live under European conditions
as though they were Europeans (see above and Batten, 1944, 47). Further, in
addition to communicating knowledge, each of these programmes must
educate people in the methods of obtaining knowledge (Batten, 1944, 46).

Principle 6. Accentuate self and voluntary help

Batten argued that developmental progress in Africa required that government
action be twinned with self- and voluntary help purposefully aimed at the

common good and at less fortunate members of communities (Batten, 1944, 23–28; 1948, 20, 79 *et al.*). Changes in orientation were required to effect this. Village action for the common good had to be extended to voluntary national action (Batten, 1944, 29 cf. Batten 1947, 12–13; 1944, 35, 38 and 39–64). He claimed that this would make significant contributions to forming nations 'out of the bewildering agglomeration of tribes and clans which at present lack even a common language' (Batten, 1947, 10–11). Later with Dickson he further developed his ideas about voluntary action and social progress (cf. Batten and Dickson, 1959).

Principle 7. Operate disinterestedly and even-handedly

From an early stage Batten consistently operated from a disinterested position with intellectual rigour, integrity and commitment to the common good. But he experienced difficulties in getting people to see and accept the impartial nature of his position and the implied working relationships consonant with it.

> *Some readers, perhaps, may disagree with statements in this book; they may doubt the author's good intention. They know that he is a white man and a civil servant. Are not his interests the interests of his own race? May not this book be some form of government propaganda? In reply to that argument and to that doubt, the author can only say that he strongly believes that Africans must and will govern themselves. He believes such development to be in the interests of the white, as much as the black, races. This book has been written in that belief, and the author alone is responsible for what it says.*
>
> (Batten, 1944, vi)

In Batten's thinking these interrelated principles prefigure the formulation of the non-directive concept, which could be seen as an eighth such principle because it emerges so naturally from them. To do this, however, would obscure two complementary relationships between the principles and the concept of a non- directive approach. The first is that the principles contribute significantly to a philosophy of the concept and a framework of cardinal reference points for the operation of the approach. The second is that the non-directive approach makes unique contributions towards translating the principles into effective practice in the realities of working with people at all levels for holistic development. The first is self-evident; the second leads to a closer look at Batten's understanding of the non-directive approach to community development.

The emergence of the non-directive approach to community development

Batten was in at the birth of community development. The concept emerged from that of 'mass education' presented in an influential report on adult education in Africa published in 1944.[4] After quoting the aim, 'to promote all forms of betterment through active participation',[5] he examined and endorsed the philosophy and principles of this movement (Batten, 1948, 78–91). He gets at the heart of the matter by focusing his attention on 'schemes, which aim chiefly at stimulating initiative among the people themselves'.

> *The aim is to get people interested in expressing their own wants – whatever they may be – and to help and encourage them to take whatever action is needed to satisfy the wants they have expressed . . . success in schemes of this sort is mainly measured in terms of community initiatives, the development of indigenous leadership, effective community planning, and an increased capacity for united community action.*
>
> (Batten 1948, 82–83)

Batten's use of the term 'a non directive approach to community development' correlates with his previous thinking and particularly with his commitment to the principle of personal and collective qualitative autonomy. The *what* of community development was familiar ground. But when he came to consider *how* to achieve such developments Batten broke entirely new ground by coming up with an original approach, which he called 'non-directive' (Batten, 1967 and 1988). Carl Rogers had used this phrase independently.[6] References to the term 'non directive' can be applied to *theory* or *philosophy* or *approaches* or *attitudes* or *intentions* or *methods* or *actions* or *being* or *presence* (cf. Kahn, 1999, 99–101 and Bozarth, 2000, 1). This can cause confusion!

Batten's non directive approach involves inner commitment to self-directivity in others and the skilful use of approaches and methods to help people to decide for themselves what their needs are in contradistinction to their wants, what they are prepared to do to meet them, and what action they are going to take and the ways and means of doing so (cf. Batten, 1967 and 1988, 11; cf. Craig, 1989, 5–6). So, it is about human freedom (cf. Lovell, 2000, 286–287). Lochhead noted:

> *Nothing, perhaps, is so characteristic of Dr Batten's approach as his belief in ordinary people's capacity for intelligent decision and choice and their*

ability to carry out by their own efforts important projects. His non-directive philosophy reflects this profound faith in human beings as people. It also reflects the evidence he collected from innumerable case studies of conflict and failure when plans are imposed without discussion and understanding.

(Lochhead, 1972, 194)

As noted earlier, during their time at the University of London, the Battens eagerly seized every opportunity to practise, test, refine and research the non-directive concept. Having demonstrated the efficacy and indispensability of the concept they produced their much-acclaimed definitive work, *The Non-Directive Approach in Group and Community Work* (Batten, 1967). In the preface he writes:

During the last eighteen years we have been working with all the many experienced administrators, trainers and field workers from 'developing' and 'developed' countries who have attended our courses either in England or overseas to get the positive roles and functions of non-directive workers and trainers specific and clear. In this book we present the conclusions which they and we have reached, in the hope that these will stimulate further thought and be of some practical help to all the many workers and trainers now experimenting in this field.

(Batten, 1967, vi)

In this book Batten defines and differentiates between the non-directive and directive approaches in the following ways:

The directive approach ... *means that the agency which adopts it itself decides, more or less specifically, whatever it thinks people need or ought to value or ought to do for their own good, and sometimes even how they ought to behave. These decisions become the agency's betterment goals for people ... Always the main initiative, and the final say, remains with them.*

(Batten, 1967 and 1988, 5)

The worker who uses **the non-directive approach** *does not attempt to decide for people, or to lead, guide, or persuade them to accept any of his own specific conclusions about what is good for them. He tries to get them to decide for themselves what their needs are: what, if anything, they are willing to do to meet them; and how they can best organize, plan*

and act to carry their project through. Thus he aims at stimulating a
process of self-determination and self-help, and he values it for all the
potential learning experiences which participation in this process provides.
He aims to encourage people to develop themselves, and it is by thinking
and acting for themselves, he believes, that they are most likely to do so.

(Batten, 1967 and 1988, 11)

The difference is illustrated by an anecdote Madge relished telling about a talk Reg gave to the local horticultural society on his most effective if idiosyncratic system of making compost. He had warmed to his subject when a member of the audience interjected, 'That is *not* how you make compost'. Without any hesitation Reg replied, 'That is how *I* do it and that is what I have been invited to talk about!' His reply was instantaneous and authoritative because it was what his life was all about, helping people to think and work out as thoroughly as they could how and why they themselves could and should do things in the light of possible consequences, intended and unintended.

The Battens designed 'facilitating structures' to help people to think through systematically and analyse human situations and their thoughts and feelings about them (Batten, 1978 and 1988, 14). These structures are sequences of interrelated questions or tasks which help workers and people to organise, order and shape *their* thinking step by step as they analyse cases, problems and situations and design work projects (Batten, 1962, Part III, 1965, 1970). These methods enabled practitioners to focus analytically on *their perspectives, their world- and work-views*[7] and to work to and with those of others. This application of Principle 2 (respectful attention to historical perspectives and world-views) is epitomised in methods the Battens' devised for studying contemporary or historical cases. They built up an extensive collection of cases subscribed over a period of some twenty years by those who attended their courses at the University of London from all parts of the world. Some were made into filmstrips and representative samples were grouped under subject headings (e.g. 'meeting requests for help', 'dealing with faction') and published with their analyses and praxis rubrics (Batten, 1962, 39–40, 113–120, 137 and 132; Batten, 1965; Batten, 1970; Batten 1967, 96–110; Lovell, 1994, 31–49).

For the Battens, both directive and non-directive approaches have their uses. Using them effectively involves, *inter alia*, assessing their respective advantages and limitations and establishing the factors, which help to choose between them. They dedicate a chapter to that in their book (cf. Batten 1967, 18–23). Later Batten redefined the kinds of situations in which workers have 'to revert to working *for*, i.e. directively':

(a) ***crisis situations*** *such as fire, flood, epidemic when people are suffering from shock;*

(b) ***holding' situations*** *when the prime need is to prevent people seriously harming themselves through ignorance or apathy or short-sightedness . . . until educational measures have had time to take effect;*

(c) ***preventative situations:*** *to prevent people, if one can, from implementing decisions they have taken with the intention of harming others for their own gain;*

(d) ***transitional situations:*** *to ease the transition from directive to a non-directive way of working with people where . . . (a total) swing from the one to the other may prove unacceptable and ineffective to the people themselves, and therefore unproductive.*

(Batten 1974 b)

Batten's educational principles and non-directive praxis

Batten's principles for education and development fall into seven categories. In the discussion that follows I will seek to illustrate how each of the 'principles' listed below were reflected in and incorporated within aspects of Batten's thinking and teaching about non-directive praxis.

Principles and approach

A summary of Batten's principles for education and development

Principle 1. Belief in human equality and potential

Principle 2. Respectful attention to historical perspectives and world-views

Principle 3. Commitment to conceptualising, factorising and contextualising

Principle 4. Commitment to qualitative autonomy

Principle 5. Focus on education

Principle 6. Accentuate self- and voluntary help

Principle 7. Operate disinterestedly and even-handedly

To use the non-directive and directive approaches with integrity, sincere belief in the equality and potential of people, Principle 1, must be bonded with youth and community work skills. Thus combined, belief gives life to the skills, and the application of the skills embodies belief in the concrete realities of human affairs. At best the result has several desirable and accumulative effects. People are enabled to engage creatively in processes of self-determination, self-direction and self-development, and this can lead to Principles 1, 2, 4, 6 and 7 being implemented (Batten 1978 and 1988, 11; Lovell and Widdicombe, 1978, 16). On the other hand, workers, become more confident and accomplished in their ability to facilitate these processes and confirmed and strengthened in their belief in the capacity of other people to think and decide for themselves and hopefully to be better able to conceptualise, factorise and contextualise; this implements Principle 3. Again, to engage in non-directive facilitation, workers need to be able to pay serious attention to the historical perspectives and world-views of the people with whom they are engaged; this implements Principle 2. To do this they have to enter into other peoples' realities: to be able 'to see things through their eyes' and to 'stand in their shoes'. Batten was a master at this. Without apparent effort, he could in quick succession view situations from the perspective of each of the participants with uncanny perception and accuracy. And, to further complicate things, as workers occupy this intimate position of self-identification with people, they have to act disinterestedly and that involves implementing Principle 7. To do this they have to be even-handed, to avoid taking sides, in order to be as neutral and objective as they can. Working with people in these ways engenders qualitative self-help action, which is most likely to produce change for the better in people and in their environment and contribute to the common good (cf. Batten 1967 and 1988, 11–12). Thus it puts into effect, Principles 3, 4 and 6 through educational processes, which is Principle 5.

Criticisms and impact

Two criticisms of *The Non-Directive Approach* are of interest here. The first, in a review article by Brian Wren (1974), was that whilst the non-directive approach had many parallels with Paulo Freire's approach to conscientisation, Batten did not have Freire's exclusive commitment to non-directivity. Wren was critical of what he referred to as Batten's 'philosophy of balance' based on choosing strategically between the approaches (cf. Batten, 1967 and 1988, Part One). This led to interesting correspondence between them in which Batten reasserted his utter commitment to non-directivity and said of the book:

> ... *my intention was to write a 'non-directive' book ... to promote objective thinking among the people who read it – not (directively) to present them with cut-and-dried conclusions about what I think they*

*ought to do. Otherwise I should be trying to 'sell' non-directive directively
. . .*

(Batten, 1974c, 2)

The second criticism appeared in an otherwise very positive review by W.W. Biddle, which included these comments:

> *It is difficult to find fault with as useful a book as this is. The Battens are widely experienced and their recommendations are both practical and consistent in a non-directive philosophy. The chief fault this reviewer would find is that they do not quote from or even refer to many authorities in the field whose writings would make the book's case even more persuasive. For example, in defending the non-directive approach, there is a wealth of literature, both psychological and philosophical which supports the Batten eloquence. For example, they have many allies in group dynamics, adult education, community development, and related fields, who could make clear that their recommendations are not distilled merely from the experiences of one couple. There is no bibliography and footnotes refer hardly at all to related literature. And unfortunately, there is no index.*

(Biddle, 1968, 54)

Biddle's criticism is entirely justifiable. From what he said about such criticisms I believe Batten's reply would be that he was describing *his own* approach (cf. the story above about compost making). Howbeit, in contrast, Batten's earlier books were impressive for the way in which they were cross-referenced with other literature and indexed (cf. Batten, 1943, 1944, 1947, 1957, 1959). Had he contextualised the approach in the way Biddle suggests, it would have helped others to do so and he may have had more overall impact. Also, it would probably have helped him and others to theorise and philosophise about the approach, something that we have seen Batten struggled and failed to do.

Beyond any doubt, Batten made profound contributions to community development and to youth and community work. He was a towering figure for half a century. It would be extremely difficult if not impossible to quantify the impact or to assess the use made of the non-directive approach in secular and religious settings. To the best of my knowledge this has not been attempted. However, the non-directive approach has impacted the field in three discernible ways: abrasively, indirectly and directly.

Abrasively, there has been a wide range of critical responses to the approach.[8] Some of these are based on one or other of several misunderstandings. They see it as an open-ended permissive leaderless approach that seriously flaws development work *or* as a sophisticated way of manipulating people *or* as a neglect of dependency needs through the emphasis on enablement (cf. Vanstone, 1982, 34–51). Others claim that it is just not possible to be non-directive or neutral. Some prefer to be democratic rather than non-directive. Then there are those who reject the approach, including some who were attracted to it, because they are disenchanted by experiences of it and its malpractice. Experiences, that is, such as: *overexposure* i.e. people revealing things they later regretted disclosing (cf. Lovell, 1973, 354–355); *misleading world and work views* accepted by workers and used as though they represent essentials of realities when they do not; *difficulties of finding time and energy* (Fitzgerald, 1993, 17; Lovell, 1973, 136, Lovell and Widdicombe, 1978 and 1986, 186, cf. Lovell, 1994, 252–253); *intellectual intimidation* by the analytical processes (cf. Lovell, 1994, 247–252 and Lovell and Widdicombe, 1978 and 1988, 186); *fear of losing control* (cf. Lovell, 1994, 253–259). However, these problems, real as they are, do not, in fact, invalidate the approach because experience has shown that they are surmountable to a greater or lesser extent in an approach which gives a vigorous lead to thinking. Then, there are some Christians who have serious theological reservations about the approach because, for them, a non-negotiable imperative of Christian mission is to tell people what they should believe, be and do and to persuade or direct them to act upon what they are told.[9]

Other criticisms variously point to ways in which the non-directive approach is limited by inappropriate circumstances, lack of competence, inadequate understanding, fallibility of workers and people. Creative praxis requires that these limitations be accepted with humility as significant aspects of all working realities and worked at through reflective practice. It also involves an approach to praxis known as *fallibilism*, 'the commitment to hold theory lightly, to live with uncertainty and ambiguity, and to be always prepared to revise our views' (Orange, 1995, 3). The word fallibilism 'emerged in the philosophy of science against the Roman Catholic declaration of papal infallibility' (Orange, 1995, 43. I owe these references to Orange to Kahn, 1999, 106). Bozarth suggests, 'The therapist's fallibility is corrected within the framework of the stance of non-directivity' (Bozarth, 2000, 6).

Critical as those responses might be, they have stimulated creative discussions about, and reflections upon, the approaches and methods appropriate to developmental work with people and measured re-consideration of non-directivity.

Secondly, the *indirect impact* of the non-directive approach is to be seen through current widespread emphases on its derivatives such as collaboration, collegiality, egalitarian participation, empowerment[10] and self-directed group-work (Mullender and Ward, 1991). Possibly these concepts have found favour because they sound more positive than the non-directive approach, appear more focussed and their praxis is easier to grasp. But these important concepts are constituent parts of non-directive praxis, which itself is part of development praxis. Good practice involves using the concepts purposively within an overall explicit praxis framework. Replacing generic concepts with implicit or subsidiary ones, such as empowerment, severs vital connections between them with serious consequences. Treating constituent parts in isolation as ends in themselves is bad practice just as it is to use objectives as purposes (Lovell, 1994, 123–125).

The non-directive approach has also impacted many other different disciplines such as counselling and adult education. Interestingly, enlightening critiques of the use of the non-directive approach in psychotherapy were more numerous than those of the use of the approach in community development. This led me to think much could be gained from a critical examination of the respective experiences of using the approach in these different disciplines: a task which I think remains outstanding.

Thirdly, there is a *direct* impact through practitioners who have adopted the approach in a thoroughgoing way as a fundamental principle, an article of faith and as a central feature of their praxis. David Thomas (1983) in his magnum opus, *The Making of Community Work*, wrote:

> The 'community' theorists and practitioners were linked to another major orthodoxy of the 1960's and 1970's – the non-directive approach, associated primarily with the work of Reg Batten. It was an orthodoxy that influenced the training of cohorts of youth and community workers but remains one of unfulfilled promise. Its adherents (with the exception of George Lovell) wrote little after 1970 and non-directiveness remained more as a guiding principle or philosophy than a clearly defined statement of tasks and behaviours. It was, too, an approach that was quickly put aside by the radical new recruits to community work in the 1970's whose concern was more often with class than with community and who were extremely suspicious of the connection of the community and non-directive theorists with colonialism.
>
> (Thomas, 1983, 91)

A brief section below indicates the impact on the churches of a particular non-directive programme of action-research, training and consultancy.

Sketchy as this overview of Batten's impact is, it indicates that the potential for development work inherent in non-directivity has not been generally recognised and acknowledged and consequently not fully realised.

Spirituality

One of the things often said to the Battens about one or other of their courses by people who did not normally use such terminology was that it had been a 'religious experience'. The Battens, who did not think of themselves as religious and were not churchgoers, were always moved and gratified by such responses because they testified to the spirituality inherent in non-directivity, which resonated with the wide range of ethical-spiritual-religious-social convictions of the participants.

Spirituality is a vogue word used of a broad range of phenomena experienced within religions and in society generally. Chile and Simpson (2004) suggest that spirituality

> *is the inner self that defines who we are . . . [it] relates to those values and beliefs that inform the meanings we make of our existence and our purpose. It . . . shapes our relationships with others and our environment.*
>
> (pp. 319, 320 and 322)

They suggest, 'community development based on spirituality includes at least the reduction of inequality, enhancement of personal security, respect for individual human rights, recognition of personal values, social justice and empowerment' (p324). Spirituality avoids being esoteric, mystical, mushy or sentimental when it emanates from deeply held beliefs, principles, purposes and values of the kind attributed to the Battens in this paper and when it suffuses being and doing (Lovell 1994, 279). Such spirituality forms reservoirs of energy in individuals and communities.

Practitioners, with this spirituality have a non-directive non-judgemental *presence*, potent and palpable but hard to describe.[11] It signals genuine altruism; its very existence mandates, encourages and creates personal and collective *freedom within people and practitioners and between them*. It causes people to feel free and to act freely because they sense that practitioners are not intent on controlling them. Consequently, they can use their energy to explore and express their freedom purposefully rather than to guard it. Non-directive practitioners, on the other hand, are able to express themselves openly because people know intuitively that they do not intend to invade or compromise their freedom. All round responsible use of these internalised and projected freedoms generates *qualitative autonomy* (Principle 4). This essential presence, variously expressed, known, appreciated and understood, is the generating power of effective non-directive practice *and* it endows it with authority and integrity. Without it, the most sophisticated methodology is counterfeit currency. Reg and Madge Batten had such a presence. I experienced it continuously and consistently in my long association with them. I covet it for myself and for all engaged in secular and religious community development and work consultancy.

Relevance to church and community work

Many people in the churches have been greatly influenced by T.R. Batten as can be seen by the references to books by Brierly, Lovell and Widdicombe. His impact upon me and my work has been profound. In the late 1960s my excited response to non-directive praxis and my enthusiastic practice of it, radically changed my approach to ministry and to church youth and community work. I remain committed to it and convinced of its relevance after forty years dedicated to practising it in all kinds of settings and situations, researching and teaching it and writing about it. However, whilst Batten's non-directive approach to community development was pivotal to me and to my work, it was not exclusively so. Gradually I established wider knowledge and praxis bases, which drew upon several disciplines: Christian biblical and pastoral theology; behavioural, psychological and social sciences, particularly studies of churches, communities, congregations, groups and group dynamics; community development; organisational studies (cf. Lovell, 1994, Chapters Seven to Ten; 2000, Part Two, 320–21; 2005, 145–152 and 263–264; Widdicombe 1994 and 2000). The resulting, essentially non-directive, praxis, I have discovered, is universally applicable to, and productive in five kinds of activities:

- *church and community work settings at all levels* (Grundy, 1995; Lovell, 1972 and 1982, 1996a and b; Lovell and Widdicombe, 1978 and 1986; Widdicombe, 1994 and 2000, 2001);
- *work and vocational consultancy*[12] (Lovell 2000 and 2005);
- *reciprocal or co-consultancy* (Copley, Lovell and New, 2000; Lovell, 2005, 164–167);
- *training for work with people in church and community* (Grundy, 1995, 31–35; Lovell, 1996a, 41–44; 1994, 204–205; 2000, 357–360 and 415–419; Lovell and Widdicombe, 1978 and 1986, 46–59; Widdicombe, 1994, 204–205, 221–222 *et al.*);

- *action-research*, which is a form of 'qualitative' research useful to reflective practice (Lovell, 1994, 219; 2000, 293, 306–307; Lovell and Widdicombe, 1978 and 1986, 14, 22, 208; 2002, 55–66).

Conclusion

Occasionally I come across significant pockets of youth, community and church work directly inspired and informed by the Batten legacy. More frequently I come across work, which resonates with much that the Battens stood for even though the practitioners do not construe it as non-directive action. But even more often I see the tragic consequences of work and relationships blighted and fouled up through well-meant but ill-conceived or inept directive or autocratic action and misplaced attempts to control people and wield power. This combination of encouraging and painful experiences along with my own experience demonstrate conclusively that Batten's principles and the non-directive approach are essential to getting people to work together creatively to make their own contributions to their own development and to the common good. Sadly, these fundamentals of good praxis are grossly neglected in the areas in which I am engaged. This may be because they differ so radically from ingrained ways of dealing with people and commonly accepted ways of using power in human and religious affairs. Or, maybe it is because their rightful contribution to the overall developmental economy has not been clearly established. But perhaps it is simply all too much against the grain and involves too much hard work. Serious attention needs to continue to be given to all such inhibitors of creativity. A renaissance of well-informed non-directive praxis is, I believe, highly desirable. A significant contribution could be made through setting collaboration, collegiality, egalitarian participation, self-directed group work and empowerment in a non-directive theoretical and philosophical praxis framework highlighting the connections between them. This could enable more people to draw upon the Battens' capital investment in human betterment, which is an important part of our inheritance.

Gratitude

My colleague Catherine Widdicombe tells how one of Batten's recurring questions on the course she attended was, 'What is your purpose?' One day she asked him privately, 'Dr Batten, what is your purpose?' Without hesitation he replied, 'To get people to think'. Daily I am reminded of that by a chair, which stood by Reg Batten's desk and now stands in our hall. It was 'my' seat during the thirty years I visited him for tutorials and consultative sessions. Simply sitting on it galvanised my thinking: it became my 'thinking chair'! It symbolises what I owe to the Battens. They helped me to cultivate and develop my desire, confidence, courage and ability to do my own thinking and to help others to do the same. That is my lasting inheritance from Reg and Madge, their gift to me and to so many others, for which I am eternally grateful.

Notes

1   There was an important review article of this book and Batten's contribution to community development in the *CDJ* (Dickson, 1958).

2   A world-view, *weltanschauung*, is an inner function of human cognition which sums up and models what we know and believe about our world and how we evaluate it emotionally and respond to it volitionally.

3   *Part I:* The geographical and historical background; The future of African Society; The problems of African economic development; The people and the land; Changing ideas about the land; Problems of individual title; From subsistence farming to cash cropping; New farming methods; Problems of animal husbandry; Forest and the future; Water for use or for waste; The destruction of the soil; Efforts to save the soil; Capital and labour as factors in African development; The case for plantations; The present and the export trade; Problems of internal trade. *Part II:* Health in a changing society; Health or disease? Prevention or cure? Education: the present situation; Problems of development; Community education; Spending policies; Taxation policies; Government: the present situation (1); The development of local government, traditional authorities, local native councils, urban and other special areas (2); The central government; Local government, general development problems; Law in a changing society; The approach to self-government.

4   *Report on Mass Education in African Society* Colonial No. 186 Advisory Committee on Education in the Colonies, HMSO.

5   (Mass education or community development is) '. . . a movement designed to promote better living for the whole community, with the active participation of and, if possible, on the initiative of, the community, but if this initiative is not forthcoming spontaneously, by the use of techniques for arousing and stimulating it in order to secure active and enthusiastic response to the movement. Mass education embraces all forms of betterment. It includes the whole range of development activities . . . whether these are undertaken by government or unofficial bodies . . .' (Batten 1948, 81).

6   It was not until Batten had been using the term for some time that he learnt that Carl R. Rogers had coined the same term for client-centred psychotherapeutic counselling (cf. Rogers, 1972) but, according to Bozarth (2000), whilst continuing to hold to the concept he ceased to use it in the 1950s 'because it was misunderstood and maligned leading to distortions of the approach'. Howbeit, in response to questions in 1975 he said that 'perhaps I enriched it (the notion of being non-directive)' (cf. Bozarth, 2000, p2). This could explain why Batten did not know of Roger's use of the term. Although Batten remained unhappy with the term he continued to use it because he could not think of a better one.

7   Over the years I have developed a way of operating through 'work-views', based on Batten's use of 'historical perspectives' and 'world-views' (cf. Principle 2) and his method of studying

organisations on his courses. A work-view, a parallel term to 'world-view' as used in sociology and philosophy, is an important inner function of human cognition which sums up, conceptualises, represents and models:

- what we believe about the nature of our work, i.e., it can have a *theological, philosophical* and *spiritual* content;
- what we know about it, i.e., it can have *cognitive* content;
- how we feel about it, i.e., it can have *affective* content;
- how we respond to it volitionally, i.e., it can have *vocational* content;
- what we know, believe and feel about the actualities of the work in which we are engaged, i.e., it can have *experiential* and *existential* content;
- the 'virtual realities' of our perspectives on our work and situations and enables others to have experiences of 'virtual insidership' of them (Lovell, 2000, 59–60; 2005, 159–160).

I have found that studying people's work-views with them non-directively enables them to revise them (Lovell, 2000, 51–71; 2005, 158–160).

8   Early in my career I researched 'critical, sceptical suspicious and confused reactions' to the non-directive approach over a period of six years in the Parchmore Project. There have been extensive internal and external evaluations of the work in which a group of us have been engaged. The internal evaluations are in the Avec Archives. There are evaluated responses in several unpublished action-research theses (Lovell, 1973 and 2006; Widdicombe, 1984; New, 1987; Mellor, 1990) and in a project report (Lovell and Widdicombe, 1978). There are several publications about the responses of people to the Avec courses and consultancy services. There is an external survey by MARC Europe (Brierly, 1990). Brierly's summary of this research appears in Lovell, 1996a, 158–171. Then there are in depth interviews, which explore the responses of eighteen quite different people (Lovell, 1996b). Several books have been published about this work (Lovell, 1972, 1994, 1996a and b, 2000 and 2005, 143–167; Widdicombe, 1994, 2000; 2001). Key documents and publications are in archives in Oxford (Lovell & Widdicombe, 2002; website http://www.avec resources.org).

9   Detailed attention has been given to these other problems related to the practice theory and theology of the non-directive approach in Lovell and Widdicombe, 1978 and 1986; Lovell, 1973, 1980, 1982, 1994, 1996a, 2000 and 2006 and in Widdicombe, 1994 and 2000.

10 Indeed, Mary Fitzgerald wrongly claims that Batten's writings are 'now considered obsolete by the users of concepts like 'empowerment' and "participation", both of which are implicit in the non-directive approach which he advocates' (1993, 17 cf. Oakley, 1998, 306 and Laverack, 2006, 4–12).

11 Halmos attributes *quality of presence* to S. Nacht and S. Viderman ('The Pre-Object Universe in the Transference Situation', *The International Journal of Psychoanalysis*, July 1963, Vol. XLIV, Part 3, 328–333) cf. Halmos, 1965, 1978, 99, 100 and 107.

12 There is now an MA in Consultancy for Mission and Ministry at York Institute for Community Theology, York St John University College with Dr Helen Cameron as Senior Tutor.

References

Batten, T.R. (1933, 6th edition1950) *Handbook on the Teaching of History and Geography in Nigeria*, Lagos, CMS.

Batten, T.R. (1934) *Koyaar Labarin Kasa da Tarihi*, C, Nigeria, CMS.

Batten, T.R. (1939/40) *Tropical Africa in World History*, Oxford University Press.

Book 1: *The Foundations of Modern History.*
Book 2: *The Growth of Europe and the British Empire.*
Book 3: *Africa: Modern History after 1800.*
Book 4: *The Modern World.*
Batten, T.R. (1941) *The British Empire and the Modern World*, Oxford University Press.
Batten, T.R. (1943) *Africa Past and Present*, Oxford University Press.
Batten, T.R. (1944) *Thoughts on African Citizenship*, Oxford University Press.
Batten, T.R. (1947) *Problems of African Development: Part I: Land and Labour*, Oxford University Press.
Batten, T.R. (1948) *Problems of African Development: Part II: Government and People*, Oxford University Press.
Batten, T.R. (1953) 'The textbook and the Teacher' in *Overseas Education*, Volume XXV, No 2, July 1953, 62–63.
Batten, T.R. (1957, fifth edition 1965) *Communities and Their Development: An Introductory Study with Special Reference to the Tropics*, Oxford University Press.
Batten, T.R. (1959) *School and Community in the Tropics*, Oxford University Press.
Batten, T.R. (1959, 1963) *Africa Past and Present*, Oxford University Press.
Batten, T.R. (1962) *Training for Community Development: A Critical Study of Method*, Oxford University Press.
Batten, T.R. (1974a) 'The Major Issues and Future Direction of Community Development', *Community Development Journal*, Oxford University Press, Vol. 9 Number 2 April 1974, 96–103. Also published in *Journal of Community Development Society*, Volume 4 No 2, Fall 1973.
Batten, T.R. (1974b) Letter to Rev Dr Brian Wren re his Review Article, 1 April 1974.
Batten, T.R. (1974c) Letter to Rev Dr Brian Wren re his Review Article, 16 May 1974.
Batten, T.R. and A.G. Dickson (1959) *Voluntary Action and Social Progress*, The British Council.
Batten, T.R. with the collaboration of Madge Batten (1965) *The Human Factor in Community Work*, Oxford University Press.
Batten, T.R. with the collaboration of Madge Batten (1967) *The Non-Directive Approach in Group and Community Work*, Oxford University Press. This is now out of print. An abridged version is available, Batten, T.R. and M. Batten (1988) *The Non-Directive Approach*, An Avec Publication.
Batten, T.R. with the collaboration of Madge Batten (1970) *The Human Factor in Youth Work*, Oxford University Press.
Biddle, William W. (1968) 'The Non-Directive Approach in Group and Community Work' in the *Community Development Journal*, Oxford University Press, Vol. 3 No. 1, January 1968, 54.
Bozarth, Jerold D. (2000) *Non-directiveness in client-centred therapy: A vexed concept*, A Paper presentation at the Eastern Psychological Association, Baltimore, Md, 25 March 2000.
Brierley, Peter (1990) *Viva l'Avec: An Evaluation of Avec's Training Ministry*, MARC Europe.
Chile, Love M and Simpson, Gareth (2004) 'Spirituality and community development: Exploring the link between the individual and the collective' in the *Community Development Journal*, Vol. 39 No. 4, October, 318–331.
Copley, D., Lovell, G. and New, C. (2000) 'Take Three Presbyters . . . The Role of Co-Consultancy' in *Epworth Review*, Vol. 27 No. 3, July, 6–9.
Craig, G. (1989) 'Community Work and The State' in *Community Development* Journal, Vol. 24 No. 1, January, 3–18.
Craig, G. and Mayo, M. (1999) 'Dr T.R 'Reg' Batten' in the *Community Development Journal*, Vol. 34, No. 4, October.

Dickson, A.G. (1958) 'Batten on Community Development' in the *Community Development Bulletin* Volume IX, No. 2. March 1958, 30–36, Community Development Clearing House, Institute of Education, University of London.

Fitzgerald, M. (1993) 'Participatory community development in Bophuthatswana' in *Community Development Journal*, Volume 28 Number 1, January 1993, 11–18.

Glickman, Harvey (1961) *Africa Report* Vol. 6 No 8 August 1961 (The African American Institute Inc.).

Goodban, G.A., Ching-lien, Chien, Batten, T.R. (1958–1961) *China in World History*, Oxford University Press:

Book 1: *The First Civilization*.

Book 2: *The Growth of China and Europe*.

Book 3: *China and the West: Development before 1900*.

Book 4: *China and the West in Recent Times*.

Grundy, M. (Ed.) (1995) *The Parchmore Partnership: George Lovell, Garth Rogers and Peter Sharrocks*, Chester House Publications.

Hailey, Lord (1938) *An African Survey*, Oxford University Press

Halmos, P. (1965, second revised edition 1978, reprinted 1981) *The Faith of the Counsellors*, London, Constable.

Kahn, E. (1999) 'A Critique of Non-directivity in the Person-centered Approach' in the *Journal of Humanistic Psychology*, Vol. 39 No. 4, Fall 1999, 94–110.

Laverack, G. (2005) 'Using a "domains" approach to build community empowerment' in *Community Development Journal*, Vol. 41 No. 1, January 2006, 4–12.

Letocha, T. (1961) *Sprawy Miedzynarodowe/International Affairs/*, No. 10, 1961.

Lochhead, A.V.S. (1972) 'Dr T R Batten' in the *Community Development Journal*, Vol. 7 No. 3, October 1972, 194–195.

Lovell, G. (1972 and 1982) *The Church and Community Development An Introduction*, An Avec Publication, Originally published in 1972 as a Grail and Chester House Publication, revised 1980 and reprinted in 1982.

Lovell, G. (1973) *An Action Research Project to Test the Applicability of the Non-Directive Concept in a Church, Youth and Community Setting*, A thesis submitted for the Degree of Doctor of Philosophy in the Institute of Education, Faculty of Arts, University of London, unpublished.

Lovell, G. (1980 and 1991) *Diagrammatic Modelling; an aid to theological reflection in church and community development work*, London, An Avec Publication 1991, originally published as Occasional Paper No. 4 1980, by the William Temple Foundation.

Lovell, G. (1982) *Human and Religious Factors in Church and Community Work*, based on the Beckley Social Service Lecture 1981 by George Lovell, London, Grail Publications.

Lovell, G. (1994) *Analysis and Design: A handbook for practitioners and consultants in church and community work*, Tunbridge Wells, Burns and Oates.

Lovell, G. (1996a) *Avec: Agency and Approach*, Pinner, An Avec Publication.

Lovell, G. (1996b) *Telling Experiences: Stories about a transforming way of working with People*, London, Chester House Publications.

Lovell, G. (2000) *Consultancy, Ministry and Mission: A Handbook for Practitioners and Work Consultants in Christian Organizations*, London, Burns and Oates, A Continuum Imprint.

Lovell, G. (2005) *Consultancy Modes and Models*, Derbyshire, Cliff College Publishing in the Cliff College Academic Series.

Lovell, G. (2006) *An Occasional Paper: A Critical Appreciation of Some Outworkings in Christian Churches and Organizations of Batten's Non-Directive Approach to Community Development*, Pinner, Available from Avec Resources, 125 Waxwell Lane, Pinner, Middx. HA5 3ER)

Lovell, G. and Widdicombe C. (1978 and 1986) *Churches and Communities: An Approach to Development in the Local Church*, Great Britain, Search Press.

Lovell, G. and Widdicombe, C. (2002) *Avec Archives: An Annotated Catalogue*, Pinner, An Avec Publication.

Mellor, H.G. (1990) *A Theological Examination of the Non-Directive Approach to Church and Community Development with a Special Reference to the Nature of Evangelism*, A thesis submitted for the degree of Master of Arts in Theology in the Theology Department, Faculty of Arts, University of Durham, unpublished.

Mullender, A. and Ward, D. (1991) *Self Directed Groupwork: Users Take Action for Empowerment* London, Whiting and Birch.

Oakley, P. (1998) 'Review Article: Community Development in the Third World in the 1990's' in the *Community Development Journal*, Vol. 33 No. 4, October 1998, 365–376.

Orange, D.M. (1995) *Emotional Understanding: Studies in Psychoanalytical Epistemology*, New York: Guildford.

Rogers, C.R. (1972) *On Becoming a Person: A Therapist's View of Psychotherapy*, London, Constable.

Thomas, D. (1983) *The Making of Community Work*, London, George Allen and Unwin.

Vanstone, W.H. (1982) *The Stature of Waiting*, London, Darton, Longman and Todd.

Wakefield, G.S. (ed) (1986 3rd impression) 'Spirituality', in *A Dictionary of Spirituality* London, SCM, 361.

Widdicombe, C. (1994 and 2000) *Meetings that Work: A Practical Guide to Team Working in Groups*, Cambridge, The Lutterworth Press, this is a republication for a wider constituency of *Group Meetings that Work*, St Paul's, 1994.

Widdicombe, C. (2001) *Small Communities in Religious Life: Making Them Work*, Cambridge, The Lutterworth Press.

Wren, B. (1974) 'Review Article: Introducing Paulo Freire', *Learning for Living*, a Christian Education Movement magazine, January 1974 issue.

Reports of the Battens' Overseas Assignments

Along with other papers and memorabilia these will eventually be housed in the Avec Archives in the Wesley Centre, Oxford, Westminster Institute of Education, Oxford Brookes University, Harcourt Hill, Oxford OX2 9AT. Contact: Methodist Heritage Coordinator (Archives and Art), Dr Peter Forsaith (details on p75 of *Avec Archives Annotated Catalogue*).

Batten, T.R. (1959) *Impressions of the Indian Training Programme and Some Suggestions for its Improvement.*

Batten, T.R. (April 1964) *Report on Community Development in Southern Rhodesia.*

Batten, T.R. (October 1966) *Some Comments on the Policy of Panchayat Development and Decentralisation in Nepal and some Suggestions for Increasing its Effectiveness.*

Bloore, K. (July 1967) *Community Development Training: A Condensation of the (July 1965) Batten Report* (Published by the Ministry of Internal Affairs).

Batten, T.R. (March 1972) *National Development in Nepal: The Decentralisation Policy: Its Purpose and Problems.*

Batten T.R. (July 1972) *The Community Development Programme in Saudi Arabia: Report Submitted by Dr T.R. Batten.*

Batten, T.R. and Batten, M. (July 1965) *Report and Recommendations by Dr T.R. Batten and Mrs M. Batten to the Rhodesia Government on Implementing the Policy of Local Government Through the Concept of Community Development.*

Batten, T.R. and Batten, M. (March 1968) *Some Suggestions Based on Work Done with the Community Development Department, Ministry of the Interior during our Visit to Thailand, January–March 1968.*

Batten, T.R. and Batten, M. (November 1966) *Suggestions for Increasing the Effectiveness of Training and some Other Activities of the Community Development Department, Ministry of the Interior, Thailand.*

Batten, T.R. and Batten, M. (February 1968) *Community Development Department Ministry of the Interior Bangkok: Report of the Community Development Department Trainers' Seminar Conducted by Dr T.R. and Madge Batten, January 15–26, (1968),* Prepared by Training Division, Community Development Department, Ministry of Interior.

Batten, T.R. and Batten, M. (February 1968) *The Non-Directive Approach in Training, An Account of the Recommendations arising from the Rose Garden Seminar for Officers of the Training Division and Technical Services' Division of the Local Administration Department, Thailand, from February 5th–16th 1968.*

Further Information

Extant copies of the reports, copies of articles and papers referred to in this chapter, which are not easily accessed and other Batten papers and memorabilia will eventually be housed in the Avec Archives in the Wesley Centre, Oxford, Westminster Institute of Education, Oxford Brookes University, Harcourt Hill, Oxford OX2 9AT. Contact: Methodist Heritage Coordinator (Archives and Art), Dr Peter Forsaith (details on p75 of catalogue).

For further information about Avec, Avec Archives and Avec Resources see http://www.avecresources.org. A brochure about Avec Resources' books, an annotated catalogue of the Archives and books by Widdicombe and Lovell are available from Miss Catherine Widdicombe, MPhil, at 125 Waxwell Lane, Pinner, Middx HA5 3ER, Tel 020 8866 2195; Fax 020 8866 1408; email: jcwiddicombe@tiscali.co.uk.

Reg Batten 1950s

CHAPTER 12

Long Walk From the Door: A History of Work with Girls and Young Women in Northern Ireland from 1969

Susan Morgan and Eliz McArdle

In 2006 a garden party was held by YouthAction Northern Ireland, to mark the end of an era. YouthAction was moving from the Hampton site, a substantial Victorian house which had been the organisation's headquarters since 1973 (Chapman, 2005), to a contemporary new building in the centre of Belfast. Scanning the sea of faces it was notable that many of the women in attendance had been involved in work with girls and young women since the 1970s up to the present day. Grabbing this novel opportunity we photographed a chronological line of those involved. This sparked an idea that it was timely to capture the rich and unique history of this work, to both record it and to acknowledge that reflection on the past may help us to shape the future.

Some of what has been revealed in the subsequent research indicates that the broader social context of the 'Troubles' has had an impact on the development of the work, meaning that at times there has been a uniqueness to work with girls and young women in the Northern Ireland context. Whilst the practice itself is noteworthy, the fact that it existed and flourished within this context is quite remarkable. Work with girls and young women has long been contested; however, a number of identifiable factors have influenced its survival and continued growth. We explore some of these factors and the relationship they have had with the backdrop of prevailing civil and political conflict and the subsequent move towards peace. We postulate on how these factors will prevail in our current 'post-conflict' society and whether the relationship between feminism and current practice is one that needs to be revisited.

Methodology

The purpose of the research was not only to capture facts, but also some of the feelings, emotions, motivations and values involved helping to shape understanding of the influences, direction, twists, turns and strategies during the last 35 years. Two main methods were employed; the first, a review of documents that had been produced in direct relation to work with girls and young women in Northern Ireland and the second, in-depth interviews of some of those who had been involved and pivotal to the work and its development. A snowballing technique was used to identify the nine interviewees whose comments have informed the analysis but with awareness that their reflections are subjective and offer specific perspectives on the development of work with girls and young women and an acknowledgement that times and dates to which they refer may be indicative rather than actual.[1] The broader context has been informed through documents, with historical reference to the recent conflict in Northern Ireland and others relating to the development of work with girls and young women within a youth policy framework.

The conflict, civil rights and the women's movement

The most recent conflict in the history of Northern Ireland faced a defining moment in 1968 when endemic discrimination, based upon religious or political persuasion, was challenged through the Civil Rights movement. In 1967, the Northern Ireland Civil Rights Association was set up. It drew its members from both communities but mainly from Nationalist Catholics who were more at a disadvantage under the Stormont government. This movement was an attempt to draw attention to grievances with regards to housing, employment and elections (Fitzduff and O'Hagan, 2000; Darby, 1995; Dunn, 1995).

Peaceful demonstrations soon spiralled into violence as clashes between the civil rights marchers and unionist supporters became more frequent and frenzied. By the summer of 1969, British troops were sent into Northern Ireland to manage the street conflict , while attempts were made between 1969 and 1971 for the British Government to offer political and social reform in response to the issues raised by the Northern Ireland Civil Rights Association. The proposed reforms were of limited value and did not quell the growing dissent amongst Catholics. In March 1972, Northern Ireland governance was taken out of the hands of the local Stormont Parliament and given over to the direct rule from Westminster. Meanwhile a pattern of housing and community segregation along religious and political lines was emerging within local communities. By this stage, the impact of conflict could already be seen among young people,

> *From 1969 many young people became involved in street riots in Northern Ireland. This chance to participate in street confrontations with the street authorities was very significant . . . and young people became involved to an alarming extent in paramilitary activity.*

(Gillespie et al., 1992, 3)

Internationally, the late 1960s and early 1970s witnessed the resurrection of the women's movement and the eruption of the black civil rights movement across America and the UK. These far-reaching movements were embraced by local civil rights activists, who felt an affinity with the aspirations and principles of their worldwide counterparts. This connection was psychologically important as it gave the Civil Rights Movement and the Catholic community access to the high moral ground and provided a greater sense of legitimacy to local civil rights activities. For women promoting and pursuing gender equality, the politicisation of a people had provided many opportunities to raise local consciousness, not only about religious and political oppression, but also of the specific political, social and economic oppression of women within Northern Ireland. This provided the springboard on which some youth and community workers began their work with girls and young women. Reflecting on the 1970s, one interviewee cited her connection to the Women's Movement and to a wider political consciousness as instrumental, saying that at the start:

> *There were lots of late night discussions . . . Thinking about what we were going to do and how we were going to organise stuff . . . there wasn't many youth centres in those days but we went into community centres knowing that you had to get the girls out of the toilets and get them participating . . .*

(Interviewee 3)

However, the relationship between the international politics of the women's movement and local civil rights activism was, for some, a double-edged sword. For feminists and those actively pursuing gender equality, association with the predominantly Catholic Civil Rights Movement, and the tacit relationship to the

Republican movement was potentially divisive. Local association with para-militaries often threatened to undermine the feminist agenda:

> *Validation on one side had a negative side effect because you did get very articulate women with republican identity attached to them and some organisations like the Association (Northern Ireland Association Of Youth Clubs – NIAYC) had to walk a very fine line . . . for the work not to be seen as over-identified with that.*

> (Interviewee 4)

For those who *were* involved in the political movements, the problems associated with promoting work with girls and young women were different. They faced the widely considered tacit opinion that the issues associated with civil and political unrest would take precedence over any other question of oppression and inequality. The 'cause' for republicans on one side and loyalists on the other was more important than gender equality – 'that' cause was for another day:

> *there was an understanding in communities that we must support each other for the cause, therefore anything that undermines your own people will be frowned upon.*

> (Interviewee 4)

The strong influence of the church and conditions of life in a conflicted society has contributed to the conservative nature of Northern Ireland and the youth sector. In places where religion is tied up with political or territorial conflict it has been argued that secularism does not easily flourish,

> *. . . religion diminishes in social significance, becomes increasingly privatised, and loses personal salience **except** where it finds work to do other than relating individuals to the supernatural.*

> (Bruce, 2002, 30)

The scarcity of secularism in this religio-political society has implications for the norms of interaction – a particular type of politeness can also be a particular feature of living in such a society. A deep seated fear of stirring conflict outside of context encourages a learned politeness which facilitates contact without conflict (Eyben, Morrow and Wilson, 2002, 15). It appears that this may have had some impact on work with girls and young women in both a positive and negative way. While work with girls and young women began its contemporary journey in an overtly political way it seems that the conservative nature of both the youth sector and wider cultural norms had a longer term impact:

People wanted to focus on what they shared rather than on what was different, its almost common courtesy . . . You're not going to bring up the things that divide you.

(Interviewee 2)

The developments in the late 1960s and early 1970s, including the influence of international social movements, the dominating influence of the growing conflict, increasing segregation between the Catholic and Protestant communities, and the conservative nature within Northern Ireland, all had a measurable influence on the direction of the youth sector and the development of work with girls and young women in the following decades.

Youth service response-policy and practice

The 1944 Youth Welfare Act (NI) introduced a more comprehensive youth service than ever before, with the Youth Committee acting as grant-maker to both local authority youth services and voluntary youth organisations. Following the introduction of Direct Rule in 1972 an administrative structure emerged which was intended to be apolitical. This included the establishment of Education and Library Boards to run key services alongside the downgrading and virtual exclusion of elected councillors and councils from the running of the country. It had the effect of virtually eliminating any overt party political influence on policy in youth work (McCready, 2001, 37).

The Recreation and Youth Service (NI) Order 1973, replaced the Youth Welfare Physical Training and Recreation Act of 1962 and effectively enabled the establishment of a statutory Youth Service for Northern Ireland, decreeing that,

each (Education and Library) Board shall secure the provision for its area, of adequate facilities of recreational, social, physical, cultural youth service activities and for services ancillary to education.

(Youth Council for Northern Ireland (YCNI), 1973)

The 1973 policy directive was very much a state response to the visible engagement of young people in the street conflict. The seriousness of this government intervention is best illustrated by the finances which followed the legislation involving centralised funding for the youth service,

It is impossible to exaggerate the significance of an increase in annual allocation from £125,500 in 1972 to £3.5 million during 1975/76. Until 1980 there was a steady growth in the amount of capital and recurrent

provision for voluntary and statutory agencies alike bringing the total of about £8 million.

(Department of Education Northern Ireland [DENI], 1987)

The impact of such resourcing has been long-term. Between 1974 and 1981, 143 purpose built youth facilities were completed including youth centres, residential centres, premises for uniformed organisations and school based youth wings (DENI, 1987). A raft of full-time youth work posts were created and professional training was developed to meet the need. On the face of it, the scale of the intervention offered opportunities for young women and young men throughout Northern Ireland; but due to the original impetus for the government response, the reality was that this new youth service had an underlying emphasis towards working with young men (Trimble, 1990):

> *you reach out to people you perceive to be on the cutting edge ... the forefront of it, which were usually young men, young men who were being killed, young men who were killing and it was usually men who were running the paramilitaries.*

(Interviewee 1)

Within the climate of the day, working to create a safer environment for young men was a goal which was readily subscribed to by all. Yet it meant that the place of young women was relegated to second-best:

> *The civil and political situation made it harder to raise issues about girls and young women as it felt like there were more life and death issues and bigger economic issues around at the time.*

(Interviewee 5)

In programme terms, there was often an over-emphasis on sport and recreation aimed at catering for the 'assumed' needs of young men (Harland and Morgan, 2003). The focus on getting young men off the streets had a huge impact on the youth centres which, as a result, were dominated by groups of young men. This is best illustrated in the physical layout of a traditional youth centre with social areas filled with pool tables, young men playing football in the sports hall and sport on the TV. Young women, if they were to come into the centre, had to make the courageous and uncomfortable journey from the entrance, to reach the safe territory with their female counterparts at the café or tuck-shop:

> *the interior was very much small rooms; the first thing you would encounter would've been the pool table for instance ... Then you'd talk*

*to the young women about the **long walk from the door** to where the café area was . . .*

(Interviewee 1)

Young women's ownership of spaces in the clubs, visibility, and feelings of safety in the clubs were compromised and almost tangible. Regardless of how uninviting the youth centres were for young women, there were few options outside the home that were considered safe. When reflecting on what was available at the time one former participant stated that there was:

nothing, literally nothing; the troubles were active, you were not allowed into town, your parents were concerned that you stayed close.

(Interviewee 8)

So there is no doubt that the youth centres offered both young women and young men refuge from a very threatening external environment:

I can remember in some instances a poorly lighted environment. Para-militaries were putting the lights out for whatever activities went on at night . . . So the environment was not hospitable in the evenings . . . the exterior wasn't the sort of place that had young people walking about safely . . . if you were a young woman it was all the more dangerous . . .

(Interviewee 1)

Whilst a new policy and practice agenda was beginning to emerge within the youth sector the cementing of youth work to youth centres at this time shows a narrowness in the government approach to the so called 'troubles'. However, a number of women were pushing the agenda for girls and young women in an environment where inequality was becoming increasingly apparent. It seems that during this era work with girls and young women was not really presenting much of a threat and it began to thrive, albeit without any targeted resources. The voluntary sector in the form of Youth Action Northern Ireland (YANI) was largely influential in the emerging strategy, policy and practice of work with girls and young women throughout the following decades.

The work and the workers

Northern Ireland Association of Youth Clubs (NIAYC) now YouthAction Northern Ireland, was (and is) a developmental youth organisation working regionally. NIAYC had strong connections with the broader community sector and wider social movements and attracted staff with like-minded aspirations. The inclination of staff towards politics with a small 'p' and social change appears to have led the agency to gender equality work. One of the key concerns of this agency became 'to improve the equality of participation of girls and young women in the Northern Ireland Youth Sector'. The need was identified in 1979 for support and training to achieve this (YANI, 1997) and between 1979 and 1984 this work became integral to YANI. However, this was not a position that was replicated throughout the youth sector where gender equality work and aspirations were at best, challenged and at worst, disparaged:

If I reflect my impressions were that everywhere you went there was a maleness, a maleness about the work, a maleness about personnel in key positions and very much a lack of awareness about the broader needs of young women and I think that was completely understandable in a society that was in the throws and turmoils of conflict . . .

(Interviewee 1)

The appetite for work with women and young women was marginal during the late 1960s and early 1970s, with a small number of women working in the sector to improve not only provision for young women but also tackle wider issues of inequality. Centres remained male dominated from leaders to members, and men disproportionately filled the managerial positions within the service (Trimble, 1990; Harland *et al.*, 2003). It was suggested by one interviewee that women at this time were not in 'powerful positions to influence' (interviewee 4) which made progress slow and cumbersome. So where work with girls and young women did take place, it was largely down to the commitment of the dedicated few:

the low participation of young women in the youth service is left to the interest and commitment of the individual worker.

(Trimble, 1990, 26)

Moving into the 1980s the 'gender equality' debate was gaining some strength overall. There were a number of important community development initiatives and government schemes in this era which supported the infrastructure of work with girls and young women. Examples include the Action for Community Employment Scheme which gave resources and staff to many youth work projects; the prominence of women's groups within community centres and the financing by Belfast City Council of the Women's Development Project under Belfast Area of Needs (BAN) (McCready, 2001, 64). The work of YANI was connected to these wider social movements and arguably was one of the few places where the youth service was connecting outside its own age groupings on a wider community front. In 1984 YANI successfully presented a case to the Department of Education (DENI) for a full time development officer post to support and develop work with girls and young women. The statutory endorsement of this post was financially and psychologically important for the work. There was by then a much broader recognition of how societal gender roles and behaviours impacted on how girls and young women presented themselves in the youth sector:

> *only by understanding the individual in the community can you come to terms with the individual in the club.*
>
> (Waiting Our Turn, 1978, 3)

It was becoming increasingly recognised that young women were not using the service to the same extent as young men. A youth sector review was undertaken in 1986, and the subsequent *Policy for the Youth Service in Northern Ireland* (DENI, 1986) outlined a curriculum for youth work with nine core requirements to be taken into account in the planning and delivery of youth programmes. The first of these core requirements specified the need for 'encouragement and preparation for participation on an equal basis by young men and young women' (DENI, 1986). These policy developments were perhaps a reflection of a sea-change on the ground:

> *the issues that women were facing were starting to be recognised and then I think it was women youth and community workers . . . doing a mix of work as their own consciousness and own awareness increased.*
>
> (Interviewee 3)

YANI was an agency trying to address the gaps in provision and this was having a broader impact on the youth sector. Reflections from interviewees reveal a positive change in the sector during the mid-1980s which saw the introduction of 'girls only' nights, single sex groups and developments to create environments where girls could meet in relative safety and freely access the facilities offered by the youth centres. The development of anti-sexist training for both male and female workers during this period offered opportunities for exploring issues, raising awareness that in turn influenced practice. YANI had a strong 'Work with Girls' sub-group, made up of young women, workers, funders and policy-makers, who brought both support and direction. The work seemed to be emanating virtually exclusively from within the voluntary sector not as a haphazard and random response to gender inequality, but rather as a strategic and considered practice with an ideological underpinning. Policy, practice and training were coming together at one time, and were influenced by the considered discussions going on with, and between, mainly female workers and the young women. However, while YANI was at the forefront of these developments, it was not without its internal struggles. For example,

> *the director . . . was very young person focused, but at the same time would have been quite conservative. (He) would see the need of working with young girls on one level but once it started pushing the boundaries . . . being a wee bit overtly political . . ., (he) . . . would have had a lot of wariness about it. The case for working with girls and young women had to be made both internally and externally as in 'Why single girls out? What's so special about girls?*

(Interviewee 4)

Conferences for girls and young women were held regularly organised by NIAYC, supported by other community based projects and training, support, resources and publications such as *Waiting Our Turn* (1984) were being offered to those working with young women. Building upon this energy and activity YANI published a seminal report called *Equality of Opportunity* (1990). This report reviewed the position of girls and young women in the full time sector of the Northern Ireland Youth Service finding that,

> *The vast majority of girls are leaving the full time sector of the youth service as early as thirteen years of age . . . Many are not attending because they are not actively encouraged to take up opportunities or because programmes are unattractive to them. Those who do attend are frequently harassed and intimidated by boys when they attempt to participate in activities. The traditional style and layout of many Youth Centres, with large open spaces accommodating general equipment used mainly by young men is another factor which contributes to young women being less visibly active. A lack of willingness to assess the needs of girls and young women, plus a reflection of the many negative attitudes towards females generally in society, appear to prevail in the sector of the Northern Ireland Youth Service researched in this project.*

(Trimble, 1990, 47)

At this stage work with girls and young women was gathering momentum. The earlier work was showing signs of coming to fruition and the feeling on the ground was one of optimism whilst still recognising that a lot of work had to be done. The damning 'Equality of Opportunity' report provided an impetus to drive the agenda forward and it was shortly followed by *Into the Mainstream* (Youth Council for Northern Ireland, 1994), which provided curriculum guidelines on how to promote the participation of girls and young women in the youth sector. Nevertheless, the impact of both these discerning documents and the evolution of the practice itself were undermined in the subsequent years by a growing hostility and resistance to feminism and feminist practice.

Backlash, hostility and competing agendas

Hostility has been a consistent feature of the work with girls and young women. A number of the interviewees made reference to the growing resistance from other workers, male workers, young men and young women themselves. It seems there was an almost constant need to justify the work. One interviewee who had a dedicated position to develop work with girls and young women commented that,

> *People questioned the post dedicated to girls and young women, yet when I explained it they felt under threat.*
>
> (Interviewee 3)

She referred to meetings where there were many deliberate sexist remarks directed at her and talked about the struggle she had with herself whether to challenge these or not, often feeling that she was in a no-win situation. This problem was clearly not exclusive to Northern Ireland as another of the interviewees discussed a conference she had attended in England where she had been asked to look at the Thompson Report, *Experience and Participation* (HMSO, 1982) from the perspective of young women. She said that this generated a lot of hostility from the men in the audience 'even when we were trying to bend over ourselves not to be confrontational' (Interviewee 5). Another commented:

> *I well remember going into various training or doing presentations where the audience would have been really very hostile where there were the smart ass questions and comments . . . it was very common for remarks about either my post or about women in front of me just to see what the reaction would be.*
>
> (Interviewee 3)

In the mid to late 1990s the institutionalisation of gender equality through policy initiatives put into place legislation which could suggest that equality was now achievable. This left little room for feminist action on the ground and a growing hostility to feminism in popular culture giving the impression that feminism was no longer necessary, had either gone too far or had achieved what is set out to do (Faludi, 1992). This had a local impact on the work in YANI and in local communities, moving work with girls and women from a position of strength, to less stable ground. In the Government Review of the Youth Service Policy and Curriculum which lasted from 1996 to 1999 (DENI, 1997; DENI, 1999), the gender equality message of the 1987 policy was watered down for the more generic core principles of 'preparation for participation, testing values and beliefs and acceptance and understanding of others' (DENI, 1997). Losing the specific reference to young women within the resulting policy document was detrimental for the work, the workers and ultimately young women themselves. The emerging context proved to be a much less fertile ground for work with girls and young women.

This 'anti-feminist' sentiment was also evident in the wider political context in Northern Ireland. For example, the Northern Ireland Women's Coalition was established (1996) to attempt to redress the lack of women involved in politics in Northern Ireland which was abysmally low. However when Monica McWilliams, co-founder of the party, was elected to her assembly seat (1998) she encountered a great deal of sexist abuse. At the time members of the party elected to the assembly would tell of how she would be ordered by other assembly members to go back to where she belonged (at home) or she 'should stay at home and breed for Ulster' rather than be in the Assembly (Galligan, 2001). The creation and expansion (although short-lived) of the Women's Coalition was an eye-opener revealing the absence of women in politics and the traditional values still prevalent in Northern Ireland. It also showed how sexism could be exposed and so explicit when the power base of the men was overtly challenged.

Just as individual workers and the feminist movement were seeing strategic gains in terms of the convergence of youth policy, practice, training, funding and political engagement, new challenges were arising. The workers found themselves facing organisational and personal hostility and responded by moderating their overt feminist expression to gain acceptance. To avoid negative stereotyping one interviewee spoke of how she talked about her life and her children in order to avoid the feminist label and therefore be dismissed as a 'radical'. This appeared to place an additional pressure upon the worker to be 'the conscience' of the youth service in relation to women and young women,

when I went to meetings I never wore what would be perceived as . . .
feminist (the) kind of clothes like dungarees and badges and stuff like that,
I always avoided stuff like that cause I didn't want the label, it was bad
enough that I had a label.

(Interviewee 3)

A number of those interviewed made similar comments, illustrating how taking on the resistance to feminist ideology was a constant struggle for those trying to introduce girls' nights or specific work with girls and young women in clubs. One interviewee suggested that 'there was need to build relationships to be both personally and professionally accepted' (Interviewee 3), and another commented that her approach involved 'trying to bring people with you rather than be confrontational . . . It was about trying, in a way, to win people over' (Interviewee 6). In order to make any impact, people needed to be almost persuaded to acknowledge the issue of equality and young women. This was firstly about working to encourage them of the merits and value of working with young women and secondly about working with female workers so that they did not become despondent with the work and the place of women within the youth service. The resistance faced by the workers resulted in their flagging energy and a question regarding connection between the practice and feminist principles. Those working with girls and young women were coming under increasing pressure to justify the value of their practice in ideological terms. Rather than justifying the work in feminist terms, this was achieved through the suppression of feminist rhetoric. It was clearly not exclusive to feminism and work with girls and young women in Northern Ireland. Spence, in her analysis of feminist practice with young women in the North-East of England discussed the implications of feminist suppression:

One of the outcomes of moderation is that the only issues which are
pursued are those which can be accommodated without too much
disruption to the status quo.

(Spence, 1996, 44)

Trying to retain a foothold against the hostility meant that in some ways the practice moved from the political to the personal, from the structural to the individual. Consequently, there remains a question around whether feminism was ever really acknowledged as legitimate in youth work practice with girls and young women in Northern Ireland.

The boys are back in town

A question which dogged the work from the early 1970s onwards, when issues were being raised and addressed for young women, was 'what about the boys?' In the 1990s this argument evolved from one of resistance to a more strategic approach; the emphasis being that the youth service, whilst catering for the interests of young men, was not necessarily addressing their needs (Lloyd, 1997; Harland, 1997, 2001). This prompted the emergence of non-traditional work with boys and young men, which in Northern Ireland had its roots firmly in feminist youth work practice (Harland and Morgan, 2003). There was a move away from a recreational focus and more attention given to the mental health and emotional needs of young men again connected to the reality of living in a conflict society (Harland and Morgan, 2003). Whilst work with young men was rooted in feminist practice, it also became a competing agenda. The work gained momentum within the context of a broader sociological discourse on a crisis in masculinity (Whitehead and Barrett, 2002), the attention given to the underachievement of boys in schools (Mills, 2003), and much published social problems such as the high suicide rates of young men (Beattie et al., 2006). The wider prevailing mood can be represented by the 'Fathers for Justice' Superhero campaign for child custody and visitation rights, which could be characterised by the principle 'if they're getting it, why not me?' This discourse has caused particular difficulties for work with girls and young women in that it can be construed that the equal treatment of young women and young men will balance up a systemic historical gender inequality. This is reflected through the equal opportunities legislation and policies, which demand parity between the sexes rather than focusing on the discrimination and oppression of women. It also shifts the focus of girls and young women's workers, who in raising issues relevant to young women, were forced at the same time to pay credit to the corresponding issues for young men and the work with young men:

> As part of the 90s and the 00s with the advent of the Young Men's resurgence, there was an issue of equality and legislation which threatened the existence of any single-sex provision – there could be a challenge to the legitimacy of single sex work on the grounds that it was discriminatory towards the other sex. This has had a major effect of undermining work . . . single sex work, as it has to then address how the needs of the other sex are not being overlooked.

(Interviewee 3)

The message being presented is that gender inequality is being faced equally by men and women, which negates the statistical picture of differences in status, power and prestige (Walter, 1998; Greer, 2000; Whelehan, 2000; OFMDFM, 2006) and undervalues specific female issues.

Whilst radical feminism conjures up images of military engagement – advance, retreat and resistance – work with girls and young women in Northern Ireland has had a more conservative edge. Only one interviewee referred to the 'sledge hammer end of change' whereby some of the approaches were very challenging. On the other hand, there was a more concerted move away from the sledgehammer, with one interviewee referring to the need for a 'sophisticated approach' (Interviewee 5), while another spoke of how raising consciousness about inequality switched on a light bulb that couldn't be switched off (Interviewee 3). Another interviewee concurs with this awareness-raising strategy:

> . . . I think what always motivated young people is fairness and unfairness you know, people can really be moved to do things because they . . . something's unfair and not justified or 'Why Me?'
>
> (Interviewee 2)

The methodology to achieve gender equality has separated radical and liberal feminists for decades, but the tension which exists in pulling from both ideologies is one which may have merit – the radical feminists being reined in to some extent, while liberal feminists are pushed into greater activism than might be expected. It is this debate and the dialogue of ideologies which has been a crucial part of the strategy, and the accountability to other people or groups who will challenge your actions, motivations and principles. This tension caused more considered action connected to the potential consequences, forming an effective strategy, which sets the work up for the phase to come.

The peace dividend and the equality agenda

On the 31 August 1994 the Irish Republican Army declared a complete cessation to military operations. This was followed by a ceasefire of the UDA, UVF and Red Hand Commandos, the loyalist paramilitary groupings in October of the same year (Kilmurray, 2004). However twenty five years of violent conflict and inter-community tension had left Northern Ireland polarised and damaged. Nearly one half of the population of Northern Ireland lived in areas that were now more than 90 per cent Protestant or 95 per cent Catholic ('A Citizens Inquiry', The Opsahl Report 1993 – cited in Kilmurray, 2004).

Thirty-two per cent of 14–17 year olds living in Northern Ireland had witnessed people being killed or seriously injured (Community Conflict, Impact on Children, 2000 cited in Kilmurray, 2004). The ceasefire therefore heralded a new dawn with a prevailing mood of cautious optimism:

> The first cautious welcome for a reduction in paramilitary violence has developed into a collective community sigh of relief . . . there is the sense that change is now possible-whatever form that may take-that the absolutism of the gun can be replaced by a process characterised by inclusive participation.
>
> (Open Letter to the Community Foundation Northern Ireland, September 1994)

At a UK and European level, economic arrangements were being put into place in anticipation or as an incentive to continue on the road to 'Peace'. In 1989 the International Fund for Ireland was established and the European Union saw their third anti-poverty programme from 1989–1994 and the European Special Support programme for Peace and Reconciliation provide a major influx of money to the voluntary and community sector. With this funding stream, came a new language of targets, outputs, outcomes and beneficiaries, arising from a deep seated culture of accountability and measurability. Whilst the finance was welcome, the managerialism with which it was accompanied potentially led to the demotion of youth work approaches with less clearly defined outcomes in favour of more 'sellable' options. In the context of work with girls and young women YANI had both the structure and the strategy to reap the benefits of this funding deluge, bringing with it new opportunities for some young women who existed in relative isolation to mainstream society such as young mothers or young women with disability. However, as single issue groups and single issue approaches such as work with young mothers flourished in this new world, it became more difficult to make a case for generic work with young women:

> The government and the state are very outcome driven and they're looking in terms of solving problems of individual young people if they can be grouped fair enough . . . they're not really interested in generic provision . . .
>
> (Interviewee 4)

This system fosters a problem centred approach with a delivery emphasis on programmes rather than provision, and as a result sidelines the generality of work with girls and young women. This culture of targeted work became strongly embedded in the community and voluntary sector in Northern Ireland not only because of the breadth of the funding stream but also due to the raft of local legislative developments accompanying peace and UK Social Policy Directives driven by New Labour's Social Exclusion Unit. Locally, the Good Friday Agreement and Section 75 of the subsequent Northern Ireland Act (1998) included a directive stating that public bodies, public policies and consequently public funds must not discriminate. More recently, the Gender Equality Strategy for Northern Ireland (2006–2016) promised 'the mainstreaming of gender equality into all of our policies and service delivery to tackle the causes of gender inequality' (OFMDFM, 2005.) Adding to this, 'New Targeting Social Need' policy (1998) highlights the principle of 'equal access for all' with measures to counteract discrimination on the grounds of gender among others.

It could be suggested that the impact of such anti-discrimination measures, rather than having the desired effect of inclusion of marginalised groupings into mainstream collectives and activities, has involved targeting selective and hard-to-reach groups for 'separate rather than integrated' work.

> *I think something else is happening; it is nearly the tick box. I think it would be harder to make the case for single identity work with girls and young women unless they were specific groupings . . . the problem groupings.*
>
> (Interviewee 4)

Ironically the 'equality agenda' has challenged the legitimacy of single sex work on the grounds that it was discriminating towards the other sex. The outcome of this is that the argument for working with young women must be made afresh:

> *and so the question has then come, come up again 30 years later, why women only, why girls only, why young women only and I think the equality legislation should have been, and fundamentally is, there to protect all that . . . but I think actually that becomes questioned ye know in terms of . . . what about men's rights and boys' rights and young men's rights?*
>
> (Interviewee 3)

Yet the confines of the peace dividend in terms of funding streams aligned to peace-building and sustainability and the possible restrictions caused by the 'Equality Agenda' have not, it seems, hampered the underpinning principles and practice of work with girls and young women for the women workers who have been involved. Work with girls and young women has demonstrated throughout four decades tactical adaptation to the changes in policy, funding and social and economic trends. Conversely, what has changed is that the work is not recognised as feminist and the feminist understanding which motivated the work in the first place is suppressed.

Surviving against the odds

In spite of a range of difficulties, new challenges and growing resistance to feminist ideology and practice, work with girls and young women has continued to thrive and develop. This was connected to a number of identifiable factors by interviewees. Firstly, the work was always being driven by a powerful force of women:

> *structurally there was a very strong work with girls subgroup and they were quite leading influential women from across the voluntary, statutory and education sectors so the big plus . . . was that it was always well thought out. It was well thought through in terms of a strategy, of how you deliver and how push the boundaries of working with young women and staff . . . and in how you press levers of policy, and that should not be underestimated.*

(Interviewee 4)

Secondly the women's sector in Northern Ireland (comprising community-based groups, women's centres, and lobbying groups) was organised as a strong, politicised and vibrant movement. This had an influence on the work with girls and young women in a number of ways. For example it was possible through the mid to late 1990s to draw from the strength of the women's sector in terms of ideological support – offering a space to develop and strengthen thinking whereas the youth sector by contrast had a more conservative edge. However, the women's sector suffered particularly from the 'anti-feminist backlash' due to its overtly political nature, whilst the reper-cussions of the 'equality agenda' involved a weakening of the female-centredness of some work. In the process, some Women's Centres became Community Centres and a local domestic violence helpline changed to offer a service to both women and men in order to accommodate statutory funders.

Despite the dilution of the women's sector, work with girls and young women continued 'under the radar' of a highly consuming political conflict and was able was able to continue to a certain degree as a feature of the youth sector, 'perhaps [because] it was seen as non-threatening, which in itself is an interesting proposal' (Interviewee 1).

The pattern which evolved from the 1970s onwards was one of push, then retreat, adapt, regroup and then push forward again each time with different terms of reference. The energy required to sustain such a pattern over concerted periods meant that 'passing on the mantle' became an important part of an overall feminist strategy. This required greater attention in terms of how younger or newer workers became engaged, educated or radicalised and how space and attention was given to the mentoring process. Frustrations arose not only from the barriers presented to the work and the workers, but also from the painstakingly slow pace of movement, coupled with the 'forward-backward' pattern. Both Interviewee 1 and Interviewee 8 made comments which reflected a disappointment at the slow progress and a professional frustration at the limited fruits of much labour.

Although these frustrations existed, there was nothing to suggest within the interviews that workers were deterred in any way from their commitment to working with girls and young women. For example, although not necessarily directly involved in work with girls and young women at the time of the interviews, the interviewees had carried the spirit and the priorities of the work into policy, funding and practice arenas. One (Interviewee 8) described how her involvement with YANI had informed her life and her practice ever since 'in whatever I have done'.

The determination and the passion of the central protagonists is a key element in the persistence of youth work with girls and young women in Northern Ireland. The drive of the workers was not only important in keeping young women on the agenda, but increasingly their positioning in places of greater power afforded them a wider sphere of influence in policy, funding, training and practice. For example, three interviewees have developed formidable careers in funding organisations. The potential for having direct impact on the lives of young women in Northern Ireland, through funding opportunities is inescapable. In terms of future strategy the movement of workers into key work areas and positions offers potential dividends for work with girls and young women. While these workers move on, new workers take their place in the 'grass roots' and so it continues.

Conclusion

The legislative, political, policy and practice developments of the past four decades are very much bound up in the contemporary picture of young women's lives and work with girls and young women in Northern Ireland. YouthAction Northern Ireland's report *Still Waiting* (McAlister, Gray and Neill,

2007) offers an in-depth perspective on the lives of young women living in Northern Ireland at the beginning of the 21st century.

The contentious title, *Still Waiting* was chosen to echo *Waiting our Turn* (NIAYC, 1978) a documentary resource created almost thirty years previously to address the low levels of participation by young women in youth provision and community activity. The connection reflects the relatively limited advances which have been achieved for and by young women in the intervening period. But it also points to a strong emerging theme in the research presented here about the persistence of passive attitudes presented by working class young women towards gender equality, whilst highlighting continuing levels of inequality. There is a stark disparity between the reality of young women's lives and the rhetoric about gender equality which relies on an erroneous belief that equality has been achieved. This position leads to apathy and complacency. The impact of this for those young women who do not achieve as they might have hoped, is to individualise the problems, difficulties and failures, even where there are clear structural explanations.

This reflects a wider social policy trend which has since the 1980s persistently moved approaches to social problems and inequalities away from the political and back to the personal. Such an individualistic approach can be seen in what is referred to as a 'post-feminist' era when many young women seem to have rejected feminism. McAlister, Neill and Gray (2007a) in their research with young women acknowledge this development among research participants. However, they argue that it is the feminist label rather than feminist principles that have been rejected (McAlister, Neill, Gray, 2007b, 18). This insight may offer opportunities for a new chapter in the journey whereby those pivotal to work with girls and young women can again reflect, regroup and advance.

As Northern Ireland continues its move away from conflict, the youth sector will increasingly need to justify its existence and its contribution to peace. There are opportunities for work and workers who are strategic in their approach, advocating and implementing practice which is sound and well established with clearly identifiable outcomes. History tells us that this is an enduring strength within the practice and ideology of work with girls and young women.

The use of the historical perspective has provided the long view. Just like '*the long walk from the door*' for young women in the youth clubs, the journey of youth work practice with girls and young women has equally required persistence and courage. The pivotal place and positioning of the workers and the passing on of the 'mantle' both horizontally and vertically have proven to be highly productive for the continuation of work with girls from a female perspective. The feminist principles of the earlier decades continue to be an ideological, if silent force. The need for stamina and strength, constancy and sustained action and for continuous reflection on ideology, vision and practice, all continue to be necessary for a future strategy of work with girls and young women in Northern Ireland.

Acknowledgements

The authors would also like to acknowledge, in particular, the contribution and support provided by Sam McCready and Jean Spence in compiling this chapter.

Notes

1   The interviewees were: Marie Abbott, Kate Campbell, Maggie Jardine, Sheila Jane Malley, Mary Marken, Sam McCready, Denis Palmer, Julie Townsend, June Trimble. All interviewees have been involved in the development of work with girls and young women throughout the 1970s and 1980s, either as participants, practitioners, trainers or managers. In the interests of confidentiality quotes in the text are not specifically attributed to individuals.

References

Beattie, K., Harland, K. and McCready, S. (2006) *Mental Health and young men, suicide and self-harm*, Centre for Young Men's Studies Research Update No. 2. Belfast, University of Ulster.

Bruce, S. (2002) *God is Dead, Secularization in the West*, London, Blackwell.

Chapman, T. (2005) *The Journey and opportunities, A history of YouthAction Northern Ireland 1944–2005*, YouthAction Northern Ireland.

Darby, J. (1995) 'Conflict in Northern Ireland, A Background Essay', in S. Dunn (ed.) *Facets of the Conflict in Northern Ireland*. London, Macmillan Press Ltd.

Department of Education for Northern Ireland (1986) *Northern Ireland Youth Service, A Review.* DENI.

Department of Education for Northern Ireland (1987) *Policy for the Youth Service in Northern Ireland*. DENI.

Department of Education for Northern Ireland (1997) *Youth Work, A model for Effective Practice*. DENI.

Department of Education for Northern Ireland (1999) *A Youth Service for a new Millennium – Youth Service Policy Review*. DENI.

Department of Education and Science (1982) *Experience and Participation. Review Group on the Youth Service in England* (The Thompson Report), London, HMSO.

Dunn, S. (1995) 'The Conflict as a Set of Problems,' in S. Dunn (ed.) *Facets of the Conflict in Northern Ireland*, London: Macmillan.

Eyben, K., Morrow, D. and Wilson, D.A. (2002), *The Equity, Diversity and Interdependence Framework, A Framework for Organisational Learning and Change*, Belfast, University of Ulster.

Faludi, S. (1992) *Backlash, The Undeclared War against Women.* London, Chatto and Windus.

Fitzduff, M. and O'Hagan, L. (2000) The Northern Ireland Troubles, INCORE background paper, www.cain.ulst.ac.uk/othelem/incorepaper.htm accessed 4 February 2007.

Galligan, Y. (22–11–2001) *Women's Representation in Northern Ireland and the Republic of Ireland*. Paper presented at John Whyte Memorial Lecture, University College Dublin.

Gillespie, N., Lovett, T. and Gardner, W. (1992) *Youth Work and Working Class Youth Culture – Rules and Resistance in West Belfast*, Buckingham, Open University Press.

Greer, G. (2000) *The Whole Woman*, London, Anchor.

Harland, K. (1997) *Young Men Talking – Voices from Belfast*. London, YouthAction Northern Ireland and Working with Men Publications.

Harland, K. (2001) 'The Challenges and potential of developing a more effective youth work curriculum with young men', *Journal of Child Care Practice* Vol 7 No. 4, 288–300.

Harland, K., Harvey, C., Morgan, T. and McCready, S. (2003) *'Worth Their Weight in Gold': An investigation into the career paths and views of Community Youth Graduates in Northern Ireland [1972–2001]*. Belfast, University of Ulster and the Youth Council for Northern Ireland.

Harland, K. and Morgan, S. (2003) 'Youth work with young men in Northern Ireland: An Advocacy Approach', *Youth and Policy*, 81, 74–85.

Kilmurray, A. (2004) *Building a Foundation for Change – A personal reflection on 25 years of Community Foundation support for community action*. Belfast, The Community Foundation for Northern Ireland.

Mills, M. (2003) 'Shaping the boys agenda, the backlash blockbusters', *International Journal of Inclusive Education*. vol. 7 (1), 55–74.

Morgan, S. and Harland, K. (in press, 2008) The 'Lens Model': A practical tool for developing and understanding gender conscious practice', *Youth and Policy*, 102, Spring.

McAlister, S., Gray, A. and Neill, G. (2007a) *Still Waiting – The stories behind the statistics of young women growing up in Northern Ireland*. Belfast, YouthAction Northern Ireland.

McAlister, S., Neill, G. and Gray, A. (2007b) 'I'm not a Feminist . . . I believe in equality for everyone' in *Women's News*. Belfast.

McCready, S. (2001) *Empowering People, Community Development and Conflict 1969–1999*. Belfast, HMSO, The Stationery Office.

Northern Ireland Association of Youth Clubs (1978) *Waiting Our Turn*. Belfast, NIAYC.

Northern Ireland Youth Committee (1973) *Northern Ireland Youth Services Act*. Belfast, HMSO.

Lloyd, T. (1997) *Let's get changed lads: Developing work with boys and young men*. London, Working with Men Publications.

OFMDFM (2006) *Gender Equality Strategy for Northern Ireland*. Belfast, OFMDFM.

Spence, J. (1996) 'Feminism in Work with Girls and Young Women', *Youth and Policy*, Special Issue on Young Women. Issue No, 52, 38–53.

Trimble, J. (1990) *'A Report on Equality of Opportunity – Provision for girls and young women in the full time sector of the Northern Ireland Youth Service'*. Belfast, YouthAction Northern Ireland.

Walter, N, (1998) *The New Feminism*. London, Little, Brown.

Whelehan, I. (2000) *Overloaded, Popular Culture and the Future of Feminism*. London, Women's Press.

Whitehead, S.M. and Barrett, F.J. (2002) *The Masculinities Reader*, Cambridge, Polity Press.

YouthAction Northern Ireland (1997) *Girls and Young Women's Support Project Evaluation* Report, Youth Action Northern Ireland.

YouthAction Northern Ireland (2006) *Gender Conscious Work with Young People. An occasional youth work practice*, Paper 2. Belfast, YouthAction Northern Ireland, University of Ulster, Curriculum Development Unit.

Youth Council for Northern Ireland (1994) *Into the Mainstream. Equality of Opportunity-Gender*. Youth Curriculum Guidelines. Belfast, YCNI.

Glossary of terms

- Belfast Area of Needs – A Government-led scheme to target funding for areas of Belfast in the greatest social need.
- DENI – Department of Education for Northern Ireland.
- Education and Library Boards – Statutory education authority and library authority for a specific area, including statutory responsibility for the provision of youth services in the geographical area.
- Loyalist – In Northern Ireland, one who is loyal to the British Crown with aspirations to maintain existing sovereignty.
- Northern Ireland Association of Youth Clubs – Currently known as YouthAction Northern Ireland, a regional voluntary organisation of Northern Ireland.
- Northern Ireland Civil Rights Association – The main organisation involved in the civil rights movement from the late 1960s to the 1970s in Northern Ireland.
- Nationalist – In Northern Ireland, one who supports the reunification of Ireland.
- OFM/DFM – Office of the First Minister and Deputy First Minister – Primary Department of the Northern Ireland Administration, established through the Belfast Agreement and the subsequent Northern Ireland Act (1998).
- Republican – A person who supports the style of government based on a republic over a monarchy. In Northern Ireland, it refers to an aspiration toward a United, 32 county, Ireland.
- Unionist – In Northern Ireland, one who wants to see the union with Britain maintained.
- Youth Council for Northern Ireland – A non-departmental public body to promote work with young people.

Girls and young women workers – past and present at Youth Action Northern Ireland Garden Party, 12 September 2006

CHAPTER 13

The Counter-Cultural Revolution and the *OZ* School Kids Issue: the Establishment Versus the Underground Press

Keith Popple

> *Come mothers and fathers throughout the land*
> *Don't criticise what you can't understand*
> *Your sons and daughters are beyond your command*
> *Your old road is rapidly ageing*
> *Please get out of the new one if you can't lend a hand*
> *For the times they are a-changing.*

(Bob Dylan, 1964)

During the summer of 1971 a highly publicised and celebrated court case took place at the Old Bailey, London which proved to be pivotal in the development of the UK's post-war counter-cultural revolution. The case brought together a number of key people in a growing movement that was ranged against the values and power of the British Establishment. It was to highlight varying alternative views of society and life styles. At the same time the media reported and commented on the views of young people, views that had steadily developed and grown powerful during the 1960s.

The court case involved three people, Richard Neville, Jim Anderson and Felix Dennis, who were accused on five charges of conspiring to publish and distribute for gain an issue of *OZ* (Number 28 – the *School Kids Issue*) which was considered by the police to be obscene. *OZ*, which was first published in the UK in 1967, was a satirical, humorous magazine that reflected the fluid and sometimes outrageous views of a hippy, youthful, bohemian strand in

British life. However, there were powerful sections of the Establishment who wanted to suppress these views and remove the publication from circulation.

This essay will contextualise the emergence of OZ with the growth of an increasing vociferous group of people who will be termed here as the 'Young Turks'. Since the early 20th century the term 'Young Turks' has come to be a used as a short-hand to mean those in society who hold progressive views, and who are not part of any one political group, organisation or movement but have opinions and life styles at odds with the status quo. These developments will be linked here with the emergence of counter-cultural revolution, including the 'underground press' of which OZ was a part, and which proved to be a challenge to the Establishment. The term 'The Establishment' is frequently used as a pejorative term to refer to the traditional British ruling elite and the structures that they either directly or indirectly control. During the period examined here the Establishment was often viewed as paternalistic, restrictive and authoritarian. During the 1960s and early 1970s the Establishment was seen as being dominated and populated by the generation who played a significant leading role during the Second World War (1939–1945) and who were finding it difficult to accept or adapt to the major societal movements taking place in the post-war period.

The essay will then consider in more detail the 1971 OZ trial before concluding with reflections on the significance of the court judgment and the subsequent developments.

The 1960s: the cultural revolution

Before examining the counter-cultural revolution it is important to recognise that at the same time a wider cultural revolution or change was taking place in the UK. According to Arthur Marwick (2000) the UK post-war cultural revolution was at its zenith during the country's affluent period from roughly 1958 to 1974, and significant and influential elements of it were located in London which was dubbed by the media as 'Swinging London'. It was primarily in London (and mainly in Chelsea, Mayfair, South Kensington and Soho) that dynamic and progressive forces of change were emerging in the areas of music, fashion, ideas, art, films, theatre, television and literature. These forces of change contained a mixture of both cultural creativity and consumer demand. Salaries for many, particularly those working in London and the south-east of England, rose ahead of prices and enabled workers to purchase an increasing range of different artistic and cultural experiences. Central to many of the changes in style and spending patterns emerging from London, was the capital's role in reinventing itself from *the* major city in a once powerful British Empire, to one of the key sites in the development of western cultural taste. Hence the term adopted for it of 'Swinging London' or the 'Swinging City', and the expression the 'Swinging Sixties'.

A key feature of the cultural revolution was the role of celebrities drawn from the British working-class. This is well expressed by Donnelly.

> *Photographers such as David Bailey, Brian Duffy and Terrance Donovan were East-End working class . . . while actors such as Michael Caine and Terence Stamp were drawn from a similar social milieu. Now they could afford to drive Rolls-Royces and mix easily with the youthful offspring of Britain's major titled families, whose acquiescence in the development of classless relations was seen as crucial to the 'swinging London' phenomenon.*
>
> (Donnelly, 2005, 92)

The BBC also employed working class writers such as Johnny Speight whose televised *Till Death us to Part* (launched in 1966) was to present in comic form an under belly of East End London working class life that celebrated racism through the fictional character of the bigoted former dockworker Alf Garnett. The television comedy had a regular viewing audience of over 17 million people. At the same time British funded and produced films were portraying changing working class life in the North of England through movies such as *Saturday Night and Sunday Morning* (1960), *A Taste of Honey* (1961) and *A Kind of Loving* (1962). Lindsay Anderson's much acclaimed film *This Sporting Life* (1963) was particularly reflective of working class life with Richard Harris and Rachel Roberts giving outstanding performances as tragic working class heroes and heroines. A little later in the decade the BBC's Wednesday Night Plays were to offer controversial examinations of the working class life. For example *Up the Junction* (1965) was to portray an abortion scene which caused considerable public outcry and negative comment on working class communities and young people in contemporary Britain.

> *However, the sensation was Cathy Come Home (November 1966), written by Jeremy Sandford and directed by Ken Loach, the story of a young mother moving from one a squalid lodging to another, then into a hostel for the homeless before finally being evicted and having her children taken away from her.*
>
> (Marwick, 2000, 245)

Nevertheless, the majority of the people who played a central role in the 1960s cultural revolution were primarily drawn from creative elements in the middle classes. If we examine the backgrounds of just a small number of people who were influential in the cultural revolution such as the artist David Hockney, the fashion designer Mary Quant, the actors David Hemmings and Edward Fox, playwright Harold Pinter, theatre director Peter Brook and writer and social commentator Germaine Greer we can note the influence of Bohemian and progressive middle class values. In many cases the new 'Young Turks' had enjoyed independent school education and a number of significant economic and social privileges. Even the Rolling Stones were draw from largely middle class backgrounds whilst John Lennon was from a lower middle class background. However, it has been pointed out that Lennon knew that emphasising the Beatles as being drawn from the industrial working class was a key to their fame and financial success. Commenting on the success of the Beatles in the USA in the early 1960s Goldman (1988) states:

> *What explained the Beatles' triumph? The answer goes back to Elvis, who had established the precedent for Beatlemania only eight years earlier. Elvis's phenomenal success in Britain had been based on the fact that he was a working-class hero, and that was equally true of the Beatles, hailed as simple lads from Liverpool who had struck it rich. John was shrewd enough to recognise the value of this delusion; he urged his mates to exploit it by putting on their scouse accents and acting as if they had been born to be lorry drivers. Aunt Mimi was horrified the first time she heard her carefully reared ward speaking like a dock worker. When she demanded an explanation, John went into his crookbacked imitation of Fagin, the Jew, rubbing his fingers together greedily and lisping, 'Money! Money!'*
>
> (Goldman, 1988, 162)

In the early 1960s it was those from comfortable middle class backgrounds, and in particular young men who had benefited from an Oxbridge education, who launched a significant satirical movement. In an impressive attack on the Establishment through surreal, topical and usually politically focused revues firstly at the Edinburgh Festival and later in London, satirists such as Peter Cook, Jonathan Miller, Dudley Moore and Alan Bennnet wrote and performed material that continues to have resonance today. In October 1961 Richard Ingrams, William Rushton, and its first editor Christopher Booker launched *Private Eye*, the fortnightly satirical magazine which is now the most influential of its kind in the UK (Decharne, 2006). In the same month Peter Cook opened in Greek Street, Soho a satirical nightclub with the 'tongue-in-cheek' title of 'The Establishment'. The venue quickly became the haunt of those who were to influence London's and the UK's growing satire scene.

The most influential and high profile satirical television programme of this period was '*That Was the Week That Was*' (*TW3*). Produced by the satirist Ned Sherrin and first shown on BBC TV in November 1962, the weekly programme reflected a concern among many that the country's leaders were out of touch with a population who often viewed politicians as benign but incompetent.

> *With a mixture of sketches, impressions and slick observations on the oddities of the week just passed, TW3 devoted at least part of each programme to showing people that is was no longer obligatory for them to respect their political leaders.*
>
> (Donnelly, 2005, 50)

However the programme was not without its critics, in particular Mary Whitehouse who in 1964 set up the National Viewers' and Listeners' Association to counter what she and members of the Association claimed was the pernicious influence of TV and other parts of the press and media. Whitehouse argued that the anti-religious, anti-authority and anti-patriotism of programmes such as *TW3* were undermining British values. However her ultra-conservative views were not met with great popularity as there was growing but quiet discontent towards the moral straight-jacket views of the Establishment, views that were for many no longer applicable (Sandbrook, 2006).

The underground press

It was at this time that another important strand of the cultural revolution was evolving: the counter-cultural revolution. Unlike the protagonists engaged in the cultural revolution the loosely associated vanguard of the counter-culture revolution did not have similar access and leverage in mainstream activities. However what they did create which was to prove powerful in communicating their ideas and views was the underground press. During the 1960s a number of alternative newspapers and magazines, emerged to attack the Establishment. Termed the underground press, and mainly created and produced in London, these publications were vehicles for the alternative views and opinions of those engaged in the counter-culture. The counter-culture movement was made up of the more radical elements of the cultural revolution's *Young Turks*. Not only did these *Young Turks* want to influence contemporary styles and attitudes, as they held political views at odds with the Establishment, they wanted to be part of a loose cultural and political movement that demanded major changes in British society; in particular they wanted to reduce, and if possible remove, the power and influence of the Establishment. The counter-cultural strand used a number of strategies. One was to offer cutting-edge radical left wing political thinking and another was to parody and satirise contemporary issues. Sometimes it was a mixture of the two and sometimes it included elements deliberately intended to shock and to attract attention.

Sociologically, counter-culture is considered to be the cultural equivalent of political opposition. According to Goffman and Joy (2004) counter-cultural undercurrents exist in many societies with the term normally referring to a visible phenomenon that reaches critical mass and persists for a period of time. Certainly that is what the role the underground press performed in the UK in the 1960s.

Briefly, some of the main underground press publications launched in the1960s, again which were principally based in London, included:

- *International Times* (later, *IT*). A key underground publication it first appeared in 1966 with a launch party at the Round House in Camden, London which included Paul McCartney, the film director Michelangelo Antonioni who a year later was to release *Blow Up* a film that reflected 'Swinging London', and a psychedelic light show and live music from the Pink Floyd and Soft Machine. *IT* featured relatively serious contributions on sexual liberation, drugs and avant-garde theatre. Two years later it enjoyed a circulation of over 40,000 every fortnight. During that year however, there was a *coup* in the magazine by a 'group of younger contributors who wanted a more aggressive tone reflecting the spirit of the barricades, rather than earnest tributes to avant-garde poetry' (Sandbrook, 2006, 528).
- *Time Out* which started life as an underground counter-culture listings magazine in 1968 under the ownership of Tony Elliot. Since the 1970s *Time Out* has established itself as a weekly high circulation mainstream listings and comment magazine with it's major publication serving the capital city as well as publishing listings guides for other cities. *The Sunday Times* 'Richlist 2008' values the Time Out Group, which is still controlled by Tony Elliot, as something in the region of £40 million.
- *Black Dwarf* was launched in 1968 by the Marxist commentator and activist Tariq Ali. Its radical left political stance included fierce opposition to the USA's involvement in the war in South East Asia, in particular its confrontation with the Vietcong in Vietnam. The paper had a revolutionary message of 'Paris, London, Rome, Berlin. We will fight. We shall win'. According to Donnelly the security forces,

> *responded to the apparent threat by bugging telephones, intercepting mail and raiding the offices of fringe political groups who had been infiltrated by the Special Branch.*
>
> (Donnelly, 2005, 148)

- *Friends* was launched in London as a radical offshoot from the UK edition of *Rolling Stone*. The magazine was first published in 1969 as *Friends of Rolling Stone*. It was later re-titled *Friends* and, from May 1971, *Frendz*. The magazine was intimately connected with other publications in the UK underground press such as *Oz* and *Time Out*. It ceased publication in August, 1972.

One of the most significant publications of the underground press of this period was *OZ* which was first launched in 1963 in Sydney, Australia as a satirical magazine and which continued publishing there until 1969. The Australia *OZ* gave prominence to views on contentious issues such as censorship, homosexuality, abortion, police brutality, the Australian government's White Australia policy and Australia's involvement in the Vietnam War. The magazine also lampooned Establishment figures including the Prime Minister Robert Menzies. However two obscenity charges were made against *OZ* and led two of the editors, Richard Neville and Martin Sharp, to leave Australia in 1966 for the UK in the hope they would receive a more sympathetic audience for their counter-culture views.

Early in 1967, Neville and Sharp, along with a fellow Australian, Jim Anderson, founded *OZ* in London. The new *OZ* quickly became one of the more visually exciting of the British underground magazines. Using new colour printing techniques and employing Martin Sharp's creative talents OZ became viewed as an irreverent and at times highly provocative icon in the counter-culture. Among the magazine contributors were Germaine Greer and Shelia Rowbotham, and later *OZ*'s supporters included John Lennon, Yoko Ono and Mick Jagger (Neville, 1996).

During 1968 Sharp left the magazine to try other ventures and his place was to be taken by a young Londoner, Felix Dennis, who had been successfully selling the magazine on the streets of the capital.

The 'School-Kids' issue April 1970

According to Travis (2000) by the end of the 1960s the editors of *OZ*, Neville, Dennis and Anderson, were 'becoming increasingly fractious, bored and exhausted by the regular rhythm of magazine production' (p. 238) and decided to advertise in the magazine for young people to join them in producing an issue reflecting their interests. According to Neville (1996) school students wrote into the magazine offering to contribute about the horrors of school exams, bullying and corporal punishment. Most of the respondents to the *OZ* advert were middle-class most of whom were attending public school and eventually some 20 young people, all 18 years and under, worked with the editors to produce *OZ* No. 28 the 'School-Kids' issue.

According to Neville (1996) the young people that worked with the three editors seemed cheerful, confident and sceptical. Neville remembers one of the young people, Robb Douglas, an 18 year-old from Hornsey, London, talking in favour of compromise rather than conflict, and wanting to reach an accord and agreement with teachers. Most had a growing political awareness and Neville remembered that Douglas, had a fantasy that the controversial Tory MP Enoch Powell, who had rallied against further black immigration to the UK, would divorce his wife and marry a black woman.

In April 1970 the 'School-kids' issue was published. The issue is ably described by Tony Palmer:

> *OZ 28 has 48 pages, all two-tone in colour. It is typographically ingenious, with the usual tendency thereby towards illegibility. Apart from the front and back cover, it has 31 pages of text, 11 pages of advertisements and 4 pages of photos. In all, these contain some 35 different photos, 30 cartoons and 20 separate articles, not including an editorial and various biographies of the contributors and editors.*
>
> (Palmer, 1971, 38)

The front cover however was the feature that attracted considerable attention as it

> *showed a naked black girl in eight different erotic poses, featuring not only the use of sex toys but the participation of other girls and even some sort of creature that might be a rat or a lizard.*
>
> (Sandbrook, 2007, 542)

Responding to 45 complaints against *OZ* 28, on the 8 June 1970, ten days before the general election that brought to office the Conservative Government led by Ted Heath, the Obscene Publications Squad of the Metropolitan Police force headed by Detective Inspector (DI) Frederick Luff raided the *OZ* offices in Princedale Road, London and removed the offending copies. As a consequence *OZ* Publications Ltd represented by Neville, Dennis and Anderson were prosecuted under a 1657 Act of a 'conspiracy to corrupt pubic morals', a charge that if found guilty carried unlimited penalties, together with charges relating to the 1959 Obscene Publication Act. It was clear that this was going to lead to a high profile and important trial as according to Palmer 'the Establishment was obviously gunning for magazines like *OZ*' (Palmer, 1971, 10). *Private Eye* at the time reported that the Tory Home Secretary, Reginald Maudling, was heard to say 'I think it's time we did a Dutschke on Neville' (Neville, 1996, 262). In 1968, Rudi Dutschke, a student activist, had been shot in the head after leading a student uprising in Berlin. He was admitted to Britain for surgery and then permitted by the Labour government to undertake post-graduate studies at Cambridge University. Dutschke's visa came up for review after the Tories were elected to office in June 1970 and the new administration was less tolerant than the previous Labour government of his political views and he was summarily deported.

The court case

After an earlier uproarious appearance at Marylebone Magistrates Court in October 1970 when the defendants donned school blazers and caps, striped ties, school satchels and short trousers, hired from a theatrical costumier's, the trial against *OZ* opened at the Old Bailey on 23 June 1971. Lasting six weeks, which at the time was the longest obscenity trial in British legal history, the successfully popular playwright and novelist John Mortimer QC, supported by Geoffrey Robertson, represented Felix Dennis and Jim Anderson. Richard Neville represented himself in court. The prosecution counsel was led by Brian Leary and among those who attended the first day of the trial was Mary Whitehouse.

The Crown prosecution had two witnesses: D.I. Luff and Vivian Berger, aged 16, who was one of the school students involved in the production of Issue 28. The judge was Justice Michael Argyle QC, a devout Christian and supporter of capital punishment who had stood as a Conservative Party prospective parliamentary candidate in the general elections of 1950 and 1955. According to Palmer (1971) Argyle was known in legal circles for the severity of his sentencing (p. 248). In 1971 only those who owned property could serve as jurors making it very difficult for a 'jury of peers' to be sworn in for the trial. As Lord Devlin once stated juries are 'male, middle-aged, middle-minded and middle class' (Neville, 1996, 283).

A short time into the case John Mortimer asked Vivian Berger, son of Grace Berger, Chair of the National Council for Civil Liberties, why he had created a six-panel Rupert Bear strip in Issue 28 which portrayed Rupert in a vivid sexual parody. According to Neville (1996, 289) this is how the interchange occurred:

Berger: I think that, looking back on it, I subconsciously wanted to shock your generation – and to portray our attitudes as different than yours. Also it seemed to me very funny.

Mortimer: Was it part of your intention to show there was a more down-to-earth side of childhood than grown-ups are prepared to think?

Berger: Oh yes. This is the kind of drawing that goes around in every classroom every day in every school.

Berger explained that he used Rupert Bear as a figure or symbol as the bear was well known to generations as a friendly, benign 'fairy tale' character. However in Berger's strip Rupert was portrayed engaging in sexual activity. When Vivian Berger was cross examined by Brian Leary for the prosecution the school student revealed that *OZ* was circulated openly at his school and without complaint from the head teacher. Berger then went on to disclose to the court that since the publication of *OZ* Issue 28 he had been regularly stopped and searched in the street by the police. He also revealed that he had been beaten up by the police. According to Neville (1996) this confirmed the three editors' views that there was a police campaign against the magazine and its supporters.

The *OZ* witnesses and supporters

As the trial unfolded it was evident that *OZ* had a number of significant and influential supporters drawn from the wider cultural revolution. In fact the list of defence witnesses for the magazine at the court case reads as a roll-call of the *Young Turks* including some nationally known individuals as well as those less well-know and working more directly with young people. Those who appeared in court as defence witnesses included:

- *Caroline Coon*: who according to Neville was 'an active figure in the punk era, is now a prolific painter' (p. 363) and was at the time of the trial founder of 'Release', an organisation that offered information and support to those arrested for drug offences.
- *Michael Schofield*: social psychologist and the author of *The Sexual Behaviour of Young People* and *The Strange Case of Pot*. He was a member of the government advisory committee on drug dependence.
- *Josephine Klein*: Warden of Goldsmith College, University of London and involved with the National Association of Youth Clubs. Klein's view was that there was no danger to young people reading *OZ* Issue 28 and advocated that it would assist them to see what was going on in society.

- *Edward de Bono*: University of Cambridge lecturer and author of *The Use of Lateral Thinking* he was well known as the advocate of solving problems obliquely rather than logically. Considered to be an expert on how children and young people think de Bono argued in court that *OZ* was important as a platform for sounding off ideas, rather like a soap box at Speakers Corner in Hyde Park, London. His view was that the contributors to Issue 28 were more interested in saying what they had to say rather than trying to affect or influence readers.

- *Hans Eynseck*: Professor of Psychology at the University of London. Known for his controversial work on IQ variations between different racial groups Eynseck stated in court that it was extremely unlikely that exposure to Issue 28 would influence a young person. Claiming that sex was used in a semi-political manner in the 'School-Kids' issue Eynseck argued that

  > Since the Establishment tends to be against free love and the open expression of sex, sex is brought in as one of the issues to beat the Establishment with. The only effect that the use of the words like 'cunt' or 'bollocks' might have is a worsening of their prose style. The acts of sadism and masochism portrayed certainly don't make them very attract-ive, and, again, I doubt if they would have much influence.

  (Palmer, 1971, 148)

- *Leila Berger*: mother and author of nearly 30 books for children had drawn up a provisional 'Charter for Children's Rights'. This charter demanded the end of caning of children and young people; the abolishment of censoring young people's letters as occurred in some boarding schools; and the Establishment of a charter of children's rights. Berger wanted to encourage a debate on how children and young people were treated in society and how they *could* be treated. She argued that children and young people should have the right of freedom from religious and political indoctrination; no discrimination based on religion, race, gender or disability; a right of expression; and the right for age appropriate information and knowledge as is necessary to understand and participate in society. Her view was that this would include knowledge of sex, contraception, religion, and drugs (including alcohol and tobacco). In court Berger argued that Issue 28 could have only a positive effect on young people.

- *Michael Segal*: former probation officer and Head of Children's Programmes at Rediffusion Television. Segal advocated on behalf of *OZ* and stated in court that young people should have more say in the conduct of their own lives and in their relationship with authority, in particular school and their parents.

- *Michael Duawe*: ex-head teacher at Risinghill Comprehensive School said in court that young people could express the most extraordinary fantasies as seen in Issue 28, and if they were repressed they would cause the young person difficulties later in life.
- *John Peel*: Radio 1 disc-jockey who also gave lectures on music in schools. Peel stated that many of the articles in *OZ* Issue 28 were well written and could be described as art.
- *Marty Feldman*: scriptwriter and comic actor. When Feldman refused to take the oath on the Bible he was asked why by Judge Argyle. 'Because I think there are more obscene things in the Bible than in this issue of OZ' Feldman replied (Palmer, 1971, 163). His court appearance turned out to be a hilarious interlude although Feldman gave examples of how his own (he was a script writer for *TW3*) and others' work was censored, in particular by the BBC. In response to Richard Neville's questioning on the Rupert Bear cartoons Feldman said:

> *It seems to me that the Establishment's getting uptight about Rupert, in some ways, represents their own childhood; the Establishment's being attacked, and it's okay for anybody to attack authority. If authority is secure, it does not fear attack. Ridicule is valid weapon, I think. In a dictatorship, one of the first things they try to do is outlaw ridicule. Hitler did this and Franco did this, and there are some who're trying to do this today.*
>
> (Palmer, 1971, 164)

- *Ronald Dworkin*: Professor of Jurisprudence, University of Oxford. Neville asked the academically talented and nationally known Dworkin whether he thought *OZ* could debauch or corrupt public morality. The Professor gave a long and legalistic response to which the Judge retorted the court was not a lecture theatre. Dworkin cut short his response and concluded that it was the prosecution's case which was a corruption not Issue 28.
- *George Melly*: professional jazz musician and singer, art critic and social commentator. Melly was one of Neville's witnesses and argued that the alleged pornography in Issue 28 was no more than could be seen elsewhere and the trial was about an attitude to life. He said that some of the words used in *OZ* were used in common parlance in many circles.

The verdict

After six weeks of argument and presentations it was considered by most commentators that the defence had made a powerful and convincing case.

However, the illuminating and compelling book by the defence lawyer Geoffrey Robertson, who has since been associated with many legal cases of social significance, recalls the pivotal role that the Judge was to play in this case.

> *Judge Argyle's views were unconsciously signalled to the jury through tone of voice and body language, which did not show up on the transcript for the Court of Appeal. Whenever he dealt with the defence his tone could not help but be scathing and contemptuous: the prosecution arguments he repeated with respect. Frequently, he expressed his own opinion – usually to the detriment of the defence, but always with the appeal-proof formula '. . . but it's a matter entirely for you, members of the jury'. He would recite a piece of evidence favourable to the defence, in somewhat surprised tones, then return to the jury: 'Well, there it is!' At this point he might hold up the magazine, and slowly let it drop – thump – onto the desk, as if it were a thing of infinite toxicity. He could hardly have made his views more clear had he actually held his nose and raised his arm as if pulling a toilet chain.*
>
> (Robertson, 1999, 38)

The Judge also wrongly directed the jury. Several hours after being sent to consider their verdicts the jury returned to ask Argyle what obscene meant. It was, Argyle replied quoting the Oxford English Dictionary, 'indecent'; a point thrown out by the Court of Appeal and which was to invalidate any conviction related to publishing an obscene article. On their return to court however, the jury found the three editors not guilty of the conspiracy charge. Nevertheless they were found guilty of the other four charges that related to publishing, sending and profiting from the sale of Issue 28.

In an emotional and packed court the Judge remanded the three in custody at Wormwood Scrubs Prison for 'medical and psychiatric reports'. The Judge ruled that Anderson and Neville, after serving their sentence, would be deported back to Australia. The verdict was to make the front pages of national newspapers and was a leading story on television and radio news. Demonstrations and marches, one led by John Lennon and Yoko Ono, took place in an outburst of public anger at the outcome. Robertson (1999) recalls that it was the next development that was to turn public sympathy against the verdict and to question the prosecution's case and the actions of a gleeful Judge Argyle.

The outcome

Robertson visited the three *OZ* editors in prison the morning after the verdict and was shocked to discover that, as per prison regulations, they had all their hair shaved off. The lawyer recalled that:

> the State had wreaked its atavistic revenge by stripping them of their hippie symbol of insolence.
>
> (Robertson, 1999, 40)

The following morning the national press carried artists impressions of the shaven OZ trio.

> At breakfast tables throughout the land, generation gaps widened as the old exulted and the young exploded. At this breaking point, something happened. Something very English, really: an unspoken recognition that things had gone too far, that it was time for moderation to reassert itself.
>
> (Robertson, 1999, 40)

It was then that a growing section of the more progressive elements of the Establishment began to attempt to limit the damage done and the embarrassment caused by the events of the trial and the custody of the OZ editors. Members of Parliament put down early-day motions criticising Judge Argyle for sending the three to prison for psychiatric reports, Bernard Levin wrote an article for *The Times* which included a scathing attack on the prosecution, and the Tory Home Secretary quickly changed prison rules so that in future remand prisoners would not be subject to prison haircut regulations.

This wider furore which did not include *The Daily Telegraph* which gave the three no sympathy what so ever (Sandbrook, 2007, 544), had no impact on Judge Argyle who at the sentencing and, although having studied very positive psychiatric reports of the three, sent them all down with custodial sentences. Arguing that as the defendants were relatively poor, fines were out of the question, Argyle sentenced Richard Neville for 15 months, Jim Anderson for 12 months, and Felix Dennis, who the Judge considered 'less intelligent' than the others, received a nine month sentence. The court erupted in shock and a demonstration involving several hundred people took place immediately outside the court building where an effigy of the Judge was burnt.

Within three days the editors were released on bail pending an appeal which took place a few months later in November 1971. By then there was growing concern at the way that Establishment through the judicial system had attempted to smother the views of what many considered to be a foolish but harmless prank by the trio. At the three day appeal the court heard the defendants' seventy-eight grounds of appeal against Judge Argyle's summing up. The Lord Chief Justice Lord Widgery, who said he was concerned by Argyle's constant denigration of the expert witnesses, found in favour of the defendants and quashed the original verdict including the order of deportation.

What gains were made?

The OZ case was to become a watershed in the way that obscenity was viewed and interpreted by UK society and the law. The narrow definition Argyle directed the jurors to use in considering Issue 28 was replaced after the Court of Appeal decision that obscenity is something that legally or culturally is not easy to identify or agree upon.

The case was a recognition both by the Establishment and wider society that young people's views and those who had alternative interpretations of the world were valid and had a place in a country that was beginning to feel secure in its new post-war identity. As the UK developed its new forms of art and culture, some of it proving to be financially profitable, so it was recognised that views that did not correspond with the status quo were important in offering an inclusive home to an increasingly diverse society.

Over time the Establishment changed and adapted to the evolving patterns of behaviour, language, and interpretation. Whilst many Establishment figures did not readily accept the changes and developments, and later in the 1970s hit back in the political form of the New Right and Margaret Thatcher, it was recognised that as Bob Dylan had written 10 years earlier 'The Times They Are a-Changin'. It was increasingly recognised and commented upon more openly that British society was based upon a set of undemocratic power structures which were designed to maintain the status quo and to perpetuate a conservative agenda based on self interest. *OZ* and other protagonists in the counter-culture did much to challenge and lampoon the Establishment although of course it would be unwise to attribute too much to their influence in securing much needed changes in our society. Nevertheless, the OZ court case was a significant event that did much to challenge the unspoken power and influence of the Establishment.

References

Decharne, M. (2006) *King's Road: The Rise and Fall of the Hippest Street in the World*. London, Orion Books.

Donnelly, M. (2005) *Sixties Britain: Culture, Society and Politics*. Harlow, Pearson.

Dylan, B. (1964) *The Times They Are a-Changin*. Columbia Records.

Goffman, K. and Joy, D. (2004) *Counterculture through the Ages: Abraham to Acid House*. New York, Villard Books.

Goldman, A. (1988) *The Lives of John Lennon*. London, Bantam Press.

Hewson, R. (1986) *Too Much: Art and Society in the Sixties 1960–1975*. London, Methuen.

Marwick, A. (2000) *A History of the Modern British Isles 1914–1999*. Oxford, Blackwell.

Neville, R. (1996) *Hippie Hippie Shake: the dreams, the trips, the trials, the love ins, the screw ups . . . the sixties*. London, Bloomsbury.

Palmer, T. (1971) *The Trials of OZ*. London, Blond and Briggs.

Robertson, G. (1999) *The Justice Game*. London, Vintage.

Sandbrook, D. (2007) *White Heat: A History of Britain in the Swinging Sixties*. London, Abacus.

Travis, A. (2000) *Bound and Gagged: A Secret History of Obscenity in Britain*. London, Profile Books.

CHAPTER 14

Withywood Youth Club

Sue Robertson

Withywood Youth Club, opened in 1963, was probably the first purpose-built youth centre to be completed following publication of the Albemarle Report (Ministry of Education, 1960). As such it represented a new beginning for club-based youth work and marked the onset of a period when money and resources were made available to allow for a rapid expansion in the number of youth centres. This chapter celebrates the work of Ray Sharpe its first leader and tells the story of the centre which was eventually demolished in 2005.

When Sharpe was appointed in 1962, Withywood Youth Club was his first post following graduation from the National College for the Training of Youth Leaders (Leicester), and he was anxious to put the ideas he encountered there into practice. In particular, according to his memoir published in 2004, Sharpe wanted the young people to run their own club. The extent to which he succeeded in achieving this ambition is demonstrated in the way many of them, now in their 60s, recall the great times they had there. Certainly for many who were members during the time Sharpe was in charge, Withywood Youth Centre remains an important part of their lives – a place where they met their future husband or wife, acquired a new skill, made lasting friendships, and had a good time. As one explained, the opening of the club meant

> *No more wandering aimlessly round the streets, causing damage and being a nuisance. It kept us out of mischief. We were safe, and we had entertainment and something to do every night. It made me a more responsible person. We could talk about anything. The club not only helped us, it helped our parents and teachers too.*
>
> (quoted in Sharpe, 2004, 27)

The building was centrally located within the Withywood estate newly built on the outskirts of Bristol. It was designed to serve as a youth club in the evenings and community centre during the day. In this respect the centre was not unique, but its physical design was innovatory and became well-known as the prototype for many similar youth club buildings constructed in the decade following publication of Albemarle. It was constructed as a result of a recommendation contained within Albemarle that the Development Group of the Architects and Buildings Branch of the Ministry of Education undertake a study of the type of premises required for effective youth work. Members of this group visited a number of youth centres to discover what design features might help workers seeking to respond to Albemarle's recommendation that association, training and challenge should reside at the heart of youth work practice. The group summarised their findings in two pamphlets, *Youth Club Buildings, General Mixed Clubs* (Ministry of Education, 1961) and *Youth Club, Withywood, Bristol* (Ministry of Education, 1963), recommending that the basis for new building should be for:

> . . . *a general mixed club for 14 to 20 year olds, open six or seven nights a week and perhaps one or two afternoons, the average attendance is usually a third of the total membership. A club should not be too small or its facilities will not be sufficiently varied to sustain a vigorous club life.*
>
> *The first and most important function of the general mixed club is social. It must provide a place where friends can meet, talk and enjoy each others company, and where they can feel that they are in a place of their own.*
>
> (Ministry of Education, 1961, 9)

Building design was one of the few mechanisms via which the Ministry of Education could shape the policies of the then largely autonomous local education authorities (LEAs). For only if the Ministry of Education approved the design might LEAs acquire permission to build a new youth centre and LEAs usually played safe by adopting the guidelines issued by the Architects and Buildings Branch. Consequently the Withywood model was frequently replicated, often without much thought as to whether or not it suited the needs of the young people in a given locality.

Withywood – the place

Withywood is a large post war housing estate covering 330 acres, five miles south of Bristol city centre within the Hartcliffe and Withywood administrative district of the City Council. By 1946 Bristol's housing problem was chronic. In the 1920s and 30s housing demand consistently outstripped supply, despite the attempts of the City Council to alleviate the problem with a programme of social housing. War damage exacerbated this situation and 30,000 people were in urgent need of housing by 1945. Insufficient city centre land forced the local authority to build on peripheral green field sites and the land for the

Withywood development was acquired via compulsory purchase in 1949. The first families moved in five years later. Apart from a number of three story blocks of flats most units were semi detached houses with gardens. By September 1962, Withywood had a population of 9,181 (45 per cent of whom were under 21) served by seven primary schools, one secondary school for 1,000 pupils, three churches, five public houses and a community centre. The population was expected to peak at 11,000. In 1989 the *Bristol Evening Post* in a series 'My bit of Bristol' suggested that Withywood lacked coherence and character and that planners had not given it a focal point or open square around which a community could grow. The article described what existed as 'a slab of shops . . . dumped in Queen's Road; a few more and a post office nearly half a mile away; the school and church in opposite corners' (*Bristol Evening Post*, 12/12/89). Yet despite poor planning, a genuine community appears to have formed over the years, with the secondary school acting as a focus for community activity, the creation of active youth groups through co-operation between the Methodist and Anglican churches, and the growth of a thriving Community Association. Even the 'slab' of Queen's Road shops came to be described as 'earthy, warm and unpretentious' (ACTA, 2002).

Youth work

In the early days two local churches ran small youth clubs and these plus a Scout group were the only provision for young people. Poor public transport and large numbers of young people on the streets persuaded residents and planners that Withywood needed a youth centre. The Community Council began to address this by recruiting volunteer leaders to run a youth group in the semi-derelict buildings of Oakhill Farm, situated on a main thoroughfare near the estate's centre. Eventually it was this club that provided the core membership of the new LEA centre built on the site of the original farm. It was expected the new Withywood Youth Club would become a place

> *where young people will find opportunities for friendship and recreation and training in contemporary surroundings under sympathetic adult guidance; a place where they can continue with some of the interests and activities to which they have been introduced at school, such as music, drama, sports and D. of E. Award.*

('Youth Service', 2, 1962)

There were also to be opportunities for informal social mixing, with a coffee bar/canteen as the focal point. It was hoped the centre would serve as an important influence and growing point in the new community. Building costs were set at not more than £30,000.

The building

What made Withywood Centre architecturally significant was its embodiment of the thinking that under-pinned the aspirations for youth work outlined in Albemarle. *Ministry of Education Building Bulletin* No. 22 was devoted exclusively to Withywood because this was viewed as the model for a building that would enable youth work to progress along the lines envisaged by the authors of the report (Ministry of Education, 1963).

Albemarle believed most existing buildings were inadequate with far too much youth work occurring in drab and dreary unheated rooms and shared premises (Evans, 1965). The Report stressed the importance of providing practical, cultural and social facilities alongside the usual diet of sport, and called for an imaginative approach with regard to any future building programme. As noted earlier it also recommended that the Development Group of the Architects and Building Branch of the Ministry of Education undertake a study of the type of premises required for youth work. In 1961 the results of this were published in *Building Bulletin* No. 20 (Ministry of Education). Concentrating on 'general mixed clubs', because they were the type most frequently in demand, the authors set the limits of net cost per nightly attendance at £170. They understood the core function of the club to be 'social', a place where friends could meet, talk and enjoy each others' company, where they could feel they were in a place of their own. They wanted youth centres to provide a wide range of facilities and activities, but not sufficient to compete with specialist clubs. Overall it was assumed they would be informal, and inductive rather than instructive.

Three Ministry architects, John Kitchen (senior architect), Frank Jackson and Len Holland worked on the Withywood project in association with members of Bristol City Architects Department. Before work commenced these three visited over 30 clubs around the country and interviewed a number of youth officers to clarify their thinking regarding what a post-Albemarle centre would contain and look like. What emerged from this process was a desire to create a building that offered young people a place of their own that was cheerful, convenient and colourful. The architects believed the external aspect must be such that it ensured the centre acquired good standing in the community. Therefore the approach was to be well lit and paved, leading to an entrance calculated to look like a busy hotel – bright, accessible, attractive and at all times visible from the road. One idea embodied in the design was that seeing and being seen were important 'the first thing girls or boys will do after coming in to the club is to hang up their coat and comb their hair or check their make up' (Ministry of Education, 1961: 13). The bulletin devoted to Withywood developed this theme arguing that:

> *young people tend to resent conditions of membership and imposed standards of behaviour. Young people who enter a youth club should be able to enter into the general fun and enjoy each others' company without necessarily engaging in a definite activity. The lounge should be seen from outside so it presents no barriers or unknown areas for those coming in for the first time. A corporate spirit may emerge rather than be imposed.*
>
> (ibid., 4)

It was envisaged young people would gather in small groups in the entrance hall, reading notices, booking games tables and waiting for friends before moving on to one of the various activities offered within. The idea was that the surroundings should be 'adult' and 'sophisticated' and that the club should look and sound busy and engaging, with activities and interests arising spontaneously from 'the corporate life of the group'. The same bulletin argued that facilities which could not be seen or heard from other parts of a club are less often used as members engaging in them tend to feel 'out of it', isolated from the life of the club both because they do not know if something interesting or spontaneous is happening elsewhere, and because their friends do not know where to find them. The 'psychological environment' was thought to be important and this was to be addressed by creating 'an uninterrupted space or series of linked spaces, sub-divided by partial or discontinuous screens, within which social, practical, physical and cultural activities can be pursued in proximity and harmony' (Ministry of Education, 1961, 11). This would allow different strands to be drawn together thereby solving the problem of capturing young people's interest whilst simultaneously enabling discrete supervision of the club.

The design for Withywood drew upon current modernist thinking about 'social space', avoiding ornamentation and using contemporary materials to create a 'modern' environment. Two key words relating to this new architecture were 'honesty' and 'function'. Architects implied that by being 'honest' buildings could help people to become so. This was to be achieved by breaking with architectural tradition and moving towards more simple unadorned buildings. Amongst the most commonly used materials at this time were glass for the facade, steel for exterior support and concrete for the floors and interior supports. Floor plans were functional and logical (Hitchcock, 1968). One of the central principles was that form would follow from function and this approach is reflected in the way Withywood was designed to allow maximum flexibility with regard the use of space. Withywood was not unique, for many schools opened in the 1960s also used this format. In *Architecture of Schools* Dudek (2000) describes how the new school he attended in the 1960s had a multi-purpose hall with a sprung beech floor with signs saying 'And No Stiletto Heels'. Withyood sported the same sign and a film about the centre adopted this instruction as its title (Bristol University, 1966). Dudek suggests that school building design during this period encompassed a set of changing educational theories which acknowledged the subtle spatial and psychological requirements of children. At Withywood a variety of architectural devices were used within an open plan idea, such as changes of level, lighting, floor and ceiling texture, glaze partitions and screens. The club was a compact two-storey construction but a single central space was constructed with a gallery to avoid isolating the floors. In the central social space, normally used for table tennis and dancing, a sunken floor provided storage space for the platforms when not in use for concerts, drama productions and other 'events'. The open plan allowed for the large clear areas to be divided up by partitions – whilst upholstered bench seats were placed back-to-back by a wall to create small intimate spaces. Screens, bookstands and plant troughs were used for the same purpose. Staff and young people were able to see the whole space, which was compact and flexible. There was only one entrance and exit for members whilst outside a floodlit games court with viewing terrace was constructed.

Withywood: central space

The final design incorporated many features that reflected the architects' recognition of the importance of activities within youth work. They concluded that activities could be divided into five categories and that each should be allocated an equal share of the total floor area. The five activity groupings were:

1. *The physical* – provision being made for a games court, alongside space for members to observe an activity, because the architects understood that, 'watching can be a stepping stone between inactivity and activity' (Ministry of Education, 1963, 6).
2. *The practical* – space designed to cater for different activities and structured to allow for multiple use. For example, the dining area could easily be adapted to provide a place for dressmaking. Some practical areas were

upstairs whilst others like woodwork, where anything from bird boxes to tables might be made, were on the ground floor.

3. *The social* – social areas were focused on the entrance, coffee bar and servery. In keeping with the wish to make space flexible the central sunken floor area was used for table tennis and socialising but could be filled with linoleum topped plywood units, two foot square by one foot deep, to make either staging or seating.

4. *The cultural* – comprised a collection of rooms accessible from the gallery that were able to accommodate around a 100. Windows allowed those outside and inside to view each other at all times. Designated rooms included a girl's sitting room with an en-suite a powder room to 'act as a bait for the girl whose interests have so far narrowed that her concern is solely for her own appearance!' (Ministry of Education, 1961, 6). There were also a committee room, group rooms, a quiet room for homework, music room and gallery seating for conversation which also provided a display area for pictures lent by Bristol City Art Gallery.

5. *The administrative* – this included offices, toilets, a cloakroom and changing rooms with showers.

Such was the flexibility of the building, Sharpe (2004) reports, that during his time there, it was able to accommodate 72 discrete activities – including soccer, weight training, table tennis, badminton, netball, photography, judo, drama, fencing, concerts, a performance by trainees from the Royal Ballet and folk music evenings.

The staff

Sharpe, Withywood's first full time youth worker, was aged 38 when he arrived. His previous occupation had been as a law court clerk. Besides Sharpe there was a fulltime deputy, Ros Taylor, and numerous volunteers. The centre retained two full-time staff until the demise of the Avon authority in 1996. Volunteers were often involved for long periods of time. For example, as one ex-member told the author:

> My dad worked down here for 29 years, I came up to help, and my mum. Then me, I qualified as a part time worker and then was married to the full time one here. A great sense of ownership. Excitement of being involved. A national football team and nationally known bands. All the young families from the cities mixed. The staff were always on the floor – never in the office.

> (Ex member, personal communication)

The building was officially opened on Friday, 27 September 1963 by Christopher Chataway MP, Parliamentary Secretary to the Ministry of Education. The following day the *Bristol Evening Post* described it as an experimental club already attracting over 300 members (28/9/63). Chataway spoke about 'the race to keep pace with youth' and how during the previous four years LEA expenditure on the youth service had doubled and Ministry grants increased from below £250,000 to over £1million. Dingy premises and draughty halls, he promised, were on their way out. He told the audience that in order

> to attract the unattached there must be more clubs for young people who want – initially at least – no more than friendship and a place to meet, but the club is more than a dancehall or snack bar with opportunities for young people to choose activities for themselves. There is room for more clubs – where, in entering the door, young people feel that no commitment is involved, and yet, once inside can, with adult leadership that is unobtrusive, make choices of activities for themselves.

> (*Bristol Evening Post*, 28/9/63)

In 1967, when Ray Sharpe moved to a post in Somerset, the same paper celebrated the success of Withywood under the headline 'Club beat doubters', reporting that over 13,000 young people had visited the club in the first five years and 750 were currently regularly attenders (*Bristol Evening Post* 27/3/67). This attendance rate was made possible partly by the fact it was officially open six days a week from 09.00 to 22.00hrs. 'Officially' because on Sunday mornings Sharpe always went to the centre to catch up with his administration tasks where he was joined by young people who undertook, on a voluntary basis, much of the repair and maintenance work needed to keep the club in good order. Visitors came from all over the world to look at a centre that appeared to function more like a Students' Union than a youth club, operating as it did without a nightly programme, with members deciding what to do when they arrived. This was a place where workers helped young people to arrange their own activities and then left these to run them for themselves thereby freeing staff to undertake what they viewed as the more important task of supporting and helping young people when needed (Sharpe, 2004).

Sharpe believed the informal atmosphere attracted a lot of young people who might otherwise have never gone to a youth club. The aim was for a 'family' atmosphere conducive to encouraging young people to talk about their concerns and problems. Conversation with young people was the bedrock of the work for Sharpe who had 76 conversations per hour in the club according to a Tavistock House researcher (cited Sharpe, 2005). Sharpe lived on the estate and was involved in a range of sporting and community groups. He describes his six years at Withywood as the 'best of my life'. Fortunately we have a visual record of the life of the club to augment those left by staff and members in the form of two films, one by made by Bristol University Drama Department for HTV entitled *And No Stiletto Heels* and a second presented by Julian Pettifer that was part of the BBC *Working with Young People* series (Davies and Rogers, 1972).[1]

Membership

The club was designed for an average nightly attendance of 190 (Ministry of Education, 1963) a figure reached most evenings during the first decade. Initially information about this new facility was circulated round the estate and as 'there was no membership scheme, we took the first hundred, just names and addresses' (Sharpe, 2005). From these a group of eight, comprising equal numbers of girls and boys, were asked serve on a Members' Committee on the understanding that elections would be held when everyone was prepared for them. This committee met weekly and left Ray notes about their decisions. Members didn't want rules, membership or a joining fee. Subs were collected by committee members whenever an individual attended the centre and the committee enjoyed full responsibility for the disposal of this money along with the right to determine which groups were to be given access to the building during the daytime. They also devised the programme and were theoretically responsible for discipline. However discipline was never a serious issue with only three members barred during Shape's tenure. Elections for the committee were held at six monthly intervals. Many felt they benefited from involvement, as the former members' committee chair told Ray:

> you made me a leader of men . . . I learned how to handle people, back then. Used it in the Union. Became a shop steward. Instead of going back in the nick. Changed my life, that did.

(Sharpe, 2004, 28)

Management

When Sharpe arrived he inherited a management committee of local people who had been responsible for the part time club previously located on the site and who believed they should now control the new centre. In particular this committee were enthusiastic about things like a boxing ring – where boys could 'knock some of the bad behaviour out of each other' (Sharpe, 2004, 15). Ray's approach differed radically from theirs and he found it impossible to work with them. Consequently after a turbulent second meeting the old committee resigned and a new one formed comprising six professionals resident on the estate, plus parents. They accepted that day-to-day management must be left to the warden, staff and young people. The new management committee focused on issues relating to the centre's role in the community. Around the same time a supporters' club was founded the members of which undertook fundraising and helping in the centre, especially at Friday night discos in order to give the members' committee a break.

Partnership

In the early days probation officers used the coffee bar for outreach work with groups and individuals living on the estate. Other professionals living and working in the area such as the clergy, beat policeman and youth workers also regularly met at the centre for lunch. Relationships with the neighbours were sometimes less than cordial and even occasionally problematic but generally Sharpe arranged for young people from the members' committee to visit them and this usually produced an amiable solution. Good links with schools were forged even before the centre opened, leading to Ray Sharpe attending assemblies and refereeing school soccer matches. Likewise positive relationships were fostered with local pub landlords, the owner of the 'chippy' and other businesses serving the estate. Wisely the LEA at that time allowed clubs such as Withywood to employ local tradesmen to undertake small repairs which helped the centre accumulate goodwill. All youth centres need to fit into their local community and as a consequence of Sharpe's sensitive engagement with local people a substantial proportion of those living on the estate acquired a stake in making the centre a success and keeping it safe. For them it became an important part of local life, providing a place for mother and toddler groups to meet as well as a home for a choir, keep fit classes, a seniors' club, a junior club and a ballroom dancing society.

Withywood in the 1970s

Ray Sharpe was only at Withywood Youth Centre for six years. Following advice from Ted Sidebottam, his old college principal, who said, 'at the end of 5 years step back, ask yourself have you done all you can, could someone else do something new?' (Sharpe, 2005), he left. He took a position as a youth officer in Exmoor before becoming Director of Youth Work for the London Union of Youth Clubs. Within a year the deputy leader also left and almost overnight the club dramatically changed. Rules and regulations were introduced and the member's committee was allowed to fade away.

Following local government reorganisation in 1974, Avon County Council took over responsibility for the centre from Bristol City Council. For various reasons during the next decade funding became less generous and the physical state of the building began to deteriorate. This was an era of punk and urban decay but Withywood was 'not really urban or decayed enough' (Nesbitt, 2006). A tobacco factory was built nearby in the early 70s, the largest in Europe, and this helped prevent unemployment in the neighbourhood rising to levels encountered in many other areas. Perhaps because of this, the estate failed to receive the funding for certain long promised facilities and gradually conditions deteriorated. During this time Withywood Youth Centre found it increasingly difficult to recruit and retain staff. A succession of full-time leaders came and went, some of whom found the building difficult to work in, notably the balcony area and staircases. According to a local youth officer (Nesbitt, 2005) it was also difficult for new workers to fit in with the group of local people involved in the centre. Some new initiatives did occur in the 1970s and 1980s such as the Withywood Intermediate Treatment Forum; but nationally the upsurge of interest and commitment of resources that characterised youth work in the 1960s was evaporating (Davies, 1999). Local authorities had to severely restrict their youth service expenditure – these were years of budget capping and reduction. Growing concern about 'unattached youth' linked to mounting pressure to target specific groups of young people encouraged a shift of resources away from building-based work. During the 1980s Avon County Council abolished local management committees. Neighbourhood support, involvement and a sense of ownership in relation to the centres generally ebbed away. Consequently there were few voices lobbying for youth work and youth centres at a neighbourhood level, both in Withywood and elsewhere.

Youth unemployment grew after 1980 in Withywood as the Wills tobacco factory first stopped recruiting, then laid people off and finally closed in 1990. In response an MSC training scheme, the Dundry Slopes Project, was established at the centre. Other initiatives launched during this period included the strengthening of the upstairs floor for weight-lifting, a programme of foreign visits, theatre residencies and a print workshop (ACTA, 2002).

In 1989 a community profile produced by youth service staff found under-usage of the Withywood Centre and a negative attitude towards it amongst residents, many of whom viewed the place as depressing, resembling a car park, off-putting and 'usually surrounded by a group of fairly aggressive looking blokes'. The building looked uncared for and was now a target for vandalism. According to Nesbitt (2006) around this time it was judged unfit for use following a health and safety audit but Avon County Council neither closed nor refurbished it. There were even suggestions of illegal drinking and drug use taking place on site. Certainly some parents reported they wouldn't allow their children to use the club. Others suggested that the youth centre reflected the current local environment and was failing to offer anything different; hence young people hung around on the streets. Indeed the young people told interviewers they wanted more activities and only used the club if it was cold and wet. However a subsequent leaders' report presented in 1993 (Thurtell, 2004) suggests that during this period there was an increase in young people using the centre because a difficult group of young men who had been meeting outside departed. It now opened on Saturday mornings for 8–12 year olds, Tuesday evenings for the 10 to 15 year olds and for Seniors on Thursday night. In addition there was a designated girls' night attracting an average attendance of 27 compared with the 35 for the mixed senior session.

In 1997 there was an overall reduction of £267,000 in the youth service budget for Bristol and decisions were made to prioritise detached and inter-agency work. Withywood staff discussed whether they had the resources to continue operating at current levels and eventually opted to offer one 'inters' and one 'senior' night' but lacking any budget for marketing they had to rely on word of mouth to publicise the revised programme (Thurtell, 2004). When discussing this era ex-Withywood members and staff often remark that both the fun and the politics tended to go out of youth work:

> *youth workers were really radical in the 70s! Now evaluation forms, paperwork; no time for thinking about young people. Before it was about young people – you were there for them, less monitored.*
>
> (Interview with Withywood ex member of staff, 2004)

Post-1990 the building also changed. In 1992 a glass partition was installed to close off the gallery because the balcony had become used for name calling and missile throwing. The spiral staircases were initially covered in to stop access, then removed. The upstairs was now rarely used due to lack of staff and the building had, when the author visited it in 1996, become oppressive, dark and uninviting. One major change in the layout was justified on the grounds of health and safety this was the filling-in of the block-floor. As an ex-staff member explained (interview, 2004) it 'was about health and safety', a 'trip hazard', and 'it was hard work moving that floor, blisters, caught fingers, it doubled as stage and seating and was a real feature'. Adapting this area for different usage always needed a lot of willing helpers which the club no longer had. A further difficulty was that during this period Hartcliffe Club for Young People (or boys club as it was then) was re-developed on a more central school site up the road from the Withywood Centre. The new facility proved to be popular with young people and many parents who saw it as being a safer environment.

The future

In 1995, Hartcliffe and Withywood received £12.15 million pounds from the Single Regeneration Budget, the largest such award in the region. On the back of this a number of projects were developed linked to other programmes such as the Education Action Zone, Sure Start and URBAN 2. The following year the South Bristol Church and Community Trust was formed out of the Withywood Church and Community Project, with the intention of developing church land and buildings for church and community facilities. Shortly afterwards plans to demolish the Withywood Youth Centre and replace it with a new building were aired. The old building was finally demolished in 2005 to make way for a £4.5m replacement. This comprises a community facility, healthy living centre and church as well as youth provision. Based at the new centre are a Strategic Youth Manager and two sessional Youth Support Workers with responsibility for developing work with young people for the church as well as the management of the youth café run by the local authority within the centre.

Conclusion

Withywood was a creature of its time, a product of a unique combination of political will, evident nationally and locally, to develop new forms of youth work and the buildings required to make these a reality. It involved a committed community, keen young people and a clear conception of what comprised good youth work. Sharpe recalls that the inspiring design came from enthusiastic architects who 'came up every three months to get comments on the building, sat in the coffee bar, talked to kids. They felt it was the best job they ever did, they enjoyed it' (2005, 12). As a result the club 'really put Withywood on the map', becoming a place where

> *if you had a problem you could talk to the leaders. Kids are still looking for the same good facilities and leadership that we had. They're no different today.*
> *I used to come every day. My mum wasn't happy about the baby, and my Dad wouldn't talk to me. I brought the baby to everything. I felt accepted there. I don't know what would have happened to us without that place. I couldn't have coped, none of us could.*
>
> (Sharpe, 2004, 30)

An ex-member recalls it in a similar vein. Jackie tells how:

> *It was around 1967. There was gang war between mods and rockers. Withywood young people had come to the Maritas café in Bedminster and someone had bad mouthed me, we went to Withywood to take them on. But ended up being shown round the club, they were really friendly. I walked up every night, I don't know where I got the money for my subs, sometimes I sold things to the rag and bone man, there was never any money, I had 9 brothers and sisters. There were 150–200 young people, it was the place to be. I formed great friendships and fell in love with the youth club.*
>
> (personal communication)

A philosophy of involvement and encouraging responsibility lay at the heart of club life within Withywood. Although Withywood Youth Centre has gone, the idea of generic, preventative work remains as important today as when the centre opened in the 1960s (Merton, 2004; Robertson, 2005). Similar clubs still operate, for instance the Bolton Lads Clubs, was recently refurbished at a cost of over £4 million. Open seven nights a week, it attracts up to 250 per session (Wylie, 2006). Young people still need somewhere to go, something to do and someone to talk to (DfES, 2006), and often where better than a local youth club?

Ray Sharpe, now living in Wales, remains actively involved in his local community 'busy supervising a youth team and centre work for families with special needs children and young people' and was recently awarded an MBE, which he accepted 'for all those young people and adults who have shared my life for 60 years' (Sharpe, 2005). Youth work is full of characters like Ray who willingly give time and effort on both a paid and voluntary basis, who enjoy the company of young people and understand the importance of the club. In these days of short term outcomes and measurements it is important to recognise the value of a place to meet in young people's lives. A place that may be the only fixed point in a chaotic life.

Note

1   Copies of the film *And No Stiletto Heels* produced by Bristol University Drama Department can be obtained on application. Unfortunately film made to accompany the BBC series *Working with Young People* is currently unavailable due to copyright restrictions.

References

ACTA (2002) *At home on the slopes. A history of Hartcliffe and Withywood*, Bristol, ACTA Community Theatre.

Bristol Evening Post (1967) *An Experiment Succeeds*, 21 March.

Bristol Evening Post (1989) *My Bit of Bristol*, 12 December.

Bristol University (19660 *And no stiletto heels*, Bristol University Drama Department (copies of this programme are available from the author on application).

Davies, B. and Rogers, J. (1972) *Working with Youth*, London, BBC Publications.

Davies, B. (1999) *A History of the Youth Service in England*, Volumes One and Two. Leicester, Youth Work Press.

DfES (2006) *Youth Matters*, London, Stationery Office.

Dudek, M. (2000) *Architecture of Schools*, Oxford Architectural Press.

Evans, W.M. (1965) *Young People in Society*, London, Basil Blackwell.

Hitchcock, H. (1968) *Architecture: Nineteenth and Twentieth Centuries*, Harmondsworth, Penguin.

Merton, B., Smith, D. and Payne, M. (2004) *The Impact of Youth Work*, Nottingham, DfES.

Ministry of Education (1961) *Bulletin 20: Youth Service Building: General Mixed Clubs*, London, Ministry of Education.

Ministry of Education (1963) *Bulletin 22: Youth Club, Withywood, Bristol*, London, Ministry of Education.

Ministry of Education (1960) *The Youth Service in England and Wales (Albemarle Report)*, London, HMSO.

Nesbitt, T. (2005) Tom Nesbitt personal communication.

Ofsted (2000) *Bristol Youth Service Inspection Report* (www.ofsted.uk).

Robertson, S. (2005) *Youth Clubs: Participation: Association: Friendship and Fun!* Lyme Regis, Russell House Publishing.

Seaborne, M. (1977) The English School its Architecture and Organisation Volume 2 1870 to 1970), London: Routledge and Kegan Paul.

Sharpe, R. (2004) *The Withywood Experiment*, (available from tricia@Sharpesolutions.com).

Sharpe, R. (2005) Personal communication.

Thurtell, M. (2004) Youth work reports and personal communication.

Trueman, J. and Brent, J. (1995) *Alive and Kicking: the Life and Times of Southmead Youth Centre*, Bristol, Redcliffe Press.

'Youth Service' Issue Number 2 1962 London, Ministry of Education.

Withywood ex staff and members (2004) Personal communication.

Wylie, T. (2006) 'Let them go to Bolton' *Young People Now*, 17 November.

Ray Sharpe

CHAPTER 15

Club, Class and Clothes: The Origins of Scouting in Sunderland

Jean Spence

This chapter charts the origins and development of Scouting in Sunderland in the aftermath of Robert Baden Powell's nationwide tour to promote his new publication *Scouting for Boys*, serialised in fortnightly parts from 15 January 1908. It focuses particularly on the creation and progress of the Vaux's Own Scouts. Major (later Lieut. Col.) Ernest Vaux was co-owner of a Sunderland brewery founded in 1805 (Pearson, ud, c. 1998) and which until its closure in 1999 was a significant source of employment in the town. The beginnings of the Scout troop which bears Vaux's name are recorded in the minutes of the Sunderland Waifs' Rescue Agency and Street Vendors' Club. There is additional evidence in the reports in the *Sunderland Daily Echo* (the Echo) which offers a more general picture of the organisation of Scouting in Sunderland. These sources are not exhaustive but they do provide the narrative outlines and some significant moments in a local history which dates to the very earliest months of Scouting.

The Vaux's Own Scouts have a claim not only to be one of the first troops to form, but also to be one of the longest surviving. Wade's official history, *Twenty One Years of Scouting* published in 1929, indicates that:

> The first Troop ... which the Chief notes in his diary as having been inspected by himself was at Sunderland. On February 22nd 1908, he notes in his diary: 'Inspected Boy Scouts at Sunderland (Col. Vaux)'.
>
> (1929, 64)

Wade gives an account of the creation of the Vaux's Own Scouts from information provided by the troop's Scoutmaster derived 'from his own investigations' (p. 64). It is likely that this account was offered by Douglas Caws who, as secretary of the Waifs' Rescue Agency management committee, was present at the formation of the Vaux's Own Scouts and who had eventually become a District Commissioner for the Scouts (Interview, Frank Caws, Jnr. 24/11/1998). Caws, who had exemption from military service, had taken primary responsibility for the Vaux's Own Scouts during the First World War. With the help of the club's resident Superintendent, Jim Smith, who did not join the services until late in the war, and Smith's wife, the Lambton Street Club had been kept open by taking advantage of the formal recognition of the Scouts role in the war effort on the home front (Rosenthal, 1986, 228). If Caws was the source of Wade's information, his memories were probably as important as his investigations and as such, his narrative should be treated with care. Nevertheless this information, supplemented by a small amount of detail included in the club's half-centenary publication *Fifty Years in Lambton Street* (Smith, 1952)[1] helps to fill in some of the details of the story.

Inevitably there are gaps and slippages in the sources of information. For example, the Scoutmaster's account reproduced by Wade implies, without being explicit, that Baden Powell visited the Lambton Street Club. There is no record in the minutes of any such visit to the club's premises. Smith's description makes no claim other than the 'Vaux's Own Scouting corps' was 'a pioneer force in the National Scouting Movement'. When he refers to the Lambton Street Troop being inspected by Baden Powell in May 1908, Smith omits the fact that this inspection, which simply *included* Lambton Street boys, took place in the Victoria Hall (Min. 21 May 2008; Smith, 1952, 5). Vaux made his first visit to the Lambton Street club to propose the formation of a Scout troop there on 20 February 1908, but whoever Baden Powell inspected in Sunderland two days later, and whatever their relationship with the Lambton Street Club, it was not until 1 April 1908 that the first meeting *with boys* took place to form the Vaux's Own Troop.

The gaps and inconsistencies of the evidence are problematic for those who are keen to establish the provenance of the Sunderland Scouts as 'the longest continuing existing' troop. Although the narrative in Wade implies such continuity, Smith, having described the formation of the troop in 1908, then tells of nothing until 1914. After the first flurry of activity during 1908, both the minutes and the newspaper reports suggest there was a falling away of interest in Scouting at Lambton Street. Indeed there is a complete silence in the minutes between March 1909 and November 1910 when it appears the troop was being re-formed, and it is not clear that even then it was sustained; a further silence in 1911 is followed by a discussion, on 25 January 1912, which indicates yet another attempt to rejuvenate the troop and it is likely that only then did the uninterrupted history begin.

Given the silences in the sources, there is no doubt debate will continue about which was the first and which has the claim to be the longest continuously surviving Scout troop. But such debates are rather sterile. What is of more interest is not so much the provenance of the Vaux's Own Troop, but rather the conditions in which it was created, and its struggle for survival. Indeed, it is the probable fact of the demise of the troop by the end of 1908 and the discussions surrounding its reformation which are of most interest. It is possible to trace here significant class dimensions and contradictions in the progress of the movement in the context of the pre-existing club. The presenting problems for survival at Lambton Street always included the question of the uniform. The ideals incorporated in *Scouting for Boys* assumed an inclusive and universal approach to boyhood in which the common uniform played an important part (Proctor, 1998). These ideals were stalled and diverted in the face of the realities of the cost of clothing and the poverty of the boys for whom the Vaux's Own Troop was intended. Yet this troop was promoted and supported by Scouting enthusiasts precisely because of the poverty of the boys involved.

The beginnings

The *Echo* reported that Baden Powell was to speak at the Victoria Hall in Sunderland on 13 February 1908 in a meeting organised under the auspices of the YMCA. The notice drew attention to the General's gallantry at Mafeking and the purpose of his new scheme of Scouting 'to awaken more interest in the training of boys of all grades of society to a better citizen' (*Echo*, 12 February 1908). It promised an interesting and amusing lecture, a large and enthusiastic crowd and the added interest of lantern slides. The lecture was to be supported by a performance by the band of the Wellesley Training Ship. The very short report of the event the following day suggested that:

> *Lieut.-General Baden-Powell, who hopes by his new national game of Red Indianism to bring about a better citizenship in the near future, possesses all the necessaries within himself to make the scheme a success.*
>
> (*Echo*, 13 February 1908)

Referring to Baden Powell's visit to Sunderland, the Scoutmaster's story in Wade's history relates that:

> *In February 1908 Lieut.-General Baden-Powell discussed his early dream of the formation of the Boy Scout Movement with Lieut.-Colonel Ernest*

Vaux, with whom he was staying at his residence at Grindon near Sunderland.

Colonel Vaux drew the General's attention to work amongst boys already carried out by the Sunderland Waifs' Rescue Agency and Street Vendors' club and induced him to pay us a visit.

This visit was the beginning of our Scouts in Sunderland . . .'

(Quoted in Wade, 1929, 64)

It is likely that Vaux and Baden Powell were acquainted as army officers as both served in the Boer War. There is no evidence the two met each other in South Africa, although there is a suggestion in the *Echo* (21 May 1900, 4) that a Sunderland contingent was 'probably at Mafeking'. The military connection, reinforced by Baden Powell taking command of the Northumbrian Division of the Territorial Army, facilitated use of the Sunderland Drill Hall as the venue for the earliest town-wide meetings concerned with the organisation of Scouting, and as Baden Powell himself indicated, his territorial responsibility meant that he could give particular attention to Scouting in Sunderland:

> *As Sunderland is in my district I shall hope to give an eye personally to the development of the Boy Scouts should they be started in your city.*
>
> (Letter from B.P. to Secretary of YMCA quoted in the *Echo*, 5 March 1908)[2]

In 1908, it would have been difficult for Vaux not to have been aware of the work of the Waifs' Rescue Agency. The club was well known and it was supported by a range of respectable and prominent professional people in the town (Spence, 2001a). However, the minutes report no previous contact with Major Vaux prior to his visit there on 20 February with the specific purpose of proposing:

> *that a certain number of gentlemen each take half a dozen boys under their care with the endeavour to help them to dress better etc., in short to smarten them up generally, in order to make them more useful citizens in after life.*
>
> *Mr Vaux stated that he had a dozen gentlemen already, who were willing to take over 6 boys each, and to do all in their power to improve the conditions of their lives, by generally taking an interest in the boys, and by helping them in various practical ways, should they require such help.*
>
> *These 72 boys to be banded together as 'Baden Powell's Scouts'.*
>
> (Min. 20 February 1908)

Vaux further suggested that the Scouts would need to meet together one night a week. He wanted the Lambton Street Club to be the headquarters of the new movement, 'more especially as he desired only to deal with the ragged street boy, and to form his Scouting Corps exclusively out of this class' (Min. 20 February 1908). The questions asked by committee were mainly about finance and the impact upon the other work of the club. The Major was keen to reassure them:

> *. . . In reply to certain questions by members of the Committee Major Vaux explained that his scheme would be entirely self-supporting, and that any money that should be received over and above the Scouting corps' expenses, he considered ought to be handed over to the benefit of the Institution as being the headquarters of the Scouts . . . He also expressed his willingness to put the Grindon Estate at the disposal of the Corps, for camping purposes etc. . . .*
>
> (Min. 20 February 1908)

The value of what Vaux was offering has to be seen both in the light of the constant struggle of the club for subscriptions and contributions, and with reference to the problem of space for boys to engage in outdoor activities in the vicinity of the club. Nevertheless the committee did not agree immediately to the scheme:

> *The chairman having expressed the committee's pleasure, at these generous proposals on the part of Major Vaux and his friends, it was decided that the committee reserve their decision till Friday Feb. 28th.*
>
> (Min. 20 February 1908)

The fact that Vaux said that he already had 'a dozen gentlemen' who were 'ready to take over six boys each' (approximating to the total active membership of the Waifs Rescue Agency)[3] implies that some activity had already taken place prior to his visit to Lambton Street. There was further discussion during the week of 20–27 February between Vaux and Eustace Charlton who was one of the most influential members of the club committee. Charlton had been keen to organise the Scouts on the meeting of the 20th:

> *Mr Charlton suggested that a sub committee of 12 might be formed of his friends to organise Major Vaux's proposed movement, one of their number being appointed a member of the Executive Committee.*
>
> (Min. 20 February 1908)

On the basis of agreed terms reached during the week between Vaux and Charlton, the committee agreed to accept the proposal for the development of Scouting in the club at their meeting of 27 February. They did so mainly on grounds which were practical rather than philosophical, and they were very careful about the conditions. There was no reference to the contents of *Scouting for Boys*; rather, here was an opportunity to extend the opening hours of the club and to gain additional resources. In particular, it was reported that Vaux had said that if the club rooms were kept open all day for the purpose of Scouting, he would 'provide a lathe, bench and tools whereby the boys could receive instruction in joinery from the Superintendent' (Min. 27 February 1908). Given that one of the primary purposes of the work in Lambton Street was to encourage boys towards the adoption of a trade, this was a promise which could only have provided further encouragement to the committee to support his scheme (Spence, 2001). They agreed to write to him as follows:

Major Ernest Vaux D.S.O.
Dear Sir,
   Referring to your interview with our committee, we shall be very pleased to do all we can to help on your Boy Scouts' Scheme, in any way in our power, and would make the following suggestions for your consideration.
   i. *The Boy Scouts be for the present at any rate, a Branch of this Agency subject to its rules and regulations and under the direction of our Executive Committee.*
   ii. *That a Boys' Scouts Sub committee be formed by you out of your body of helpers, with one or two representatives, on our Executive Committee.*
   iii. *That all Boy Scouts must be or become members of this agency and the Rooms of the Agency, be for their use each evening from 7 till 9 as may from time to time be arranged by the Executive committee.*
   iv. *That if it be desirable to have the rooms open all day instead of only between those hours (as at present) the Committee will endeavour to arrange for a Superintendent to give the whole of his time instead of a portion of it (as at present) to the work, in such case the committee would require the promise of further Annual subscriptions amounting to at least £26 to defray the actual extra cost to them of same as their present Subscription List only brings in an Income sufficient to defray currant [sic] expenses*

*for running the agency on its present lines. As soon as you are in
a position to say anything further on the subject, the Committee
will be glad to meet you again.*
  Yours faithfully,
    F. Douglas Caws
  Hon. Sec.

The managers clearly did not perceive Scouting as a change to their work, but rather as an addition, and one which came within their jurisdiction.

Although they made their decision within one week, the impetus to centre Sunderland Scouting in Lambton Street subsided as Baden Powell's ideas rapidly took hold across the town – a pattern repeated in other parts of the country (see e.g. Jeal, 1989). Vaux's attention was quickly distracted: it was becoming clear that Scouting was not only relevant to poor ragged boys from the east end, but had a much wider appeal. The already cramped Lambton Street club rooms situated at the edge of Sunderland's poor east end on the south side of the river must have begun to seem less suitable as a headquarters for the new movement, and first the Artillery Drill Hall in the centre of the town and then a building in nearby Mary Street owned by Vaux became the organising centres. It was only at the beginning of April that Vaux returned to Lambton Street to meet with the boys who might wish to join his proposed troop. Meanwhile other people were busy organising in the wider Sunderland area.

A conference to bring together those interested in Scouting was organised by the YMCA for 6 March 1908 at the Town Hall. At this event, presided over by the Mayor, both Ernest Vaux and his brother Cuthbert were present. So too were representatives from a range of organisations, including the chair of the Waifs' Rescue Agency, Mr C.E. Thompson and Eustace Charlton. The Secretary of the YMCA, Mr Johnson, affirmed Baden Powell's intention that Scouting should not grow in opposition to other organisations and movements, stating that:

> *It was proposed to organise branches in various parts of the town, and it
> is hoped to have all existing boys' organisations such as the Church Lads
> Brigade, Boys Brigade, the Y.M.C.A., the telegraph boys and the Waifs'
> and Strays' club.*
>
> (*Echo*, 7 March 1908)

In this spirit, a central committee of 24 individuals was created from those present, including the Lambton Street representatives, to oversee developments in Sunderland. Vaux referred to the agreement which he had made with the 'Waifs' and Strays' Rescue Agency' and intimated that 'Lambton Street was now open from six to nine every night, but they would open it all day, and the services of their instructor would also be given to assist in the Scout scheme there' (*Echo*, 7 March 1908). But already the effort to organise in Lambton Street was being superseded by something much larger and thereafter the development of the Vaux's Own Scouts ran alongside those in other areas of the town. Before Vaux returned to Lambton Street, he presided over another meeting in the Drill Hall on 18 March which was the first to be attended by boys from across Sunderland. The *Echo* reported that:

> *The chairman expressed his pleasure at meeting so many lads present, and saw in the numerous gathering promise of the scheme being taken up in Sunderland. That meeting was practically the first meeting for Scouts proper, and the lads were there to learn something of what would be expected of them.*
>
> (*Echo*, 19 March 1908)

The following week saw Vaux addressing a meeting at Ford, to the west of the town, where members of prominent ship-building families, including Sir Theodore Doxford and Mr Bartram were organising a 'Boy Scout brigade' (*Echo*, 26 March 1908). Vaux was elected vice-president of this initiative. On 1 April at the Drill Hall he presided over 'a crowded meeting of patrol leaders and others interested in the Boy Scouts' where 'Lieut. Frank Pickersgill gave a brief lecture on "Scout Law" and was followed by Lieut. Webb, who gave demonstrations in knot tying and a description of the Union Jack' (*Echo* 2 April 1908). Clearly Vaux, responding to the widespread interest, was extending his ambition beyond his original intention to 'only deal with the ragged street boy' (Min. 20 February 1908). However, he did not abandon Lambton Street, returning there on 2 April 1908 to 'a crowded meeting of boy street vendors' (*Echo*, 3 April 1908) with the express purpose of organising them into a Scout troop.

Lambton Street and Scouting

Vaux was keen to continue to nurture his 'own' troop in Lambton Street mainly because those who were associated with the Waifs Rescue Agency were 'boys from the poorer classes' (Smith, 1952, 5). These were the boys who were thought to be those most in danger of becoming what Baden Powell himself described as 'Wasters' or 'Loafers' (*Echo*, 28 May 1908; 16 December 1908). The possibility of influencing such boys was central to the intentions of

Scouting (Rosenthal, 1986). According to Mr Johnson of the YMCA, the purpose of the Scouts was to:

> . . . *train them in clean living, and to have endurance and patriotism . . . to remove artificial barriers between class and class, thus [to] stop the snarling between classes that was a danger to society.*

(Echo, 7 March 1908)

The Lambton Street Club was an attractive proposition for the development of Scouting because it catered exactly to the type of boy whose unfitness as a representative of British citizenry had been keenly exercising the conscience of the nation particularly since the near-disaster of the Boer War and since it had been discovered that 'three out of every five recruits were unfit for armed service' (Rosenthal, 1986, 3). The Waifs Rescue Agency and Street Vendors Club itself had been formed in a climate of increasing concern about the condition of the nation's urban children as had been highlighted by the work of Barnardo and others (Spence, 2003, 102). The club's chairman, affirmed the complementarity of purpose with Scouting when he asserted at the Town Hall meeting of 6 March 1908 that 'in the boys they worked among, the leaders of the scheme would find plenty of the right kind of material for their efforts' (*Echo*, 7 March 1908).

If Scouting was to be successful in Lambton Street, it was necessary that it contributed to, or at the very least did not contradict, the practices which the club had established to win the loyalty and influence the behaviour and attitudes of the boy street vendors. And at first consideration, it seemed that the organisation of a Scout troop might enhance and even rationalise the efforts of the club to mould respectable citizens from the back alleys of the east end. However, Scouting made little provision for the realities of working with such boys. For example, the 7th Scout law, to obey parents, made sense if parents were 'respectable'. But a constant concern of the work in Lambton Street was to woo boys away from the attitudes and values of parents who were found wanting in this matter. The evidence indicates that the first efforts to focus the benefits of Scouting upon 'the right kind of material' floundered at a number of levels: first because resources were inadequate from Scout sponsors, from the club and from the boys' families; second because consistency of time and effort could not be sustained either by the boys or the new volunteers who would be Scoutmasters; and third because the level of cleanliness and smartness required by the Scouts was constantly undermined by the battle with dirt, hunger and raggedness which was part of the everyday life of casual industrial labour linked to the main local industries of shipbuilding and mining. These difficulties weave in and out of those aspects of the work where it might have been considered that Scouting would be most useful and complementary to the underlying intentions of the work in the Waifs' Rescue Agency.

An alternative to the streets?

In Lambton Street, a great deal of emphasis was put on the idea of keeping the club homely, clean and welcoming. The promise of 'a warm, safe space' (Robertson, 2000/2001) where a boy might find refuge and relaxation, was integral to the ideal of the 'club and found its corollary in *Scouting for Boys* in Baden Powell's emphasis on the possibilities for comfortable camping and the cosiness of the 'scout hut' (Baden-Powell, 1932, 33–34). There were however some issues around the question of sleeping in the open air. It might be acceptable for Baden Powell to sleep outside on the veranda of his private home in all climates (Jeal, 1989, 459), but poor, ragged boys who slept outdoor in a town such as Sunderland were likely to be identified either as 'waifs' (to be rescued by clubs such as that in Lambton Street) or 'vagrants' and arrested for 'loitering' (min. 9 June 1910) or simply for 'sleeping out, as were some of the members of the club in 1902:

> *Mr Caws reported that 4 members of the Club viz. No's 74 [Portland], 96, 24 [Wm Potts] and 128 had been lodged in the police cells for sleeping out at nights. But the Magistrates had let them off for one month's trial understanding that they were members of the Street Vendors Club.*
>
> (Min. 14 August 1902. See also Min. 16 April 1914)

Jim Smith was particularly keen to develop organised activities, including drama and sport as a means of training and improving the health of the boys but his club building offered no room for expansion beyond covering the back yard, and had no immediate access to open space in its built-up urban environment.[4] There were beaches to the north of the river, well used by the local population, but the club had struggled to find regular, accessible outdoor space for organised activities. So the invitation to use Vaux's Grindon estate, within walking distance of the club, to facilitate Scouting, must have been viewed as an excellent opportunity both for boys to gain access to outdoor living away from the street and for the expansion of the activities agenda.

At the first town meeting of 6 March 1908, Vaux said that:

> *He thought those interested might begin by selecting their boys, say six in number, get to know them and their characters and take them for walks*

in the country. He was willing that they should walk round his farm at Grindon, where they would find something of interest. In the coming summer he would like a weekend camp, and would gladly let them have it on his land at Grindon, if they thought it suitable. The Waifs' and Strays' club might, he thought, be their basis, and beginning there they could afterwards form branches.

(*Echo*, 7 March 1908)

The proposed camp at Grindon was to be extended to become the primary focus for the establishment of the Vaux's Own Scouts. Although subsequently more attention has been given to the Humshaugh camp near Hexham held in August 1908, partly because Baden Powell stayed there (e.g. Reynolds, 1942, 135, 148; Jeal, 1989, 399), Grindon was the probably the first of its type to be held after the 1907 Brownsea Island experiment (Wade, 1929, 66). It was planned as a means of preparing the boys for greater things. Baden Powell had written to Vaux before the end of April 'asking for 8 of the Scouts to be selected and trained, to travel around with him and give demonstrations at his lectures on the subject of the Scouts Scheme' (Min. 30 April 1908). The *Echo* reported that, 'This was considered a great honour for the town. Major Vaux to raise this patrol' (*Echo* 2 May 1908).

Twenty-four Scouts from Lambton Street were drilled during May 'at Mr Wood's gymnasium' in preparation for the camp. In opening access to the gymnasium, Scouting was already promising to widen the facilities accessible to boys from Lambton Street.

The camp was eventually held over a three week period in June and shared with a troop from Hampstead, 'raised from a similar class of boys'. Captain Pearce, who brought the Hampstead troop, was charged with 'training' the boys so that 'they will be able to give exhibitions all over England of the methods of the scheme'.[5] It appears that the camp accommodated eight boys from Sunderland (chosen, according to the *Echo* from 'about one hundred' Lambton Street 'Scouts') and eight from Hampstead, although Wade suggests that there were 12 boys from Hampstead and the minutes record that:

Mr Smith reported that 14 of the Club Scouts had gone to camp at Grindon ... Thirty boys who were instructed at the Gymnasium by General Baden Powell who expressed his satisfaction at the progress made by the local corps, are going to camp at Grindon shortly.

(Min. 28 May 1908)

Each camper was to be paid five shillings per week to attend (ibid.). It is not clear from the accounts if any of them ever actually eventually toured with Baden Powell.

Paying the boys to participate in the Grindon camp had probably not been within Vaux's original plan, but 'keeping them off the streets' via Scouting was to be no easy option with regard to street vendors. The five shillings which they received was probably just slightly less than they would have earned per week selling newspapers, but about equivalent if their food was taken into consideration. There was probably no possibility that some of those boys could have attended the camp without such a subsidy. It had also been necessary for Vaux to subsidise their preparation for the camp. The report of the Scoutmaster in Wade tells us that:

> *Lieut.-col. Vaux secured the services of Captain W. Webb and Mr Fred Wood. These gentlemen came down every week to train the boys in Scouting. This went on with great success.*
>
> *At this time during their training it was very difficult for these poor boys to attend regularly owing to the sale of their papers etc.*
>
> *The philanthropic mind of Colonel Vaux soon overrode this difficulty. He agreed to pay for all the returns these boys had after seven o'clock so that they could take up their training. This went on under the able instructors mentioned until May, when a month's camp was held at Grindon under the charge of Captain Pearce, who brought twelve boys from other districts.*
>
> (Wade, 1929, 65)

The involvement of poor boys in this camp was important to the promotion of the idea of the beneficial impact upon those deemed most socially problematic, as was later made clear in the *Echo* report:

> *Lieut. General Baden-Powell intends to have 30 boys under canvas during the summer at a holiday camp and the boys at Grindon are a portion of those being trained for it. He also intends to use these lads in the way of demonstration at his lectures in different parts of the country. Another object he has in view is to utilise the class of boy who generally develops into a loafer. These lads for whom the camp is held are of the waif and stray type. The Sunderland eight are from the Lambton Street Institute and have shown marked aptitude for their Scout work. The London eight are of the same class.*
>
> (*Echo*, 28 May 1908)

Clearly the prospect of subsidising the boys to promote the ideals of Scouting at the outset of the venture was one thing, but continuing such subsidy to enable them to maintain their involvement was another matter. The expectations of regularity and discipline demanded by Scouting went well beyond the basic 'No smoking, swearing or gambling' and no 'disorderly conduct' required for general membership of Lambton Street. To sustain the level of organised drill and 'training' demanded by Scouting was probably impossible for most street vendors no matter how willing, because of the irregular time structures and unpredictability of their everyday lives.

Inevitably, once the subsidies which addressed these issues were spent, so too did enthusiasm for Scouting begin to wane amongst the Lambton Street boys. They returned to selling their newspapers, were unable to commit to regular troop meetings and the boundaries between Scouting and ordinary club membership began to collapse. Vaux was forced to shift his perspective in order to retain any hope of continuing to influence 'ragged street boys'. His Grindon estate continued to be used by Scouts, and his Vaux's Own Scouts used it once more over the weekend of 20 June 1908, but he also found himself playing host to organised visits from the general membership of Lambton Street. For example, a telling photograph from a 1911 newspaper report (*Illustrated Chronical*, 20 July 1911) shows a large number of club members, some of whom were barefoot, and none of whom wore Scout attire, during a visit to the Grindon estate. In a similar fashion, Capt. Webb, who had offered his services specifically as a Scout leader, found himself working on a broader platform through his association with the club, agreeing in August to 'allow the street Vendors to play matches on the Barracks ground' (Min. 20 August 1908).

The Scouts thus became the means whereby 'an alternative to the streets' could be to extended more successfully into the organised use of the outdoors and open spaces which were previously inaccessible to the Lambton Street boys, but this in itself was insufficient to sustain Scouting in the context of their poverty.

Influencing boys?

From its inception, the Waifs' Rescue Agency imposed some basic but very general rules regarding behaviour. The emphasis was mainly upon the question of orderliness, with the threat that 'If any member of the club is guilty of disorderly conduct he is liable to expulsion' (Min. 9 December 1901). Within five months of the opening, the rules were extended to 'absolutely' forbid 'spitting or dirty or disorderly conduct' (Min. 15 May 1902). The relationship between dirt and disorder in the minds of the club managers was no accident.

Physical cleanliness was central to the achievement of working class respect-ability and carried meanings about values and morality. Boys were expected to be physically clean on entering the club, and soap and towels were provided by the back yard tap to enable them to wash. We are told in *Fifty Years of Lambton Street* that washing the boys was one of the tasks undertaken by Mrs Smith (Martin in Smith, 1952, 14). As late as 1934 The Echo ran a headline which read 'A Club Where a CLEAN FACE Is the Only "Subscription"' (19 April 1934) and yet later, the Annual Reports were inscripted with the motto: 'Live Clean, Think Clean, Be Clean' (e.g. 1950 et passim – 1975).

The expectation that Scouting might contribute to social order and promote 'clean living', and the 10th Scout Law: 'A Scout is clean in thought, word and deed', would have been experienced simply as a reinforcement of the ethos which was already centrally engrained in the Lambton Street approach in 1908. However, the Scout law was concerned mainly with the morality of dirt rather than its physicality, and to achieve this was a second order level of influence. Certainly those who wished to sponsor Scouting did not imagine themselves having to *deal directly* with dirt as the following telling excerpt suggests:

> *I pictured myself as the benevolent patron into whose pocket the Scoutmaster might dip with reason, and I saw myself going occasionally to their meetings, say once a quarter, and with a benevolent smile saying, 'Well, boys, and how are we getting on, eh?' and patting the smallest on the head, if clean enough'.*

(cited in Reynolds, 1942, 147)

Yet in order to exert any influence in the matter of attitudes and behaviour it was apparent that those working with the children of the poor had to firstly address some absolutely fundamental practical concerns. How could it be possible to press upon dirty children the virtues of clean living and purity of thought? Scouting provided a charter for training and the terms of reference for influencing boys' attitudes, but it did not address the fundamental manifestations of poverty which predetermined the possibility of boys partici-pating. Such boys needed to be washed!

Of course at the start, Baden Powell did not imagine that Scouting would become a movement in its own right, but rather that it would be grafted onto pre-exiting provision, as an additional means of working with some boys. He was not concerned therefore with first order problems. Scouting was intended as a means of reinforcing influences which were already at play, of deepening the training of boys who were already subject to the rules of organisations such as the YMCA, the Boys' Brigade, or the Waifs' Rescue Agency. Advocates of the scheme such as Vaux, who had never previously been involved in such work, could not in the early stages of the movement have imagined the levels of commitment and the practical application necessary to win the trust and compliance of those they desired to influence and train. In Lambton Street, Smith and his wife clearly applied themselves to the task not only of demanding that boys observe the rules, but also of helping them to achieve such observance. Both offered sympathetic help to the boys (and informally to the girls who were excluded from club membership) (Interview, Bridget Brewster, 1999), who wanted to participate. In so doing, they were able to win the loyalty which was necessary to exert a deeper influence. In this, their stability and dependability were essential factors.

Smith was a practising (non-conformist) Christian, a time-served joiner, and an athlete. His credentials as a resident Superintendent were excellent. He was a self-consciously respectable, skilled, family man but working class nevertheless. As such, he could act as a 'bridge' between the professional middle class men of the committee whose values he shared, and the lower working class families whose boys attended the club, whose values he understood (Putnam, 2000). However, Smith's own class status seemed to place him outside the expectation that the leaders of Scouts would be 'gentlemen', as initially envisaged by Vaux. Whilst he was responsible for opening the Lambton Street rooms for the Scouts, he was not considered as a potential Scoutmaster. Yet the 'dozen gentlemen' whom Vaux had claimed to be ready to organise the Scouts in Lambton Street do not seem to have materialised in practice.

According to the account in Wade, the first Scout leaders in Lambton Street were Capt. W. Webb and Mr Fred Wood, who owned the gymnasium where the boys trained for the Grindon camp, and it is recorded in the minutes of 16 April 1908 that 'during the week, three gentlemen had taken Scout Patrols, 6 boys being in each patrol'. To lead a Scout patrol for one week was one thing, to work with these boys in order to achieve a lasting influence in the longer term was quite something else. It appears that Wood at least continued to work with the Vaux's Own Scouts during the summer of 1908, but at his gymnasium rather than in the Lambton Street premises (min. 18 June 1908) and no doubt someone was with the troop when they participated in the Dispensary Sports Day in August 'but failed to win any prizes for races etc' (Min. 6 August 1908). However, after this last entry to the minutes, the record of participation of Scout leaders in Lambton Street goes dead. Captain Webb's involvement shifted to a town-wide role, and he introduced Baden Powell at a Scout concert in the Avenue Theatre on 16 December 1908. Although boys from Lambton Street were present at this concert (min. 17 December 1908), in Webb's introduction he mentions the strength of Scouting in Hylton, Offerton and Seaham, but of the Vaux's Own Scouts there is only silence.

No other leader is mentioned until the minutes of January 1912 when

> *Mr Caws reported that with regard to a troupe* [sic] *of boy Scouts for the club, there had been a meeting of gentlemen interested in the same on 22nd at 15 Lambton Street. – Mr Oliver the Secretary of the Boy Scouts was present, and explained many features of the movement. Captain Farrow and Captain Walker expressed themselves willing to take charge of the Lambton Street Troupe* [sic].
>
> (Min. 25 January 1912)

On 15 February 1912, it was reported that, 'Messrs Walker, Farrow, Caws and Robinson met at the Club on Monday the 12th inst when 10 of our boys were selected to be drilled at the Scouts in Mary Street'. This records the beginning of the direct interest by Douglas Caws in the Scouts, but notably, the boys were required to meet in the Mary Street Scout headquarters rather than in Lambton Street and it is later noted that 'three of the boys resigned on the second night and one new boy started. The bigger boys do not seem eager to join' (Min. 22 February 1912). Nevertheless, there seemed to be steady development of Scouting in the club from this point onwards.

Probably the Vaux Own Scouts began to settle in 1912 because the idea that it would be mainly external 'gentlemen' who would run the patrols or troops, and sponsors such as Vaux who would fund them, began to give way. The club assumed in-house responsibility for developing the Vaux's Own Troop. In the summer of 1912, at a Scout camp at Whitburn, a local village to the north of Sunderland, 'the boys were in charge of Scoutmaster Sam Hardy and the superintendent of the agency Mr J.A. Smith, Mr Douglas Caws, secretary and Mr W. Robinson, member to the committee were also in camp' (Unattributed newspaper cutting pasted in Minutes, 1 August 1912). Caws and Smith were thenceforth to maintain their commitment to the Vaux's Own Scouts as a lifetime project and the Souvenir Invitation Programme for the 1958 Jubilee lists Smith as 'First Acting Scoutmaster'. Other 'gentlemen' came and went. For example, on 14 November 1912, (Min.) Caws 'advised the Committee that he was endeavouring to get some friends to assist with the management of the Scouts, Mr Walker having been too busy to attend since he has acquired a new appointment'. By 1913, 'Mr Burnet and Mr Meek are drilling the Scouts once a week with Mr Smith's assistance' (Min. 20 February 1913). In May of that year 'the Agency Scouts are parading weekly in charge of Lionel Bennett (min.

22 May 1913). Bennett was the Scoutmaster in charge during the summer camp on the Pemberton Estate at Hawthorn that year. By 4 September it is recorded that Mr Hardy joined him as an assistant, but by 14 May 1914 'Mr Lionel Bennett has recently been unable to attend the Troupe and has resigned his position as Scoutmaster. Mr J. Whitfield Parker who has for some time been keenly interested in the Club work is at present acting as Scoutmaster, being assisted by Edward Bell (one of our old boys) and Mr Mackin who acts as drill instructor'. Again, in the summer camp at Hawthorn in 1914, Jim Smith attended. On the return from the camp, war broke out and Mr Parker joined the forces. At this point, Smith and Caws assumed complete responsibility for the Scouts, and in line with the interest of younger boys, Smith took advantage of the innovation within Scouting to work with young boys and organised a Wolf Cub pack (Min. 5 November 1914).

The direct commitment made by Smith and Caws in 1912 to Scouting in Lambton Street, and their adoption of Scouting as integral to the ethos of the wider work of the club enabled the Scouts to thrive. But their first commitment was to the generic work of Lambton Street. They could only exert 'influence' through the Scouts if the generic work of the club was first established and maintained. The role of the Scouts would be mainly to extend and rationalise this influence amongst the boys who were most amenable to the possibilities, in a manner somewhat akin to what Baden Powell had originally intended in his desire that troops should be sponsored by existing organisations.

This strategy secured the survival of the Waifs' Rescue Agency during the First World War because the Scouts provided a legitimate, and state recognised role, for Smith and Caws 'on the home front'. The military connections and the overt patriotism inscribed within Scouting were a particular attraction for poor boys who found in them a means of expressing loyalties, and gaining recognition for their efforts which transcended class difference in a time of war. So the Scouts therefore became a central and established aspect of the work of Lambton Street, much more nearly approaching Vaux's original vision and in the process, generic club work and Scouting methods became much more closely aligned (Spence, 2001b). The Scouts became accepted as a 'progressive' dimension of the work, membership of which was available to those who had already accepted some of the basic principles of behaviour and attitude promoted by the club, and in the process, the Lambton Street Club itself began to serve a wider population than its original east end constituency. Henceforth, the Lambton Street Club would develop into a town-wide resource for Sunderland boys.

Hunger and raggedness

Many of the boys who used the Lambton Street Club must have found in it simply a refuge from the daily struggle for survival in an unforgiving industrial landscape. For such boys, the possibilities of bettering themselves in the future through the influences exerted by the club were, at the very least, secondary to finding the everyday necessaries of life. If the workers and managers of the club were make a long term impact on life chances, character and values, then, just as they provided soap and towels to deal with dirt, so too was it necessary to recognise the primacy of hunger and raggedness.

Again there was a role here for Mrs Smith:

> *It was Mrs Smith who made the soup, mended the rags and, in the early days, often washed the boys as first step in their initiation into a better standard of life.*
>
> (G.H. Martin, in Smith, 1952, 14)

The 'treats' and 'special occasions' which framed the timetable of club life invariably included food, which was usually donated by an individual member of the management committee or a sponsoring organisation, such as the Co-operative Society. Mainly such food was associated with social and religious rituals and was offered on a collective basis. For example, Mr Thompson supplied a basket of Hot Cross Buns every Easter. Free food was not explicitly conceived as one of the benefits of membership and early in the club's life there had been debate about 'the immorality of indiscriminate giving' when the caretaker had given free cocoa, coffee and biscuits to some members who could not produce the half penny normally charged (Min. 22 January 1903; Spence, 2006, 284). Nevertheless, despite the rhetoric, free food was an essential aspect of club life and in the December preceding the introduction of Scouting, the management committee had conceded its necessity when they agreed to open a soup kitchen in the face of a cyclical economic crisis in Sunderland:

> *A lengthy discussion followed concerning an offer from Mr Ingram to start giving soup suppers at the Club twice a week whilst the present distress in the town lasted. He stated that he had already consulted Smith about these proposed suppers, and that Smith had expressed himself willing to help and to make the soup. The Chairman advised Mr Ingram not to apply for Daily Mail funds as he felt that they were doing real harm to Sunderland and Mr Ingram replied that he heartily agreed with Mr*

Thompson regarding the effect of these funds and had no intention of applying to them for cash to supply the boys with soup. He desired simply to start giving these suppers two nights per week, at his own expense, plus any offers of help he might receive from his friends as time went on.

It was suggested by Mr Kirby that the boys might contribute a small amount for basins of soup and bread, but Mr Ingram said he could not agree to carry the thing forward on these lines. Smith on being consulted by the Committee, stated that he was in favour of giving the club-members this benefit, since the wretchedness he found at their homes was appalling, and that in many cases it was really not the result of drunkeness, or wilful neglect. The committee finally agreed to this proposal, and the Chairman thanked Mr Ingram for his kind offer and expressed the Committee's pleasure at his interest in the Institution and Smith was authorised to start the soup kitchen next week on those nights which best suited himself and Mr Ingram.

(Min. 5 December 1907)

Invariably the discussion about food was accompanied by discussion about clothing. Like food, the provision of clothes was rendered morally acceptable if it was associated with ritual or special occasions or cases. Here, the main ritual was that of a boy leaving school and starting work. Except in the most extreme circumstances, (such as a boy having no trousers (Min. 24 October 1907), clothing was normally provided by the club only to enable boys to take up an offer of employment. Even then Jim Smith and the committee members negotiated with both families and employers in an effort to minimise costs to the club, but often it was the Lambton Street coffers which bore the main cost (Spence, 2001a, 2006). But just as it had encouraged the offer of soup, the hardship of the boys and their families in the winter of 1907–1908 seems to have softened their approach and an appeal was made for second hand clothing to distribute to boys in need:

The following persons had contributed bundles of clothing Miss Todd, Mrs Pumphrey, Mrs Ezra Miller, and Smith gave the following list of boys whom his investigations had proved worthy of clothing, MacLaney, 121, brothers Hanlon 17 & 18, brothers MacMann 85 & 86, Dowd 89, brothers Turner, 14 & 13. The Committee authorised him to distribute clothes to these members.

A p.c. was read from the Reverend Rees of the Grange church stating that he regretted that he could not find any old clothes for the Waifs and

Street Vendors at the present time, as his congregation was already taxed in this respect by their own Missions and Sunday Schools.

(Min. 5 December 2007)

It was into this environment of general hardship and local 'distress' that Major Vaux introduced the new Scouting movement. It is noticeable that the occasions associated with Scouting were generally accompanied by food, thus encouraging the idea that this was a 'special' activity. For example, at the end of their first evening of training at Mr Wood's gymnasium, the Scouts preparing to camp in Grindon were offered coffee and buns by Mrs Wood (Min. 7 May 1908).[6] Later that month it was reported that 26 of the Lambton Street Scouts had visited Grindon with Mr Smith where after being supplied with 'tea and sandwiches' they were shown around the farm and grounds by Major Vaux. Significantly, the provision of refreshments was accompanied by a further inducement for the boys to remain involved. As a further reward, 'uniforms had been given out to a certain number who are going on Friday night to meet General Baden Powell at the Victoria Hall' (Min. 21 May 1908).

The Scout uniform was desirable but clearly out of reach as an item of expenditure for the families of the boys who frequented Lambton Street. For the club to contribute to Scout uniforms was beyond the terms of reference which associated clothing with work, and the second hand clothing provided in response to special need did not fit the case. It is recorded in the minutes of 23 April 1908 that Vaux had given some of the boys 'red ties' to distinguish them as Scouts. Free uniforms were supplied to those who were chosen to attend the Grindon camp in June and the minutes of 18 June 1908 record Baden-Powell's 'satisfaction at their smartness' when he inspected them at the camp. The achievement of smartness as a signifier of the success of the work of the club was to become particularly evident when the boys who joined the forces in 1914 made an appearance in the club in their newly acquired uniforms (Spence, 2001b). For 'smart' was what they could never be in the rags which characterised their childhood dress.

After the initial donations from Vaux, there is no record of any further contributions to the clothing needed by Scouts. In an *Echo* report in December, which focuses on the Scouts as 'well dressed boys marching', there is an assumption that the Vaux's Own Scouts were involved:

This morning Major Vaux received a letter from a gentleman who expressed his delight tin the practical result of the Baden Powell scheme in Sunderland as seen in the well-dressed boys marching in time in Holmeside last night. The letter says that doubtless many of these boys were last year uncared for, and says the result of the work in Sunderland does Major Vaux credit. A cheque for 10 guineas in aid of the movement was enclosed.

(*Echo*, 16 December 1908)

However there is no suggestion of the involvement of Lambton Street boys in such activity in the minutes. By this time the engagement with Scouting seemed to be more tangential. After the summer camp, the Vaux's Own Scouts struggled to survive and in this, the uniform was an important consideration. In early September it is recorded that:

Many of the Club Members are unable to join the Scouting Movement, because they cannot afford to buy their uniforms, and no more are being given out by the Scout Leaders at the present time.

(Min. 3 September 1908)

Jim Smith reported that the cost of a uniform 'without boots' was ten shillings and sixpence and in response, the minutes note that 'The boot question has, and is hampering the Scout leaders a good deal since they find it difficult to drill boys with bare feet'.

(Min. 17 September 1908)

By the spring of 1909 the AGM report stated that:

Major Ernest Vaux had been elected a member of the committee and it was due to him that the club had its own corps of Baden Powell Scouts. Owing to the cost of the uniforms, which did not come out of the income of the agency, it had only been found possible to enrol a comparatively small number. Judging by the good results already effected by major Vaux and his officers, the committee felt that there was good work to be done by the scheme.

(*Echo*, 26 March 1909)

Thereafter, the minutes go silent on the Vaux's Own Scouts until 16 November 1910 in which a newspaper article pasted into the minutes book quotes Major Vaux as saying that 'he was glad to hear that they were going to start a troop of Boy Scouts and hoped that the secretary's anticipation of being able to obtain the funds to provide them with uniforms would be realised'.

Then there is a complete silence during 1911 and it is not until January 1912 that they re-appear in the records. It is at a meeting of 25 January 1912 that the continuous recorded history of the Vaux's Own Scouts in Lambton Street begins and notably, Vaux himself was absent. At this meeting the committee suggested that the boys 'should be drilled without any uniform for say a month or 6 weeks' and that 'the Committee be responsible for the first batch of uniforms required but that apart from this initial help the troupe [*sic*] to be absolutely self-supporting'. They agreed to 'be responsible for uniforms from £7-10-0 to £10-0-0'. By 21 March they were agreeing to 'pay 1/= per pair for having the men's trousers supplied by Lt. Col. Vaux cut down to fit the boys' and were authorising Smith to 'get the necessary materials and make the lockers for the Scouts' clothes as required'. This suggests that the boys who were given uniforms were expected to keep them in the club between meetings. On 4 April the minutes note that eight boys had been provided with uniforms, that a knife and whistle had been given to one boy and a knife to another who had come out top in a Scout examination. The committee then agreed to buy new trousers for the Scouts at 1/6 per pair. In July they reaped their reward when having attended a Scouts Association Display at the Garrison Field, the troop 'were specially commended for their smartness by Col. Surtees'.

In an article focusing upon the meaning of the uniform amongst the Scouts and guides, particularly between the wars, Proctor (1998) argues it was a major factor in the Scout identity and developed into a highly nuanced marker of class and status as well as a means of generational distinctiveness. She makes but passing reference to the fact that some young people had no access at all to a uniform. Yet this was certainly the circumstances confronting most of the boys who were associated with the Lambton Street Club. Their absolute exclusion from the pleasure of smart clothes and the status of the uniform would have made the Scouting both more desirable and at the same time more inaccessible to them from the very start. It is frequently noted that in some towns the Scouts attracted negative attention from their peers, and to some of this might be understood with reference to the exclusion experienced by those without the means to participate. Yet there is no record of this having happened in the east end of Sunderland or of there being any antagonism to Scouting in the Lambton Street Club. Possibly this is because of the way in which the line between the Scouts and the regular members of the club were allowed to blur, and because the resources offered by Vaux initially in support of Scouting were mobilised by Jim Smith and his management committee towards the more general benefit of club members.

Vaux, scouting and the generic work in Lambton Street

The Vaux Brewery had been a growing source of employment in Sunderland for over a hundred years by the time the Scouts were conceived. Yet until the advent of Scouting, the Vaux family never seem to have sponsored the employment of boys from Lambton Street. However, after his election to the committee there are records from May of 1908 of Ernest Vaux accepting boys for work on his farms, in his stables, as a trap driver and in one case as a jockey at his racing stables in Middleham. He does seem to have employed some boys who might have been difficult to place and been prepared to put up with some difficulties which others might not have tolerated, but the process was fraught. For example:

> Major Vaux had found it necessary to take H.F. away from his home and lodge him elsewhere, on account of his ill-fed and dirty condition. At the Major's request, Mr Smith had visited the lad's home and found the parents agreeable to this arrangement.

(Min. 15 October 1908)

And then, two weeks later:

> There was a long discussion . . . concerning F. who is not contented with his lodgings, and desires to return to his home . . . Major Vaux has stated that he cannot employ the lad if he returns home, since before he left his home he was so dirty and ill-fed.

(Min. 29 October 1908)

Vaux was no different from other employers in realising gain from the employment of boys from the Lambton Street Club (Spence, 2001a). In 1908, he was paying to boys six to seven shillings for farm work, and eight shillings for driving a traveller's trap (Min. May date 1908; October date 1908). In April 1911, he was offering three shillings per week plus board to a boy who had accepted farm work.

During 1909 there was a minor tussle between Vaux and the Lambton Street committee over paying for the outfit required by the boy whom Vaux had recruited from the club to become a jockey for him. Vaux had contributed 10/- towards the required outfit, and paid the boy's train fare. Later it was reported that the boy was required to have more clothes which would cost according to Jim Smith's estimates, £1.15.0. Vaux said he would pay some of this but asked the club to also make a contribution. They said they could not pay any more as they had already contributed nearly £3.0.0 towards the cost of fitting out the boy. In the end, Vaux paid for the clothes and Mr Smith went and bought them.

There is little evidence that Vaux ever became a fully committed working member of the management committee. Rather, he seems to have interpreted his role as a sort of benefactor who, as well as providing work, could offer 'treats' to the boys. By the end of 1908, this seems to have been his major role in relation to Lambton Street. His Scouting interests were increasingly being expressed in the growth of the town-wide movement and in Lambton Street he was rather inconsistently spreading goodwill and largess, mainly through food, to the regular members:

> *On Wednesday evening Major Vaux gave the first of a promised series of coffee suppers. After coffee and buns an excellent gramophone was set going, Major Vaux having bought the same for the purpose, and the lads enjoyed the evening thoroughly joining in the various chorus songs with great gusto. Before the close of this entertainment Major Vaux announced that he had arranged with Mr Smith to cook some potatoes for them next Wednesday, and also that if they were good lads and behaved themselves, he might even give them a Christmas dinner at Grindon. The latter announcement produced deafening cheers.*
>
> (Min. 19 November 1908)

Whilst the generous intentions of Vaux were welcomed, his inconsistency was something of a problem for the management committee. The evening entertainment mentioned above had been long promised, but had only materialised when he was reminded of his promise. He became enthusiastic for a while as the club members practised some singing for the concert in aid of the Scouts to be held in the Avenue Theatre in December. Then he seems to have forgotten the promise of the Christmas dinner and once again, Mr Smith had to remind him. Whilst he responded positively, hosting a dinner for 112 club members in January 1909 (Min. 7 January, 1909) it seems that he was never going to fully understand the ethos of the club in practice.

His lack of awareness of the day to day principles of the work in Lambton Street was made evident shortly after his election to the committee. He made an embarrassing but significant *faux pas* when he wrote to the committee with the suggestion that he might provide some of the boys with articles to sell on the streets. In response:

> *Mr Kirby moved Capt Foster seconded and the motion was carried that these proposals should not be adopted at the present time. Mr Caws was requested to write Major Vaux to this effect and to explain to him that one of the prime objects of the Club was to reduce Street Vending in the town rather than aid it.*
>
> (Min. 21 May 1908)

The slightly jagged relationship which Vaux developed with the club before the First World War might have been smoother had Scouting taken off in the way that he had hoped at the outset. He seems to have maintained his involvement with regard to the potential of the club to introduce Scout principles to the poorest boys, but his interest seems to have been not so much in work with young people per se, but rather in the success of Scouting to win boys to his own values which he saw reflected in the Scouting scheme. In this context, it is perhaps unsurprising that some of his difficulties with Lambton Street were resolved by the integration of Scouting into the central work of the club during the First World War, and after the war, Vaux was honoured with the role of chairman. But in the meantime, the introduction of Scouting to the poorest of boys was no straightforward matter.

Conclusion

The Vaux's Own Scouts are testimony to both the success and the failure of Scouting. The longevity of the troop and their survival for most of the twentieth century in the poorest part of an industrial town is indicative of the reach of the movement and its power to speak to boys from all walks of life. During the First World War, the Lambton Street Scouts were partnered and supported by a richer troop from Offerton and this is indicative of the possibilities of the idea of 'brotherhood' and friendship through shared beliefs and values. However, the story of the early years of the development of the troop demonstrates something of the idealism of the scheme as far as the poorest boys were concerned. Baden Powell's original idea that Scouting would be organised within pre-existing organisations meant that at the outset he did not address some of the very practical problems and difficulties encountered by boys whose lives were ruled by poverty. But nor did he consider how his uniformed troops would relate to those organisations in which they were developed. The managers of the Lambton Street Club adopted the scheme in the hope of a contribution to their work and only on the clear understanding that it would not cost them anything, but ultimately it was necessary for them to invest money and energy in order to stabilise Scouting. For 'gentlemen' such as Vaux were neither able nor willing to undertake the personal and financial commitment required to sustain a troop whose members were in no position to meet some of the basic requirements of Scouting for regularity, cleanliness, thrift and most of all, smartness through uniformity.

Scouting might only have continued as a minor part of the work of the Waifs' Rescue Agency and Street Vendors' Club had it not been for the particular circumstances, and the opportunities for establishment offered by the First World War. As a movement favoured by government and recognised for its usefulness in organising children to help and support the war effort, Scouting was able to move centre stage in Lambton Street. In doing so, the Vaux's Own Scouts not only helped the club to survive, but probably helped some children to survive the privations of the time. Ultimately though it was the club that provided the necessary practical and interpersonal foundation for a Scout troop for the 'ragged street boy', without its sponsorship, no such troop would have been possible in Sunderland.

Notes

1 Authorship is not attributed on the actual publication but the Annual Report, 1951–1952 describes 'the publication of a Jubilee Handbook, "50 years at Lambton Street" from writings by our superintendent Jim Smith, whose connection with the Club extends to within a month or two of its foundation' (p. 4).
2 Of course this letter suggests that as far as B.P. was concerned, Scouting had not yet started in Sunderland by 5 March.
3 For example, attendance at the club during the last week of March 1908 ranged from 21 to 84, with an average over the week of 57 (Min. 9 April 1908).
4 Over one hundred years later, the club retains this influence, and its new building has been designed especially to facilitate sporting activity.
5 Pearce had started the 1st Hampstead Troop which Jeal notes was also one of the first to form in the country. Pearse, who was an officer in the volunteers, also helped at the Humshaugh camp (Jeal, 1989, 399).
6 The minutes report that 'Major Vaux had also started a savings bank for the boys and has promised to double anything they save'. This could not have been a great sum in the circumstances.

References

Baden-Powell, R. (1932 edition) *Scouting for Boys: Boy's Edition*, London, C. Arthur Pearson.
Eager, W. McG. (1953) *Making Men: Being a History of Boys' Clubs and Related Movements in Great Britain*, London, University of London Press.
Jeal, T. (1989) *Baden-Powell*, London, Hutchinson.
Proctor, T.M. (1998) '(Uni)forming youth: Girl Guides and Boy Scouts in Britain, 1908–39', *History Workshop Journal*, 45, Spring, 103–134.
Putnam, R.D. (2000) *Bowling Alone: The collapse and revival of American community*, New York, Simon and Schuster.
Reynolds, E.E. (1942) *Baden-Powell*, London, Oxford University Press.
Rosenthal, M. (1986) *The Character Factory: Baden-Powell and the Origins of the Boy Scout Movement*, London, Collins.
Robertson, S. (2000/2001) 'A Warm, Safe Space', *Youth and Policy*, 70, Winter, 71–77.

Smith, J. (1952) *Fifty Years at Lambton Street*, Private Publication.

Spence, J. (2001a) 'Edwardian Boys and Labour in the East End of Sunderland: Welfare and Work' in R. Gilchrist, T. Jeffs and J. Spence (eds.), *Essays in the History of Community and Youth Work*, Leicester, Youth Work Press.

Spence, J. (2001b) 'The Impact of the First World War on the Development of Youth Work: The case of the Sunderland Waifs' Rescue Agency and Street Vendors' Club' in R. Gilchrist, T. Jeffs and J. Spence (eds.) *Essays in the History of Community and Youth Work*, Leicester: Youth Work Press.

Spence, J. (2003) 'Frank Caws and the Development of Work with Boys in Sunderland' in R. Gilchrist, T. Jeffs and J. Spence (eds.) *Architects of Change: Studies in the History of Community and Youth Work*, Leicester, NYA.

Spence, J. (2006) 'Gender and Class Negotiations in an Edwardian Welfare Organisation: a Tale of Two Women, *Women's History Review*, 15 (2) April, 277–295.

Wade, E.K. (1929) *Twenty-One Years of Scouting*, London: Pearson.

Primary sources

Minutes of the Management Committee and other ephemera in the archives of the Sunderland Waifs' Rescue Agency and Street Vendors' Club, 1901–1929. Lambton Street Fellowship Centre, Sunderland.

The *Sunderland Daily Echo*, 1908–1914, and 1934, Sunderland Reference Library.

Interviews with:

Mr Frank Caws Jnr. (son of Douglas Caws), 24 November 1998

Mrs Elaine Amundsen (daughter of Douglas Caws), December 1998

Mrs Bridget Brewster whose family used the Lambton Street Club in its early years, 24 March 1999.

Douglas Caws

CHAPTER 16

'Forgotten Corners': A Reflection on Radical Youth Work in Britain, 1940–1990

Tania de St Croix

> *There has always been a radical tradition within youth work, of workers committed to not merely working with young people, but working with young people in order to try and create a better society.*
>
> (Jeffs, 2002, 4)

This chapter aims to explore evidence of radical youth work practice in the history of 'modern' youth work. The term 'radical' can be rather vague so, to be clear, I am focusing here on youth work that comes from broadly socialist or anarchist perspectives, while recognising that many who share similar values refuse labels. The immediate difficulty is the lack of youth work literature that positions itself politically. There are few references to radical youth work and even fewer examples of what this has amounted to in practice; radical youth work tends to be vaguely defined, broadly interpreted and under-analysed. This is in contrast to schooling, adult education, social work and community work, where radical approaches have been more widely explored, debated and documented (see for example, Wright, 1989; Lovett, 1988; Bailey and Brake, 1975; Curno 1978).

The paucity of radical youth work literature can partly be explained by a more general lack of critical youth work theory (Gilchrist *et al.*, 2003), but may also point to the limited influence of radicalism in youth work's history. There are various possible reasons for this, not least that youth work's frequently precarious situation has meant that fighting for radical approaches has often been seen as a distraction. This position assumes that youth work itself is by its very nature a 'good thing', worth preserving in whatever form. Investment in youth work is inevitably offered with strings attached, for example Gordon Brown's promise of £670 million for new youth centres as a means of tackling 'anti-social behaviour' (Brown, 2007). Youth work is once again being presented as soft policing, and young people as a nuisance to their community rather than a part of it.

For those of us who oppose authoritarianism, capitalism and their effects on young people, it is useful to look at how youth workers of the past have worked against or despite of oppressive social policy, to be inspired by past contributions and possibly to learn lessons. This chapter presents an inevitably lopsided view of radical youth work history; by focusing on projects which inspire me I will undoubtedly omit examples that others view as important. While making no claims to be comprehensive, I aim at least to contribute to a debate that is sorely lacking, can there be, and has there ever been, such a thing as radical youth work? As Jeffs and Smith (2006, 36) argue:

> For youth work to survive with any integrity it will be necessary to exploit niches and forgotten corners; and to hide from, or at least stay out of sight of, key state surveillance systems.

This chapter is written in search of these 'forgotten corners' where adults and young people have worked together to create spaces for genuine collaboration.

Context, the origins of radical youth work

In his paper 'Whatever happened to radical youth work?' Jeffs (2002) equates radicalism with working towards change and a better society, tracing a radical tradition of youth work back to anti-slavery campaigner and educator Hannah More in the 1780s. This concept of radicalism encompasses most liberal youth work, whereas I wish to focus specifically on more controversial forms. Rather than aligning radical youth work with a certain ideology, I define it here as a particular combination of values, methods and attitudes,

> Radical youth workers work informally with young people and take them seriously. Their daily work is informed by political and moral values, opposition to capitalism and authoritarianism, belief in equality and respect for the environment. They question 'common sense' and reflect critically on their work. They attempt to practice youth work in a spirit of debate, struggle and fun.[1]

This definition of radical youth work applies most strongly to 'modern' youth work since the start of the youth service in 1939. However, it is important to look at some of the origins of radical practice.

Youth work is a loosely defined activity with disparate origins. Many early youth work organisations had explicitly colonial and conservative values and aims, for example boys and girls clubs, the Boys Brigade, the Girls Friendly Society, Scouts, Guides, YWCA, and YMCA. Boys were prepared for war or the workplace, and girls to be housewives and mothers. The Scouts, for example, were set up to promote militaristic and public school values, loyalty, courage, obedience and 'playing the game' (Boehmer, 2004). These organisations can be included in a loose definition of 'youth work' because they took place in young people's leisure time and attendance was voluntary, but their strong ideologies required strict adherence to a set of rules, behaviour and often a uniform. Even the principle of voluntary attendance did not necessarily come from any belief in freedom of choice, but was a pragmatic attempt to win popular 'voluntary' consent for adherence to establishment values (Davies, 1986).

These broadly conservative organisations appear to dominate the early history of youth work, but during the same period there were also left-wing youth groups and organisations. Clarion Clubs in the late nineteenth century were explicitly socialist, and offered 'fellowship' and activities such as singing, hiking, cycling and drama. The Clarion Clubs valued the outdoors and nature, and individual development was the aim. As Prynn (1976, 65) writes, 'The intellectual and moral regeneration of the working class was seen as the essential counterpoint to any social and economic reorganisation'. Similarly, Kibbo Kift Kindred and the Woodcraft Folk were set up with pacifist and socialist values, sharing the environmental values and many of the methods of Scouting but opposing its imperialist origins (Davis, 2000). The Socialist Party, Communist Party and Co-operative Union also set up youth sections. Radical youth work may also have been influenced by early alternative approaches to schooling such as Homer Lane's Little Commonwealth and A.S. Neill's Summerhill (Bazeley, 1969; Neill, 1971).

There has not always been a consensus on the left that youth work is inherently 'a good thing'. Working class organisations did not necessarily approve of early benevolent or state-sponsored youth work, and neither did many young people (Davies, 1986; Humphries, 1981). There have always been those who do not attend any youth groups. Many of these young people educated themselves through activity and discussion, through playing and talking in public spaces, such as in this description of Edwardian Salford street group,

During each nightly meeting the young worker, once fully integrated, listened, questioned, argued and received unawares an informal education ... From first-hand experience, often bitter, youths compared wages, hours, conditions, considered labour prospects, were advised on whom to ask for when seeking a job and what to say. All this was bread and butter talk vital at times to the listener, talk that had an economic scope and variety to be heard nowhere else.

(Roberts, 1971, 157)

This description is probably near to many radical worker's ideal of a youth group, but with no youth worker in sight!

Mavericks and dissidents (1940–1970)

During the war, conscientious objectors and peace activists became involved in voluntary work of various kinds including youth work. This may have been an attempt to regain a place and sense of value in a society in which their views and actions were controversial. But their main motivation was probably to contribute towards improving life in some small parts of the world. These volunteers tended to be 'articulate, stubbornly principled and prepared to accept the consequences of refusing to obey the directions of the state. Whilst suffering self-imposed social exile, they came to identify with another stigmatised group' (Cohen, 1998, 7). These workers were sometimes seen as mavericks or dissidents, and had the confidence and belief to run experimental projects. The growth of the welfare state following the war enabled the growth of youth work through increased funding and recognition, and this included left-wing and alternative youth projects.

An outstanding example of a somewhat maverick youth worker during this period is Marie Paneth (Paneth, 1944). The Branch Street project started life in a bomb shelter in a 'slum' area of London, later occupying a semi-derelict house due for demolition. Paneth aimed to provide a free space and basic resources for young people's activities with minimal rules or interference from adults. The programme was typical of its time, consisting of arts and crafts, games, informal fighting and intermittent trips and camps, but its anti-authoritarian approach was distinctive and controversial. It was largely staffed by conscientious objectors with occasional input from women from an un-named voluntary organisation. As Paneth herself was an Austrian immigrant, the 'outsider' status of the core workers made them vulnerable to criticism, but they fought to retain their libertarian approach to the young people,

> *we were utterly unconcerned about their behaviour but enormously*
> *concerned with being 'on their side', seeing their side of the question,*
> *bringing them things which they might want or need, so that they might*
> *find out and become convinced that we were really for them.*
>
> (ibid., 47)

This concept of being 'on people's side' is also emphasised in an oral history of Peace Service Unit volunteers (Cohen, 1998) and seems to have been of great importance to radical workers during this period.

The Branch Street workers had to fight off considerable pressure from their voluntary organisation supervisors to make the project more conventional and structured, but Paneth fought for her beliefs, writing, 'I believed my methods to be the right ones and therefore I could not change them, but had to go through with them until I was either dismissed or had proved successful and achieved my aims' (Paneth, 1944, 24–5). While Paneth does not at any time claim to be radical, nor call herself a youth worker, many of the values and methods portrayed in her book could inspire radical youth workers today. However, it is unclear what motivates Paneth, and some of her language suggests the conservative aim of 'civilising' these young people. On the other hand, the involvement of conscientious objectors and pacifists suggests a left-wing bias to the project, and some passages suggest anarchist principles;

> *I had thought it should provide the roof under which this little group of*
> *youngsters could find their own form of community life, by starting from*
> *scratch and developing their own rules, finding their own way of doing*
> *things.*
>
> (ibid., 59)

Paneth's book is full of honesty, self-criticism and genuine affection for the young people she works with; even if she originally aimed for them to take on her values, she appears to learn as much from them as they do from her.

Branch Street concludes with a proposal for an old bomb-site to be used as a play area where children can build huts and make gardens. At the same time, a 'junk playground' was being created along the same lines on a Copenhagen housing estate. The adventure playground movement spread to Britain, based on the principle of giving children a space to use freely during their leisure time. A Danish play leader explained that 'to organise and arrange programmes is to stifle imagination and initiative and preclude children whose lively curiosity and interests constantly demand new outlets' (Lambert and Pearson, 1974, 18). British adventure playground worker Jack Lambert saw his role not as a leader but 'a liberator, to show the children that the playground really is *their* domain' (ibid., 159). Like Paneth, Lambert fought for his unconventional principles while being honestly self-critical. He writes of one London project in which adult planners proposed improvements to the children's playground which 'looked more like a plan to take over their space and occupy it' (ibid., 54). The plans went ahead despite his opposition, and his own actions were affected;

> *I was caught out. I found myself saying, 'Get off the fences. Get off the roof. Stop throwing things at the windows!' I was becoming part of the new order. The children realised that I was no longer an ally.*
>
> (ibid., 55)

With reflection, time and experience, Lambert gained the confidence to use less authority with the children while being more assertive with his supervisors.

This period was no golden era for radicalism, but there were probably many more workers like Marie Paneth and Jack Lambert who never recorded their stories. Both Paneth and Lambert were suspicious of 'theory', ran busy and chaotic projects, and had to spend much of their energy defending their work against sceptics. Both were persuaded by others to write up their experiences, Lambert being assisted by a freelance journalist. It is surely likely that there were workers with similar beliefs and ideas during this period who never found time or confidence to write and be pubished. It is difficult to establish how much influence such workers had beyond their own projects, but mainstream youth work has taken on some aspects of these pioneers' ideas, in particular the principles of being on young people's side and involving them in planning their own activities. On the other hand, continued emphasis on 'youth provision' betrays the general assumption that youth work should be organised for young people rather than by them.

Activists and troublemakers (1970–1990)

By the beginning of the 1970s the state's role in youth work was firmly entrenched, although the heavy investment of the 1960s had tailed off. The youth service was well established and most voluntary-managed organisations were funded, at least in part, by local or national government. Radical forms of youth work took place either with the tacit support of local government or away from its gaze, and in either case were particularly vulnerable during the Thatcherite attacks on the welfare state in the 1980s. At the same time, wider social struggles had significant impact on youth policy and youth work, in particular feminism, anti-racism and gay rights activism.

Radical youth projects hardly flourished during the 1970s and 1980s, but the majority of overtly political youth work literature comes from this period. Welfare state workers discussed and wrote about the contradictions of working *In and Against the State* (LEWRG, 1980). Books were published discussing approaches to radical education, social work and community work. Although there is less literature directly relating to radical youth work, overtly political issues played an increasing role in discussions and publications during this time. As one reader commented in a letter to the main youth work magazine *Youth in Society*, 'Youth Service spokesmen certainly have been moving to the left!' (Marsland, 1980). Some youth work publications of the time came from an explicitly radical perspective, including Butters and Newell's (1978) investigation of part-time youth worker training. Butters and Newell argued that youth workers should make a 'critical break' with the dominant social education model of youth work, and instead support young people's emancipation so they can overthrow the institutions and ideologies of the powerful classes. It does not appear that this recommendation was widely taken up! However, the review was influential in dispelling the myth of political consensus amongst youth workers, and was followed by a series of local training courses in which youth workers were actively encouraged to identify their political and ideological motivations (Leigh and Smart, 1985).

Many youth workers of this period took part in wider struggles, whether supporting striking miners or being involved in anti-racist, feminist and gay rights activism. The political potential of youth work was sometimes viewed optimistically at an organisational level, and some socialist local education authorities such as Inner London and Sheffield saw youth work as a part of their progressive policies. Political education became recognised as a valid aspect of youth work, and projects were formed to support and empower marginalised groups of young people. Some local authorities made efforts to take young people's views seriously even where this brought youth workers into conflict with authority, such as a Manchester Youth Service policy which banned the police from youth clubs.

Youth workers became involved in libertarian alternatives to formal education such as the Sutton Centre and Free Schools (Shotton, 1992; Wright, 1989). The Paint House was run on similar principles but situated itself in young people's leisure time, and was documented by its workers and members (Daniel and McGuire, 1972). Two youth workers somehow acquired a building in Stepney and encouraged local young people to use it freely, hoping they would take responsibility for it. To give an idea of the workers' hands-off approach, it seems to have been trashed by young people even more frequently and thoroughly than the Branch Street project! One member explained,

> We 'ad nowhere else to go. Fix the place up, wreck it and then build it up again, that was the Paint House. We was curious about the place, it was funny. It was nothing like any place I'd been in before. No one to tell you what to do.

(ibid., 54)

The youth workers interpreted the destruction as the gang's way of dealing with a level of freedom they were unaccustomed to. The young people later repaired and decorated the building, using it as a social space and even an occasional place to sleep, and organised all the activities themselves for eighteen months. As one member commented,

> When we first come 'ere you told us that this was our place, to do what we liked but we didn't believe you. We tried to force you to tell us what to do . . . we didn't realise that this was the type of place we were looking for.

(ibid., 55)

The workers used the anti-authoritarian values they shared with the young people as a focus for informal education, gradually attempting to influence them on issues such as racism where their views differed.

However, the Paint House was not typical of its time, and as Taylor (1987, 133–4) argues, the character-building model 'the indoctrination of obedience to the capitalist imperative' continued to dominate the average youth club. Other radical critiques accused youth work of being inherently and institutionally sexist (Nava, 1984; NOW, 1983) and racist (John, 1981; Williams, 1988). John (1981) argued that young people were more politically aware and active than the youth workers who were supposed to be educating them, and that youth workers,

> function to coerce young blacks back into passive acceptance of class domination and racist oppression, to acquiesce in the perpetuation of their underclass status, to condemn them to powerlessness, and to deny them the space they have won for themselves.

(ibid., 205)

John's study found that black young people took active steps to avoid youth work interference in their lives, many preferring to pay for commercial provision, and most avoiding writing their names as they entered the youth club. Individualised resistance to youth work was not confined to black young people. Ball and Ball (1973) cite the example of Glasgow young people burning down a youth club, arguing this was because young people felt no ownership of the club. The young people from the Paint House are also cynical about mainstream youth clubs, admitting to breaking windows and causing other damage. Although one Paint House member argues in favour of a local youth club where some members pass rules through committee, his friends disagree, 'They pass what? Like you can smoke, silly things like that . . . you could always get into the Paint House, you were never turned away from the door' (Daniel and McGuire, 1972, 58).

Much of the room for politicised work with young people was closed off during the Thatcher years. Youth work faced financial cuts, socialist LEAs were abolished and controversial projects disbanded (Davies, 1999). The Woodcraft Folk, for example, were vilified by the Conservative Party and right-wing press because of links to the Co-operative movement, and became increasingly apolitical as a result (Davis, 2000). Thatcher's government required the youth service to meet state objectives, particularly through job skills and crime prevention schemes for young people on the margins. As Davies (1986, 110) put it, 'The Youth Service was being set a test, in these hard times, contribute effectively to the socialisation and containment of the young or forfeit state endorsement and material sponsorship'. Even relatively uncontroversial political comment had dire consequences, one youth group published a report saying that unemployment was a problem and lost its funding five days later (Ingram, 1987). On the other hand, many politically motivated voluntary sector projects were set up during the 1970s and 1980s, and other new grassroots groups were less politicised but challenged the benevolent models of the past, primarily by being set up by local working-class communities themselves rather than by middle-class professionals or philanthropists. Many of these organisations still exist today, continuing to bring rich variety to the youth work voluntary sector. The residual strength of local authorities combined with new grassroots initiatives has allowed a certain amount of space for radical approaches to youth work; space which has continued to shrink ever since.

A radical legacy?

The context in which youth workers operate is increasingly regulated, and any radical pockets of practice have survived in a very different environment to the relative freedom of the 1950s or the politically charged 1970s. The neo-liberal ideologies of new managerialism and marketisation have affected youth work more gradually than other sectors such as schooling, but both youth workers and young people are increasingly monitored and controlled. In particular, computerised systems such as Contact Point and their local equivalents record unprecedented levels of information on young people and the projects they attend. Quantitative evidence of youth work's effectiveness is the order of the day, with youth services required to achieve accredited qualifications for five percent of the local youth population (Flint , 2005). At the same time, left-wing political movements have diminished in influence during eighteen years of Conservative rule followed by neo-liberal New Labour. Direct action environmental and anti-capitalist movements are an exception, but it remains to be seen how far these will influence youth work.

Radical and alternative youth work practice has survived in places, particularly where young people have genuine opportunities to influence projects. Detached youth work, for example, while by no means always radical, enables a freedom of practice that is difficult to achieve in more regulated settings. This form of youth work is based on youth workers meeting young people on the streets in their local area, and originated in an experimental project in the 1960s in which young adults attempted to befriend young people who were disengaged from society (Morse, 1965). From marginal beginnings, detached work has grown in popularity with youth work managers because it is seen as cheap and able to reach individuals who are excluded from society (and those who have the greatest potential to cause trouble through civil unrest or low level crime). From one perspective, the growing acceptance of detached youth work is the recuperation of radical practice, in which even young people's own spaces are monitored by friendly agents of the state. Alternatively it could be viewed as a rarely surviving opportunity to work with young people in a relatively unstructured and autonomous manner. As Tiffany (2007, 48) argues, there is,

> a historical tendency for detached youth workers to 'bend' (or subvert) social policy parameters in order to secure the greatest benefit for young people. This 'space for subversion' has shrunk to such an extent that detached youth workers' 'room for manoeuvre' is increasingly restricted. Ironically, this deprives them of the very flexibility that has, until now, been the hallmark of effective practice.

In detached youth work then, 'success' is conditional on a high level of autonomy for workers and participants.

It could be expected that environmental youth work might experience a resurgence given that it is a growing arena of both radical activism and government policy, but it has tended to be overwhelmingly liberal with a rather 'goody-two-shoes' image. It continues to have middle-class connotations, despite the greater impact of environmental problems on the least privileged in society. A recent National Youth Agency report on youth work and climate change betrays a distinctly reformist perspective, arguing, 'What is required is merely a shift in approach rather than a major reorientation' (Francique, 2007, 15). Dearling and Armstrong (1997, 3) attempt a more critical approach, asking 'Should youth work stick to the 'safe' areas such as recycling and tree planting, or can empowerment embrace the Do it Yourself culture of the road and tree protesters?' However, groups which approach environmental youth work from a social equality perspective tend to be marginalised from mainstream youth work and the growth in environmental activism of the 1990s has not yet had a significant influence.

This contrast between liberal and radical approaches is also apparent in the field of youth participation. Magnuson (2005) argues that political education in youth work is more often reformist than radical;

> *Instead of politics, we have created niches where we allow youth to participate, and we have created new languages, for example, civic engagement, character education, and public work. These niches and languages distract us – and youth – from participation in decisions about substantive political issues, and they allow us to avoid the real conflicts and divides that are part of politics.*

(ibid., 164)

Youth forums and youth councils are inherently neither liberal nor radical in nature. Their effectiveness depends on how much real influence young people are given, in terms of organising the project itself as well as how much power they have in wider decision making. If these structures ape adult institutions they risk being training grounds for future politicians, suitably trained in fudged answers and spin, or democracies of pretence where decisions are of no consequence.

Conclusion

It would be simplistic to argue that radical youth work is disappearing, but the spaces for experimentation are diminishing. Managerialism, surveillance and marketisation have affected all welfare and educational endeavours over the last thirty years, and youth work is not exempt. In addition, the right-wing attacks on socialism and trade unions during the Thatcher era have left a legacy of silence and suspicion, where it is controversial even to discuss politics. No clear picture emerges; no tidy rise and fall of radical youth work, few battles heroically lost or won. If youth work is 'an incorrigibly heterogeneous and contradictory field of activities' (Butters and Newell, 1978, 17), then its radical elements are also laced with these contradictions. But despite the messy picture, some themes emerge, of politically marginalised workers working with socially marginalised young people; of honest self-criticism and learning from mistakes; of adults who situate themselves firmly on the side of the young people they work with; of workers who are prepared to fight for strong beliefs over their values and methods; of young people seen as 'creators not consumers' (Smith, 1982).

In many accounts of radical youth work there is a sense of marginalisation, of perceiving oneself as a maverick or a troublemaker; I have found that learning from and being inspired by the past can help address this feeling of isolation. It will surely benefit radical youth workers in the future if those of us who see ourselves as radical attempt to record our own recent youth work histories, either individually or with colleagues and young people. The dearth of radical perspectives in youth work literature will continue if controversial projects are never written down except as bland numbers, aims and outcomes. Writing publicly about political beliefs can have consequences, but radical youth workers should develop ways of sharing their experiences. Networks of support and critical discussion have an important role to play here.

Radical youth work 'inside the system' will always be contradictory. As Bailey and Brake put it,

> the development and success of welfare schemes within a capitalist society can only be understood if it is realised that, as long as the unions and others act as pressure groups within the state context, they tend to sustain rather than undermine the established situation.

(1975, 2)

On the other hand, some aspects of youth work are useful to young people and communities, but less useful to capitalism – in particular, informality, voluntary participation, confidentiality, non-intrusive monitoring, valuing the group and the individual, and, crucially, the genuine respect for young people's views. These are inevitably the most frequently threatened and defended, youth work today is the result of struggle, and lack of struggle, by youth workers and young people against its use as overt social control or formal education. For the future and in respect for those who struggled before us, radical youth workers should grasp at opportunities to talk, reflect, write, support each other, take action when needed, and support young people's critical discussions and actions where we can.

Note

1   I developed this definition following a discussion at a workshop entitled 'Is there such a thing as radical youth work?' at the British History of Youth and Community Work Conference 2007 in Durham.

References

Bailey, R. and Brake, M. (1975) *Radical Social Work*, London, Edward Arnold.

Ball, C. and Ball, M. (1973) *Education for a Change, Community Action and the School*. Middlesex, Penguin.

Bazeley, E.T. (1969) *Homer Lane and the Little Commonwealth*, New York, Shocken.

Boehmer, E. (ed.) (2004) Introduction in, R. Baden-Powell, *Scouting for Boys*, Oxford, Oxford University Press.

Brown, G. (2007) *Gordon Brown Speaks to Conference*, accessed 13/12/07 at http,//www.labour.org.uk/conference/brown_speech.

Butters, S. and Newell, S. (1978) *Realities of Training, A Review of the Training of Adults who Volunteer to Work with Young People in the Youth and Community Service*, London, National Youth Bureau.

Cohen, A. (1998) *The Revolution in Post-War Family Casework, The Story of Pacifist Service Units and Family Units 1940–1959*, Lancaster, Centre for North-West Regional Studies.

Curno, P. (ed.) (1978) *Political Issues and Community Work*, London, Routledge and Kegan Paul.

Daniel, S. and McGuire, P. (1972) *The Paint House, Words From an East End Gang*, Harmondsworth, Penguin.

Davies, B. (1986) *Threatening Youth, Towards a National Youth Policy*, Milton Keynes, Open University Press.

Davies, B. (1999) *From Thatcherism to New Labour, A History of the Youth Service in England, volume 2 1979–1999*, Leicester, Youth Work Press.

Davis, M. (2000) *Fashioning a New World, A History of the Woodcraft Folk*, Loughborough, Holyoake Books.

Dearling, A. and Armstrong, H. (1997) *Youth Action and the Environment*, Lyme Regis, Russell House Publishing.

De St Croix, T. (2007) *Taking Sides, Dilemmas and Possibilities for Radical Youth Work*, available at http,//critically-chatting.0catch.com/recentarticles/index.html.

Flint, W. (2005) *Recording Young People's Progress and Accreditation in Youth Work*, Leicester, National Youth Agency.

Francique, M. (2007) *Working With Young People to Create a Climate of Change*, Leicester, National Youth Agency.

Gilchrist, R., Jeffs, T. and Spence, J. (2003) *Architects of Change, Studies in the History of Community and Youth Work*, Leicester, National Youth Agency.

Humphries, S. (1981) *Hooligans or Rebels? An Oral History of Working-Class Youth and Childhood 1889–1939*, Oxford, Basil Blackwell.

Ingram, G. (1987) 'Youth workers as entrepreneurs', in, T. Jeffs and M. Smith (eds.) *Youth Work*, London, MacMillan.

Jeffs, T. (2002) Whatever happened to radical youth work? *Concept* 12 (2), 4–8.

Jeffs, T. and Smith, M. (2006) Where is Youth Matters Taking Us? *Youth and Policy* 91, 23–39.

John, G. (1981) *In the Service of Black Youth*, Leicester, National Association of Youth Clubs.

Lambert, J. and Pearson, J. (1974) *Adventure Playgrounds*, Harmondsworth, Penguin.

Leigh, M. and Smart, A. (1985) *Interpretation and Change, The Emerging Crisis of Purpose in Social Education*, Leicester, National Youth Bureau.

LEWRG (London Edinburgh Weekend Return Group) (1980) *In and Against the State*, London, Pluto Press.

Lovett, T. (1988) *Radical Approaches to Adult Education*, London, Routledge.

Magnuson, D. (2005) Response to, 'captured by capital', *Child and Youth Care Forum* 34 (2), 163–166.

Marsland, D. (1980) Letter in, *Youth in Society* 49, 7.

Morse, M. (1965) *The Unattached*, Harmondsworth, Penguin.

Nava, M. (1984) Youth service provision, social order and the question of girls, in, A. McRobbie and M. Nava (eds.) *Gender and Generation*, Basingstoke, MacMillan.

Neill, A.S. (1971) *Summerhill*, Harmondsworth, Penguin.

NOW (National Organisation for Work with Girls and Young Women) (1983) Reclaiming the past, *Youth in Society*, 79, 18–19.

Paneth, M. (1944) *Branch Street*, London, George Allen and Unwin.

Prynn, D. (1976) The Clarion Clubs, rambling and the holiday associations in Britain since the 1890s, *Journal of Contemporary History* 11, 65–77.

Roberts, R. (1971) *The Classic Slum*, Harmondsworth, Penguin.

Shotton, J. (1992) Libertarian education and state schooling in England 1918–90, *Educational Review* 44(1), 81–91.

Smith, M. (1982) *Creators Not Consumers, Rediscovering Social Education*, available at http,//www.infed.org/archives/creators/default.htm.

Taylor, T. (1987) 'Youth workers as character builders, constructing a socialist alternative', in, T. Jeffs and M. Smith (eds.) *Youth work*, London, MacMillan.

Tiffany, G. (2007) *Reconnecting Detached Youth Work, Guidelines and Standards for Excellence*, Leicester, Federation for Detached Youth Work.

Williams, L. (1988) *Partial Surrender, Race and Resistance in the Youth Service*, Lewes, The Falmer Press.

Wright, N. (1989) *Assessing Radical Education*, Milton Keynes, Open University Press.

CHAPTER 17

Youth Work and Class: The Struggle That Dare Not Speak Its Name

Tony Taylor

This chapter will seek to explore the relationship between youth work and class, albeit with trepidation. Nowadays simply to mouth the phrase 'the class struggle' is to invite derision and disbelief, not least from those within youth work (and I was taken aback by how many there were), who danced in the streets over a decade ago as New Labour came into government. The renovated, former socialist party's message was clear – class struggle politics were redundant, consigned to the dustbin of history. The then revitalised, now sometime reviled leader, Tony Blair declared infamously, 'the class war is over' (Davies, 2008, 108). This evidently persuasive posture continues to be contemporary common-sense. In challenging this fantastic fabrication I shall draw significantly on my own history within Youth work over the last 40 years, drawing inspiration from Lucio Magri's observation that all of us can say, if we wish, 'I am, then, a living private archive in storage' (2008, 62) and from the radical tradition of unearthing and respecting personal accounts as a rich and legitimate historical source (Samuel, 1981; Roberts, 1995). This is not, I hope, egotistical indulgence. Reflections on the relationship between youth work and class are few and far between. Given this absence and allowing for my fading memory, my own history is the history I know best, the history I have lived. As Magri puts it, 'I cannot claim I was not there, I did not know' (2008, 62). Thus I have a record of sometimes subtly, at times stupidly and always stubbornly arguing the class corner, perhaps most pretentiously in a piece, *Youth Workers as Character-Builders, Constructing a Socialist Alternative* (1987), a call to arms which fell on petrified pastures.

Now the reader may be forgiven for wondering whether such an impression-istic approach is a case of clinging on to the past for fear of the present; whether my self-centred stance supports Williamson's depiction of the radicals of yesteryear as 'afflicted by ideological myopia' (2008) or is guilty of being what has been referred to ironically as an unrepresentative 'sample of one' (Stanley and Wise, 1983, 168). For example, was there any relationship in 1984 between my activity as Chair of the Leicester Miners' Support Group, my interventions into the Community and Youth Workers Union (CYWU) and my practices as a Youth Development Officer? Is there any resonance between the rhythm of the struggle of Capital versus Labour and the changing character of youth work? Is it fanciful to wonder whether the defeat of the miners foreshadowed the retreat within youth work from the promise of social education to the predictability of social engineering? These may seem absurd questions, reflecting no more than wistful sentiment, whether for a fighting working class or for youth workers committed to 'voluntary association'. Nowadays it seems that both are deemed to be obsolete.

Nevertheless, despite the odds, my position is fortified by evidence that the New World Order is in disarray, the 2008 'credit crunch' being a crisis of deregulation and so-called financial innovation (Blackburn, 2008), a case of corporate capitalist greed. Therefore I shall argue that the relationship of youth work to class haunts the youth work project, influencing significantly what we think we are up to with young people. Furthermore the failure to take this on board has undermined fatally thus far the possibility of a holistic youth work practice opposed to all oppression and exploitation, which is unequivocally on the side of the struggle for genuine equality and authentic democracy. I am unapologetic that this aspiration runs counter to post-modernism's dismissal of efforts to think about social order and history in their entirety, its rejection of 'universals' and 'speaking for others' and thus its withdrawal from politics (Bauman, 1995).

Reflections on class

The following is a touch crude, but serves its purpose. During the twentieth century class politics has revealed itself primarily in three ways, roughly equivalent to the much-used and abused notions of right, centre and left:

1. On the right, a conservative politics which sees class divisions as inevitable and utterly necessary to the well-being of society. In theory the laws of the market should govern everything, guided by an all-knowing and all-seeing capitalist class.
2. In the centre, a liberal democratic politics which desires to soften class divisions by a judicious mix of the Market and the state's intervention into the economy, hoping to curb capitalism's excesses.

3. On the left, a reformist social democratic or state capitalist perspective which seeks to gradually erode class divisions through the use of the state under the socialist party's control.

Despite appearances there isn't a decisive division between these competing currents, each of which is wedded till death do them part to capitalism. Essentially they differ only about how to manage the system, which is not to deny the significance of past ideological clashes and compromises – witness the rise and demise of the welfare state (Gough, 1979; Fraser, 2008). However the post-war settlement forged under pressure from the working class was welcomed by all parties, whilst the Thatcherite assault upon its collective premises has been pursued most relentlessly by New Labour, the Tory's supposed adversary. It is not just pub talk to suggest it is increasingly difficult to put a cigarette paper between any of them. This is symbolised by Gordon Brown's journey from the reforming socialist of 1989, who complained of an unacceptable 'extraordinary transfer of resources from the poor to the rich' to today's 'champion of privatisation, the market, of the interests of the super-rich, of globalisation, of the whole neo-liberal agenda' (Newsinger, 2007).

Yet, outside of this spectacle, boundaries are also blurred within the marginal milieu of the revolutionary left. The Leninist groups in the main have never freed themselves from their infatuation with Labour as the party of the working class, and thus in practice have often been indistinguishable from the reformist social democratic left. Meanwhile the small forces of libertarian socialism and anarchism are accused of a supposedly naive commitment to an emancipatory politics premised on the inventiveness of the masses, in their insistence that radical change must be the creative endeavour of the people themselves or else they will just be changing their masters.

There is some explanatory merit in this sketch, but constructing political categories can mask as much as it reveals. In particular it fails to capture the ebb and flow of an individual's political loyalty. Take myself: when I entered youth work I was a middle of the road Labour supporter, dabbling with liberalism, only to be converted dramatically to Trotskyism in the mid-70s, a creed of which I was a heretical disciple through to the Miners' Strike. After this traumatic working class defeat I trod a tortuous path away from determinist Marxism to a libertarian viewpoint, informed and inspired by the council communist tradition (Pannekoek, 1936) and by the autonomist project proposed by Cornelius Castoriadis (Taylor, 2008). These shifts were reflected in how I did youth work. My instinct is that any questioning practitioner will endure similar ups and downs in trying to understand the world. And yet, amidst this apparent promiscuity, there is a continuity and fidelity, amongst those I respect and admire, for whom I shall generate yet another label, the 'critical left'! To my mind what binds this eclectic group of activists together is a vision of a future beyond capitalism, an unceasing hostility to functionaries, bureaucrats and party machines, a determination to think radically beyond dogma and a commitment to a democratic political practice beyond elitism and substitutionism. In wondering which class perspectives, right, centre, or left have impinged upon youth work, it is the impression made by this critical left, of which I'd like to be thought a member, that fascinates me the most.

Whatever happened to class?

In hoping to stimulate discussion, our reference point is the sixth chapter of Volume 2 in Bernard Davies' seminal 'History of the Youth Service in England' (1999). Whilst exploring the fate of issue-based youth work in a Thatcherite climate, he asks, 'Whatever Happened to Class?' In the very moment of pondering the question, he recognises its irony, noting that historically youth work 'has been preoccupied with reaching working-class youth and countering their worst excesses' (1999, 94). He provides the answer to his own question here. Traditionally youth work has accepted its part in implementing the class struggle from above, its task being to integrate youth into an acceptance of the capitalist system. Putting this into the context of the post-war situation, Davies reflects on two contrasting periods:

- Through the 50s and 60 the view was cultivated that society was becoming 'classless', symbolised by the slogan, 'we've never had it so good'. As for young people, they ought to have been making the most of the rich opportunities available to them.
- Across the 70s and 80s there followed a significant shift in the economic and social conditions, which underlined once more the enormous disparity between the richest and poorest in society and 'the extended period of relative poverty and dependency' experienced by large numbers of young people (1999, 94–95).

As for the Youth Service's response to this rapidly changing scenario, he marks its failure 'to construct a practice, theory and ideology for responding to the class roots of the disadvantage experienced by young people' (1999, 96). He calls our attention to the pertinent questions, still utterly relevant today, posed by Tony Jeffs and Mark Smith 15 years ago:

Do youth workers . . . seek to encourage working-class young people to reflect critically on their experiences of the labour market? Or do they simply seek to ameliorate the situation?

(1990, 221)

For what it's worth, my own experience, interpreted of course in the light of my own politics – from the early 70s as a part-time worker through being a Training Officer in the early 80s to the absurdity of being a Chief Youth and Community Officer in the 90s, up to and including present-day conversations with workers on the ground – has been overwhelmingly one of arguing within a profession that, rare exceptions aside, has poured oil uncritically on the troubled waters of class exploitation. Certainly Davies is right to stress youth work's failure to construct an ideology, a politics supportive of working-class youth, but he stops short of putting his finger on the reason for this shortcoming. For the creation of an educational practice supportive of working-class young men and women would need to rupture a professional culture, which has seldom questioned its uncritical acceptance of the market, the state and its bureaucracy (Schmidt, 2000). When we talk of the youth service, perhaps we ought to speak of an agency in the service not of young people, but of capital. Not that, obviously, the profession would recognise itself in the picture thus drawn.

However I am in danger of reifying both youth service and youth work. In reality both are composed of people thinking and acting within their differing frames of reference. There are those, who embrace explicitly the capitalist agenda, supported by an overwhelming majority, who accommodate to its authority, professing ignorance, disinterest or despair set against a miniscule minority, who overtly resist. The overarching passivity is all the harder to take when youth workers claim to possess a special insight into the condition of young people, compared, for example, to teachers. In the early 90s youth workers in Wigan refused initially to work from the same base as neighbourhood social workers on the grounds that the latter, unlike themselves, were agents of social control. In practice this posture proved unsustainable. On what basis do youth workers possess a more insightful critique than others of inequality and injustice in the workplace, never mind the insidious way in which capitalism burrows into every nook and cranny of all our lives?

Following Cleaver (2006) it is sobering to recognise that education is structured as an industry and that even youth work is increasingly managed along the lines of a factory, reproducing the social relations of capitalism. This is all the more poignant, given that the post-Albemarle youth service sought to be an island of informal education separate from the needs of the economy. That this was ever so is highly debatable. From school-leavers' courses in the 70s through involvement in Youth Opportunities Programmes in the 80s to incorporation in the Connexions initiative of this decade we can trace an underlying acceptance of the rules of the game. Certainly today youth work is openly instructed to reproduce 'labour power' – the willingness and ability to work – with little in the way of collective protest from within its ranks. Inevitably though there is always some resistance on the factory floor. Thirty years ago some of us talked of 'contradictory spaces', 'prefigurative practices' and of being 'In and Against the State' (London-Edinburgh WRG, 1980), utilising Marxist analyses of the subordination of humanity to the extortion of profit. Such insights have been largely lost, leaving today's alienated workers in something of a theoretical vacuum. Contrary to the hopes expressed by Jeffs and Smith (1990) youth workers are floundering in a sea of capitalism and, not knowing how to swim against the tide, appear to be drowning.

Of course this unfolding argument is heading for trouble. In the year 2008, don't working people (in the widest sense) share the same shrug of their shoulders with youth workers? Many might well agree that things ought to be better, but feel little can be done about it. They are hardly straining at the leash to throw off their chains. In an apparent acceptance of the status quo, many have retreated into a 'privatised' world of individual rather than collective concern. A cloud of cautious conformity seems to hang in the air. It is taken-for-granted that a minute minority rule over the vast majority and that this is called democracy. Readers with long memories might remember the 7:84 Theatre Company formed by John McGrath, who in 1979 performed in a youth centre for which I was responsible. The ratio from which they took their name remains close to the mark, 7 per cent of the world's population possesses 84 per cent of the world's wealth. Yet this obscenity seems to elicit no more than a sigh of helpless resignation from the bulk of the country's citizens. Is it time to admit, despite my emotional attachment to the notion, that the class struggle is lost, and that youth workers can hardly be chastised for reflecting this reality? To recover our bearings we need to pass back the dilemma to a time when nobody could claim the class war was done and dusted.

We must return to Davies's articulation of a post-1974 shift in the social and economic conditions and its consequences for youth work. To be blunt his formulation is a euphemism for a sometimes bloody battle between Capital and Labour, a period of sustained attack upon a working-class too big for its own clogs by a ruling class desperate to regain its own control and profitability. Across this period the ascendant neo-liberal fraction within the ruling class fought to undermine and fracture the institutions and achievements, however partial, of class struggle and solidarity, from the trade unions through to the right to free education for all, including the very character of the post-Albermarle youth service itself. Indeed it was Davies himself who led a critical response to the attack on youth work, posed, in particular, by the emergence of the Manpower Services Commission (MSC), via his prescient pamphlets, *In Whose Interests?* (1979) and *The State We're In* (1981). Writing around the same time, I accused the MSC in suitably melodramatic terms of desiring nothing less than 'the behavioural modification of the young proletariat' (Taylor, 1981). Proletariat indeed – given the post-modernist 'war on totality', there's a word that has gone out of fashion! And, I should add, this is with some justification if it is construed as meaning simply the offspring of the disappearing industrial working class. Whatever, in Davies' greatest achieve-ment, *Threatening Youth* (1986), he was at pains to recognise the class conflict underlying the fluctuations in social policy towards young people, urging trade union resistance to both the undermining of the idea of social education and of workers' pay and conditions. Yet this critical and combative example is exceptional. Across this harrowing period youth work remained a spectator at the theatre of class war unfolding before its eyes. Despite its pretension to being a source of social and even political awareness, as an institution, as a profession, it contributed little to the struggles of those years. Anxious, perchance, about its own survival, given the threat posed by the MSC, it shrugged its shoulders back then. This clavicular compliance was not by chance.

It is necessary to give a semblance of substance to these sweeping assertions. In trying to do so, I need to stress that my primary purpose is to catalyse a debate and to bring out into the open alternative memories and interpreta-tions, especially as my recollections hardly rival for accuracy, those of dedicated diarists such as Tony Benn. When I finished work I relaxed with a few pints and the evening paper rather than a cup of tea and a dictaphone! In essence my argument is that the taken-for-granted class outlook within youth work has been capitalist in its intent and the dilemma is to locate any opposition to this *fait accompli*. Nevertheless this hegemonic grip has been challenged, as we shall see, in training, analysis and practice by a motley collection of critics and practitioners, who, in doing so, identify themselves as the salt of the earth.

Training the cadre?

The liberal democratic inspired training of the initial vanguard of full-time youth workers in the 60s, with its acceptance that class dilemmas were melting away, aimed at supporting young people stripped of their structurally understood class, gender, race, sexuality and disability identities. The emancipatory potential of this training's emphasis on a person-centred process was diminished greatly by its failure to root its subjects (both youth workers and young people) in the relations of class, in relations of power. The only superficial reference to class in the influential BBC pamphlet, *Working with Youth* (1972) comes in Bernard Davies's concluding chapter, where he ponders the impact upon practice of the notion of immediate working class or delayed middle class gratification. My own training as a primary teacher in the same period (1965–1968) mirrored the same illusion that class was on the wane. My sole memory is that of being lectured on Bernstein's (1971) theory of elaborated (read sophisticated middle-class) and restricted (read backward working-class) codes of expression. In retrospect the thrust of my higher education seemed intent on undermining my very sense of being working-class. My respectable journey to becoming a professional ignored working class creativity, and working class struggle.

From the late 70s onwards I came into contact with full-time qualifying courses either as a visiting lecturer, a practice-based supervisor or as an external examiner. Ironically, having discovered Marxism on the picket line rather than in the lecture hall, I found myself arguing for the inclusion of a class analysis in the curriculum. This special pleading in youth work circles contrasted strongly with the influence of Marxism in many Social and Community Work Departments, out of which sprang texts such as *Social Work: Reform or Revolution* (Pritchard and Taylor, 1978). In 1980 I did an MA in Community Work Studies at Bradford, where, for example, I wrote a scathing critique of Ivan Illich and Paulo Freire. The university was rife with a creative energy and tension around 'The Unhappy Marriage of Marxism and Feminism' (Sargent, 1981). But, to my knowledge, this was not the mood in the majority of youth work training agencies. The exceptions that may or may not prove the case were to be found in the North-East of England, where both Newcastle Polytechnic and Durham University were linked directly to the class-conscious Community Development Projects at North Shields and Benwell respectively (1972–1977). Reports emanating from these controversial initiatives included *The Making of the Ruling Class*, *Organising for Change in a Working Class Area* and *Women's Work*, all of which inspired in addition the class orientation of the Sunderland Polytechnic Community and Youth Work course.

Contrary to this 70s working class feminist emphasis, as youth work training was being radicalised in the 80s, class was seen as less significant than gender and race, and later sexuality and disability. If class did appear on the agenda, it was via a functionalist sociological analysis stressing status, occupation and culture rather than by way of a model of political conflict. Indeed, much later, in 1997, whilst lecturing at the Manchester Metropolitan University, I found myself arguing in its significant absence for the inclusion of a session on class in the opening Social Divisions module, seen as an ideological cornerstone of the course. My contention is that the necessary shift in the make-up of the staff in the institutions through the 80s and 90s saw the recruitment of men and women, black and white, gay and straight, whose ideological priorities were gender, race and sexuality. By and large, class was not accorded equal status, dashing hopes of an integrated analysis. Indeed to talk of class, to be a Marxist, never mind an anarchist, became less and less chic, even more so as post-modernism's superficial sophistication gained in prestige and the dis-course of Anti-Oppressive/Anti-Discriminatory Practice became institutionalised (McLaughlin, 2005).

Over in the arena of part-time youth worker training, as a fledgling tutor in the mid-70s, I walked into the same battle about class. In Lancashire the Bessey model of part-time training ruled. It seemed that those organising and delivering the course thought that power had something to do with the Electricity Board. Collision was inevitable. Although accusing the Youth Service staff team of 'class treachery' was not perhaps one of my more astute tactical observations. Later, as a Training Officer, in first a metropolitan then a county council, from around 1978 through to 1985, I was involved in a number of efforts to introduce a class struggle dimension (not forgetting gender, race and sexuality) into the curriculum. The raw material of these courses was supplied by the students' own biographies, out of which flowed the social and political issues. This said, the first sortie into 'the personal is political' had pursued the slogan intrusively. Yet whilst we were to review this process harshly, leading to a less intense, structured approach, its premise that the consciousness of the worker is at the heart of the youth work relationship remains correct. In neither of these cases, within Wigan and Leicester, did anyone contest the content of the courses directly. In retrospect, for a time, those hostile to this attempted politicisation of the work tended to keep quiet in public, intimidated by our apparent theoretical confidence. Such opponents contented themselves with undermining the purpose of the courses on the shop-floor, buttressing the conservatism of the workplace itself. Thus, whilst these training experiences were unpredictable hot-beds of argument, in tune with our views of what youth work ought to be, their impact on evening-to-evening practice was severely constrained. Unsurprisingly these attempts to shift the focus of training were shelved with relief sooner or later, as the principal architects moved on.

On the other side of the coin I must mention being involved as an external with the Sheffield Community Work Apprentice Scheme from 1987–1990, a product of Sheffield Council's flirtation with municipal socialism. To the consternation of senior local government officers the scheme sought to recruit to the course 'activists committed to acting in the interests of the class' – brave and noble sentiments indeed. Under the guidance of Jan Docking, a Marxist-Feminist out of the University of Warwick's Social Work course, where both Peter Leonard (1978) and Bernard Davies were tutors, the scheme grappled seriously with tensions around class, gender and race, particularly as the composition of the students reflected the old Labour movement in the 'steel city', the growing confidence of working-class women and the rise of an increasingly belligerent Black presence in Sheffield. As the mood turned against 'socialism in one council', the 1987–1990 course was the last run of this grounded, class-conscious and innovative undertaking.

My contention is that youth work training since Albemarle, scattered instances aside, has not confronted class from the perspective of the dominated. By default it has sided with the dominant class, failing to recognise 'the class nature of the experiences generated' in the work and the widespread and insidious acceptance of the superiority of bourgeois norms (Jeffs and Smith, 1990, 220–221).

Arguing and thinking

On the wider front than just training, we can mark what used to be a favourite pastime within youth work, 'arguing endlessly about what we were doing, what we would like to do and what others ought not to be doing': the arenas within which purpose, policy and practice were discussed. These arguments were dismissed by their detractors, the 'doers', as indulgent navel-gazing. However, through the late 70s and the 80s this internal deliberation saw a range of attempts to influence practice from a working-class perspective. These efforts comprised articles, pamphlets and books written with class tensions in mind; individuals and groups intervening in staff meetings, in-service training and in the trade unions/professional associations; and even the organisation of independent discussion outside of the system. It was a rich period of argument, bedeviled by the question of how many people, what percentage of the youth service workforce were ever actually involved in this ferment? Crucially this intensity of debate was related intimately to the climate of political tension shaped by the living struggles of working-class women and men and working-class youth across that period – health workers, local government officers, fire-fighters, steelworkers, miners, Asian women at Grunwicks, black and white young people in Brixton and Toxteth. The space to think critically was opened up by working people refusing to lie down in the face of capitalist provocation. Inspired by this resistance, individuals and groups within youth work put in their pennyworth in different ways.

As mentioned earlier, Bernard Davies produced a series of insightful pamphlets beginning with his *Part-time youth work in an industrial town* (1976) through to the book *Threatening Youth* (1986) which sought to stress the significance of class relations for youth work. In particular his writing was catalytic in the Community and Youth Workers' Union (CYWU) resistance to the attempted colonisation of work with young people by the Manpower Service Commission (MSC). Indeed I was Chair of the CYWU's MSC Working Group, which monitored and opposed the Commission's attempts both to undermine wages and conditions and to impose an explicit employer-led agenda on practice with young people.

In 1978 the National Youth Bureau published *Realities of Training*, a skewed, yet searching interrogation of the relationship between youth work training and practice, written by Steve Butters and Sue Newell. Given youth work's suspicion of theory and politics, the impact of this remarkable piece of analysis was initially muted in its impact: not all that astonishing, given that its concluding proposal was for a Radical Paradigm for youth work founded on the vanguard role of a working-class youth contesting its subordinate position in society. Except that extraordinarily, a National Youth Bureau initiative (sponsored by the Brewers' Society), the 'Enfranchisement Project' (1980–82), under the influence of such as Steve Bolger, Alec Oxford and Andy Smart, adopted the 'Five Models of Youth Work' delineated in *Realities of Training* as the basis of a critical dialogue with youth workers across fifty Authorities and Voluntary Organisations in England and the Six Counties of Northern Ireland.

The five models were firstly, Character-Building, then secondly, the three elements of the Social Education Repertoire, namely Cultural Adjustment, Community Development and Institutional Reform, and thirdly the Radical Paradigm. The latter, in seeking to make a qualitative break from the politics of class compromise contained in the other models, identified itself in the following statement:

> *It's no good being naïve about the police, the school system or youth unemployment. Too many campaigns and pressure groups overlook the ways in which these institutions reflect the interlocking systems of capitalism, patriarchy and racism. If we are really going to make a*

difference to young people's lives then we have to work with them to overthrow these systems. For us as youth workers this will involve consciousness raising and political action. For some of us the way forward lies in building alliances with the organised working class in their historic struggle, not for more crumbs, but for the whole bloody bakery.

Others of us see the labour and trade union movement as so deeply sexist and racist that our commitment is to a programme of radical self-emancipation, breaking down conditioning and de-legitimising authority.

For us the usual channels are a con, which we may choose to exploit but we reject the cosiness of reform. Real change means struggle and conflict.

(Leigh and Smart, 1985, 168)

Heady stuff methinks! Anyone involved in this Enfranchisement experience could not fail to be moved by the stark and complex differences it illustrated between youth workers. Initially I was part of the Wigan working group, but my most emotional experience came on a Leicestershire Community Education staff training weekend, where staff were asked to situate themselves in different rooms according to their political/professional allegiance to one of the five approaches to working with young people. The exercise pressured workers to identify their ideological commitment. It was painful and tears flowed. Whatever its faults, it remains one of the few courageous efforts in youth work to cut through a self-congratulatory 'do-goodery', the illusion that we're all on the same side. It confronted people hiding their politics under a tarpaulin. It posed the right question from a class-conscious outlook: 'In whose interests are you doing this work?' When the money ran out, the initiative contrived to die what seemed a natural death. Nevertheless, on the ground, some workers strove to maintain the momentum.

As perhaps an eccentric example it led in Leicestershire to the creation of a workers' group, SYRUP (embarrassingly, the Socialist Youth Workers Revolutionary United Party!), made up of socialists, anarchists and feminists. The group met regularly in people's homes, in people's own time, to discuss policy and practice, the strategy and tactics for change. It was instrumental in winning support for one of the part-time workers' courses mentioned earlier, which asserted that helping young people makes sense only if we have a firm grasp of how a young person's class, her gender and her race influence the choices available to her. In my opinion, at that time and now, such groupings which refuse professional boundaries, bringing together part-time and full-time youth workers, community tutors, officers, the Youth Training Scheme instructors of the past, the Connexions advisers and Advanced Practitioners or whomever of today, and, if possible, administrative staff are essential to developing collective, oppositional practice. This particular East Midlands group drew much energy from its involvement in supporting the Leicestershire striking miners, the 'Dirty Thirty'. In significant contrast I remember arguing in 1984 with leading feminists within youth work who refused to be involved in the dispute, citing the unacceptable sexism of the miners – thus tragically cutting themselves off from all the possibilities of working with the women, the young and not so young women of the Great Strike.

The Leicestershire grouping and others with which I've been involved, particularly in Wigan in the late 70s, desired and invited support from fellow travellers. Indeed the Wigan Community and Youth Service Association (CYSA) in 1981 organised independently a conference, *Youth Work and the Crisis*, in Manchester, which impacted upon the unionisation of youth workers and perhaps even contributed to the birth of *Youth and Policy* as an independent critical journal. After all, it was Frank Booton, a founder member of *Y and P*, who described the gathering of 40 or so people as 'an historic event'! This acknowledged that the overtures of these small, but lively groupings were not widely applauded. A broader network of youth workers dedicated to organising a collective Critical Left practice never materialised.

The reality of practice

This reality has proved perturbing. Initially I felt fragile about the seemingly incestuous nature of the smattering of initiatives I identified as anti-capitalist. Whilst I know there were and are other workers ploughing a similar furrow, there is little in the way of documented evidence to support such an assertion. So I returned to our starting point, the question 'Whatever Happened to Class?' which might well be reinterpreted as meaning, 'Why has there been no visible working class-conscious youth work?' Given the thrust of my argument thus far, the answer is plain. Such an oppositional practice, even at the height of 1980s municipal socialism, was and is institutionally unacceptable. The consequence is that this minority practice, largely unrecorded, is hidden from history. In this context it is clear that painstaking research, particularly via tracing and interviewing those involved, is required to bring some of this practice back to life and up for scrutiny. I shall return to this necessity in my conclusion.

For the moment, therefore, I wish to do no more than pose some questions with regard to Critical Left youth work, supported by reference to examples from my own history. It will become obvious that my illustrations are almost all drawn from the 1980s when our efforts were connected umbilically to the wider working class struggle itself.

- How many initiatives of an unambiguous Critical Left disposition have won funding and mainstream support? In Wigan, inspired by the pioneering efforts of Roy Ratcliffe, the Twist Lane Youth Co-operative was set up in the early 80s as part of the Council's educational provision. Run by young people themselves, it provided material support, e.g. free driving lessons and starter grants, to young men and women wanting to set up collective ventures. Inevitably the course of its existence was turbulent and in its later days it lost its political momentum, having failed to reach out to similar projects elsewhere.
- On more traditional terrain, what youth centres or detached projects can be said to have pursued a Critical Left direction? On a Wigan council estate, where I lived for a time, over a decade of intervention from socialists and feminists such as Tim Warren and Julie Hart, which privileged both the views and direct action from the local working-class community, witnessed a roller-coaster ride from detached youth work project to the euphoric opening and tragic closure of a purpose-built youth club. In Derbyshire a mining village youth centre, supported by Cliff Williams, a former rebel Clay Cross councillor, was a rallying point of dissent and a constant irritation to the ruling Labour Group in the County Council. In Lewisham the positive and trusting relationship with black working class youth built over years by white workers born and bred on the same estates poses a classic, yet insufficiently discussed question: what is the significance for a Critical Left practice of workers continuing to live in their own communities rather than moving on to professional pastures new?
- To what extent have youth workers and young people together identified with and supported working class protest on demonstrations and even picket lines? I drove the classic mini-bus of young people to 'Right to Work' and 'A Woman's Right to Choose' demonstrations, to Anti-Nazi League rallies, meeting up with other workers and their 'kids'. So too back 30 years, the rise of punk and reggae allowed me to accompany young folk to see and argue about the politics of the Clash, Stiff Little Fingers and Linton Kwesi Johnson . . . and have some fun! What we told our managers and employers varied, and again is unrecorded. Is such explicit activity seen as breaking some professional code of political neutrality, to which the majority of workers adhere, even as they flout it themselves in the name of God, the Duke of Edinburgh's Award and Britishness?

- What was the significance of the agit-prop theatre groups, exemplified by the Red Ladder Company, all of whom toured youth and community centres, performing plays with a clear political commitment to the working class? In the aftermath of those vibrant evenings, where the actors and young people mingled in animated conversation, what was the bearing upon youth work practice?
- Is a class struggle practice at its sharpest when control over policy and resources is contested full on by youth on behalf of all young people, whatever their gender, race, sexuality or disability? It is an expression of my compromised past that I've only been involved in a couple of pieces of practice where young people took on both the profession itself, the Council bureaucracy and the ruling politicians? The first was a fight over their control of a youth centre, their right to decide how it was run. The second surrounded their effort to set up a Youth Council with genuine autonomy, able to criticise both the youth service itself and the local state. After a tense tussle these initiatives were closed down and the workers disciplined, although unusually an effort to analyse and learn from our errors was written up in the pages of the short-lived, progressive journal, 'Schooling and Culture' (Ratcliffe and Taylor, 1981). Mention of this Inner London Education publication touches on another historical silence relating to the character and impact of youth projects initiated under the banner of municipal socialism and the rhetoric of equal opportunities across the 80s. What is their balance of achievement?
- Given its battering at different times over the last 50 years, the recurring cycle of cuts and the repetitious restructurings, how often have youth workers and young people organised together militant resistance to the attack on youth work provision as a whole? In 1994 the onslaught on the youth service in Wigan precipitated the biggest demonstration in the town for nigh on 20 years. Yet this energy and anger did not spill over into direct action, into occupations of the threatened premises and increased pressure on the local authority. In hindsight it seems likely that as workers we were fearful of being accused of manipulating young people and scared that rebellious activity outside of the norm would worsen the situation. Such a politics of appeasement rather than struggle permeates youth work. It is why our history lacks its class heroes and heroines – sacked workers and proscribed groups of young people.
- The above example takes us inexorably to the relationship of youth work to trade unionism. Certainly I believe the diverse voices of a Critical Left impacted decisively on the transition from Community and Youth Service

Association (CYSA) to Community and Youth Workers Union (CYWU). It is sobering to reflect that the newly born union adopted a radical, democratic constitution, which I played a part in writing. Within its pages you will find that the newly named National Organiser was to be an elected three year post paid on JNC 4, the pay scale of the membership: you will discover that the right to caucus 'for any group of like-minded individuals within the union' was seen as a key to openness and transparency, closing the door on backroom intrigue. A quarter of a century later the appointed National Secretary has been in charge of the CYWU for over 20 years and the right to caucus has been replaced by orthodox structures such as an Equal Rights Committee. Yet the period from the late 70s in the association/ union was one of turmoil. It provides a fascinating case study, which ought to shed light on the politics of youth work and its relationship to the broader social and political movements, which were yet to be exhausted. In this respect I am committed to writing a piece exploring in depth the metamorphosis of the CYSA into the CYWU, hopefully to be presented to a future history conference.

Anti-classist youth work?

In the discourse of youth work, since the 70s, sexism and racism have been central, but no mention of classism is to be found. As for sexism there is little doubt that youth work has rightly recognised its responsibility to be anti-sexist. Whilst 40 years ago you would have found youth workers openly saying 'a woman's place is in the home', this would be deeply frowned upon today. Similarly, you would have come across mainstream youth organisations that communicated the idea of the superiority of 'Anglo-Saxon' culture. From an anti-racist perspective this is rightly inadmissible and would be off limits today. None of which is to say that sexism and racism are now sorted within youth work's agenda, far from it. In this context, though, if the word classism was allowed, what might being anti-classist mean?

It is necessary to return to the notions of anti-sexist and anti-racist practice in search of an answer. An anti-sexist practice seeks to contest and indeed end the domination of women by men. It aspires to challenge this abuse of power on a personal level (eg. prejudiced language, attitudes) and on an institutional level. An anti-racist practice seeks to confront and indeed undermine utterly white power over black people. Again it strives to do so at a personal and institutional level. So, what about an anti-classist practice? It seems logical that such a practice seeks to oppose and indeed overthrow the domination of the working-class (widely defined) by the ruling capitalist class. It would attempt to do so on a personal and an institutional level.

It is important to recognise that anti-classist practice directed at the individual would differ somewhat from anti-racist/anti-sexist practice at the personal level. In the case of the latter, oppressor and oppressed, male/female, white/black, so to speak, rub shoulders together in the youth project, in the training group and in the staff meeting. Neither can escape the task of dealing with one another. Unfortunately, perhaps, because it would be therapeutic to give them some grief, members of the ruling class don't attend in person the youth project or, as a rule, even become youth workers. Thus what an anti-classist practice proposes is that the attitudes and prejudices challenged are those that are *within and against* the class, those that undermine class solidarity and resistance. For certain, questioning sexist, racist and homophobic attitudes would be integral to an anti-classist practice, but in addition all manner of stereotyping other young people, for example, according to which estate, neighbourhood, village or town they come from, would be confronted.

Perhaps it is obvious why anti-classism isn't a feature of youth work practice. Whilst introducing an anti-classist perspective would enrich anti-racism and anti-sexism, it would create a chaos of contradiction. If youth workers are opposed to classism and the ruling class imperative, how do we rationalise youth work's increasing involvement in preparing young people to be exploited on training schemes or in the workplace? How can this be consistent with an anti-classist practice?

The struggle continues

In focusing on a notion of the class struggle and youth work's willful dismissal of its relevance, I risk being seen as an historical leftover, trying obstinately to resurrect the discredited idea that class is primary, relegating the significance of other social relations. This is not at all my desire. My point is no more and no less than that the political struggle for equality, freedom and justice must have a rounded and interrelated sense of the relations of class, gender, race, sexuality and disability. None of them make proper sense without reference to each other. If this inextricable knot is recognised, the silence about class within most youth work is deeply disturbing.

In one way, it would be refreshing never to mention the class struggle in a separate sense ever again. For the title of this chapter could have been *Youth Work and Politics: The Relationship That Dare Not Speak Its Name*. By politics is not meant tiresome gossip about the personality clashes inside New Labour's

Central Committee, the contemporary version of the wrangles of the Elizabethan court. Rather we mean the crucial questions of who has power, in whose interests do they use that power, what power do we have to change the situation if we disagree? At this historical moment, we are led to ask, specifically in terms of youth work and the youth service

- What power do youth workers have in terms of the purpose and content of the work?
- What power do young people have in terms of arguing the case for what they see as their needs in a critical dialogue with youth workers and the state?

Despite the recurring rhetoric about participation it would seem very little. Leave aside the situation facing young women and men, the profession itself seems reluctant to oppose this state of affairs. By and large youth workers are perceived to be doing as they are told. Yet history illustrates that obeying orders is a class and political question. There is the world of difference between a capitalist system in which the greed of capital is contested at every turn by Labour; in which the right of management to manage is questioned and resisted; in which a male hierarchy is challenged in the name of girls' work (back 30 years!) *and* a capitalist system within which there is severely diminished working class opposition; in which management does as it wishes; in which the gains of the past, such as girls' work and black youth work, are divested of their radical edge, recuperated and rendered safe. In this latter scenario, which corresponds to the situation today, the powerful, their self-serving political and bureaucratic sycophants, and even layers of youth work management itself, increase the ideological pressure, insisting that youth workers, forgetting their class, should transform themselves into social entrepreneurs, all the more so to influence young people in the same direction. Whatever happened to class? Youth work's amnesia aside, it never went away.

It is acknowledged that this account is subjective, fragmented and incomplete. However, it is hoped despite its ignorance and its shortcomings that it will encourage others to interrogate the past with class in mind. This is vital in the sense that my memory needs to be mediated by the memory of others, aided by the further unearthing of documentary evidence. In this way our collective memory gives us the best chance of treating 'our own experience as if one were dealing with someone else's life' (Magri 2008, 60), enabling us to move nearer to our best plausible explanation for what did and didn't happen. Reflecting on youth work and class underlines the urgency of (re)creating networks and collectives committed to bloody-minded argument and resistance in the face of the 'Enemy Within' – capitalist values, ideas and practices. Forgive the invocation of an old class struggle slogan, but yet again it's time to 'Educate, Agitate and Organise'.

References

Baumann, Z. (1995) *Life in Fragments: Essays in Post-Modern Morality*, London, Blackwell.

Bernstein, B. (1971*) Class, Codes and Control*, London, RKP.

Blackburn, R. (2008) 'The Subprime Crisis', *New Left Review*, (50) March/April.

Butters, S. with Newell, S. (1978) *Realities of Training*, Leicester, NYB.

Castoriadis, C. (1997) *World in Fragments* ed. David Ames Curtis, Stanford, Stanford University Press

Cleaver, H. (2006) *On Schoolwork and the Struggle against It*, at http://www.eco.utexas.edu/facstaff/Cleaver/hmchtmlpapers.html

Corrigan, P. and Leonard, P. (1978) *Social Work Practice under Capitalism: A Marxist Approach*, London, Macmillan.

Davies, B. and Rogers, J. (1972) *Working with Youth*, London, BBC.

Davies, B. (1976) *Part-Time youth work in an industrial town*, Leicester, NYB.

Davies, B. (1979 *In Whose Interests? From Social Education to Social and Life Skills Training*, Leicester, NYB.

Davies, B. (1981) *The State We're In*, Leicester, NYB.

Davies, B. (1986) *Threatening Youth*, Buckingham, OUP.

Davies, B. (1999) *From Thatcherism to New Labour: A History of the Youth Service in England*, Volume 2, 1979–1999, Leicester, NYA.

Davies, B. (2008) *The New Labour Years: A History of Youth Service in England*, Volume 3, 1997–2007, Leicester, NYA.

Fraser, G. (2008) 'Neo-liberal welfare: the politics of the voluntary sector', *Concept*, Volume 18, 2.

Gough, I. (1979) *The Political Economy of the Welfare State*, London: Macmillan.

Jeffs, T. and Smith, M. (1990) 'Young People, Class Inequality and Youth Work' in T. Jeffs and M. Smith (eds.) *Young People, Inequality and Youth Work*, London, Macmillan.

London-Edinburgh Weekend Return Group (1980) *In and Against the State*, London, Pluto.

Leigh, M. and Smart, A. (1985) *Interpretation and Change*, Leicester, NYB.

Magri, L. (2008) 'The Tailor of Ulm', *New Left Review*, 51.

McLaughlin, K. (2005) 'From ridicule to institutionalization: anti-oppression, the state and social work' *Critical Social Policy*, 25.

Newsinger, J. (2007) 'Gordon Brown: From Reformism to Neo-Liberalism', *International Socialism*, Summer, 115.

Pannekoek, A. (1936) *Party and the Working Class* at http://www.libcom.org/library-party-and-working-class-pannekoek

Pritchard, C. and Taylor, R. (1978) *Social Work: Reform or Revolution?* London, RKP.

Ratcliffe, R. and Taylor, T. (1981) 'Stuttering Steps in Political Education', *Schooling and Culture*, Issue 9.

Roberts, E. (1995) *A Woman's Place: An Oral History of Working Class Women 1890–1940*, London: Blackwell.

Samuel, R. (1981) *People's History and Socialist Theory*, London, RKP.

Sargent, L. (ed.) (1981) *Women and Revolution: The Unhappy Marriage of Marxism and Feminism*, London, Pluto Press.

Schmidt, J. (2000) *Disciplined Minds*, Oxford, Rowman and Littlefield.

Stanley, L. and Wise S. (1983) *Breaking Out: Feminist Consciousness and Feminist Research*, London, RKP.

Taylor, T. (1981) 'Youth Opportunities, The Argument for Resistance', *The Bulletin of Social Policy*, 8.

Taylor, T. (1987) 'Youth Workers as Character Builders: Constructing a Socialist Alternative' in T. Jeffs and M. Smith (eds.) *Youth Work*, London, Macmillan.

Taylor, T. (2009) 'What Has Cornelius Castoriadis Got to Say About Youth Work?' *Youth and Policy*, (101).

Williamson H. (2008) *Let's protect Youth Work's distinctiveness* at http://www.cypnow.co.uk/Archive/786404/Lets-protect-youth-works-distinctiveness

Web site

Critically Chatting Collective: http://www.critically-chatting.0catch.com, co-ordinated by Tony Taylor.

CHAPTER 18

The Origins and Development of the National Youth Agency

Tom Wylie

Origins

As with several other aspects of contemporary youth work, the origins of The National Youth Agency lie in the Albemarle Report (1960). Albemarle envisaged that the new Youth Service Development Council would require an 'intelligence unit' to serve both it, and the growing youth service field, by judging how far policy was being implemented and by encouraging research and experiment to meet the needs of young people. These proposed functions were reinforced and extended by the Bessey Report (1962) which suggested that the proposed intelligence unit should also gather information and ideas about how to run training courses, principally those for part-timers, and collate for training purposes some of the basic research in the fields of psychology, social group work and other relevant areas. In 1963 the governors of the National College for the Training of Youth Leaders (NCTYL) based in Leicester responded formally to the request of the (then) Ministry of Education to establish such an intelligence unit at the College. The unit would be called the Youth Service Information Centre (YSIC), would cover both England and Wales, and have several functions:

1. the accumulation of teaching material, especially for use in the training of part-time youth leaders, full-time youth leaders and trainers;
2. the investigation and dissemination of information about experimental work already undertaken in this country, and about experience and practice in other countries;
3. listing and abstracting from useful publications;
4. the identification of suitable projects for research and the submission of these for consideration by the Research and Intelligence Branch of the Ministry of Education;

5. maintaining a close working contact with the Ministry of Education in the publication of the journal 'Youth Service'.

By April 1964 the YSIC was established with Alan Gibson moving from the National College to be its first Head, accountable to the Principal of the NCTYL, Ted Sidebottom. In 1967 Gibson was reporting to the Youth Service Development Council that various activities had been undertaken by the Centre in line with the original remit. These included the production of training materials, information about experimental and other forms of innovative youth work, answering field enquiries (some 450 per annum) from the YSIC's own gathering of documentation, the production of various publications (including annotated book and film lists and written contributions to the Ministry's 'Youth Service' monthly magazine), and the identification of research needs for Ministry action (Gibson, 1967).

In the same report, however, Gibson hinted at a wider role for YSIC. He identified the need for a stronger 'conceptual standpoint' in youth work, 'drawing conclusions in relation to certain concepts of the purposes of Youth Service, interpreting significance . . . giving more weight to this finding and less to that, reconciling conflicting conclusions . . .' An explicit expression of Gibson's approach lies in the seminal work he co-authored with Bernard Davies, *The Social Education of the Adolescent* (Davies and Gibson, 1967). This influential work may be viewed as offering the first major approach to defining the purposes of youth work in secular terms. It began to offer both a set of principles and a methodology to the growing local authority youth sector which had not yet assembled the theoretical or ideological underpinning, often faith-based, which underlay existing programmes in much of the voluntary youth sector, still less those of formal schooling.

In his major report to the YSDC, Gibson went on to suggest:

> *It may even be appropriate to change the Centre's basic field of reference to include several of those common, informal-education approaches made by workers in a variety of administrative sectors – secondary teachers of 14 and 15 year olds, liberal studies tutors, student welfare officers, recreation leaders, adult education organisers, community workers, some social workers – who draw to a large extent on the same subject-matters, methods and philosophies as the youth worker, and on the same sources of knowledge in the social sciences including education. Such a change of focus may entail a change of title and perhaps of governance of the Centre; but it may be especially important now to offer such an agency to this wider field as a vehicle for promoting informed practice, since the*

rapid development which justified an Information Centre for 'Youth Service' is being paralleled in these other areas, and since the interchange of ideas and methods now involves this much wider circle of personnel and services.

(Gibson, 1967)

Gibson's visionary proposals went further than those of purposes, scope and title but encompassed a new governance – cutting loose from the governors of the National college (in any case this college had only been seen as having a limited lifespan as 'emergency training'); new funding arrangements, including from local authorities; more staffing; and a new headquarters location, London. The new body would, in Gibson's specification, have four main functions:

1. an information service on new developments;
2. the promotion of the evaluation of research and experiment;
3. the promotion of higher standards in training, especially of part-timers, and the co-operative development of training aids and advanced courses;
4. liaison with other educational and welfare bodies within and beyond the UK.

From YSIC to NYB

By 1969 when Gibson left to join HM Inspectorate, the YSIC had grown to six full-time staff and his grand design for a reconstructed national institution was in the process of being established as the National Youth Bureau (NYB) with a representative governing structure based in a new location, though still in Leicester.

John Ewen, the incoming Director, was comfortable with the grand design. Indeed, all the subsequent Directors of the NYB/NYA (David Howie 1977–87, Janet Paraskeva 1988–95, and Tom Wylie 1996–2007), sought to be passionate advocates for taking a wide look at young people's lives and for a range of services to be developed to meet their needs including, but not restricted to, traditional youth services. In consequence the NYB, not always comfortably, sought to thread a path between the generality of policies on youth affairs, the distinctive form of social education practice known as 'youth work', and the set of loose institutional arrangements called 'The Youth Service'. It began also to move increasingly from the principles – and – practice orientation which had been the hallmark of YSIC to the arena of policy-making which would become characteristic of NYB and NYA's work. The YSIC began in a time when, thanks to the Albemarle Report, the direction of policy for youth work was clear; its successor bodies would not be so fortunate.

The NYB did not come into being as a constitutional entity until 1973. After four years of struggle to bring it into life, Ewen saw its formation as being against the background of a high degree of suspicion in the youth work field – both voluntary and local authority – of the putative Bureau's empire-building tendencies. As Ewen remarked, the NYB was 'dragged screaming into existence rather than celebrated'. His sense of embattlement was reflected in the first leaflet the new Bureau issued to describe its role. This had a paragraph entitled 'Some Fears' and another entitled 'Firstly, what NYB is NOT'. The first of the 'nots' was, 'a controlling agency . . . to tell people what to do . . . to dictate policy, or to interfere with other organisations about their work'. The second 'not' was, 'a professional institute' and the third 'a youth organisation with field workers or field projects' (NYB, 1974 [a]). Its first Annual Report identified two broad aims:

> to assist the emergence of a forum on a generic and multi-professional basis between all those concerned with the social education of young people . . . and, secondly, to offer relevant services (information, training and research) to those who are assisting that process.
>
> (NYB, 1974b)

Accordingly, in its early years the new Bureau gave much attention to its 'Forum' function – in the shape of its widely drawn Council which included teacher unions, social work and community-based organisations as well as youth service bodies. The 'Forum' role was also expected to be developed via national consultative groups – on Youth Research and on Youth and Community Work Training. The latter was to prove the more enduring. As the 1970s unfolded, the NYB was able to add to its generic services in information, publications and forums by establishing specialist units for Youth Social Work (principally in respect of the then fashionable 'Intermediate Treatment' for young offenders); for Young Volunteering; for Youth Unemployment and, eventually, for Youth Work. Indeed, by 1980, the National Council of Voluntary Youth Services (NCVYS) was co-located in the NYB's premises as was the National Association of Young People's Counselling and Advisory Services (NAYPCAS). The NYB continued to seek to influence policy and was associated with some notable events including the Youth Charter Conference held at Wembley in 1978. The Bureau's Consultative Group on Youth and Community Work Training metamorphosed over several years into a separately governed but related and co-located Council for Education and Training in Youth and

Community Work (CETYCW) with extensive responsibilities for the professional endorsement of initial, in-service and part-timer training. This gradual accretion of the validation functions for training youth workers represented a major achievement for NYB and was due in no small measure to the support of allies in HM Inspectorate, notably Edwin Sims, in convincing DES officials that the NYB could be trusted to develop this role as competently as any academically-based validating body – as indeed it proved. Alan Gibson's original 'grand design' had taken two decades to negotiate and construct but, by the early 1980s, was now nearly in place, with a total staffing exceeding 70.

Financing was never easy. The original plan had been for shared central and local government funding but the principle, established in 1972, that the Local Authority Associations would also financially support the Bureau's work did not materialise for another 25 years. In consequence, the NYB depended almost entirely on central government finance, principally from the then Department for Education and Science though it also had time-limited support for particular projects or specialist units from other government departments. Both the 'forum' function and the reliance on national government funding nearly brought the NYB to its knees. Ewen, Howie and Paraskeva, in their different ways, understood the Bureau to have a mandate to address youth questions proactively and to take up committed positions on the youth issues of the day. This stance was maintained into the Thatcher era when quangos had ceased to be in fashion and the expression of a concern for, say, rising levels of youth unemployment or about police harassment of young black people or levels of spending on youth services all risked putting the advocates onto a collision course with government. Following a review of youth service provision (the 'Thompson Report', 1982) which made some critical comments on the NYB's current activities, the NYB faced the first of several reviews, initiated by the DES and undertaken by the scrutineers it selected. The Cockerill Report of September 1983 commended the NYB for its publications; thought that it should collect better data; doubted the wisdom of it having a policy stance – 'it should not be any sort of campaigning body'; and advocated the end of NYB's existing structure of specialist units which risked taking the Bureau towards a more federal structure. Cockerill also sought a greater regional dimension to the NYB's work, though the development of such units as did emerge relied heavily on finance from relevant local authorities rather than national funding. He did, however, note in respect of the NYB's scope that it was 'axiomatic in the 1980s that we are talking about youth affairs rather than the youth service of the traditional kind' (Cockerill, 1983). The NYB adjusted itself to these imperatives – and survived when others, such as the Schools Council, did not.

A bureau becomes the agency

By 1991, following another DES scrutiny, the NYB was re-shaped again – into the National Youth Agency. This time the Department's intention was to merge the national youth bodies it grant-aided (NCVYS, BYC and NAYPCAS) and its most obvious direct clients (NYB and CETYCW) into one body. The vision was flawed, not necessarily in its goals but in its construction. It fell apart on the unwillingness of the voluntary sector bodies to be swept into a quango, especially one which seemed bent on having some form of 'core curriculum' for youth work. They decided to head for the open seas and to survive as best they could until the tide turned and the DES began to value them once more (as indeed it did). By 1992 the outcome of the Department's inadequate diplomacy, therefore, was a national support system for youth policy and youth work which not only had not advanced but, as a result of the departure of NCVYS and NAYPCAS, had even lost the synergy of co-location which had previously been available. (More understandably, however, it had already 'lost' any responsibility for youth work in Wales which had been a remit of the original YSIC and of NYB. Policy responsibility for the youth service in Wales had already been transferred from the DES to the Welsh Office in1978 and Wales eventually established its own Wales Youth Agency, but would close it just over a decade later.)

By 1995 the Department for Education was back for another scrutiny of the Agency it had just created. As Bernard Davies records,

> *Though involving consultations with some 84 interested bodies, the DfE sought to keep maximum control over this new review by carrying it out internally. In ways which did little to displease DfE officials, it nonetheless acted as a release valve for the kinds of, albeit often contradictory, critical comment which a central resourcing body like NYA was always liable to attract. The process thus provided ample 'evidence' for unconvinced central government officials to interpret unfavourably if they so chose. Thus, the Agency's information and library services, its promotion of equal opportunities, its co-ordination of Youth Work Week and its response to individual enquiries were all well regarded. Somewhat contradictorily, however, it was seen as 'remote from the field'. It was also judged to be offering inadequate support to the voluntary-statutory partnership and 'not sufficiently committed to the ethos of the voluntary sector'. As the NYA carried a brief for voluntary sector development (though with limited resources for fulfilling it), it was wide open to such complaints, notably*

from NCVYS which itself had suffered at NYA's expense in the 1990–91 reorganisation.

(Davies, 1999, vol. 2, 126)

Although the field itself had offered some of these hostages to fortune, enough members of it, particularly in the local authority sector, saw the implications of the Department's intended financial re-structuring of the Agency and rallied sufficiently to divert the full thrust of the Department's blade from The Agency's heart. The outcome was that the Department reduced its own funding – essentially back to the old YSIC information functions with which it had always been most comfortable. The Local Authority Associations stepped into the breach and picked up much of the Agency's core costs by accepting a transfer from DES into the national system of local authority finance and then 'top slicing' this Revenue Support to make an annual direct grant to The National Youth Agency for specific purposes, particularly those of a more developmental nature.

A new agency emerges, as New Labour takes power

By 1996 a new NYA had emerged: no longer a quango but a partnership body with its governance and direction shared between local authorities, voluntary sector and young people themselves. A body which sought to build on the work of its predecessors – hence, information for practitioners, and for young people; a commitment to the improvement of practice through publications and short courses for service managers and field workers; forums and networks for specialist groups; developmental activity, for instance in supporting young people's voluntary action and through grants for innovative work of national significance; arrangements to validate initial professional training and staff development. Not least, freed from the constraints of excessive dependence on government income, there was a renewed endeavour to 'speak truth to power' – to communicate to national and local policy-makers the distinctive contribution of youth work within a range of services for young people. It retained its belief that adolescence is a distinctive period in people's lives and that young people have needs and potential as well as deficits, and that those who try to work with them in many different settings, especially in youth work, deserve effective support and advocacy. The Agency in its latest guise thus saw important continuities with YSIC and NYB in its work and in its values as well as making the functional changes needed to respond to new contexts, not least the arrival of a new government.

The year after the NYA had been re-shaped in its funding and governance and had acquired a new Chief Executive (the present author), the policy world was changed by the arrival in May 1997, of a new Labour government with some apparent commitment to the needs of young people, especially the young unemployed. In opposition, the Labour Party had used a task force to study youth issues in preparation for being in government and the Party's spokesman, Peter Kilfoyle, had not only taken a close interest in the youth service but was himself a former youth worker. Surely the sun was about to shine on youth work after long years in the shadows?

Regrettably not. Although the New Deal on employment was launched in 1998 and work was set in hand to reform the youth justice system, Labour never published its internal task force paper on youth issues and Kilfoyle was not given the youth brief in government but was despatched to other ministerial duties. The youth (in Education) post was taken instead by Kim Howells, MP for Pontypridd, and a man with no discernible knowledge of, or concern for, current youth issues.

It was evident that any political impetus to strengthen youth work had leached from New Labour's immediate agenda. Happily, the few civil servants immediately concerned had had some thoughts of their own. One of these was to map current youth service provision in English local authorities. This was undertaken by the NYA and published in September 1998 as 'England's Youth Service: the 1998 Audit' (NYA, 1998). It achieved a 100 per cent return from local authorities and could be described as a 'Doomsday Book' of the scale of provision in this part of the youth sector. Its commentary, written by Mary Marken a former member of NYB staff, underlined the longstanding wide variations regarding provision across the land, reflecting the different funding and other commitments of local authorities. It showed that the very fabric of the youth services was so weak in many areas that it found it hard to sustain either innovation or its continuing work: the Albemarle inheritance had been allowed to erode.

The findings of this first Audit were inherited by a new Minister, George Mudie, a street-savvy Scot with a trade union background representing a disadvantaged constituency in Leeds. Mudie was personally sympathetic to youth work and wanted to improve matters. But he was thwarted by two factors. First, he became pre-occupied by the task of reshaping the Further Education Funding Council (FEFC) and existing Training and Enterprise Councils (TEC). Second, a key DfES policy adviser, Tom Bentley, was interested in reconstructing the support services for young people along the lines he had set out in his book, *Destination Unknown* – with hindsight, an appropriate title for the policies set in train (Bentley and Gurumurthy, 1999).

At this point disjunctures occurred in the policy-making process and several years of turbulence followed as various attempts were made to better align services for young people, initially through the creation of a Connexions Service. In this process little consideration was given to the needs and potential role of youth work. Mudie had despaired of getting a properly focussed paper on the Youth Service from his officials or political advisers and turned to the NYA (and this author) to draft a possible 'green paper'. But Mudie was not able to push this document with its proposals on youth work past the policy guardians in other parts of the DfES and in No 10: it was kicked into the long grass, from where it would eventually be retrieved (see Wylie, 2004 for a fuller assessment of this period).

The National Youth Agency and many in the field accepted that there needed to be a radical re-configuration of local services with and for the young. But they saw limits to the capacity of information and advice to produce changes in individuals, never mind in their peer groups and communities; they argued that it needed the full range of youth work – including detached work and work with small groups – to be deployed by skilled personnel qualified on courses which had robust external validation (NYA, 2001).

The youth work sector declined to roll over, but the arrival of Connexions (and, later, Children's Trusts) presented the field with some difficult choices. It also presented some difficulties for the NYA since Connexions was becoming a flagship of government youth policy. Had the NYA still been a quango with virtually a single stream of government funding via the DfES it probably could not have articulated as sharply and consistently as it sought to do, the flaws as it saw them in the design of Connexions and its operational construction and practice. The NYA asserted that 'The key decisions about the delivery of services to address the complex needs of young people must be made locally'. It also urged that 'whatever decisions are taken on the structural shape of a Connexions Partnership and its local management, questions remain about the delivery of locally accessible youth provision of the type consistently identified as desirable by young people in consultation exercises – ''Somewhere to keep warm and safe'''; 'where we can mix with others and make new friends'; 'our own space' (NYA, 2001).

Youth work re-discovered

In any event, after several years in the doldrums, youth work itself had re-emerged into the policy spotlight. This was partly prompted by the growing recognition that Connexions would need all the friends it could get if it was to deliver. It was greatly helped by the arrival of new DfES officials who were open to the NYA's arguments that an effective Connexions strategy required a wider infrastructure of youth support and development. They now sought help to develop the youth service in its own right and as a partner to Connexions.

Youth work benefited from a suite of governmental interventions designed to build its capacity, reform its organisational arrangements and specify standards for local provision. Government began to advance this 'Transforming Youth Work' agenda as a consultative paper in March 2001 (DfES, 2001) and produced a definitive policy document – 'Resourcing Excellent Youth Services' in December 2002 (DfES, 2002).

To reach this point there was an important confluence between three key elements: the whole-hearted political commitment of the relevant Minister, now Ivan Lewis; the skilled drafting and dedication of DfES officials; and the ready availability of policy and operational material created by the NYA, notably the expression of a proposed Youth Pledge (NYA, 1999) and detailed draft standards which identified what would constitute a sufficient youth service. These latter elements had been set out in 'Quality Develops' published by the NYA in May 2001; by December 2002 they were government policy. This suite of developments provided a clear specification of the range of youth service provision which should be secured by local authorities; a common planning system, targets and performance indicators; a programme of management training; and an ambitious set of proposals for workforce development. Not least, there was additional, ring-fenced funding. All this represented a bold new architecture for youth work with a national framework establishing the basis for local co-ordination and delivery.

The NYA extends its role

As the new century opened, the National Youth Agency stepped up its own support to the field as well as to national policy-making. The DfES was once more in developmental mode and keen to support the Agency's broader activities. The NYA thus reshaped its information services, developed a pattern of management training and of consultancy support, particularly for those local authorities which had been judged poor performers by Ofsted. It also secured new grant management programmes to take youth work skills into areas of disadvantage and to deploy them on the growing agenda of young people's health needs and their entry to employment. This developmental work included a more rigorous attempt to analyse the nature of effective youth work and to embed it through standard-setting, publications, training and on-site visiting. It extended its long-standing work on the validation of initial professional training courses in higher education and for continued professional development, and the accreditation of young people's learning. With the goal of helping the voices of young people to emerge in local and national decision-making, it created a set of standards, 'Hear by Right', and provided direct support to young people's-led organisations, notably YouthBank. It also began to play a larger role in European youth policy work, though it had a limited locus in this arena since the responsibility for running EU programmes in the UK had been given by government to the British Council.

These different interventions were built on the original YSIC platform but had extended the NYA's role beyond information-gathering, analysis and dissemination into an agency which was more overtly developmental in seeking to embed good practice and to use projects to generate systemic change. The Agency developed a partnership with Haymarket Press for the latter to take over NYA's monthly magazine, *Young People Now* and produce it as a weekly journal for the burgeoning youth sector. It had also become more explicit in seeking to influence policy and to promote the role of a particular approach – that of 'youth work' – within the broader landscape of services for and with young people.

As well as distinctive approaches and skills, youth work brings an explicit set of values and, following wide consultation, the Agency codified these with a defined statement of ethical conduct (NYA, 2000). Those who have immense skills in working with the least biddable young are not often the best at form-filling, tracking, or toeing a party line: if they were good at paperwork, they would work in an office or for the civil service. Despite the efforts of the NYA and others down the years, youth work overall had not been good at researching and evaluating its own practice, still less at the hype and persuasive engagement seemingly necessary to win funding battles. The NYA tried to fill this gap.

And, of course, the youth sector inclines to debate and disputation. This was even evident on the publication of *Resourcing Excellent Youth Services*, which was almost wholly a good news story but was regarded by some as representing a 'new managerialism'. It is no surprise that some should have found criticisms to make of aspects of government's policies for resourcing youth work, notably any concern for targets and the accreditation of learning. What did seem rather naïve was the proposition that youth work can get by on the basis of its ability to have convivial conversations with the young without showing how these develop into transformational relationships, experiences and outcomes. In his *History of the Youth Service*, Bernard Davies drew attention to a memorandum from the DES official responsible for youth service in 1978, Barnie Baker. Baker wrote then: 'with so many competing claims on public expenditure, an increased emphasis or justification [of the Youth Service] in terms of social objectives must be expected' (cited in Davies, Vol. 1, 192, 1999). We may disagree about what social objectives are desirable but, twenty-five years on, this condition remained an inescapable imperative for anyone who sought governmental funding for youth work. The National Youth Agency endeavoured to give youth work the confidence in its own methodology of practice and its value base – indeed, its very history – to engage with and persuade funders and policy-makers of the enduring value of its approaches. This work bore some fruit in the publication of *Youth Matters* (DfES, 2005) and to subsequent, albeit limited, stronger legislation in 2006; in the Youth Opportunity and Youth Capital Funds; and in consultation on a ten year strategy for young people's services which commenced in 2006 as part of the government's Comprehensive Spending Review to which the NYA contributed substantial evidence.

The fault-lines

Taking the long view of the past forty years, various fault lines in the YSIC/NYB/NYA's work has been evident. Over time some of these have been successfully negotiated but others remain. The first is that of its relationship to government and how far it should campaign to affect policy. The YSIC operated in a policy environment which was broadly benign to its work and the youth sector and YSIC was, in any case, more interested in practice than policies or structure. The National Youth Bureau had always taken some public and private positions to encourage youth-friendly policies but its funding and, at times, status as a non-departmental public body ('quango') inhibited full-blown campaigning. (Indeed, on at least one occasion in the 1980s, officials required the NYB to desist from continuing a piece of work, on Youth Service funding, on pain of losing its total grant). After 1996, the NYA was no longer a creature of central government, with a Board appointed by the Secretary of State for Education and a programme of activities closely scrutinised by DfES officials. Even so, the Agency remained a public body, in receipt of substantial public funds (£10m per annum by 2006), and had to take proper account of the contracts, interests and concerns of its various paymasters: in the Russian saying: 'the only free cheese is in a mousetrap'. Some of the Agency's frankness, for example on the Connexions Service, still incurred a chill factor in relationships with government but, on the whole, a closer partnership emerged in which both parties respected the other's position and constraints. Closer working also required a review of the tactics of influencing and the NYA concluded that long-term influence was not won by gesture politics or grandstanding on public platforms. It preferred to advance its case by reasoned argument and carefully assembled authoritative evidence, where possible based on research which the Agency increasingly undertook on its own account or published on behalf of major research bodies such as the Economic and Social Research Council or for the Joseph Rowntree Foundation. It also took the view that it was better to be closely involved with government's policy formation before a paper emerged for formal consultation with the field. This insider role may risk a measure of co-option into official thinking and can also result in a frustrating war of attrition, even with governments which are concerned about youth issues (although sometimes less persuaded of the efficacy of youth work in meeting them).

The NYA's relationships with the field had always been complex and occasionally taut. Some expect the Agency to be active campaigners on public policy, especially for a particular organisational construct – 'The Youth Service'; others consider that it too readily accepts a governmental line and attributes this to the Agency's funding relationship. The truth is often more layered: the field is often divided on policy issues and the Agency's Board may reflect this. Moreover, the Agency draws its own conclusions about policy, and may well conclude, on occasion, that the government's approach is correct and hence worthy of support.

The disputatious, and rebellious, nature of the youth field ensures that NYA is rarely without its critics, even opponents, especially when it seeks to offer leadership on policy matters. Some, including government, appear to see a value in diffusing the sources of influence upon the field: the fears of 'empire-building' of which John Ewen wrote twenty-five years ago still cast a shadow. Despite a governance structure which includes representatives of its principal bodies, the youth work field seems to find it difficult to give whole-hearted support to its national agency: the sector pays a political price for this begrudgery. Notwithstanding the inclusive nature of the governance, activities and staffing of the Agency, it is still seen in some quarters as being 'not relevant to the voluntary sector', or as 'not interested in local authority youth services'. The issue of the scope of the Agency – 'youth affairs, or youth work, or the youth service' – which appeared resolved by the move from YSIC to NYB in 1972 and confirmed by Cockerill's judgment in 1983, returns from time to time. By 2006, the NYA had come to focus on the professional practice of 'youth work', in whatever setting it was found.

The youth sector is diverse – in its services, structures, specialism, scale and value base. Many large national voluntary bodies provide services to their own members which the NYA could not aspire to match, even if it wanted. Some are ardent campaigners but, understandably, for their own work or perspectives rather than the sector overall. Strategically, the Agency has chosen to eschew the option of providing a direct service to young people by means of local projects but being only an intermediary body may diminish some of its influence with government and field practice even if it avoids it being in competition with other service providers. It has, partly as an alternative, sought to provide direct financial and administrative support to emerging bodies such as YouthBank and Muslim Youth Work Foundation as well as those which are more established, including the National Federation of Detached Youth Work and Youth Access (formerly NAYPCAS). The Agency sought to sustain the field's many voices by publication in print or, increasingly, on its website. Those outside the direct youth work constituency who are opinion formers on social policy expect the NYA to be more than just a champion for youth work or the youth service – they expect it to be challenging practitioners towards the improvement of services to young people and by 2006 a variety of NYA activities were deployed to that purpose. This pressure on the Agency to widen its scope and adjust its positioning was not expected to diminish.

One minor but vital fault-line has concerned the initial training of the field's practitioners. In the 1980s the NYA acquired an important responsibility to try to uphold high professional standards in youth work. It sought to do this, not through staff control but through drawing in the widest field – employers, unions, training providers – into the scrutiny and validation of courses in higher education leading to professional status. The validation process invites challenge. The NYA has a particular concern to ensure that professionals who emerge from initial training have received a formation which, above all, enables them to work effectively by deploying youth work skills and values with young people – regardless of the professional setting for such work. Down the years, the Agency has tightened its expectations of what such higher education courses should provide, though it has, so far, eschewed the creation of a comprehensive curriculum for them to adopt.

The concept of a curriculum in the wider youth work field has generated tension. The term is not one with which many youth workers are comfortable since it smacks of the classroom and hence of prescription whereas the youth work tradition is to build on the expressed interests of young people and hence grow organically in different settings. It is also a term which has been rather ambiguously used within youth services to mean both the whole range of opportunity made available by a service (which would be better described as 'provision') and the particular set of experiences or programmes which occur inside a youth work unit to promote personal and social development. Alan Gibson had contributed considerably to thinking about the youth work approach to social education, but had not used the term 'curriculum' at this point (Davies and Gibson, 1967). John Ewen was one of the first to deploy the term in youth work when he published *Curriculum Development in the Youth Club* in1975. In a later phase of the NYB's life, a distinctive project entitled 'Enfranchisement' sought to embed curricular principles and a model approach to content in youth work (Leigh and Smart, 1985). By the early 1990s the DES sought to specify a 'Core Curriculum' for youth services and enlisted the NYA's over-enthusiastic help to run what turned out to be a rather abortive set of ministerial conferences on this theme. The newly-born NYA's close identification with the government of the day on this contentious and badly expressed initiative damaged its relationship with the field. The term 'curriculum' faded nationally for a period thereafter but was increasingly used by local authority youth services as a way of carrying their purposes into unit-level practice. The NYA returned to support this work with some limited analysis of curricular principles in youth work (Merton and Wylie, 2002) and with a set of developmental projects, notably 'Getting Connected', The NYA's version of the Neighbourhood Support Fund and the Young People's Development Programme, each of which represented the Agency's 'incubation' role for new forms of practice. Associated arrangements for accrediting learning in non-formal settings linked such curriculum development with national benchmarks but generally produced more vocal critics than supporters.

Conclusion

The new financial and governing arrangements for the NYA after 1996 appear to mark a critical break with the previous thirty years.

The DfES and other government departments continued to fund NYA for specific services or projects but a substantial element of the Agency's 'core' grant now came via local government, negotiated annually with the Local Government Association. The Agency wanted to work closely with local government in order to encourage responsive local services for young people but increasingly had to do so alongside, and sometimes in competition with, other bodies in the extensive children and young people's sector. Many years before NYB's Director, John Ewen, had led a group of youth workers to meet the then Prime Minister, Edward Heath, and to urge on him the establishment of a broader set of youth policies and structures. NYB had published Ewen's seminal pamphlet along those lines, but Heath lost office before this could be taken further by government (Ewen, 1972).

Ewen's successor, David Howie, continued to make the case for some form of service integration, often based on a model of community-education. The concept of services integration became the holy grail of youth policy, re-emerging in the Connexions strategy and with even greater force in the re-structuring of local services for children and young people following the Children Act (2004) and the Labour government's call for services to be better attuned to the needs of the most disadvantaged and vulnerable. Local youth bodies, both voluntary and local authority increasingly responded to these pressures. The NYA sought to help youth work professionals and services to engage with these issues and to influence governmental thinking. But the Agency itself will face continuing challenge to its role, functions and funding in this new landscape.

As this chapter has sought to show, the National Youth Agency has regularly reshaped its activities for new times. But there are limits – and they are not simply those of funding. Responsiveness, support and advocacy nationally for young people and youth work is not helped by the lack of a coherent architecture for promoting and co-ordinating the voice of, and services to, voluntary and maintained youth work sectors. Several separate national bodies with overlapping boundaries still exist: they include the NYA, the British Youth Council, National Council of Voluntary Youth Services and the youth exchange arm of the British Council. No other European country has anything comparable. The field has colluded in the continued separation which permits the state to 'divide and rule' the sector. It is surely the moment to re-open the thinking which led, two generations ago, to the move from a YSIC to an NYB, and, a generation later, to the attempt to construct a multi-purpose, cross-sectoral National Youth Agency. But, however the Agency develops it will aspire to be based on values, shaped by powerful ideas, and committed to the young.

References

Albemarle Report (1960) *The Youth Service in England and Wales*, London, HMSO.
Bessey Report (1962) *Training of Part-time Youth Leaders and Assistants*, London, HMSO.
Bentley, T. and Gurumurthy, R. (1999) *Destination Unknown*, London, Demos.
Cockerill Report (1983) *Report of the Review of the National Youth Bureau*, London, Department of Education and Science.
Davies, B. (1999) *A History of the Youth Service in England*, Vols 1 and 2, Leicester, NYA.

Davies, B. and Gibson, A. (1967) *The Social Education of the Adolescent*, London, University of London Press.

Department for Education and Skills (2001) *Transforming Youth Work*, London.

Department for Education and Skills (2002) *Resourcing Excellent Youth Services*, London.

Department for Education and Skills (2005) *Youth Matters*, London.

Ewen, J. (1975) *Curriculum Development and the Youth Club*, Leicester, NYA.

Ewen, J. (1972) *Towards a Youth Policy*, Leicester, MBS Publications.

Gibson, A. (1967) *The Youth Service Information Centre: the terms of reference, answerability and staffing' Report to Youth Service Development Council* (YSDC, 67), Unpublished, 15.

Leigh, M. and Smart, A. (1985) *Interpretation and change: the emerging crisis of purpose in social education: a history of the Enfranchisement Development Project*, Leicester, NYB.

Merton, B. and Wylie, T. (2002) *Towards a Youth Work Curriculum*, Leicester, NYA.

National Youth Agency (1998) *England's Youth Service: the 1998 Audit*, Leicester, NYA.

National Youth Agency (1999) *Modern Services for Young People*, Leicester, NYA.

National Youth Agency (2001) *Quality Develops*, Leicester, NYA.

National Youth Agency (2000) *Ethical Conduct in Youth Work*, Leicester, NYA.

National Youth Bureau (a) (1994) *What kind of agency is the NYB?* Leicester, NYB.

National Youth Bureau (b) (1974) *Annual Report*, Leicester, NYB.

Thompson Report, (1982) *Experience and Participation. Report of the Review Group on the Youth Service in England*, London, HMSO.

Wylie, T. (2004) 'How Connexions came to terms with youth work' in *Youth and Policy*, No. 83, Spring, 19–29.

National Youth Agency

Maple Terrace. YMCA billiards 1956

A group from Ypres (West of Flanders) a division of the Christian Health Insurance Fund. They were at a camp in Switzerland, on a preventative health cure. Filip Cousée's father is one of the youth leaders in the picture (the tallest guy). He must be 17, so the picture must date back to 1959.

Photograph courtesy of Mrs. June Banks

Lambton Street Wolf Cubs, c. 1916 at their camp in Sharpley Woods. Jim Smith is at the centre of the photograph, and his son, Jim Smith jnr to the far right. Two brothers, Alfred Prett aged 9 and Austin Prett aged 11 are to the far left and right of the photograph respectively.

Thomas Binney (1798–1874)

Russell House Publishing Ltd

We publish a wide range of books on work with young people including:

Kids at the door revisited

By Bob Holman   2000   ISBN 978-1-898924-58-6

This book tells the story of a community youth work project in Bath through interviews with young people who were involved. It also tells their stories over the decade that followed.

Its core message must not be overlooked: effective support for young people at risk cannot be built in a vacuum and must be developed organically in the context of the cultures and communities to which they belong.

Young People Now

Working with Black young people

Edited by Momodou Sallah and
Carlton Howson   2007   ISBN 978-1-905541-14-0

Bringing together this work's different dimensions and perspectives, this book seeks to challenge both the accepted status quo of Black young people's **negative over-representation in most aspects of life** – including education, criminal justice, housing and health – and their **under-representation in empiric literature**. It seeks to help find ways forward.

Having their say
Young people and participation

Edited by David Crimmens and
Andrew West   2004   ISBN 978-1-898924-78-4

*An interesting and informative read for policy makers, professional and young people themselves, and indeed anyone interested in developing children and young people's participation in **political life**, citizenship and social inclusion.*

Children & Society

Secret lives: growing with substance
Working with children and young people affected by familial substance misuse
Edited by Fiona Harbin and Michael Murphy   2006   ISBN 978-1-903855-66-9

Most books of this genre discuss either how to assess the issue or how to work with it: this book does both, leaving the reader with a sense of confidence as to how they might go about working with this group of service users, as well as why they are working with them in this way . . . I recommend this book for all concerned about substance misuse.

Community Care

Respect in the neighbourhood
Why neighbourliness matters
Edited by Kevin Harris   2007   ISBN 978-1-905541-02-7

Offers an astute analysis of the nature and effects of 'respect', as it is lived out in the day to day lives of ordinary people, but also points to ways in which it might be sustained and, even more ambitiously, restored.

Professor John Pitts, Editor of the *Community Safety Journal*

For more details on these and other youth work books or to request a copy of our catalogue contact us at:

Russell House Publishing, 4 St George's House, Uplyme Road, Lyme Regis, DT7 3LS
Tel: 01297 443948
Fax: 01297 442722
Email: help@russellhouse.co.uk
website: www.russellhouse.co.uk

In North America contact:
International Specialized Book Services, 920 NE 58th Ave, Suite 300, Portland, OR 97213-3786, USA
Phone toll free within North America 1-800-944-6190 Fax 503-280-8832 Email orders@isbs.com
website www.isbscatalog.com